Invented Worlds

Invented Worlds

The Psychology of the Arts

ELLEN WINNER

HARVARD UNIVERSITY PRESS

Cambridge, Massachusetts, and London, England

1982

Library of Congress Cataloging in Publication Data

Winner, Ellen.
　　Invented worlds.

　　Bibliography: p.
　　Includes index.
　　1. Arts—Psychological aspects.　I.　Title.
NX165.W5　　　700'.1'9　　　82-1020
ISBN 0-674-46360-9　　　　　AACR2

For reasons of space, illustration credits appear on pages 391–394, which constitute a continuation of the copyright page.

Calligraphy by Jean Evans
Design by Gwen Frankfeldt

Foreword

By *Rudolf Arnheim*

When psychologists investigate the arts, two prerequisites, more than any others, are indispensable for success. The explorers need the delicate hands of good surgeons, who can penetrate a body without destroying the order and functioning of the organs; and they need respect for what Rudolf Otto, speaking of religion, called the *mysterium tremendum*—that is, the awe-inspiring secret. If they lack the delicacy of touch, they will noisily handle their data without caring enough about what they are doing to the phenomena they want to describe and explain. If they lack the respect, they may assume that they are dealing only with the ordinary, augmented perhaps a few degrees. But the arts are not more of the same; they are different.

Ellen Winner knows that. She makes her readers remember that even Sigmund Freud was not sure what makes art great and how one becomes a great artist. She heeds the lesson of Baudelaire's poetic albatross, who is pulled down to the deck and teased, not necessarily by sailors alone. Winner keeps the bird in flight but goes after its shadow which, when cast upon the ground, is reachable, measurable, two dimensional. And as she applies her tools, she glances mindfully and gratefully at that high apparition to which we owe it all.

Winner means business. She has been thoroughly trained in experimental techniques, mostly in their application to child psychology. In particular, when she tells how children look and listen and how they handle language, she is not limited to abstractions but relies on the full variety and complexity of all the real youngsters whom she and her colleagues have observed. This awareness does not make her relax the standards of the scientist. As she reports carefully, clearly, and with a minimum of technical jargon on the many theories that have been put forth in the various areas of the psychology of art, she never fails to ask, gently and insistently: But is it testable?

Thus, while her survey creates a handbook on which readers will rely for years to come, it is the handbook of a critic. There is none of the poker-face reporting that makes the users of textbooks believe that all is known and final. Winner asks questions, voices doubts, points at gaps. She arranges confrontations. She presents a field of research in the throes of productive turmoil. The reader, instead of being handed neatly packaged findings, is invited to join the puzzling and the searching.

By insisting on what is testable, measurable, and countable, the experimental psychology of art tends necessarily toward generalizations, the most relevant statements about reality as we know it and, at the same time, the most remote from that reality. All psychology does this, and so do the other sciences. But it pays here to distinguish between two kinds of remoteness. There are scientific studies dealing with minor aspects of a subject. With some effort one can relate them to the subject, but their relevance is deferred, and one is not truly enlightened. Then there are the highly abstract descriptions, far removed from what strikes the senses, in which nevertheless the very core of the topic seems to reverberate. No one can learn about Kepler's mathematical laws of planetary motion without feeling the shudder of the cosmic. In the psychology of art, a similar difference obtains.

Hundreds of studies have been made of who prefers what colors and shapes, or at what level of complexity the pleasure of interest turns into the pain of boredom; of how much spatial distance is conveyed by certain configurations of lines, or which strings of tones sound dissonant or unresolved. It is necessary to know these things, and Winner patiently collects the bricks that build this house. Yet she also makes me feel that the spirit of art is most tangibly present wherever insightful investigations confirm that by means of the arts the human mind strives for clarification and depth, and that the things we see and hear carry an eloquent symbolism whose truth afflicts us almost bodily.

Two main types of audience will reach for this book. To readers who come from psychology, the extension of their subject matter into the arts will prove welcome and wholesome. In the arts, the mind displays its passions most purely and applies the intelligence of its senses most fully. Whoever can do justice to the psychology of artists, their work, and their public is well on the way to giving an adequate account of human nature. The other audience for this book will come from the arts, from their practitioners, historians, and theorists. Accustomed to limiting their attention to the work itself, these readers will be usefully disturbed by the realization that the work of art is only the most splendid product of an ability which animates human beings at large, and that the impulse to create has its roots in an individual's motivation and cognition in general. This audience, too, is invited by the psychologist to come and take potluck.

"No path reaches the center of things," wrote Eduard Hanslick in *On the Beautiful in Music*, "but every one of them must be directed toward that center." The direction is indeed what matters. No science aspires to provide duplicates of the objects of its endeavor. It merely casts a net that will envelop the object and adhere to it in approximation. "To unravel the mysterious tangles of creative thinking," writes Winner in the midst of her many facts, "does not diminish this uniquely human activity. Rather, it renders the accomplishment even more marvelous."

Acknowledgments

In the summer of 1978, I began to develop an outline for a course on the psychology of the arts that I was slated to teach in the fall. I soon realized that no one work integrated the various theories and content areas within the field. This book was written to fill that gap. It is intended to answer the question that I posed to myself as I planned my course, and that my students posed to me as they wondered whether to register for the course: What is the psychology of the arts?

Many people have helped in this project. My deepest debt is to Howard Gardner, whose work in the psychology of the arts inspired me, whose comments on various versions of the manuscript proved invaluable, and whose companionship provided much needed sustenance throughout. Rudolf Arnheim, Roger Brown, Paval Machotka, and David Perkins read the entire manuscript and made extremely cogent suggestions. Others who offered valuable criticisms on portions of the book are Mort Achter, Jeanne Bamberger, Tom Carothers, Irvin Child, Lyle Davidson, Randolf Easton, Gary Hatfield, John Pfeiffer, William Ryan, Joseph Tecce, Irene Winner, and Dennie Wolf. I also thank my colleague at Boston College, Ali Banuazizi, who first suggested that I teach a course on the psychology of the arts.

Among those at Harvard University Press who made this book possible are Eric Wanner, who offered superb suggestions along the way, and Elyse Topalian, who contributed editorial assistance and musical expertise. I am extremely grateful to Virginia LaPlante, my editor, who not only sanded the rough edges and tightened the joints, but also skillfully clarified many points of organization and logic.

Eve Mendelsohn assembled the figures and secured the permissions. She accomplished this with such forethought and efficiency that she made an overwhelming task seem manageable. I greatly value her contribution. Thanks go to Beverlee Seronick for the drawings and diagrams; William Minty for the musical scores; Chris Miller for photographic assistance; Paula Blank, Ellie Errico, Chris Meyer, and Chris Miller for helping with the references; Ellie Errico and Chris Meyer for proofreading; and Ellen Finkelstein, Kathryn Hollenbach, David Maloof, Celia Schneider, and Linda Stuart for typing.

Some of the research discussed here was supported by grants to Harvard Project Zero from the National Institute of Education, the National Science Foundation, and the Spencer Foundation, agencies that were willing to include the arts within the areas of cognitive development that have received their support.

Contents

Illustrations

The Puzzle of Art

The psychologist will find in works of art, as well as in informal observations recorded by artists, a wealth of information, which will serve not only this special field of study but will enhance the understanding of the human mind in general.

—Rudolf Arnheim

Although artistic behavior has no obvious survival value, all known human societies have engaged in some form of artistry. Art has existed from the very beginning of human existence. Our earliest indisputably Homo sapiens ancestors, Cro-Magnon humans, engaged in painting, and possibly even music, dance, and drama. Using natural dyes from plants, these first humans covered the walls of their caves with paintings of the animals that they hunted. The depiction of masks in the paintings suggests that the germs of theater may also have existed at that time. And the discovery of flutes in the caves, carved out of the bones of animals, tells of the early invention of music. Moreover, the prevalence of all forms of art in contemporary hunting and gathering societies provides indirect, converging support for the view that Cro-Magnon humans sang and danced as well as painted.

In contemporary, industrialized societies, only a handful of people are professionally engaged in making art. However, if popular forms of artistic activity are included under the rubric of "art," almost all of us are involved in some form of artistic creation: we adorn our bodies with jewelry, plant roses in our gardens, redecorate our living rooms, and arrange food on platters in colorful, balanced patterns. Moreover, almost all of us participate in the arts as audience members: we visit museums, read novels, listen to music, take in television dramas, and watch Olympic acrobatics. Artistic activity is not simply a luxury available to the leisure classes but is a fundamental aspect of the human repertoire. Indeed, the production of art is not abandoned even in situations in which the greater part of a person's energy must be expended in the sheer struggle for survival, as the art of concentration camp inmates startlingly testifies.

In an effort to understand universal aspects of human beings, social scientists have studied such forms of behavior as language, tool use, aggression, and sexuality. Despite the universality of art, less effort has been spent in explaining artistic activity. Artistic behavior raises many puzzling questions. Why, for example, is there such a powerful urge to engage in behavior which does not contribute to our material survival? Is this urge related to what motivates us to play, fantasize, or dream? Or is it more akin to what drives us to solve a mathematical equation? And why do we experience such powerful emotions when we contemplate works of art?

These are psychological questions. Essential to them all is the underlying question of the meaning of the term *art* itself. Although we all know how to apply the term, the criteria that are used to classify something as a work of art prove extremely difficult to formulate.

Traditional Definitions of Art

We have little trouble supplying clear-cut examples of works of art and contrasting these to instances that plainly do not qualify as art. In normal contexts, a painting, but not a map, counts as a work of art; a Mozart concerto but not the sound of a car honking, and a poem but not a newspaper article qualify as art. Because we use a common word to refer to a Leonardo da Vinci painting, a Shakespeare sonnet, a Mahler symphony, and a Greek vase, we assume that all of these objects have something in common. We assume that if we can list their shared properties, we will come up with the necessary and sufficient features of art—those features that are common to all works of art and absent in all non-art objects.

Consider an indisputable example of a work of art, Leonardo da Vinci's *Mona Lisa*. By determining the characteristics of this painting, perhaps we can discover the defining features of any work of art. The *Mona Lisa* is an artifact. It was made by a human. It was made deliberately and with skill. It has no obvious utilitarian function but is intended to be contemplated. It expresses emotion, although the emotion conveyed by the smile is ambiguous. It presumably served as a vehicle of self-expression for Leonardo. And it is beautiful and pleasing to look at.

These properties, however, are not defining features of art. First, no single one of these properties is itself sufficient to make an object qualify as a work of art, for each of these properties is also common to objects that are clearly not works of art. A toothbrush is as much an artifact as a piece of sculpture; many things besides art works are made by humans, deliberately and with skill; not only works of art but many other things lack a utilitarian function (snapshots, knickknacks); many things express emotion (a newspaper photograph of an angry crowd; a weeping willow) and also serve as vehicles of self-expression (a political speech); finally, nature as well as art is beautiful to behold.

Second, no single one of these properties is necessary to a work of art, for any one of them may be missing in an art object. "Found art," such as a piece of driftwood mounted on a pedestal in an art museum, is not an artifact. A finger painting by a chimpanzee may be classified as art despite its nonhuman source. A pleasing pattern created by accidentally spilled paint may be considered art, yet the pattern was made neither deliberately nor with skill. Indeed, the nineteenth century Romantics believed that deliberation is often antithetical to art. In Shelley's "To a Skylark," the poet pours forth his soul in "unpremeditated art." And the Surrealists espoused what they called "automatic writing," in which authors surrender all conscious control of their craft so that a supernatural medium may work through them. Works of art surely may serve utilitarian functions. There is speculation that the cave paintings, for instance, were painted not simply to be contemplated but to engender luck and bravery among hunters. Some art, such as twentieth century "minimal art," may not express emotion in any ordinary sense. As for self-expression, it is questionable whether artists working within a strict tradition, such as that of ancient Egypt, are expressing themselves in any way similar to artists in a more modern, individualistic tradition, in which "norm-violation" is prized. And finally, if aesthetic appeal and beauty are necessary, this leaves out Marcel DuChamp's *Urinal*, which one would be hard pressed to call "aesthetic," or Edvard Munch's *The Scream*, which is not in any ordinary sense of the term "beautiful."

Given the difficulty of discovering a set of either necessary or sufficient features of a work of art, the attempt to define art has had a long and turbulent history. Throughout the centuries, many thinkers have tried to set out the necessary and sufficient properties of art. And each new theory has repudiated those that went before. Definitions have been criticized either for incompleteness, when they exclude some forms of art, or for overinclusiveness, when they do not clearly distinguish art from non-art. But the attempt to define art has never ceased, perhaps in part because of the unshakable notion that we cannot talk sensibly about art unless we know what all art objects share and what distinguishes them from all non-art. (Bell, 1913). Two attempts to define art, the formalist and the emotionalist, exemplify the difficulty of the question.

The English aesthetician Clive Bell (1913) argued that works of art achieve their status as art not because of their content but only because of their form. In a work of art, elements are combined in certain ways to create "significant form," and the effect of this form is to arouse "aesthetic emotions" in the observer. Only art possesses significant form, and only significant form elicits aesthetic emotion.

This definition has the advantage of including as art those abstract twentieth-century works in which the traditional, narrative, representational function has been discarded. It thus directs attention away from representation to the importance of design. Nevertheless, there are some serious problems with the definition. First, significant form, the determining property of art, is defined as that which evokes aesthetic emotion, while aesthetic emotion is defined as that which is evoked by significant form. Such a circular definition is immune to verification or falsification. Moreover, the problem of defining "aesthetic emotion" is as fraught with difficulties as is that of defining art itself.

A second problem is that the definition excludes art that fails to evoke an aesthetic response. Such a "poor" work would lack significant form and thus not qualify as art. Hence, the definition can comprehend only "good" art. It conflates evaluative terms (those that distinguish good art from bad) and descriptive ones (those that distinguish art from non-art). Thus, the definition is incomplete.

Whereas Bell regarded the formal aspects of art as critical, others, such as Leo Tolstoy (1930) and the aesthetician R. G. Collingwood (1938), focused on the emotional effect of art. The truly essential property of art, Tolstoy maintained, was not form but rather the expression of emotion in a sensuous public medium. In art, emotion is transmitted to the perceiver like a spreading infection. The more potent the infection, the better the art. And that which does not infect others with emotion fails to qualify as art.

This definition too is problematic. One shortcoming is its breadth. While art works typically express emotion, so do many other things. A scream of terror or a sob of despair is an expression of emotion in the sensuous public medium of sound no less than is a piece of music. What is needed is some way to distinguish between emotion expressed through the invented, fictional world of art and emotion expressed quite literally by a human scream or sob. A second problem is that the status of an object as a work of art is not, in fact, determined by its degree of emotional expressiveness. The geometric lines of Mondrian's paintings do not express emotion in any obvious sense. Yet surely they are works of art.

These formalist and emotionalist theories are only two of numerous philosophical attempts to define the characteristics of art. To try to resolve this hopelessly vexed issue, contemporary philosophers have taken a radical new approach. To ask what is the essence of art, it is claimed—or for that matter, to ask this with respect to a concept as ordinary as furniture or food—is to ask the wrong question.

New Definitions of Art

The traditional approach to definition, since the time of Socrates, has been to search for the necessary and sufficient properties of the term in question. This approach has permeated not only aesthetics but all fields of philosophical inquiry. Philosophers of mind have sought the defining properties of knowledge; moral philosophers have sought the defining properties of the good life; and philosophers of art have sought to discover the defining properties of art, beauty, and the aesthetic response.

This traditional notion of definition was challenged by the philosopher Ludwig Wittgenstein (1953). Wittgenstein argued that most concepts or categories do not possess a set of characteristics shared by all members of the category. Rather, category members are united by strands of similarity, or what are called "family resemblances." The concept of games, for instance, includes board games, card games, ball games, Olympic games, ring around the rosie, and games played all by oneself, such as throwing a ball against a wall. There are no features common to all of these games. Skill, competition, and amusement are part of some but not all games. One game shares properties with some games, and another game shares a different set of properties with yet another group of games. The classification of a new activity as a game is made by judging its similarity to something already established as a game, not by asking whether it is similar to all games in the same way. Concepts such as game are open concepts, which possess no set of necessary and sufficient properties but are held together by a network of overlapping and crisscrossing similarities. Many common concepts are thus open ones, as opposed to the closed concepts of math and logic, such as the class of prime numbers.

Art has since been defined as an open concept lacking any necessary or sufficient properties. The boundaries of art must be infinitely expandable in order to encompass new and previously un-dreamed-of forms of art (Weitz, 1956). Because art is expansive, adventurous, and never static, unforeseeable and entirely novel forms of art are always possible. Because the concept of art must remain infinitely expandable, the defining features of art cannot be listed. Such a list would close the concept. Accordingly there is no way, in principle, to define a work of art.

A more useful approach has been taken by the philosopher Nelson Goodman (1968, 1978). While acknowledging that art can-not be defined in terms of necessary and sufficient features, Good-man proposed that art works tend to possess certain properties. Underlying this approach is the assumption that all art works con-tain symbols and are themselves symbols. Viewed in this way, art is a manifestation of the most characteristic activity of human beings, the construction of symbols. But to state that all art works are symbols does not solve the definitional problem. Many things which are clearly not works of art are also symbols, such as maps, diagrams, traffic lights, and numbers. Moreover, all words are sym-bols, but not all language is artistic language. The difficulty of dis-tinguishing aesthetic from nonaesthetic symbols—say a painting from a traffic light, or a poem from a newspaper article—brings us right back to the problem of determining the defining properties of art.

To avoid this problem, Goodman argued that the question *"What is art?"* should be replaced with the question, *"When is an object a work of art?"* He gave the example of a stone lying in a driveway. This object is not a work of art, nor is it a symbol of any kind. The same stone in a geological museum is also not a work of art, but because it is a sample of some of the properties of stones of a given period, it functions as a symbol. Put this same stone in an art museum, and it may begin to function as a work of art. Like the stone in a geological museum, the stone in an art mu-seum is a symbol—but it is a sample of other properties than is the stone in the geological museum. The stone in the art museum exemplifies a certain shape, size, color, and texture. It may even metaphorically exemplify a mood. When people view the stone in an art museum, they attend to all of these properties, and thus the stone can be said to be functioning as a work of art.

This example demonstrates that one and the same object can function as a symbol in certain contexts but not in others, and as an aesthetic symbol in certain contexts and a nonaesthetic symbol in others. What distinguishes an object when it is functioning as an aesthetic symbol is that it tends to possess certain symptoms. These aesthetic symptoms are not necessary and sufficient proper-

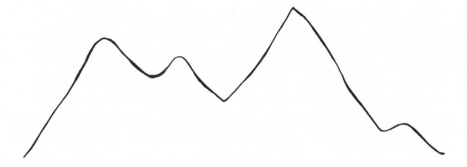

1 *Zigzag line illustrating repleteness.*

ties of works of art; they are more like clues, or like the symptoms of a disease. A disease such as influenza is usually accompanied by the symptoms of sore throat, cough, and fever. But one may have the flu and not have the symptoms, and one can have one or more of these symptoms and not have the flu. In the presence of these symptoms, it is simply a fairly safe bet that a case of the flu is indicated. So also, the presence or absence of one or more aesthetic symptoms does not qualify or disqualify a work as aesthetic. One or more of these symptoms simply tend to be present in works of art. This approach is a probabilistic one: if something has one or more aesthetic symptoms, it probably is a work of art.

One of the symptoms that works of art usually possess is "relative syntactic repleteness." Art works tend to be replete because when an object functions as a work of art, relatively more of its physical properties are important than when it is not functioning as a work of art. Consider a zigzag line (Fig. 1). If we are told that the line is an electrocardiogram, all that is important to note are the dips and peaks of the line. But if we are told that this same line is the outline of a mountain in a landscape painting, we turn our attention to more of the properties of the line, such as its thickness, brightness, or color. Similarly, if a stone is placed in an art museum, we attend to its size, shape, color, and texture. When a symbol functions aesthetically, more of its properties are relevant than when this same symbol functions outside of the arts.

Another symptom of the aesthetic is "metaphorical exemplification," also called "expression," which refers to one of the ways in which art works typically symbolize. Works of art express moods: a painting may be described as sad, a symphony as elated, a poem as gloomy. But it is not only moods that are expressed: a painting can express loudness, a symphony can express heat, a poem can express smoothness. Though the way in which a particular property is expressed may vary from culture to culture, art of all cultures expresses moods or other qualities through formal properties, such as line, color, and rhythm. Art works typically symbolize through expression; nonaesthetic symbols do not. Only paintings, but not maps and graphs, can be sad, loud, heated or calm. Moreover, the properties that a work of art expresses are different from those that a work literally possesses. A painting can be literally blue, but only metaphorically sad.

The presence of aesthetic symptoms such as these requires us to do more than look through the symbol to what it represents, as we do with nonaesthetic symbols such as maps, graphs, and traffic lights. Their presence compels us to attend to the symbol itself. Thus, works of art are nontransparent.

A work of art may lack any one of these symptoms, and any one symptom may also be found outside of a work of art. Moreover, these symptoms are differently distributed across the various art forms. If all of the symptoms are found in an object, it is most certainly a work of art. If none of the symptoms is found in an object, it cannot be a work of art. But no one of these symptoms must be present for an object to qualify as a work of art.

Such a probabilistic or symptomatic definition of art makes it easier to deal with borderline cases of art. A scribble produced by a chimpanzee may function as a work of art if the observer realizes that all of the physical properties of the lines are relevant (repleteness). But the work may not have functioned as a work of art for the chimpanzee: the precise variations in line and color may have been produced quite accidentally, and the chimpanzee may have paid these subtle variations little or no attention. Thus, a work may function as art for the observer but not for the maker, or vice versa. Works that are usually considered borderline cases of art, such as creations by children, chimpanzees, and brain-damaged or psychotic people, are potentially aesthetic objects, and a symptomatic approach may be applied in order to decide whether the object is functioning as art for either the maker or the perceiver.

Defining the Psychology of Art

The psychology of art focuses on questions related to the participants in the artistic process—namely the artist, the performer, the perceiver, and the critic. Of these, the roles of artist and perceiver have received the most attention. A psychologist of art is interested primarily in the psychological processes that make possible the creation of and response to art. Two broad questions have guided the psychological study of the artist. What motivates the artist to create? And what cognitive processes are involved in creating art? Two parallel questions have guided the investigation of the perceiver. What psychological factors motivate a person to contemplate works of art? And what kinds of cognitive skills are required to understand a work of art? These major questions provide an organizing framework in understanding the psychology of art:

	Artist	Perceiver
Motivation: the 'why' of art	What motivates the artist to create?	What motivates humans to contemplate a work of art?
Cognition: the 'how' of art	What cognitive processes are involved in artistic creation?	What cognitive skills are necessary to understand a work of art?

The philosophers of ancient Greece were the first to grapple with these overarching questions. Plato developed a theory of what drives the artist to create, as well as a view of the process of artistic creation. The poet was said to be possessed by divine inspiration, and the process of creation was one in which the poet's rational faculties yield to irrational frenzy. Aristotle proposed a less Dionysian view of artistic creation, stressing instead the careful, controlled workmanship involved. These two divergent views—art as uncontrolled madness and art as careful craft—have surfaced time and again, even today polarizing psychologists.

Plato and Aristotle also formulated theories to explain why audience members are drawn to the arts. Plato believed that the arts exert a powerful effect on the soul. Because of the potent influence of art, Plato argued that certain forms of art were dangerous and should be censored. Aristotle believed that members of the audience are attracted to dramatic tragedy enacted on stage because of its carthartic, purging effect.

From the time of the ancient Greeks, not only philosophers but artists have continued to grapple with the puzzles of artistic creation and response. Nineteenth century poets, for example, echoed Plato in their attempt to come to terms with the mystery of artistic creation. Writers such as Wordsworth, Blake, Shelley, Coleridge, Baudelaire, and Rimbaud glorified the imagination, the emotions, and the irrational—in contrast to reason—as the source of art. Art, they believed, cannot be produced by rational rules or mere "skill." Rather, it is created by irrational means. Not only was the conscious, rational mind viewed as irrelevant to artistic creation, but artistic creation was believed to be actually threatened by the intervention of reason.

In some sense, the Romantic position constituted a return to Plato's stance. Both the Greeks and the nineteenth century Romantics believed that creation can be explained only by forces independent of the rational self. But while Plato viewed artistic creation as having an external source, divine inspiration, the Romantics believed artistic creation to have an internal source, the unconscious. For this reason, the roots of creativity in dreams, drug-induced fantasies, and psychoses, as well as physical illness, were sometimes stressed. While the Greeks believed in inspiration from above, nineteenth century artists believed in inspiration from below (Arnheim, 1962). The nineteenth century insistence on the importance of the irrational not only echoes Plato but also anticipates Freud's emphasis on the role of the unconscious in artistic creation. The problem of inspiration remains a key and unsolved puzzle in the psychology of art today.

The way in which psychologists have grappled with fundamental questions about art differs from the approach of both philosophers and artists. What distinguishes psychologists' studies of the arts is not the questions asked, but rather the way in which the questions are answered. Whereas the arguments of philosophers and artists are based on introspection and logical analysis, psychologists found their answers on an empirical, sometimes experimental base.

The major questions posed by the psychology of art are treated in this book. The answers provided are by no means exhaustive but represent some of the leading, often conflicting ways that a question has been addressed. Three major art forms are considered: painting, music, and literature. These art forms were chosen for several reasons. First, psychological studies have focused more on them than on art forms such as sculpture, dance, architecture, or theater. Second, these three art forms are characterized by different ways of symbolizing: painting symbolizes through both denotation (a shape in a picture can represent an object in the world) and expression (a picture can express sadness through its colors); music rarely denotes, symbolizing instead primarily through expression (a symphony does not usually refer to any object in the world but may express elation); and in literature, the denotational function is far more prevalent than the expressive one. Thus, a comparison of these art forms clarifies the different problems posed by each form of symbolization in isolation (music versus literature) and by both forms of symbolization operating together (painting versus music and literature).

The book examines how the adult perceiver responds to and makes sense of the art form in question, how these perceptual skills develop in the child, and how the ability to produce the art form develops. It thus delineates the adult end-state of perceptual competence, the development of perceptual skills, and the development of productive skills in each art form. The book does not address the adult end-state of productive competence, because comparatively little is known about how any given type of artist produces a work of art. Psychologists have tended to focus on the perception of art rather than on its creation, probably because the former lends itself more readily to study in a laboratory or an experimental setting. Moreover, psychologists have focused on universal aspects of the artistic experience. While the perception of art is part of everybody's experience, the production of art is restricted to a relatively small number of adults, although it is part of the experience of most children.

Two pathological populations, those with focal brain-damage and those diagnosed as schizophrenic, are also considered. Psychologists have examined these groups in order to find out how artistic skills are organized in the brain, and what the relationship is between artistic creativity and mental illness. These studies provide some insight into the biological underpinnings of artistry.

Certain topics are not treated here. There is little coverage of the vast field of art education, as numerous texts on the subject already exist. Wherever possible, however, the educational implications of the research are discussed.

The social dimension of the arts is also omitted. For instance, the problem of the role of the artist and the function of art within society, and artists' changing perceptions of that role, is not treated. Nor is there a discussion of the ways in which the response to art is mediated through the culture in which one lives. The influence of sociocultural factors on the role that artists carve for themselves, and on the ways in which art works are experienced, is undeniable. However, because there has been little empirical work on these issues, the focus of the book is on the individual as a participant in the artistic process.

Finally, popular forms of art are rarely considered here. The focus instead is on the fine arts. Thus, there is little mention of television or jazz, nor of comic strips or rock and roll. The omission of the popular arts resulted from the fact that the bulk of the research in the psychology of art has focused on the fine arts.

This book has both a theoretical and a methodological bias. The theoretical bias, shaped by Rudolf Arnheim (1974), Nelson Goodman (1968), and Susanne Langer (1942), treats the arts as fundamentally cognitive domains. Both producing and perceiving art require the ability to process and manipulate symbols and to make extremely subtle discriminations. In this sense, literacy in the arts is as demanding as literacy in the sciences. Aesthetic symbols, just as scientific ones, must be read. Thus, the arts are treated not as forms of leisure, play, or amusement, nor as exclusively emotional activities. They are viewed, rather, as fundamental ways of knowing the world.

The methodological bias leans toward systematic and experimental evidence. Anecdotal, introspective, or even clinical evidence is given much less weight than is evidence gleaned from replicable empirical investigations. Only in cases where there is a dearth of experimental evidence is introspective and clinical evidence given prominence.

The psychology of art lags considerably behind the psychology of other human activities. While psychologists have devoted a great deal of attention to the type of reasoning demanded by participation in the sciences, relatively little attention has been paid to the arts. Yet over the course of human history, the arts have occupied a much more central position than the sciences. Logical, scientific thought is an invention of Western, post-Renaissance culture, and it remains restricted to a small enclave of individuals. Participation in the arts, in contrast, has been widespread for thousands of years.

The reasons for the relative dearth of investigations into the psychology of art are at least twofold. First, because the arts are often considered mysterious, investigators have assumed that they are not open to empirical study. And second, most psychologists have been relatively unfamiliar with the arts and thus unwilling to investigate them. Indeed, there is no area of psychology in which a greater distance prevails between what should be known and what has been established. It is in the hope of beginning to close that gap that this book has been written.

ONE Personality and Intellect

1 The Artist

Writing is a form of therapy; sometimes I wonder how all those who do not write, compose or paint can manage to escape the madness, the melancholia, the panic fear which is inherent in the human situation.

—Graham Greene

Why is the creative impulse never satisfied; why must one always begin anew?

—Aaron Copland

Imagine two playwrights based in New York City. They are both in their mid-forties. Each of them is a first-born son; they come from a middle class background, and both were educated at the same schools. In many respects, these men are very similar. Yet one of them is a highly creative writer, whose plays have altered the conception of theater. The other, while extremely competent, is not particularly original; his writing is derivative, and one generation hence, his plays will be forgotten.

What is the difference between these writers? Some psychologists would search for an answer in their personalities. Freud, for instance, would argue that the creative playwright possesses exceptionally powerful and frustrated instinctual drives, along with an extraordinary capacity to sublimate, or rechannel, these drives into artistic work. Other psychoanalytically oriented psychologists would point to a relatively higher degree of autonomy and ego strength in the creative playwright. For behaviorist psychologists, the difference between the two writers would be due to the way in which they have been shaped by their respective environments: the creative playwright is simply someone who by chance has discovered a style of writing which the public likes, and for which he is thus reinforced.

One might also search for differences in the intellects of these two writers. Some psychologists would focus on the ability of the creative writer to generate a greater number of unusual ideas, or to perceive connections between things ordinarily considered different. Others would suggest that the creative writer has more sheer intelligence. Still others would emphasize the fact that, whereas the ordinary writer may be skilled at solving problems that confront him in his writing, the creative writer actually sets out to discover interesting and challenging problems which he can then tackle.

The differences might also be located not in any stable personality or intellectual traits of the creative writer, but rather in the way that his mind works during the process of writing. Many artists as well as some psychologists have pointed to the special role of the unconscious during creative episodes. The creative playwright's best ideas, they would insist, are born in his unconscious, and they come to him in the form of sudden moments of inspiration. Unlike the ordinary writer who works laboriously on a regular schedule, the creative writer is said to be at the mercy of mysterious powers of inspiration that are beyond his control.

A range of factors thus may make the creative artist unique. Some theorists emphasize the motivation and the personality of the artist. Some point to external factors in the artist's life. Others focus on the intellect of the artist. And still others posit something special about the way in which the creative mind works during the actual process of creating.

Instinctual Drives

When asked why they create, artists often reply that they make art because they have to. "I could not live without devoting all my hours to it," Picasso admitted (Ghiselin, 1952). Creative endeavor in the arts as well as the sciences appears to involve a passionate attachment to one's work. Rarely does a lawyer, for instance, insist that she is driven to practice law, that she could do nothing else, that her life would be empty or unbearable if she had to enter another profession.

Just what it is that drives artists and scientists is a question that has often engaged the attention of psychologists. By far the most comprehensive theory of the source of artistic motivation is that proposed by Freud (1908, 1910, 1914, 1928). Freud's theory of the artist must be understood within the broader context of his theory of personality, which was developed on the basis of the memories, dreams, and free associations of his neurotic patients. Although his evidence was drawn from troubled individuals, Freud formulated general laws said to govern all of human behavior, both normal and abnormal. Just as the study of color blindness has helped scientists understand the workings of normal vision, so for Freud, the study of neurotic conflicts illuminated the normal human personality structure.

The basic tenet of psychoanalysis is that human behavior is the product of a conflict between powerful unconscious instinctual drives and the restraints and defenses imposed by the superego and the ego. Like an iceberg, the bulk of mental life is submerged below consciousness, housing primitive instinctual wishes whose actual fulfillment is strictly forbidden. These instinctual wishes, which are constantly pressing for release, cannot be fulfilled directly because of the restraints imposed by civilization. Thus, people must find alternative, indirect routes to the fulfillment of their deep-seated and powerful desires. If the instinctual energy is directed outward into socially acceptable channels, a person remains relatively healthy. But if the energy is blocked or turned against the self, signs of neurosis develop.

Freud argued that the instinctual wishes pressing for release are primarily sexual in nature and stem from the early years of childhood. Through his analysis of his patients and his own self-analysis, Freud came to believe that the events which befall the child during the first five years of life critically shape the development of the adult personality. By far the most important set of early experiences, which leaves its imprint on all later life, is the child's relationship to the parent of the opposite sex and the Oedipal crisis that results. Around the age of four or five, the child becomes increasingly sexually drawn to the opposite-sex parent and consequently wishes the same-sex parent out of the way. Freud tried to show that the way in which the Oedipal relationship is resolved shapes the entire course of development. The Oedipal drama becomes a recurrent theme in everyone's dreams and fantasy life; and for those who become artists, the Oedipal theme is enacted over and over again in the works of art that they produce.

Scarcely a domain of human behavior escaped the application of Freud's theory. It was used to illuminate the meaning of dreams, the function of religion, the evolution of society, and the significance of myths, fairy tales, literature, and the visual arts. The creative person, often seen by philosophers and artists as unique and inexplicable, was to be explained by the same psychological laws as those governing more mundane behavior, such as daydreaming, joke telling, or making slips of the tongue and other "trivial" mistakes. If this were not the case, Freud argued, then the products of genius would not be understood by ordinary people.

Artistic creation was seen as the artist's means of coping with unconscious Oedipal wishes which cannot be fulfilled or even consciously faced. Like creativity, neurosis also originates in response to the conflict between the press of unusually powerful instincts and the demands of civilization which inhibit the fulfillment of these instinctual desires. Both neurosis and creativity are attempts to solve this conflict. Neurotics react to the conflict by imposing defense mechanisms which repress and distort their desires, often developing a relatively rigid personality. Creative persons do not repress their socially unacceptable instinctual desires; instead they sublimate them. In sublimation, libidinal energy is not repressed but is rechanneled to fuel socially acceptable goals. These socially approved goals are not limited to the domain of the arts: an athlete striving to compete in the Olympics is as much a sublimator as the artist striving to produce works of art.

The sublimation involved in artistic creativity is thus similar to the sublimation involved in ordinary productive behavior. But artistic sublimation differs from other forms of sublimation both in its similarity to the process underlying dreams and in its kinship to play. While Freud distinguishes between the artist and neurotic, he takes pains to point out the similarity between the artist and the dreamer. Both are engaged in the same activity: they are unconsciously gratifying deep-seated wishes on the plane of fantasy. It is in precisely this sense that the artist is also like the child at play. Both child and artist create a world of their own which is taken extremely seriously and is clearly distinguished from the real world. In this invented world, their wishes can be fulfilled in fantasy and in disguised form. Children who enact a fight to the death between two sibling dolls are playing out rivalrous wishes to do away with a sibling or the same-sex parent. Artists who write a novel in which the protagonist becomes a hero, beloved by all, are playing out their own narcissistic wishes. Although only in mediocre works of art are the artist's wishes blatantly portrayed (in greater works, the wish fulfillment is more veiled), all art involves the gratification, in fantasy, of the artist's unconscious yearnings. And all wish fulfillment, even on the plane of fantasy, results in a reduction of instinctual tension.

Because Freud believed that we never relinquish anything pleasurable but merely exchange one pleasure for another, he sought to discover what children exchange for play as they grow up. In the normal adult, Freud reasoned, play has given way to the fantasy of the daydream. But in the artist, play has given way to the creation of works of art.

Strands of similarity are thus drawn between art, neurosis, play, daydreaming, nocturnal dreams, and ordinary forms of productive work. All of these forms of behavior are driven by a common ingredient: powerful wishes that cannot be fulfilled. Add to this ingredient a proclivity toward repression, and one becomes neurotic. But add to this same ingredient a proclivity toward sublimation, and one becomes an ambitious worker or, if one also possesses a mysterious ingredient called "genius," one becomes a creative artist or scientist.

Not only did Freud believe that the urge to create is determined by the unconscious conflicts of early childhood, but he felt that the content of works of art, like that of dreams, is similarly determined. Because a work of art functions as a disguised fulfillment of an unconscious childhood wish, the work, properly interpreted, becomes a window on the unconscious. Just as is the case in dreams or fantasies woven by a child at play, a painting or novel, no matter what its overt theme, at the deepest level always contains the fulfillment of the unconscious wish that fueled the work in the first place. And just as with a dream or a child's play episode, analyzing the content of a work of art and peering beneath its symbolic disguise can reveal the personality of the artist.

An example of Oedipal wish fulfillment through the latent content of a work is provided by three classics of literature: Sophocles' *Oedipus Rex*, Shakespeare's *Hamlet*, and Dostoevsky's *The Brothers Karamazov*. According to Freud (1928), all three works deal, at some level, with the theme of parricide. The longing to replace the same-sex parent is a powerful, universal wish, ignited in infancy and forbidden for all time. The three works treat this latent theme under different levels of manifest content. In the Greek play, the latent content is the most unconcealed, as the deed is actually committed by the son. In the other two works, the murder of the father is carried out by someone besides the son. But a psychoanalytic reading of the later works reveals that underlying the theme of murder is the son's wish to kill his own father: Hamlet's paralysis stems from his unconscious guilt, and the murder in *The Brothers Karamazov* is committed by someone who has a filial relation to the victim. Dostoevsky's identification with the murderer is suggested by the fact that he made the murderer an epileptic like himself, as well as by the fact that the author's own father was actually murdered when Dostoevsky was a youth. Thus, in Freud's view, Sophocles, Shakespeare, and Dostoevsky are all unconsciously playing out a forbidden Oedipal wish. No guilt follows from this, however, because their wishes are displaced onto fictional characters.

Freud's most extensive example of wish fulfillment through art was provided by Leonardo da Vinci. Freud used this Renaissance artist and inventor as a case study to support his theory of creativity, which applied to scientific as well as to artistic achievement.

Using all the evidence that he could amass from Leonardo's life, writings, and paintings, Freud (1910) constructed a coherent picture of the artist's personality and motivation.

Leonardo was an illegitimate child who lived with his mother until sometime between the ages of three and five, when he was taken away and brought to live with his father and his father's wife. Because Leonardo's mother had been abandoned by his father, and because her only love object was thus her child, Freud assumed that Leonardo's mother showered him with an excess of love. Such an intense relationship between mother and son, Freud believed, must have stimulated a precocious sexuality in Leonardo, coupled with an abnormally strong Oedipal attachment to his mother. However, because Leonardo was taken away from his mother at an early age, the normal impossibility of fulfilling Oedipal wishes was even more starkly brought home to the young Leonardo. Leonardo thus met two of the critical preconditions for becoming an artist: he had atypically powerful drives, and the fulfillment of these drives was prohibited.

These two childhood factors could have fostered neurosis rather than creativity in Leonardo. In order to defend against his abnormally strong yearning for his mother's love, Leonardo might have developed the defense mechanism of "reaction-formation," a form of repression in which his positive feelings for his mother would have been turned into their opposite, hostility, perhaps even toward all members of the female sex. Or he might have repressed his longing so severely that all other emotions were also repressed. In this case, he would have become unable to experience any strong emotion.

Yet Leonardo became an artist and inventor rather than a crippled neurotic. The reason, Freud inferred, is that Leonardo possessed an extraordinary capacity for sublimation as well as an extraordinary "talent." He thus possessed the necessary and sufficient conditions for artistry. Had his proclivity been instead toward repression, he would have become neurotic rather than creative.

Freud found support for this explanation of Leonardo's motivation in his painting *Madonna and Child with St. Anne* (Fig. 1.1). Both the Madonna and St. Anne wear the blissful smile of young motherhood. Anne is rendered almost as young as Mary, despite the fact that in the Bible she is considerably older. Moreover, all three figures are fused in a triangular mass. According to Freud, only an artist with Leonardo's childhood could have invented this picture of two young mothers, each of equal grace and charm. Unconsciously, this painting represented Leonardo's repressed wish to be

1.1 *Leonardo*, Madonna and Child with St. Anne. *In this painting, Freud argued, Leonardo was unconsciously expressing his longing for his mother and his step-mother. The outline of a vulture in Mary's drapery, with the tail leading directly to the child's mouth, was said by Freud to represent Leonardo's unconscious sexual wishes.*

nurtured and loved by both of his mothers, biological and step. Painting such a picture provided partial fulfillment of this wish. Because he could not fulfill the wish in reality, he fulfilled it unconsciously on the fantasy level of art.

Freud's theory of artistic motivation is a daring one. Perhaps because its thesis is so strong, and because one principle is used to explain all artistic drive, the theory is vulnerable to criticism. There are problems with the story of Leonardo, as well as with the general theory of the artist.

One of the most glaring weaknesses of the Leonardo story is the lack of attention paid to the sociohistorical context in which Leonardo painted. For instance, during Leonardo's time, a large cult of St. Anne flourished (Schapiro, 1962a). The Pope had handed out a prayer to Anne and Mary, illustrated with a woodcut of these three figures. In this woodcut, Mary sits on the lap of St. Anne, and the child, seated on Mary's lap, is the object of both of their attentions. Thus, it is highly likely that Leonardo did not invent the image. However, even if it could be proved that Leonardo simply availed himself of a popular image, it could be argued that Leonardo's susceptibility to this influence, rather than another, was due to his particular unconscious wishes.

Another weakness is the assumption that Leonardo's mother loved him excessively, but it is just as likely that she was hostile to her illegitimate child. If so, there are no grounds for arguing that Leonardo had abnormally strong Oedipal feelings. This possibility underscores the difficulty of constructing a psychological portrait of an historical figure who cannot be studied directly.

A more general weakness of Freud's theory is its inability to predict. The theory does not predict who will become an artist and who will succumb to neurosis. Nor does it predict or explain why some people are able to sublimate through art while others sublimate through athletics, or why one person becomes a great painter while another writes poetry.

Freud was well aware of some of these limitations. He did not claim that he could predict, on the basis of childhood evidence, which people were destined to become artists. He did not try to set forth all of the necessary and sufficient conditions for genius. Instead, he applied the laws governing normal psychological functioning to the motivation of the genius to create and to the psychological function of creativity in the life of the creative person. Psychoanalysis, Freud admitted, cannot explain genius; it can only reveal the factors that awaken genius as well as the types of subject matter that it is fated to choose. Such limitations are perhaps what Freud had in mind when he wrote, "Before the problem of the creative artist analysis must, alas, lay down its arms" (1928, p. 177).

For Freud, then, the difference between the two imaginary playwrights would rest in their Oedipal histories and their resultant personalities. The creative playwright may be fueled by stronger instinctual drives. Perhaps the drives of the creative writer were frustrated to a greater extent in childhood: thus, he is more strongly impelled to fulfill these drives by weaving fictional worlds. Or if the two playwrights possess equally strong drives, the creative one is more adept at disguising his drives in his art works, while the less creative one produces works of more blatant wish fulfillment. Perhaps, Freud would continue, the ability to produce works that reveal less obvious signs of instinctual gratification is due to genius, that mysterious quality which distinguishes the creative writer from the hack.

Ego Strength

According to popular lore, the greatest artistic geniuses are emotionally unstable, perhaps even a bit "crazy." One thinks of Van Gogh, who spent his last years in a mental institution, or of Dostoevsky, who was subject to violent epileptic fits. But there is little truth to this view. In fact, several major studies, carried out in the 1960s at the Institute for Personality Assessment and Research at Berkeley, have demonstrated just the opposite. The most creative artists, these studies suggested, are not particularly anxious or neurotic. Rather, they have considerable ego strength and are highly independent.

This view of the artist as emotionally healthy and strong is shared by Freud, who made a distinction between neurotics, who rigidly repress their instinctual energy, and artists, who sublimate this same energy into satisfying and productive work. But while Freud's characterization of the artist was based on indirect evidence, psychologists at the Institute based their claims on direct studies of creative people, including painters, writers, doctors, physicists, biologists, economists, anthropologists, architects, research scientists, engineers, and mathematicians (Barron, 1958, 1969; Gough, 1961; Helson and Crutchfield, 1970; MacKinnon, 1961, 1962, 1965). In each case, people nominated by judges as highly creative in their fields were compared to representative members of the same profession. Thus, it proved possible to distinguish between the personality traits of artists who are extraordinarily creative and artists who are more ordinary.

Typical of the research were several studies of architects (MacKinnon, 1961, 1962, 1965). Three groups were included: architects nominated by a panel of five judges as the most creative members of the field, architects chosen because they had worked with one of the "creative" architects for at least two years, and architects selected at random from a directory of architects. As a check that the three groups really differed in creativity, all subjects were rated by a large group of architects on a seven-point creativity scale. As expected, the creative architects received the highest ratings; the representative group received the lowest ratings; and those who had worked with the creative architects received intermediate scores.

Numerous personality tests were then administered. In these

tests, the subjects read a list of personality descriptions and were asked to agree or disagree with each one. From their responses, generalizations were formed about the personality of each subject. These personality checklists demonstrated that each group of architects possessed a different constellation of traits. The creative architects revealed themselves to be strong, willful, self-confident, controlling, and self-centered. For instance, they were more likely than either of the other groups to agree with statements such as, "I think I would enjoy having authority over other people," or "I have a natural talent for influencing people," They were unconcerned with the impression that they made on others and were guided solely by their own internal standards. They possessed a great deal of autonomy and ego strength. They were more likely than any other group to disagree with statements such as, "I am easily downed in an argument," and to agree with statements such as, "When someone says silly or ignorant things about something I know, I try to set him right."

In contrast, the representative architects proved much less dominant and independent. The personality traits that they displayed were far more acceptable and conventional, such as affiliation, deference, socialization, responsibility, and self-control. For instance, they were likely to agree with, "I have never done anything dangerous just for the thrill of it" (a measure of responsibility), but to disagree with, "My parents never really understood me" (a measure of socialization).

Those who were in the middle group, who themselves were not highly creative but had worked for some time with creative architects, achieved personality scores intermediate between the other two groups. They proved less dominant and self-confident than the creative group, but more so than the representative group. But on two measures they were not intermediate. They displayed the highest level of emotional conflict. For instance, they indicated a desire to control as well as to be controlled, and a desire for independence along with a wish to be included in the activities of others. And they displayed the highest level of anxiety of all three groups. Though they were not assessed as neurotic, they revealed more neurotic tendencies, such as conflict and anxiety, than either the creative or the average group.

This personality typology of architects fits the theory of creativity of Otto Rank (1945). Central to Rank's distinction between the creative and noncreative personality are the concepts of will and guilt. Children first experience the will of their parents. Later, their own will, or counterwill, begins to emerge, and this often conflicts with the parents' will. Such conflict leads to guilt and is resolved in one of three ways, which determines the type of adults that children become.

One solution is for children simply to adapt their will to the will of the parents. Once children identify their will with that of the parents, there is no longer any conflict, and there is no longer any guilt. The child who adopts such a solution becomes an adult who internalizes the norms of society. Such a person experiences little conflict and is also not particularly creative. This is the lot of the typical adult.

If children refuse to adapt their will to that of the parents, two routes are open to them. They may partially break away from their parents. Because the rebellion is only partial, they do not fully realize their independence and are left with a sense of guilt and inferiority. This kind of person, while conflicted and neurotic, is nonetheless more creative than the fully adapted adult, precisely because of having achieved some measure of independence.

The second route open to children who refuse to adapt involves the full establishment of independence. People who establish their own independent ideals and their own will have achieved the highest level of development. This is the creative individual, the artist, the man of will.

In their autonomy and ego strength, creative architects fit Rank's description of the creative person. The personality of these architects suggests that there may well be a connection between autonomy and creativity. The life histories of the creative architects provide further support for Rank's view. These architects reported that their parents had displayed extraordinary respect for them at an early age, granting them unusual freedom and expecting them to be independent. This independence was fostered by a lack of intense closeness between parent and child. And there were frequent moves to different communities, often resulting in a lonely childhood. It is precisely such experiences that would confirm Rank's theory by strengthening of the child's personal will.

The same general pattern of results was also found for the other groups of artists and scientists studied at the Institute. Over and over again the evidence supported the claim that the most creative members of a profession are also those who have ego strength, assertiveness, and independence. However, the bulk of this evidence comes from paper-and-pencil personality tests. Such tests do not necessarily provide insight into stable, inner characteristics. One cannot be sure that people will in fact behave autonomously simply because they describe themselves as autonomous on a personality inventory. Thus, these claims would be strengthened were they based on more real-life situations.

Fortunately, the social psychologist Solomon Asch (1956) devised an experimental paradigm in which a person's independence can be measured in a situation more true to life than that provided by questionnaires. Asch set up a situation in which people were asked to make very simple, straightforward perceptual judgments in a group situation. The subjects were shown a line (the target stimulus) and were asked to decide which of three other lines was closest in length to the target. One answer was clearly correct; the others were clearly wrong. All but one of the participants were "confederates" of the experimenter and received instructions to give the same wrong answer. When the one "naive" subject's turn finally came, he often succumbed to the subtle group pressure and gave an answer that denied the evidence of his senses. The experiment demonstrated a surprisingly high tendency to conform to group norms, even when a person knows full well that there is something wrong with these norms.

Frank Barron (1958), a psychologist at the Institute, administered Asch's experiment to creative and noncreative individuals. Consistent with MacKinnon's findings, Barron showed that creative people are less likely to conform and are more likely to abide by their own judgment, even in the face of subtle social coercion. Thus, with a variety of measures, researchers at the Institute have reported the same general findings. Similar findings have been reported by researchers elsewhere guided by different theoretical frameworks and using different measures (Cross, Cattell, and Butcher, 1967; Drevdahl and Cattell, 1958). For all of these psychologists, what would distinguish the two imaginary playwrights is the extent to which the personality of the outstanding playwright can be described as strong, assertive, and fiercely independent.

A word of caution is in order here. This research may merely add up to the unsurprising claim that people who are ambitious and highly achievement-oriented tend to be strong, independent, and unconventional. After all, those artists and scientists who had achieved enough eminence to be nominated by their peers as highly creative were undoubtedly extremely ambitious. Thus, while autonomy and ego strength may be necessary to "make it" in the arts or sciences, they may well be equally necessary for success in many walks of life. It is also possible that the qualities of autonomy and ego strength are not necessary to success in the arts per se, but simply to success as an artist in Western society. Little is known about the kinds of personality attributes required to thrive as an artist in a society that places less value on ambition and competition, or in a society, like that of ancient Egypt, with a strict artistic tradition within which all artists must work.

Reinforcement

The leading contemporary theorist of behaviorist psychology, B. F. Skinner, has proposed an account of artistic motivation that is much less complex than that put forth by Freud or by researchers at the Institute for Personality Assessment and Research. According to the behaviorist view of motivation, human behavior, as well as that of lower animals, is shaped entirely by external rewards. We sustain the illusion that our behavior is self-generated and that we have a measure of free will. In fact, however, our actions are entirely a product of environmental contingencies.

Behaviors, Skinner noted, always have consequences. Whenever a behavior is followed by positive consequences, we are motivated to repeat that behavior. Similarly, when an action is followed by negative consequences, we learn not to repeat that action. Thus, a bank teller who earns his supervisor's approval when he arrives at work ten minutes early will continue to be prompt, the rat who finds food at the end of a maze will run the maze over and over, and the lawyer who loses clients because she is not a good listener will become a better listener. Similarly, the playwright who is praised for a certain style of writing will continue to write in that style, and the playwright whose works are scorned will stop working or at least alter that style. "The artist," Skinner observed, "puts paint on canvas and is or is not reinforced by the results. If he is reinforced, he goes on painting" (1972, p. 335).

Skinner's artist creates in order to be reinforced. The difference between the two imaginary playwrights would therefore be explained entirely by their respective histories of reinforcement. The creative playwright by chance stumbled upon a style that the public applauded. Because of this approval, he continued to write plays in this same style. He is not more "creative" than the ordinary writer. Indeed, Skinner would shun any talk of such "unmeasurable" qualities. The fact that one writer is judged more creative reduces to the claim that the public finds his plays more reinforcing and thus reinforces him for his writing. Novel behaviors require no unusual explanation, and the motivation of the artist is no different from the motivation of the lawyer, the bank teller, or the rat.

Skinner's theory of the artist is in many ways fundamentally different from Freud's. While Freud spoke of unconscious mental forces, Skinner rejected all such talk of inner unseen processes, claiming to explain artistic activity fully in terms of observable behaviors and environmental reinforcements. No recourse to mental or emotional states is necessary to explain the artist. Like the behavior of all living creatures, the artist's behavior is shaped entirely by measurable, tangible rewards and punishments.

In some respects, however, Skinner and Freud were not entirely dissimilar. Both tried to explain artistic creativity by the same laws that account for the most mundane of human behaviors. And both viewed artists as driven to create by powerful forces over which they have no control. For Freud, the forces were internal ones, while for Skinner they were external.

Skinner's theory is open to a number of criticisms. First, the theory cannot explain why some artists but not others are reinforced for their work. What is it about the plays of the creative playwright that audience members like and which causes them to reinforce the author by attending his plays and writing positive reviews? Skinner did not answer this question. But herein may lie the heart of the difference between the two playwrights.

Second, why does the creative playwright persist when he is less reinforced than the hack, who may well be more popular? Rembrandt provides a good example. Although Rembrandt was very popular and successful in his early years, he later refused to bow to popular tastes, electing to paint in a way that shocked his contemporaries. Why did he abandon the style that had won him such acclaim? Skinner would answer that some artists are reinforced not by popularity but by the praise of a select few or by pride in their independence. But then why does the less creative artist not find the same things reinforcing and thereby become more creative? Skinner could only reply that one artist is reinforced by a sense of independence because a sense of independence is reinforcing to him; another is reinforced by the praise of many because it is the praise of many that reinforces him. Such answers reveal the circularity and lack of predictiveness of the theory.

Atypical Thinking

The arts, it is commonly held, are primarily emotional activities. The process of creation involves feeling rather than reasoning; artists do not think, they simply emote. This prevalent belief that art is primarily an emotional rather than a cognitive activity is supported by the Freudian vision of artists as dominated by instinctual drives beyond their rational control. Yet owing to the influence of thinkers such as Nelson Goodman (1968), Susanne Langer (1942), and Rudolf Arnheim (1962, 1969, 1972, 1974), a more cognitive vision of the arts has emerged. Psychologists are now studying the thought processes of the artist and seeking cognitive explanations of artistic motivation.

Psychologists interested in creativity in general, rather than in the arts in particular, have always defined creativity as involving a special form of thought, and they have made numerous attempts to lay bare the workings of the creative intellect. One such attempt was carried out by Joy P. Guilford (1967). By developing a "creativity" test, Guilford sought to demonstrate that creativity is not a unified skill but rather a collection of different component abilities. The questions on the test had no one right answer. Typical questions required subjects to produce synonyms of a given word; to produce words beginning with a specified letter; to list uses for a common object, such as a brick; or to imagine the consequences of improbable events, such as the possibility of all people becoming deaf. The more answers produced, and the more varied and unusual the responses, the higher the score achieved.

The term "divergent thinking" was coined to describe the thought processes of those who attained high scores. Divergent thinking was characterized by three separate components: fluency (measured by the sheer number of responses produced), flexibility (measured by the variety of responses), and originality (measured by the novelty of responses). Divergent thinking was opposed to convergent thinking, a type of thought oriented toward the known, correct solution.

Although both convergent and divergent thinking are often called for in the solution of a problem, Guilford hypothesized that the ability to think divergently was particularly characteristic of creative individuals. The creative mind, he believed, was fluent in the sense of having readily available a great deal of material, was flexible in its thinking, and was unconventional and original. Accordingly, the difference between the creative and ordinary playwrights would be located in their respective abilities to think fluently, flexibly, and originally. However, Guilford never empirically demonstrated a connection between divergent thinking and other measures of artistic creativity, so his studies do not permit the conclusion that creative people think divergently rather than convergently.

It was left to other investigators to determine whether such a relationship existed, and the results of their studies are in conflict. Some studies reported a positive relationship between divergent thinking and creativity. For instance, Victor Lowenfeld and Kenneth Beittel (1959) found that students rated as very creative in the visual arts scored high on a number of factors of divergent thinking. But MacKinnon (1961) found no relationship between divergent thinking and creativity in architects, and Jacob Getzels and Mihaly Csikszentmihalyi (1976) found a negative relationship between divergent thinking scores and later success as an artist.

Perhaps a clear relationship has not been established between divergent thinking and creativity in the arts because of the fact that the types of tasks used to measure divergent thinking are a far cry from the nature of creative endeavor. The ability to rattle off fifteen unusual uses for a brick, or twenty-five words beginning with *b*, suggests a mind that is clever, quick, and flexible, but not necessarily capable of the kind of deep thought which is generally associated with creativity in the arts or the sciences. Moreover, Guilford's tasks are all verbal; there is no reason to assume that verbal ability is important to creativity in the nonverbal arts.

Whereas Guilford emphasized the ability of the creative person to generate a multitude of unusual ideas at a rapid rate, other psychologists have stressed a different but perhaps related skill, the ability to perceive connections between elements ordinarily classified apart. Researchers at the Institute for Personality Assessment, who found that creative people give unusual responses to word association tests, concluded that creative people are especially good at perceiving novel connections. Sarnoff Mednick (1962) came to a similar conclusion. He devised a test called the Remote Associates Test in which subjects received several words from distant categories, such as *rat, blue,* and *cottage,* and were asked to think of a word that links them all, such as *cheese.* People assessed by other measures as high in creativity scored higher on this test than did less creative people: they responded at a faster rate, they produced more associations, and their associations were more varied and unusual. This finding supported the view that the essence of creativity involves the ability to form unusual associations.

Yet another researcher to argue that creative people perceive similarity where the ordinary mind sees only dissimilarity was Albert Rothenberg (1971). Rothenberg devised a test which required people to supply the opposites of words. He administered this task to two groups of people, one composed of subjects designated high in creativity, the other composed of subjects considered low in creativity. The creative people not only were able to perform at a much faster rate but also were able to give more opposites than were the noncreative people. The perception of resemblances between elements ordinarily considered divergent was dubbed "Janusian thinking," after Janus, the Roman god who could see in two directions at once. This finding supported the view that the creative person must be able to juxtapose and integrate elements ordinarily considered diametrically opposed. Thus, from this perspective, the creative playwright would differ from the ordinary one primarily in his ability to perceive similarity where ordinary people see only dissimilarity.

Intelligence

The finding that creative people think in atypical ways does not mean that creative people are more "intelligent" than ordinary people. It appears that, while a certain degree of intelligence is necessary for creativity, among people above the baseline, there is no relationship between degree of creativity and degree of intelligence.

Only low correlations have been reported between intelligence, as measured by school performance or IQ tests, and creativity, as measured by various kinds of creativity tests or ratings of the quality of works produced (Getzels and Jackson, 1962; Guilford, 1967; Torrance, 1962; Wallach and Kogan, 1965). For instance, some artists scored high on intelligence but were not rated as high in creativity by their peers, while others attained high creativity ratings but achieved relatively low intelligence scores (Barron, 1963a; MacKinnon, 1961). Even among mathematicians and scientists, the correlation between intelligence and creativity, though positive, is quite small (Gough, 1961). Thus, the difference between the two imaginary playwrights is not likely to be one of sheer intelligence.

To be sure, most investigators have found that a person with a low IQ cannot be highly creative in any field. Creative people tend to be of superior intelligence in comparison to the general population (Barron, 1963a). However, there are no tests which can pick out, among early high IQ scorers, those who will go on to prove exceptionally creative. And over the IQ of about 120, intelligence seems unrelated to degree of creativity. Thus, the creative person, while likely to have a relatively high IQ, is just as likely to have an IQ of 180 as 120.

At least one exception to this "baseline" rule has been reported. A group of children were identified who were characterized by low IQ's and who nonetheless scored high on tests of creativity (Wallach and Kogan, 1965). This conflict between the studies of adults and childrens can perhaps be explained. Even if there is, in fact, no relationship between IQ and creativity in childhood, those children who are creative yet lacking in intelligence may never grow up to be outstanding in a creative field such as the arts.

While creativity may exist in the absence of a high intelligence, such intelligence may be required if one is to achieve recognition in the highly competitive world of the arts.

Discovering Problems

In the process of fashioning a work of art, artists continually confront problems that must be solved. The poet must search for just the right word; the painter must figure out how to make a plane appear to recede; and the composer must decide on the chord that best completes a melody and strikes the right mood. The arts do not simply involve the emotions but also call upon the artist's cognitive, problem-solving skills.

Most traditional measures of creativity as well as intelligence assess the person's ability to solve problems. But while problem solving is undoubtedly important in the arts, it is possible that another, related skill is even more central: the ability to find problems. Perhaps the most creative artists are not simply good at solving problems but are also able to discover challenging problems.

This proposal was explored by Jacob Getzels and Mihaly Csikszentmihalyi (1976), who carried out a large-scale study of the personalities and perceptual and cognitive skills of art students at a prestigious art school. The study was based on a view of human motivation propounded by Jean Piaget (1963), Robert White (1959), Harry Harlow (1953), and Daniel Berlyne (1960). These diverse psychologists all rejected the Freudian view that people strive to reduce stimulation and that only a state of tension-free quiescence is experienced as pleasant. They proposed a new theory of motivation, based on evidence such as the fact that monkeys seek out interesting activities and often spend their free time playing with puzzles rather than scavenging for food (Harlow, 1953), or that infants spend extensive time engaging in sheer exploratory behavior which increases rather than reduces stimulation (Piaget, 1963). This evidence suggests that people are often motivated to increase rather than lower stimulation. Mental activity can thus be seen as an end in itself, and escape from boredom through novelty and stimulation can be viewed as a powerful drive.

On the assumption that humans often strive to increase stimulation, Getzels and Csikszentmihalyi hypothesized that the creative person is the stimulus-seeking person par excellence. The artist, they argued, is one who is motivated to search for and discover new problems to solve. To test this hypothesis, art students were given a set of objects and were asked to select any number of them, arrange them however they desired, and use them as the model for a still life. The experimenters observed the way in which both more and less successful art students carried out this task. In particular, they observed the degree to which the objects were handled and explored before the drawing stage, and the degree to which alterations were made after the drawing phase had begun.

The finished drawings were judged on three dimensions: technical skill, originality, and aesthetic value. Students were also asked about their subjective experience of the drawing process, including why they had chosen a particular arrangement, what they were thinking while they were drawing, and whether any elements in the drawing could be altered or eliminated without changing the basic character of the work. Their answers were scored in terms of the degree to which they reflected a concern for discovery. For instance, in response to the question of why the objects were arranged in a given way, a student who said that the objects had been arranged according to an a priori conventional principle, such as symmetry or harmony, was credited with little concern for discovery. However, a student who said that the arrangement itself was relatively unimportant, since the real structure of the drawing was to be worked out on the page, was credited with a strong concern for discovery.

The drawings judged to be the most original and highest in aesthetic value were made by those who had explored and rearranged the objects until they found a design problem which interested and challenged them; these were the same students who had scored the highest on concern for discovery in their responses to the questions posed. Those who made the least original and aesthetic drawings were more passive, simply accepted the problem as given, and went about the task of drawing the objects without exploring other possible combinations or compositions. Interestingly, no relationship was found between concern for discovery and sheer technical skill.

These findings led to the conclusion that the artist is motivated not solely by the desire to solve a problem but also often by the desire to find a problem to solve. Those who spent time rearranging the objects were searching for a visual problem whose solution would prove challenging. Those who simply drew the objects as presented were not seeking or defining a new problem but were simply solving a given one. Thus, the creative playwright would seem to be distinguished by his search for new problems which he then resolves in his writing; in contrast, the ordinary playwright does not set out to discover new problems but is content simply to work on the ones at hand.

As another facet of their research, the students were asked to explain why they were motivated to create. Over and over again, these young artists-in-the-making said that they painted in order to discover, to understand, to know. Thus, the articulated motivation behind their artistic work was very different from that proposed by Freud. Instead of citing emotional factors that drove them to paint, these artists consistently cited cognitive factors.

Talent

Ask a passerby what distinguishes the great artist from the mediocre, and none of the answers reviewed so far would be offered. The most common-sense response to such a question would probably not include instinctual drives, ego strength, reinforcement, atypical thinking, or the capacity to discover new problems. Instead, the passerby would say: "It's obvious. One has talent; the other doesn't."

Psychologists would certainly agree with this assessment. Yet few have taken this observation any further, because it is difficult to determine just what is meant by talent. No one really knows what talent is, although there are numerous tests to assess talent within the various arts (e.g. Graves, 1946; Meier, 1940; Rigg, 1942; Seashore, Lewis, and Saetveit, 1960; Wing, 1948). Freud himself despaired of ever trying to explain genius.

Clearly, the creative playwright must have more talent than the pedestrian one. But no one knows what makes someone talented, whether the brain of a gifted child is different from that of an ordinary child, or the degree to which giftedness is inherited or environmentally produced. It may be that the talented person is genetically predisposed to exhibit unusual skill in one or more of the symbol systems of the arts. These predispositions would most likely differ for different symbol systems. For example, the child born with a musical talent may possess perfect or near-perfect pitch. The child born with a talent in the visual arts may possess eidetic imagery, the ability to remember a visual scene in all its details. And the child who will become a writer may possess unusually rich intersensory connections, so that the colors of a scene evoke a mood best captured through metaphorical language.

The numerous tales of child prodigies who surprise their parents by spontaneously producing extraordinary works of art support the view that giftedness in a particular art form cannot be entirely a matter of training and environment. Nonetheless, it is exceedingly difficult to prove such a hypothesis. Moreover, even if the initial proclivity is neurologically determined at birth, few would deny that a great deal of cultural and familial support is necessary for such a gift to blossom.

In summary, certain conditions must be met to become an artist. To begin with, one needs a dose of that mysterious substance "talent." And this talent is most likely to be specific to a particular symbol system: there is no reason to assume that the person who is musically gifted also possesses talent in the visual or verbal arts. To this dose of skill within a symbol system, add several other cognitive capacities: the ability to perceive connections where others perceive only disparity, and the disposition to search for new problems where others are content to work on old ones. Finally, add a certain personality structure, one fueled by powerful drives that the individual is able to rechannel into artistic work, and one characterized by strength, independence, and the will to succeed.

While both cognitive and personality characteristics distinguish the creative artist, the relationship between cognitive and personality variables is not clear. Perhaps they are unrelated: those children who happen, for whatever reason, to develop a strong, driven personality and who also possess the requisite cognitive capacity would thus become artists. But another possibility seems more likely. Children who become aware, early in life, that they possess an unusual gift may react by developing a strong, independent, and highly motivated personality structure. Recognition of their talent may be the driving force behind the development of the personality that is typical of artists.

The Creative Thought Process

So far, the pathbreaking playwright has been distinguished from the plodding one by enduring personality and intellectual traits. Perhaps, however, the creative writer's most distinguishing characteristic is not a set of stable traits which manifest themselves in all domains but rather a special way of thinking that is deployed during the process of creative work.

Many artists as well as scientists have displayed curiosity about their thought processes during the act of creating and have introspected about this process. The attempt to lay bare the workings of the mind through introspection has a venerable history in psychology. Psychoanalytic and gestalt theorists based much of their work on introspective evidence. One of the cornerstones of Freudian theory, the Oedipus complex, grew out of Freud's painstaking self-analysis. And even the most dedicated experimental psychologists have made use of introspection in conjunction with other more objective measures.

There is, however, widespread disagreement over whether introspection provides reliable evidence. Behaviorists, for example, have always dismissed such evidence because it is based on unmeasurable processes which are not publicly observable. Other experimental psychologists have dismissed introspection on the ground that what people believe to have transpired in their minds often did not in fact occur (Nisbett and Wilson, 1977). Though it is not at all clear that people can gain accurate access into their own thought processes through introspection, experimental methods are subject to limitations as well. Both avenues are therefore necessary to gain an understanding of creativity.

Some artists have described the creative process in extreme terms, seeing it either as entirely unconscious and irrational or as wholly ordinary and rational. Among those who have described the creative process as entirely unconscious and inexplicable is the poet Amy Lowell. For Lowell, the real work involved in writing a poem transpires in the unconscious. Thus, it is a process over which the poet has no control: "It would seem that a scientific definition of a poet might put it something like this: a man of an extraordinarily sensitive and active subconscious personality, fed by, and feeding, a nonresistant consciousness. A common phrase among poets is, 'It came to me.' So hackneyed has this become that one learns to suppress the expression with care, but really it is the best description I know of the conscious arrival of a poem . . . An idea will come into my head for no apparent reason; 'The Bronze Horses,' for instance. I registered the horses as a good subject for a poem; and having so registered them, I consciously thought no more about the matter. But what I had really done was to drop my subject into the subconscious, much as one drops a letter into the mail-box. Six months later, the words of the poem began to come into my head, the poem—to use my private vocabulary—was 'there' " (Ghiselin, 1952, p. 110).

Writers are not the only ones who claim to experience no conscious control over their work. A similar account was proposed by the surrealist painter Max Ernst, who explained that when he painted, he felt as if he were a spectator observing the birth of his own work. Thus, creating a painting is like having a baby: it is a process over which one has little conscious control. Ernst also described the process of painting as similar to automatic writing, in which writers are said to surrender all conscious direction and allow a spiritual medium to work through them.

Not all artists have described the creative process as so diametrically opposed to consciousness and rationality. Edgar Allan Poe rejected such a view as a deliberate attempt to mystify the artist. Creation, he insisted, is nothing more than conscious, calculated, clever craft: "Most writers—poets in especial—prefer having it understood that they compose by a species of fine frenzy—an ecstatic intuition—and would positively shudder at letting the public take a peek behind the scenes . . . at the cautious selections and rejections—at the painful erasures and interpolations." And writing about the composition of his poem "The Raven," Poe articulated an even more rational view: "No one point in its composition is referrible either to accident or intuition . . . the work proceeded, step by step, to its completion with the precision and rigid consequence of a mathematical problem" (Rothenberg and Hausman, 1976, pp. 58–59).

Clearly, some artists have found the business of creation to be a great deal more difficult than the effortless process described by Lowell. But both extremes—creation as unconscious and irrational, and creation as conscious and deliberate—are problematical. On the rational end, it is often contended that Poe was being disengenuous when he described the process of writing a poem as involving only ordinary, calculated deliberation. At the other extreme, the view of creation as entirely unconscious and fortuitous can also be challenged. If Lowell, for instance, had been asked what aspiring writers ought to do in order to become a great poet, she would certainly not have recommended that they sit around and wait for a bolt of creative lightning to strike. More probably, she would have suggested years of training and hard work. In their attempt to convey the awesomeness of the moment of inspiration, artists such as Lowell may simply overlook the fact that a long formative process—years and years of hard work—make eventual inspiration possible.

By far the majority of artists as well as scientists have taken a position somewhere in between the view of creation as mysterious and irrational and as explicable and rational. Most report several very different stages in the creative process. In the initial phase, the problem is struggled with consciously and explored in all directions. After this laborious and often frustrating phase, creators turn their mind to something apparently unrelated to the problem they have been trying to solve. Then suddenly, as if out of the blue, inspiration strikes. The germ of a solution comes to mind, and the creators feel as if it came from nowhere. Artists and scientists commonly conclude that while their mind is directed elsewhere, their unconscious works on the problem; after a period of "incubation" in the unconscious, the solution presents itself fully formed to the conscious mind. However, the moment of fortuitous inspiration offers only the germ of a work. Following this seemingly effortless instant, a phase of conscious refining occurs in which the creator painstakingly expands the tiny seed given by inspiration.

The composer Richard Wagner described a moment of inspiration which occurred while he was half asleep and thus not in full conscious control of his thoughts, followed by a period of deliberate work in which he transformed the inspirational seed into a final work: "I fell into a kind of somnolent state, in which I suddenly felt as though I were sinking in swiftly flowing water. The rushing sound formed itself on my brain into a musical sound, the chord of E flat major, which continually echoed in broken forms . . . I awoke in sudden terror from my doze . . . I at once recognized that the orchestral overture to *The Rheingold*, which must long have laid latent within me, though it had been unable to find definite form, had at last been revealed to me . . . I decided to return to Zurich immediately, and begin the composition of my great poem" (Wagner, 1924, p. 603).

The playwright Jean Cocteau argued that inspiration supplies only the germ which must then be followed by hard work: "To write, to conquer ink and paper, accumulate letters and paragraphs, divide them with periods and commas, is a different matter from carrying around the dream of a play or of a book" (Ghiselin, 1952, p. 82). The writer Dorothy Canfield described two very different psychological and physiological states during the phases of the creative process. During the inspirational phase she lost all sense of time, her cheeks burned, her lips were parched, and her feet were cold. After two days of such intense, uninterrupted concentration came many more days of calm rewriting, in which time appeared to drag on forever, punctuated by periodic breaks from the labor of revision (Ghiselin, 1952).

Similar testimony comes from scientists. The French mathematician Henri Poincaré described the interplay of hard work and sudden inspiration in a scientific domain: "Just at this time I left Caen, where I was then living, to go on a geologic excursion . . . The changes in travel made me forget my mathematical work. Having reached Coutances, we entered an omnibus to go some place or other. At the moment when I put my foot on the step the idea came to me, without anything in my former thoughts seeming to have paved the way for it, that the transformations I had used to define the Fuchsian functions were identical with those of non-Euclidean geometry . . . On my return to Caen, for conscience's sake, I verified the result at my leisure" (Ghiselin, 1952, p. 37). Poincaré had consciously put aside the problem of Fuchsian functions.

Then, while stepping on a bus and thinking about other matters, suddenly he recognized the identity between two types of functions. The phase after inspiration, the phase described so often as one of careful reworking and refinement, was for Poincaré a trivially simple one: the process of verification merely demonstrated what he had already realized to be true. But many days of hard work preceded the brief moment of inspiration: Poincaré's discovery involved craft as well as inspiration.

The self-reports of artists and scientists suggest that during the period of creative work, a sequence of different types of thought is experienced. This sequence includes rational efforts at problem solving as well as moments of inspiration that do not seem to be the product of conscious effort alone. The different stages of thought occur in a certain order: a moment of inspiration must follow a much longer period of conscious work as well as a period in which the creator has taken a break from the work at hand. What begins as hard work eventually becomes automatic: as if from nowhere, inspiration strikes and the germ of a work is formed.

This picture of the creative process is based on only one type of evidence: the random, uncontrolled introspections of creative people who, for one reason or another, elected to write about how they worked. Psychologists have not let the case rest here. Armed with a variety of theories and methods derived from clinical practice, case studies, and studies involving large numbers of subjects and a battery of statistical tests, they have attempted to probe further into the inventive mind.

Unconscious Incubation

Based on the testimony of creative thinkers, Graham Wallas (1926) identified four stages in the creative process: preparation, in which the problem is explored; incubation, in which conscious attention turns away from the problem; illumination, in which the basic idea or solution appears with suddenness and a sense of certainty; and verification, in which the idea is tested and refined. By far the most controversial aspect of this formulation is the stage of incubation, during which the unconscious is said to work on a problem, solve it, and present a solution to the unconscious mind. Theoretical support for this view coomes from the psychoanalytic work of Ernst Kris (1952) and Lawrence Kubie (1958).

According to Kris, creative work involves a phase of inspiration followed by a period of elaboration. Each of these phases entails a very different kind of mental activity and a different level of consciousness. The inspirational phase is guided by primary-process thought, a type of thought described by Freud as irrational, chaotic, and tolerant of the contradictory and the illogical. Such thought, Freud believed, lies at the heart of dreams and dreamlike or hallucinatory states, in which bizarre connections are formed, opposites are interchanged, and the rules of time and space are violated. As Freud originally formulated the issue, primary-process thought is seated in the unconscious. In Kris's revision of psychoanalytic theory, however, primary-process thought is housed in the preconscious, a level much closer to the surface than the Freudian unconscious.

During the inspirational phase, according to Kris, the artist momentarily regresses to a preconscious, primary-process level of thinking. Such a phase corresponds to the incubational period described by Wallas. The regression entailed in creative thinking is described as "regression in the service of the ego," in order to distinguish it from the regressive thinking of the psychoses. In the case of psychotic thinking, the individual regresses to primary-process thinking and cannot resurface to ordered, logical forms of thought. In the case of the artist, however, the regression is temporary and the conscious ego remains in ultimate control.

The tolerance of contradiction made possible by a regression to primary-process thinking increases the probability of the formulation of novel combinations of images and ideas, a process that is central to creativity. The phase of regression is followed by an elaboration of the work of creation by means of conscious, logical, secondary-process thought, a phase corresponding to Wallas' verification. During this phase, the artist consciously works out the ideas supplied by the workings of the preconscious.

Kris's notion of regression in the service of the ego has received modest empirical support (e.g. Barron, 1963a; Wild, 1965). For instance, to determine whether creative people tend to have an unusual ability both to regress to primary-process thinking and to achieve control over such thinking, the Rorschach test was administered to a group of people who were also given creativity tests (Pine and Holt, 1960). Responses to the Rorschach stimuli were scored in terms both of primary-process thinking, as in aggressive, sexual, or nonlogical statements, and of control over primary-process thinking, as in socially acceptable statements. Those who achieved the highest scores for creativity were the same people who achieved the highest scores on both Rorschach measures—the expression of primary-process thoughts and control over such thoughts.

In order to test the claim that creativity is a multiphase process involving a stage of unconscious incubation, Catherine Patrick

(1935, 1937) asked poets, painters, and scientists, to think aloud while working on a creative problem. The subjects' descriptions of their mental processes provided evidence for all four stages and thus supported a multiphase view of creativity. However, as Patrick herself was aware, the studies did not allow the firm conclusion that the period labeled as incubational actually involved unconscious work. The evidence for incubation consisted of demonstrating that an idea which occurred early in the course of working on a problem was then forgotten and later remembered. But to demonstrate unconscious incubation, it would have been necessary to show that during the time in which the idea was consciously forgotten, this idea underwent changes in the unconscious, so that when it returned to the level of consciousness, it had achieved a new and more articulated form.

Other experimental studies have been carried out to test the construct of incubation. In these studies, ordinary people—that is, not ones selected for their creativity—are typically given a problem to solve. Half of the subjects are interrupted in the middle of the task and given another distracting task to perform. Subsequently, they are allowed to return to the initial problem. The question is which group will solve the problem better or faster. If the interruption and distracting task allow the initial ideas to incubate in the unconscious, then the interrupted group should perform the best.

The results of these studies are inconsistent (Olton and Johnson, 1976). Although some studies reported that the interrupted group performed better than the noninterrupted group (Dreistadt, 1969), not one of these studies has survived replication. This proved true even of a study that attempted to simulate the natural course of creative work by giving subjects a more challenging problem than those used in most incubation studies and by allowing the subjects to take a long break at whatever point they wished (Olton, 1979).

Compounding these difficulties is the fact that unconscious incubation is by no means the only way to explain superior performance in the interrupted group. In cases where the distracted group performs better, several explanations are equally plausible. The interruption may have allowed subjects to break out of a rut, a poor way of approaching the problem; it may have allowed them to return with a strengthened will; or they may simply feel refreshed and less subject to boredom as a result of the interruption (Patrick, 1935; Woodworth, 1938).

Thus, there is still no strong empirical evidence to support the recurrent claim of artists, scientists, and psychoanalytic theorists that the unconscious carries out a great deal of the work involved in the process of creation. Yet the persistence of this claim in the self-reports of creative people cannot be overlooked: the subjective impression of a period of incubation followed by illumination is itself a robust phenomenon. The discrepancy between the self-reports of the creators and the evidence from psychological laboratories may be accounted for in a number of ways. It is possible that the negative experimental findings stem from the fact that psychologists have studied ordinary individuals rather than ones selected for their creativity. Perhaps incubation occurs only in the minds of outstandingly creative people. Or perhaps the failure to demonstrate incubation in the laboratory stems from the relative artificiality of the situation in which the "creators" find themselves. It is also possible that the self-reports of inspiration following a period in which the creator's mind was directed away from the problem at hand have been exaggerated. Incubation may occur, but rarely. The awesome nature of the phenomenon when it does strike may lead creators to believe that it occurs more often than it does.

Conscious Craft

In a sharp break from both introspective accounts by creative people and psychoanalytic accounts of the creative process, some psychologists have focused on the contribution of conscious, rational processes in the creation of a work of art (e.g. Arnheim, 1962; Dewey, 1934; Ecker, 1963). According to these psychologists, to define the essence of creativity as the forging of novel links is insufficient. The "reshuffling" that occurs in primary-process thought may be important, but it cannot constitute what is essential about creativity. For instance, not all novel links prove fruitful and aesthetically appealing. Moreover, the bulk of the creative enterprise occurs after artists have had their initial moment of inspiration. Thus, instead of focusing on the illogical nature of insight, these psychologists view creation as a logical species of problem solving.

Picasso once remarked: "It would be interesting to preserve photographically, not the stages, but the metamorphoses of a picture. Possibly one might then discover the path followed by the brain in materializing a dream" (Arnheim, 1962, p. 30). The gestalt psychologist Rudolf Arhneim (1962) set out to do exactly what Picasso suggested. By scrutinizing all of the work sheets and preparatory sketches that preceded Picasso's painting *Guernica*, and by studying the stages of the canvas en route to its final composition, Arnheim provided a new view of the creative process. Instead of sudden insight after long incubation, creating a work of art was shown to involve a dialectical process in which the work grows in "erratic leaps, forward and backward" (p. 132). At the heart of this process is goal-directed "visual thinking" (p. 134)—a far cry from the inexplicable flash of inspiration described by artists in their retrospective accounts.

Two assumptions inform this approach. First, during the entire time that artists are creating, they have a final goal in mind. This goal is the artists' vision of what they ultimately want to achieve, and it provides both the energy and the direction for the creative process. And second, little that artists create is accidental. Rather, everything is produced for the purpose of more nearly approximating the final goal.

In creating a work of art, artists are struggling to solve a problem, using all of their conscious, intellectual powers. The creative process involves problem solving within a medium. For the painter, it involves visual thinking. The solutions reached are dictated by formal considerations and by the equally important need to express a particular meaning. If formal considerations were all, the artist would simply strive to find the most pleasing organization of space. But formal use of space is only a means to an end, and that end is to make visible the meaning that the artist wishes to express. Every choice of shape, line, and color functions symbolically to render this meaning visible. Thus, in the first state of *Guernica*, the fallen warrior had an arm raised at right angles to the body, which Picasso later lowered (Fig. 1.2). This decision to lower the arm had both formal and symbolic consequences. Formally, the lowered arm competes less than the upright arm with the upright form of the bull. And with respect to the meaning expressed, the upright arm renders the bull less potent, while the lowered arm, in contrast, underlines the strength of the bull. Picasso may have lowered the arm of the warrior in order to achieve these formal and symbolic consequences.

Such an explanation views the creative process as a series of deliberate, conscious, logical choices. The artist's solutions are arrived at through a lengthy dialectical process, often involving trial and error. But at all times the artist is consciously attempting to achieve a particular vision. And every decision is guided by an awareness of the formal symbolic constraints of this vision.

Arnheim's analysis of the creative process differs vastly from those analyses that emphasize the importance of unconscious insights and the perception of novel connections. Creativity, Arnheim argued, demands more than the readiness of a nimble mind to perceive new combinations. To be sure, such flexibility is necessary, but it is not sufficient. Picasso attempted many possibilities,

1.2 *Picasso, early state of* Guernica *(top), with the arm of the warrior raised at right angles to the prostrate body, and final canvas, with the arm no longer raised, perhaps to avoid competing with the potency of the bull.*

but never did he attempt novel possibilities at random. Each one was controlled by his ultimate vision; each represented a search for the final form that the artist already had in his mind. The artist's goal is not simply originality, as suggested by neo-Freudian psychologists who stress the importance of the preconscious. Originality is necessary, but the ultimate goal is to make visible the painter's vision.

The questions that Arnheim asked were not unlike those posed by Freud. However, the way in which they were answered was entirely different. Freud asked questions like, "Why did Leonardo paint this particular painting in this way?" And the answers that he supplied had to do with the personal history of the painter. Similarly, Arnheim confronted the question, "Why did Picasso paint *Guernica* in this way?" But the answers given had to do not with Picasso's personality but rather with the nature of the task in which he was engaged. While Freud explained the artistic product in terms of the artist's childhood, Arnheim explained the work in terms of the artist's vision: the artist's aesthetic goal determines the subject matter as well as the form in which this subject is represented. While Freud would have interpreted *Guernica* as ultimately a statement about Picasso, Arnheim interpreted the painting as a visual statement about the world. And while for Freud, the content of a painting was a means of disguising the artist's ultimate meaning even from the artist, for Arnheim a painting's content was a means of making visible the artist's ultimate and conscious vision.

Arnheim's approach is not without its problems. To begin with, the artist's vision may not always be there from the start. It is possible that too much is read into Picasso's first sketch for *Guernica*. Or if not, perhaps the possession of a guiding vision from the start does not characterize all paintings: artists may sometimes stumble on a solution accidentally, and as a result, their ultimate vision may change.

A second problem is that Arnheim's approach accounts for the process of the work after the initial conception but does not illuminate the source of this initial conception. Thus, the most fundamental aspect of the process remains shrouded in mystery. However, no psychological studies have yet been able to reveal much about how the artist gets the first glimmerings of an idea for a work. Some thinkers have gone so far as to say that this problem is in principle not susceptible to empirical study (e.g., Popper, 1968).

Perhaps the fundamental limitation of the approach, and one explicitly admitted by Arnheim, is that, while it has exposed the steps involved in the making of *Guernica*, it has not necessarily exposed the mental processes lurking behind the steps. It is only inference that Picasso lowered the arm of the warrior because it competed with the potent upright form of the bull. Other decisions and reasons might have resulted in the same end-product.

One way to zero in more directly on the psychological processes that occur as the artist moves step by step toward the solution of an artistic problem is to ask the artist to think aloud while creating. This technique, used by Patrick to provide evidence for incubation, was also used by the cognitive psychologist David Perkins (1981). Perkins adopted an "on-line" process-tracing method in order to explore the possibility that the creative process is not simply a matter of unconscious incubation during which ideas are juxtaposed in novel fashion, but is rather a cognitive problem-solving venture entailing a series of deliberate, nonmysterious decisions along the way.

In the studies based on this method, both poets and visual artists were asked to work on a poem or a drawing in the laboratory. Subjects were asked to think aloud, saying something every five seconds. If their minds were blank, they were instructed to say so. They were cautioned not to analyze or overexplain their thoughts but simply to verbalize them. And at moments when an idea seemed suddenly to appear, subjects were asked immediately afterward to try to remember the thoughts leading up to the idea.

It is often objected that such a technique disturbs the normal thought processes. If artists are asked to think aloud as they create, they will not create in their normal way. But as the subjects in these studies became absorbed in their work, their reporting became automatic. And in almost all cases they said that they felt they had followed their usual procedure and made approximately normal progress. Some even reported that the verbalizing helped them organize their thoughts.

The studies suggested that the creative process involves a combination of reason and intuition. What is novel about these findings is their careful exploration of the rational side of creation. Through the use of the process-tracing technique, it was possible to dissect the key moment of insight that artists and scientists write so much about. The evidence demystified the creative moment, that instant of sudden illumination when, for example, the final line of a poem appears to spring full-blown into consciousness. Careful scrutiny of these moments and the moments that immediately preceded them demonstrated something astonishing: beneath the illusory impression that an idea has arisen "out of the blue," or out of the unfathomable unconscious, can be found a series of small logical steps, quite accessible to consciousness if one bothers to look very carefully. The moment of "insight" is simply the final step in a chain of reasoning carried out so rapidly that unless the creator pays particular attention, its workings remain undetected.

Consider the case of the professional poet participating in one of the studies who arrived at the laboratory prepared to compose a poem. She began with only the vaguest of ideas—a notion that the day reminded her of an air-raid drill because of the wailing of her children. She wrote the first line: "My babies are wailing like those air-raid drills/I remember." She added some more lines about her childhood memories of air-raid drills. At this point she stopped.

She had drawn a comparison between babies and air-raid sirens at the beginning, but she had not yet shown how they were connected except through sound. She paused for a moment when unable to proceed. Suddenly she said, "Aha! It has to do with . . . preserving your own life first. I think that's what this has to do with, actually. Maybe I'll call this poem 'Self-Preservation.'"

She had discovered the deeper link between babies and air raids: both had the effect of warning her to escape somewhere to maintain her very existence. To discover how the recognition of this link arose, she was asked to recall any thoughts that occurred just before her "Aha!" She responded: "Well, I was thinking [reads] 'and I am still fighting that cold war/alone. The wailing babies. What did they signal me to do? What is it [the air raid] a signal for me to do? And actually [pause], why do you hide? It's because you're trying to preserve yourself, and that's what the babies are signaling me to do too, because basically I can't, I don't tolerate them very well, and it does me in so much that I have to leave them and go into silence, some place that's silent so I can preserve myself (pp. 67–68).

Perkins analyzed the steps that led up to the final moment in which the poet recognized the underlying similarity between air raids and babies. The poet asked herself what the wailing babies signaled her to do, and then what the sirens urged her to do. The sirens, she reasoned, signaled her to hide, in order to preserve herself. And that is what the babies signaled her to do too, and for the same reason. These steps led up to her insight. The germ of the poem was now complete, and all that followed was the work of revising, tinkering, and clarifying.

While psychoanalytic theory would view the moment of insight as a product of primary-process thinking, and the hours of subsequent elaboration as a conscious, secondary-process effort, Perkins' studies found no such dichotomy. The moment of insight was in fact the product of logical, not haphazard steps. Like Arnheim, Perkins presented a view of the creative process that runs counter to the Romantic and Platonic image of a work of art as received, rather than crafted, by the artist. And like Arnheim, Perkins sketched the creative process as being very much constrained by the artist's goal and engaging the logical faculties of the mind in a problem-solving situation.

But if the moment of insight is not mysterious after all, and if it really consists of a rapid chain of reasoning, the question arises as to why most creative people insist on the crucial role of sudden insights which come upon them "from out of the blue." It is possible, Perkins argued, that there is really no conflict between these two positions. Reasoning is as natural and spontaneous a process as walking across the room. The brain is designed to reason, and it does so fluently. The reasoning process is laborious only when a problem is very difficult, just as walking is laborious only when the path to be traversed is very steep. Rational effort may thus be laborious or spontaneous. Artists and scientists who report moments of sudden insight may have just gone through a rapid process of spontaneous reasoning. It is not necessary to invoke mysterious, unconscious processes to explain thinking that appears spontaneous.

Using a similar approach, the psychologist Howard Gruber (1974, 1978) explored the thought processes of Charles Darwin. Gruber analyzed Darwin's notebooks in order to lay bare the stages through which a creative mind passes in the construction of a revolutionary theory. Although this work illuminates creativity in the sciences, the findings may also tell something about creativity in the arts.

The picture of the creative process that emerged from the notebooks is far closer to the view proposed by Arnheim and Perkins than to the self-reports of artists and scientists claiming inexplicable moments of insight. Darwin's thought was a slow, constructive process involving rational, directed thought and many small insights rather than one great moment of insight. Darwin was engaged in a "network of enterprises" (Gardner, 1981, p. 64). Instead of focusing on only one problem, he worked on many problems at the same time. Some of these areas of inquiry were connected in his mind; others may have seemed unconnected. As a result, Darwin had to juggle the pursuit of a number of areas of inquiry. But by virtue of this network of enterprises, one domain of inquiry might eventually shed light on another as connections between disparate domains were discovered.

According to Gruber, the creative mind is often guided by "images of wide scope," in which diverse elements are joined so as to allow a reconceptualization of a field of knowledge (Gardner, 1981, p. 67). These images need not be visual ones. Those of Piaget, for instance, were not. Examples of such unifying images are Freud's image of the mind as an iceberg with the submerged bulk as the unconscious and the tip as the conscious mind, or Darwin's image of the branching tree of nature.

Like the researchers at the Institute for Personality Assessment and Research, Gruber found that the creative thinker possesses exceptional courage and autonomy. And like Arnheim, Gruber stressed the importance of the creator's guiding goal. Creative thinkers do not work randomly on one problem or the other;

rather, everything they do is in the service of achieving an ultimate goal. One is reminded of the English landscape painter Constable, who said: "Painting is a science and should be pursued as an inquiry into the laws of nature. Why, then, may not landscape painting be considered as a branch of natural philosophy, of which pictures are but the experiments?" (Gombrich, 1960, p. 33). Or one thinks of Picasso, who said: "Paintings are but research and experiment. I never do a painting as a work of art. All of them are researches. I search constantly and there is a logical sequence in all this research" (Liberman, 1960, p. 33).

These analyses do not permit the conclusion that the unconscious plays no role in the creative process. One can never prove that the unconscious is not involved. Perhaps Perkins' poet, for instance, achieved her insight by nonrational thought processes, and it was only her discovery of the origin of the insight that was logical. The ambiguity of these findings underscores the difficulty of the effort to crack the problem of creativity. But by focusing on the contributions of the conscious mind, this research has shown that there is little need to invoke unconscious processes. At least the bulk of the creative effort can be explained by goal-directed logical thought. These studies serve to demystify, without demeaning, the process of creation. In place of a sense that certain moments in the creative process are beyond understanding, they suggest that these moments are indeed explicable if one looks with enough care.

Arnheim, Perkins, and Gruber were only the first explorers in a perilous terrain. They adopted two different means of untangling the creative process: examining the tracks left by the creator in the process of composing a particular work, or probing the thought processes during the period of creative work. To unravel the mysterious tangles of creative thinking does not diminish this uniquely human activity. Rather, it renders the accomplishment even more marvelous. For it may be that, with just the ordinary cognitive tools of logic, reason, and goal-directed decision-making, the creative person is able to achieve works that are anything but ordinary.

A word of caution is in order. There is probably no such thing as "the" creative process. Undoubtedly a great deal of variation among creative people exists. Some artists may use more conscious craft, others perhaps use more irrational, primary-process thought. Any single theory designed to explain creativity as if it were one process, used alike by all artists and scientists, is likely to be incomplete.

Tentative conclusions can now be drawn about what it is that differentiates the creative and the ordinary playwright. To begin with, they probably differ in terms of temperament. It is a good guess that the creative playwright is more driven, more independent, and more dominant. He may well have come from a family who fostered his autonomy. The playwrights probably also differ in cognitive traits. The creative playwright may be better able to perceive relationships among domains ordinarily considered unrelated, and more likely to set out to discover new problems rather than simply to solve old ones.

If the creative playwright were asked to describe the workings of his mind while he is writing, he might well say that his best dramatic ideas just come to him out of the blue, while he is brushing his teeth or falling asleep. He might, like the film-maker Ingmar Bergman, say that he makes all his decisions on the basis of sheer intuition (*New York Times*, May 8, 1981, p. C7). Yet such testimony must be taken with some skepticism. To be sure, the playwright may genuinely feel that his insights emerge out of nowhere, or from the depths of his unconscious. However, if his thought processes are closely examined, it will probably appear that a great deal of logical, rational, conscious hard work led up to these insights. They were perhaps made possible by the writer's network of enterprises. That is, because he is most likely thinking of his next play while writing the current one, insights from one domain may illuminate problems in another domain.

Despite the fact that the artist's insights are built upon hard work and goal-directed problem solving, these insights nonetheless remain qualitatively different from those of ordinary people. Both the genius and the ordinary person make use of logical rational thought, yet only the genius is able to revolutionize our way of seeing the world. Over and above the hard work, reason, and care, creative people do have the possibility of coming up with great metaphors, melodies, paintings, or scientific theories. And it is that extra something which may forever defy rational explanation.

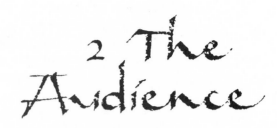

2 The Audience

Poetry is indispensable, if I only knew what for.

—Jean Cocteau

All art is quite useless.

—Oscar Wilde

In 1914, Freud confessed that no piece of sculpture had ever exerted so powerful an effect on him as the *Moses* of Michelangelo. When Freud visited Rome, he was repeatedly drawn to the deserted church that housed the *Moses*. For Freud, there was something inscrutable about this work, something not readily understood. He puzzled over the meaning of the facial expression— whether it is meant to reveal a stable character trait or to be read as the portrayal of a particular mood at a highly significant moment. If the latter, he wondered what the moment might be— whether the sculpture represents a Moses about to spring to his feet, wrathful at the sight of pagan worship, or whether his expression contains the final rather than the initial traces of a violent gust of passion. Focusing on details as minute as the precise position of Moses' right thumb when it comes in contact with his beard, Freud evaluated a number of hypotheses, arriving finally at an interpretation that seemed best to fit all the evidence.

There are several possible reasons why Freud was so strongly attracted to Michelangelo's *Moses*. Perhaps his study of the work served deep-seated emotional needs, allowing him to identify unconsciously with Moses, both men unappreciated by their people but ultimately vindicated. Possibly Freud simply derived pleasure from the sheer beauty of the sculpted form. Or the experience may have served more cognitive needs, allowing Freud to test his wits in the solution of a challenging intellectual problem.

To explain Freud's attraction to the *Moses* requires facing the more general question of the source of art's appeal. The sounds of a Beethoven symphony rivet our attention; we spend hours in a museum staring at colored canvases on a wall; and we experience the full range of human feeling while reading Tolstoy's *Anna Karenina*, a novel about people who existed only in a Russian author's imagination. Why do we do these apparently useless things?

This question, in turn, raises the question whether the source of art's appeal is universal, or whether art serves different needs for different kinds of people. Perhaps not everyone would experience Freud's powerful attraction to *Moses*. It may be that people's reaction to a work of art is determined, in part, by their familiarity with the arts, their "cognitive style," or their personality.

Various theories of the needs served by art have been proposed by philosophers and psychologists. One of the most common-sense views is that the function of art is to communicate. By expressing their inner feelings, artists convey important messages to the spectator through the work. The essence of the aesthetic experience is to apprehend the often hidden message.

This explanation, however, fails to tell how the arts are unique. No one can deny the fact that a work of art carries information. But there are many ways to communicate other than through the arts. What is needed is an understanding of why people so eagerly seek aesthetic messages.

Another approach, which owes something to the Darwinian tradition, views the function of art as adaptation. The experience of art is said to provide training in skills that ultimately affect the chances of human survival. For instance, it is argued that art sharpens the powers of discrimination, renders important messages more memorable because of their aesthetic wrapping, enhances sociability and self-assertion (Dissanayake, 1974), and fosters a willingness to be innovative and break out of old ruts (Peckham, 1965). Art, thus, is said to have contributed to human survival and evolution. Unfortunately, however, such evolutionary propositions are extremely difficult to test.

Still another long-standing view in the history of philosophy is that the essence of the aesthetic experience is the apprehension of beauty. The contemplation of the beautiful is said to provide a unique kind of pleasure, often called "the aesthetic emotion." On this account, art serves to satisfy the need for pleasure.

There are two problems with this view. First, some independent definition of aesthetic pleasure is needed, for to say that aesthetic pleasure is that pleasure yielded by an aesthetic object is not very revealing. Second, if aesthetic pleasure comes from the contemplation of beauty, this fails to explain the experience of pleasure when people witness art that does not appear beautiful, such as a play depicting violent bloodshed, or a portrait of a man whose face is distorted by anger. Clearly, if art's effect is pleasure, pleasure does not derive solely from the perception of beauty.

The arts have also long been viewed as therapeutic. Plato believed that some forms of music have a calming effect on the soul; others suggested that art has a moral effect on human character. One of the earliest expositions of the view that art is essentially therapeutic is Aristotle's theory that the function of tragedy is to arouse the emotions of pity and fear in order to discharge these passions and leave the audience purified and purged.

Like theories stressing the pleasure derived from beauty, the therapeutic theories grant a central role to pleasure. However, here the pleasure derives not from the effect of beauty but from catharsis, relief, and consequent healing. Unlike theories based on beauty, therapeutic theories can handle the paradox of ugliness and tragedy.

To ask what humans "get" out of exposure to art is to ask a motivational and therefore a psychological question. Within the field of psychology, two major attempts have been made to explain the source of art's appeal. The psychoanalytic theory of art espouses the view that art is therapeutic. According to Freud, people are irresistibly attracted to art because of its power to rechannel and thereby relieve overpowering instinctual demands. This discharge of instinctual energy is both pleasurable and therapeutic. A very different tradition, that of experimental aesthetics, maintains that people are drawn to art because of the capacity of its formal properties to elicit pleasure.

The Release of the Repressed

Freud's theory of the need served by exposure to art is part and parcel of his theory of the artist's need to create. Just as Leonardo unconsciously acted out forbidden wishes on a symbolic plane when he painted the *Madonna and Child with St. Anne*, the perceiver of this painting also unconsciously gratifies forbidden wishes. Thus, both making and perceiving art allow forbidden wishes to be gratified.

According to Freud (1911, 1913a, 1913c, 1925), the process by which the audience achieves unconscious gratification involves two steps. The perceiver's first response is one of pleasure given by the sheer formal properties of the work, such as color and form in the case of painting, rhythm and rhyme in the case of literature. These properties elicit pleasure because they are beautiful. And underlying the pleasure derived from the experience of the beautiful is the pleasure derived from sexuality. "There is to my mind no doubt," Freud wrote, "that the concept of 'beautiful' has its roots in sexual excitation and that its original meaning was 'sexually stimulating' (1905, p. 156).

Only for the connoisseur, however, do the formal properties of a work constitute the strongest source of aesthetic pleasure. For the ordinary perceiver, the pleasure from the beauty of a work of art is only the "fore-pleasure," and a relatively superficial one at that. It is essentially a bribe, enticing the perceiver to experience a second, more powerful source of pleasure.

The second source of pleasure is yielded by the content of the work. Consider Dostoevsky's *The Brothers Karamazov*. This novel deals with the theme of parricide, focusing on a murder committed by someone with a filial relation to the victim. Freud (1928) presented evidence to suggest that Dostoevsky chose this theme because of his own unconscious Oedipal anger toward his father. And Dostoevsky's parricidal wish, Freud argued, is also every reader's Oedipal wish. Readers, by unconsciously identifying with the novel's characters and by projecting their own wishes onto these characters, achieve the same gratification as did the author.

The gratification of instinctual desires discharges the unpleasant tension of these unallayed wishes, and this discharge is experienced as pleasurable. Because such a release of tension, for both artist and audience member, provides psychic balance, art's ultimate effect is therapeutic. If people were not able to act out their forbidden fantasies in such an indirect way, these wishes would press for their release in other, more threatening ways.

Art is not, for Freud, the only arena in which forbidden wishes can be symbolically gratified. The same process underlies nocturnal dreams and daydreams, slips of the tongue, jokes, and neurotic symptoms. But wish fulfillment through art provides a much more potent source of pleasure for two reasons. First, there is the pleasure in the formal properties—the beauty—of the work. And second, a work of art contains more of what Freud called "secondary elaboration" than do dreams or fantasies. Secondary elaboration refers to the disguise with which the artist unconsciously conceals the latent content of a work. If Dostoevsky had said outright that he harbored a wish to kill his father, readers would feel revulsion. And if they allowed themselves to have a daydream in which they carried out this deed, they would feel guilty and anxious. But in *The Brothers Karamazov*, the latent content—Dostoevsky's parricidal wish—is concealed by the manifest content—a fictional character murders another character who is not his biological father but to whom he bears a filial relationship. In this way, readers are prevented from becoming conscious of their own wishes and thus are spared both revulsion and guilt. It was precisely because of the importance Freud attributed to the secondary elaboration of art that he professed a dislike for expressionism and surrealism—schools of painting which he felt depicted primary-process imagery too directly, as in a dream.

Freud's theory of art's appeal is not without its Achilles' heel. There are three major weaknesses in the theory: the dichotomy between form and content, the lack of conclusive evidence that art is therapeutic, and the general difficulty of testing the theory.

Freud's sharp division between the form and content of a work is problematical in two respects. First, such a radical distinction is philosophically untenable, since there is no way to decide where form leaves off and content begins (e.g. Goodman, 1975). Is *Moses'* facial expression part of the form or the content? Is the intensity of Dostoevsky's language separable from the themes of his novels? And even if such a division were possible, it is difficult to imagine how one could respond to these two aspects separately, as Freud maintained. Second, in dividing form and content, Freud undervalued the formal aspects of art, conceiving of them as sheer technical properties which play only a minor role. His focus on representational content to the exclusion of other aspects renders his theory helpless to explain the appeal of nonrepresentational art, such as music, architecture, and abstract painting or sculpture. This is a serious weakness. The experience of nonrepresentational art does not differ so markedly that it must be accounted for by an entirely different set of principles.

Freud's view that beholding a work of art has a therapeutic effect or provides a catharsis by which instinctual tensions are allayed is also lacking in evidence. Several studies by social psychologists bear on this issue. In the typical experiment, subjects are shown aggressive films in order to determine whether the possibility of acting out their aggressive impulses vicariously through projection has the effect of diminishing overt aggressive behavior. The results of these studies conflict (Murray, 1973). Many have found no effect on overt aggression, and only one study reported a positive effect (Feschbach and Singer, 1971). In this study, boys who watched only aggressive television programs reduced their overt aggression more, over the course of seven weeks, than boys who were given a diet of nonaggressive programs. Although these results applied only to lower class boys, they suggest that catharsis can occur. However, a later study reported the reverse finding: extensive viewing of aggression on television correlated with a high degree of aggression in preschool children (Singer and Singer, 1979).

Not only do the results of these studies conflict, but they may not be the best way to test Freud's theory. After all, psychological experiments do not come close to the experience of reading *The Brothers Karamazov* or attending a performance of *Oedipus Rex*. Moreover, it is not at all self-evident that catharsis is measurable by degree of overt aggression (Machotka, 1979). Perhaps art provides a subtler measure of relief.

This illustrates a more general problem with Freud's theory. Because he posed questions of the broadest, most fundamental kind, and because he proposed answers framed in terms that would be very difficult to measure in a psychological laboratory, the theory is extremely difficult to test. Freud himself never attempted to subject his theory of the aesthetic response to direct experimental test. Instead, he relied on indirect evidence—namely the consistency of his arguments with the theoretical edifice that he had constructed on the basis of years of clinical experience to explain all of mental life.

Aesthetics from Below

An entirely different approach to the psychology of the audience member originated with Gustav Fechner (1876) at the end of the nineteenth century. Unlike Freud, Fechner restricted himself to questions about the arts that could be answered in an experimental laboratory. Rather than posing the broad question of the needs served by art, Fechner set out to determine, through rigorous experimental procedure, those formal properties of art that people find pleasing. He believed that he was founding an "aesthetics from below." Unlike philosophers who speculated about the nature of the beautiful (e.g. Kant, 1892), Fechner hoped to furnish the missing factual base of aesthetics by determining what people in fact find beautiful.

The method used to answer this question was disarmingly simple. Two stimuli differing in only one respect were presented to subjects, who were asked to indicate which stimulus they preferred. The properties of the stimuli receiving the highest number of votes were then regarded as properties yielding aesthetic pleasure. The stimuli used in these experiments were often isolated components of works of art, such as simple geometric patterns, rather than whole works of art. This choice of materials was motivated by the desire to determine the precise basis of any preference: since any two works of art differ in innumerable respects, a choice of one over the other cannot unambiguously reveal the basis of that preference.

This methodology was thus based on a stimulus-response model: the stimulus was a simple pattern; the response was a vote of preference. Such stimuli and responses proved easy to measure in the laboratory. This paradigm became the prototype of investigations carried out in the twentieth century under the rubric of "experimental aesthetics." Researchers in this tradition studied the psychophysical properties of visual and auditory stimuli—their brightness, loudness, smoothness—in order to determine which properties were preferred by the typical individual. The findings were then generalized to the arts.

The research produced abundant findings. For instance, it showed that brighter hues are preferred to duller ones (Guilford, 1934); that the green-blue area on the color spectrum is the most pleasing, with a secondary peak at the red end and a trough between yellow and green (Guilford, 1940); that color combinations in which the colors are quite different from each other are preferred (Granger, 1955a); and that moderate levels of loudness are the most pleasing, with tones becoming less pleasing as loudness increases from 50 to 90 decibels (Vitz and Todd, 1971; see also Child, 1968–69, 1978; Francès, 1968; Kreitler and Kreitler, 1972; Pickford, 1972; Valentine, 1962).

Researchers in the field of experimental aesthetics posed questions much more susceptible to empirical investigation than did Freud. It is far easier to determine the properties of art objects that are liked and disliked by the typical person than it is to answer the fundamental question of why people like art. By transforming the psychology of art into an experimental field, Fechner and his colleagues made an invaluable contribution. Some might argue, however, that the cost, at least initially, was a focus on questions too narrow in scope. As the psychologist Henry Murray quipped about the field of psychology in general, "Academic psychologists are looking critically at the wrong things. Psychoanalysts are looking with reeling brains at the right things" (1981, p. 343). This is a disturbingly apt characterization of the relationship between experimental aesthetics in its early stages and psychoanalytic approaches to the psychology of art: Fechner used rigorous methods to answer narrow questions; Freud used imprecise methods to answer overarching questions.

The field of experimental aesthetics remained relatively bereft of theory during the first half of the twentieth century. Although consistent preferences were found, little explanation was offered to account for these preferences. One exception was the work of the mathematician George Birkhoff (1933), who devised a formula to predict aesthetic value based on two factors, complexity and order. Using four kinds of stimuli—polygons, vase outlines, melodies, and lines of poetry—Birkhoff argued that patterns highest in order, harmony, and symmetry were the highest in aesthetic value. However, whether this theory accounts for the aesthetic merit of more complex works of art was not demonstrated. Moreover, other studies have thrown these results into question (e.g. Beebe-Center and Pratt, 1937; Davis, 1936; Eysenck and Castle, 1970).

The Arousal Theory

The psychologist Daniel Berlyne (1971) demonstrated that the relation between order and aesthetic pleasure is more complicated than Birkhoff's linear formula. Berlyne fashioned a comprehensive theory of the nature of aesthetic pleasure and of the properties of stimuli that optimize the aesthetic response, which he called the "new" experimental aesthetics. At the heart of his theory of art is the claim that art elicits pleasure by acting on arousal, that is, on a person's level of attention, alertness, or excitement. Berlyne was not the first to point to the role of arousal in aesthetic response; this idea was stressed centuries earlier by Aristotle in his theory of the response to tragedy. But while Aristotle focused on the relation between arousal and catharsis, Berlyne sought to discover the link between arousal and aesthetic pleasure.

According to the arousal theory, aesthetic pleasure can be achieved either by an arousal "boost," a moderate elevation of arousal until an optimal range is reached, or by an arousal "jag," a sharp rise in arousal beyond the optimal range followed by the pleasurable relief when arousal is reduced. The view that pleasure is to be had from both moderate increases in tension and sharp relief from tension is not unlike Freud's view that fore-pleasure is given by a moderate rise in tension and end-pleasure is given by a total relief of tension.

Berlyne argued that art affects arousal through three different properties. First, its psychophysical properties, such as brightness, saturation, size, loudness, or pitch, affect arousal. These were the properties studied in the "old" experimental aesthetics. The second way in which art affects arousal is through its ecological properties, its association with experiences recognized as helpful or harmful to survival, such as food, war, sex, or death. These were the properties studied by Freud, and they have to do only with the representational content of a work. The third and by far the most important way in which art affects arousal is through the "collative" variables of its formal properties, which had not previously been subjected to systematic scrutiny. Collative variables are such arousal-heightening devices as novelty, or the newness of elements; surprise, or the frustration of expectations; and complexity, or the heterogeneity, irregularity, and asymmetry of elements. These variables are called "collative" because, in order to determine the novelty, surprise, or complexity inherent in a pattern, the perceiver must compare; or collate, information from more than one source. The new experimental aesthetics is distinguished from the old by its focus on collative variables of form.

According to the arousal theory, artists manipulate collative variables in order to affect arousal in two very different ways. An arousal boost is achieved through the use of familiar, regular patterns, such as ones high in symmetry. An arousal jag is achieved through the use of patterns high in novelty, surprise, or complexity which cannot be immediately assimilated. A complex pattern, such as an asymmetrical one or one containing heterogeneous forms, elicits uncertainty in the perceiver, which is correlated with a sharp elevation of arousal. Because one of the fundamental human drives is to explore and thereby satisfy one's curiosity (Harlow, 1953; Piaget, 1963; White, 1959), the perceiver is then motivated to explore the pattern until it is understood. This assimilation and consequent resolution of uncertainty is accompanied by a reduction in arousal, which is experienced as pleasure.

In studies of this dual relationship between collative properties, arousal, and hedonic value, Berlyne did not use actual works of art but constructed patterns composed of discrete, countable units, such as dots, triangles, and lines. The decision to use artificial stimuli was based on the difficulty of precisely measuring a collative property, such as complexity, in an actual work of art. With artificial stimuli composed of discrete units that could be counted, the components of complexity, such as symmetry or heterogeneity, could be more precisely measured and manipulated. Though such stimuli were a far cry from works of art, the results obtained were argued to be generalizable to art. Moreover, a few studies used actual art works in order to corroborate the results obtained from simple stimuli (Berlyne, 1974). While most of the work focused on visual patterns, some research on auditory patterns and poetry was also carried out (Berlyne, 1974; Kamman, 1966).

In one study (Berlyne, 1970), the patterns were arranged in pairs whose members differed in complexity (Fig. 2.1). The degree of complexity was measured objectively in terms of physical char-

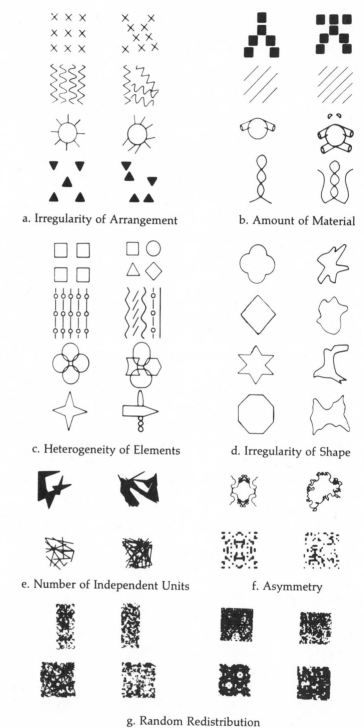

a. Irregularity of Arrangement

b. Amount of Material

c. Heterogeneity of Elements

d. Irregularity of Shape

e. Number of Independent Units

f. Asymmetry

2.1 Patterns used to test aesthetic preference. The left member of each pair, possessing either low or moderate complexity, is the preferred pattern.

g. Random Redistribution

acteristics, such as irregularity (symmetrical versus asymmetrical arrangement of the same units), amount (less versus more of the same units), and heterogeneity (same versus different units), as well as subjectively by asking subjects to rank the patterns by their complexity (Day, 1965). The subjective ranking demonstrated four levels of complexity: the left-hand members of categories a–d were the simplest (level one); next in complexity were the right-hand members of categories a–d (level two); more complex were the left-hand members of categories e–g (level three); and most complex were the right-hand members of categories e–g (level four).

Use of these stimuli made it possible to test predictions about the relationship between complexity, arousal, and hedonic value. For example, the arousal theory predicts that two types of patterns will be experienced as most pleasing: ones low in complexity, which cause only moderate arousal elevation, and ones moderately complex, which are complex enough to elevate arousal sharply but not so complex as never to be assimilated. When subjects were asked to rank the patterns for pleasingness, the two levels of complexity yielding the highest pleasure were indeed level one, the simplest, and level three, the moderately complex. These two levels of complexity, however, yielded different types of pleasure. With repeated viewing of the simple patterns, subjects reported that these patterns became steadily less pleasing. With repeated viewing of the more complex patterns, subjects reported that the patterns first became even more pleasing and then began to decline in appeal. As a result, the subjects rapidly became bored with the simple patterns. In the case of the more complex patterns, which were not immediately assimilated, their appeal rose until they had been fully understood, and only then did a pattern become boring.

For ratings of interestingness, a simpler relationship was found: as patterns increased in complexity, interestingness rose, peaked at level three, and then declined. The patterns of level four were too chaotic ever to be understood; thus, they proved neither pleasing nor interesting.

The finding that interestingness rises steadily until an optimal level of complexity is reached, after which point interestingness declines, is supported by other evidence. For instance, complex patterns engender greater looking time than do simple ones (Berlyne and Lawrence, 1964). The patterns in levels one to three engender increasingly long looking times, but viewing time begins to decline at level four, the most complex level (Day, 1966). These findings support the theory that complex patterns elevate arousal through the uncertainty that they elicit; the perceiver is then motivated to explore the pattern until it is understood. However, given a pattern so complex that it cannot be assimilated, the perceiver will not look at it for a long time, because longer looking does not result in greater understanding.

Judgments of pleasingness thus have a curvilinear relationship to degree of complexity. Very simple and moderately complex patterns are equally preferred. Moderately complex patterns, however, are judged to be more interesting than simple ones and rivet attention for a longer time. Moreover, the pleasingness of simple and moderately complex patterns has different causes. The motivation to look at simple patterns is "diversive," that is, pleasure seeking, whereas the urge to look at and explore more complex patterns is "epistemic," that is, knowledge seeking. Moderately complex patterns stimulate the perceiver's curiosity and elicit knowledge-seeking behavior, challenging the perceiver to explore until the pattern is understood.

These findings led to the generalization that art yields pleasure by acting on arousal in the same two ways. Moreover, they suggested that other activities also yield pleasure by sharply elevating and then reducing arousal. Such activities include scientific inquiry and other forms of problem solving, as well as play and humor. All of these domains pose a challenge which people are motivated to resolve. Thus, the arousal theory places art within the context of other fundamentally important human activities.

Let us return for a moment to the figure of Freud absorbed in contemplation of the *Moses*, to determine whether his attraction to this sculpture can now be understood. Applying the psychoanalytic theory alone to this situation would lead to the conclusion that Freud was attracted to the sculpture primarily because of its content. Perhaps there was something about it that he could unconsciously identify with and project onto. The similarity between Moses, the lawgiver, who handed down a new religion and was unappreciated by his people, and the founder of psychoanalysis, who handed down a revolutionary "creed" and was spurned by his contemporaries, probably did not escape Freud. And underlying this identification was perhaps an unconscious wish to replace his father by becoming a father himself—the father of psychoanalysis.

The arousal theory offers an alternative, but not necessarily conflicting, explanation. On this account, Freud was drawn to the *Moses* because of its complexity and mystery. The uncertainty and the conflicting hypotheses yielded by the sculpture provided a challenge for Freud to make sense of the work. In ultimately achieving an understanding of *Moses*, Freud experienced a pleasurable sense of relief. Thus, the motivation to study the *Moses* was the anticipated reward of relief to be gained from clarification.

Whether or not Freud was unconsciously identifying with Moses or Michelangelo in order to play out a forbidden wish, he was clearly and undeniably engaged in a problem-solving venture. In stressing the involvement of the intellect in the aesthetic experience, the arousal theory made a valuable contribution.

Nevertheless, the arousal theory faces a number of problems. One is the questionable generalizability of the empirical findings. There is a wide gulf between the stimuli studied and actual works of art. Although it is possible to measure complexity in an art form such as music or literature, that is analyzable into discrete symbols, complexity cannot be so easily measured in an art form such as painting, in which the symbols are "dense" rather than discrete (Goodman, 1968). Hence, for visual stimuli Berlyne was for the most part forced to use simple geometric patterns that were analyzable into units. Whether people would find the patterns particularly pleasing or interesting outside of an experimental situation is questionable. The attraction of these patterns is not inherent in the stimuli themselves. Outside of the experiment, probably, these stimuli would be relatively neutral. What may have motivated the subjects to express a preference is that they were asked to make such a decision and were thus challenged to display their aesthetic expertise, despite their indifference to the stimuli available (Hochberg, 1978). As one subject protested, "How can a dot be beautiful?" (Normore, 1974, p. 119).

Another question about the generalizability of the arousal theory to art arises not from the stimuli but from the method used. Asking subjects to rank their preferences for stimuli having a wide range of complexity may inadvertently elicit a "central tendency effect," in which subjects show a preference for stimuli in the middle of any given series (Woodworth, 1938). People also prefer things just moderately different from the level to which they have adapted (Helson, 1948). Thus, preference for any given pattern presented in a set would depend not on any of its inherent properties but on its relative complexity within the particular set in which it happens to be presented (Kennedy, 1961; Steck and Machotka, 1975). If it occupies a middle level within a set, it will be preferred, but if it is placed within another set in which it occupies an extreme level, another pattern will be preferred.

Thus, a liking for moderately complex patterns may not predict preference for any particular work of art, since complexity is entirely relative to the context in which the work is viewed—either its relation to the perceiver's previous encounters with art, or its relation to other works present at the same time. To try to predict preferences for individual works of art from the arousal theory would lead to odd conclusions. For instance, since more complex patterns engender longer looking times, people should look longer at any painting with a fairly high level of heterogeneity than at a painting by Mondrian consisting simply of several perpendicular lines and two or three colors. This should be true even if the more complex work is not well executed. Clearly, however, people may look for hours at a Mondrian, never tiring of it despite its simplicity. Complexity as measured by number, heterogeneity, or arrangement of units omits a great deal of what rivets the observer's attention in art.

The other problem with the arousal theory is its failure to specify what is unique about the aesthetic experience. Many stimuli affect arousal levels. An extremely aversive stimulus, such as the sight of a dead animal, may elevate arousal; averting one's gaze may bring relief. This suggests that arousal by itself is neither pleasant nor painful. Rather, whether people enjoy a state of arousal depends on the meaning that they attribute to the eliciting stimulus. The arousal theory does not deal with this, and thus cannot account for the fact that people may feel pleasure from the tension afforded by looking at a painting, but pain from the same level of tension produced by a frightening experience. For the same reason, the theory cannot explain why people feel very different kinds of pleasure from the arousal-stimulating properties of art and of domains outside of art, such as sports (Kreitler and Kreitler, 1972).

To be sure, the arousal theory links art to other challenging activities, such as humor, play, and problem solving. But while it is important for any theory of art to demonstrate that the arts are not a domain set entirely apart from the rest of human life, such a theory must also demonstrate what is unique about the aesthetic experience. Freud went to great lengths to point out the kinship between art and the imaginary worlds constructed by the dreamer or the child at play. But he also insisted on the uniqueness of aesthetic pleasure given by art's formal properties as well as its higher level of concealment of primary-process imagery through secondary elaboration. The arousal theory, however, does not explain the difference between art and other exploratory activities.

Beyond the Pleasure Principle

Despite the importance Berlyne granted to the involvement of the intellect in the aesthetic experience, the ultimate motivation to witness a work of art was, for him, the pleasure it afforded: cognition rested squarely in the service of hedonism. Other philosophers and psychologists have gone beyond the pleasure-centered theories of Freud and Berlyne to insist that art serves the human need for knowledge quite apart from any pleasure that such understanding may yield (Arnheim, 1969, 1972, 1974; Cassirer, 1957). According to these theories, art functions ultimately to reveal and clarify reality.

For example, Susanne Langer (1942) proposed that art serves to objectify human feeling so that people can contemplate and understand the world of inner experience. Making a distinction between discursive symbols (those used outside of the arts, such as literal language and numbers) and presentational symbols (those used in the arts), Langer argued that only the presentational kind can describe inner reality. The world of feeling is incommensurate with nonartistic, discursive symbols. Presentational symbols, on the contrary, are able to mirror the structure of feeling. Art thus becomes the only way that people understand and reflect upon feeling. Because of this, art yields insight into the mind. For theories like Langer's, this cognitive function is unique to art and is far more important than any other need served by art, such as pleasure or excitement.

Perhaps there is no sharp dichotomy between emotional and cognitive responses to art. According to the arousal theory, after all, emotion and knowledge are intertwined: knowledge yields pleasure. For Langer, the two are also linked: art enables people to understand the world of feeling.

Yet another relationship between emotion and understanding was proposed by Nelson Goodman (1968), who argued that in the arts, as well as sometimes in the sciences, the emotions function cognitively. The arts are fundamentally a way of knowing: art works must be "read," and subtle discriminations made. This reading of a work of art is carried out by the emotions as well as the cognitive faculties. "Emotion in an aesthetic experience is a means of discerning what properties a work has and expresses," Goodman noted (p. 248). Thus, not only does understanding yield pleasure, but pleasure can stimulate people to make further discriminations. And further discriminations allow understanding of both the work and the worlds to which it refers.

Freud's contemplation of *Moses* again serves to clarify what is meant by the cognitive functioning of the emotions in art. *Moses* elicited powerful emotions in Freud. Indeed, it was these feelings that brought Freud back to the sculpture again and again. These emotions stimulated Freud to try to understand the work, to try to unravel its mystery. And the more he came to understand the sculpture, the greater the pleasure he felt. It is impossible to separate the contributions of Freud's emotions and reasoning powers in his response to Michelangelo's *Moses*.

The cognitive function of the emotions dissolves the paradox of tragedy and ugliness. The therapeutic value of catharsis, or the pleasure derived from arousal, need not explain why people expose themselves to violence and pain in art. Their revulsion at Oedipus' murder of his father functions in the service of their understanding of the play, and the satisfaction that accompanies this understanding may well account for the appeal of art.

Individual Differences in Aesthetic Response

Whatever their differences, the various theories of the response to art converge in at least one important respect: they all assume that art serves the same need, or set of needs, for all people. And because any given work of art satisfies the same need in all individuals, there should be minimal disagreement about which works are the most satisfying. The *Moses* should have the same powerful effect on everyone as it did on Freud.

A number of studies have been carried out to explore the degree to which people agree or disagree in their response to works of art. Some of these studies support the view that people respond to art in the same way; others demonstrate considerable individual variation in response owing to a person's degree of familiarity with the arts as well as to deep-seated aspects of personality and temperament.

There is considerable evidence that people agree in their aesthetic preferences and judgments (Beebe-Center, 1932; Eysenck, 1940, 1940–41, 1941a, 1942; Francès, 1968; Granger, 1955a-c; Soueif and Eysenck, 1972). Hans Eysenck and his colleagues demonstrated high agreement both within and across cultures when people were asked to judge which of two patterns was better (Götz, Borisy, Lynn, and Eysenck, 1979; Iwawaki, Eysenck, and Götz, 1979). The test devised consisted of forty-two pairs of nonrepresentational pictures (Fig. 2.2). The members of each pair were identical except for the fact that one member had been altered so that eight artists unanimously considered it to be inferior in design. Subjects were not asked to select the design they preferred, but to select the better gestalt, or more harmonious design. The test was administered to people of different sexes, different ages, and different cultures (Japan and England).

2.2 Forms used to test aesthetic judgment. The left member of each pair is seen as superior in design.

The results demonstrated a high level of agreement across individuals, largely independent of sex, intelligence, personality traits, and culture. As for age, while adults scored higher than children, within the group of children there were no correlations with age. The researchers accounted for these results in terms of a single aesthetic ability possessed to different degrees by different people. They posited the existence of an innate aesthetic sense, rooted in the structure of the nervous system. Thus, the minor variations that obtain among individuals would presumably be due to genetic factors in aesthetic sensitivity rather than to any factors such as intelligence, personality, training, or culture.

These findings demonstrate that, given certain types of stimuli, people tend to agree in their evaluative judgments, but the agreement is not perfect. The question is whether individual deviations from the norm are purely random events, or are systematically related to certain factors such as familiarity with art or even to personality and cognitive style. While Eysenck found no relationship between individual differences and personality, other researchers, using more complicated stimuli than Eysenck, have obtained very different results.

Determinants of Preference

How familiar a person is with the arts may influence the kind of art that is preferred. In Eysenck's studies, the subjects' background in the arts was not controlled. However, other studies have shown that people familiar with the arts, such as artists and students of art history, have aesthetic preferences that diverge consistently from those of people lacking familiarity with the arts. For instance, people who are knowledgable about the arts base their aesthetic judgments on goodness of composition, while those without special knowledge of the arts base their judgments on degree of realism and type of subject matter (Peel, 1944, 1946). This finding was confirmed in another study showing that average people prefer paintings that are realistic, while specialists are indifferent to this dimension (Francès and Voillaume, 1964).

The most extensive program of research demonstrating the role of familiarity with the arts was conducted by Irvin Child, who devised a test consisting of reproductions of paintings, drawings, and prints, arranged in pairs. Members of each pair were similar in obvious respects, such as representational content and medium used, but diverged in aesthetic merit as determined by twelve specialists. For example, Hans Holbein's *A Lady of the Cromwell Family*, paired with Hans Krell's *Portrait of Queen Mary of Hungary*, was judged superior by the twelve specialists (Fig. 2.3). When this test was administered to "connoisseurs of art," defined simply as people with some familiarity with the arts, there was considerable agreement with the experts about which work was preferred, both within cultures and between cultures as diverse as the United States and Africa, Fiji, Japan, Pakistan, and Greece (Anwar and Child, 1972; Child, 1962, 1965; Child and Siroto, 1965; Ford, Prothro, and Child, 1966; Haritos-Fatouros and Child, 1977; Iwao and Child, 1966; Iwao, Child, and Garcia, 1969). But when the test was given to people with no expertise in the arts, their evaluations differed significantly from the connoisseurs.

These results are in direct contrast to those of Eysenck. Although Eysenck did not compare connoisseurs to nonconnoisseurs, his test items were constructed by connoisseurs, and the subjects tended to agree with the connoisseurs' preferences. One possible explanation of this divergence lies in the stimuli used. Whereas

2.3   Holbein, A Lady of the Cromwell Family, *and Krell,* Portrait of Queen Maria of Hungary. *The Holbein is preferred by people who are familiar with the arts.*

Eysenck used simple abstract stimuli, Child used works of art in all their complexity. Here it appears that experience in exploring works of art affects evaluative judgment.

The use of different types of stimuli may also have interacted with the different instructions given. Whereas Child asked subjects to pick the picture they preferred, Eysenck asked subjects to select the more harmonious gestalt. Responses to these two types of instruction usually correlate highly (Götz et al, 1979), except in cases of psychoses, when people often prefer the composition considered less harmonious (Eysenck and Eysenck, 1976). However, it is possible that responses to these two instructions do not correlate when complex representational stimuli are used. Had Child's subjects been asked to select the better gestalt, higher agreement might have been obtained. In short, experience with art may affect one's preferences, but not one's ability to perceive harmony.

What is needed is a study in which ordinary subjects and connoisseurs are given abstract stimuli and representational stimuli, and are asked both to select the ones preferred and the better ges-

talts. High agreement would probably be found for the better gestalts among both types of stimuli; but in the case of preference,
agreement would probably be found only for abstract stimuli.
Such findings would lead to the conclusion that individuals agree
about what is considered harmonious, and that harmony dictates
preference in the case of simple, abstract designs but not in the
case of complex, representational works.

Familiarity with the arts is not the only factor that determines
aesthetic judgment. In fact, art background may be secondary in
importance to the particular cognitive style with which a person
approaches experience.

Child (1965) hypothesized that certain cognitive styles determine aesthetic taste. For instance, since works of art are complex
stimuli that require exploration, a high tolerance of complexity
might lead to superior aesthetic judgment. It might also be that individuals with greater independence of judgment arrive at superior
aesthetic evaluations. Or greater access to fantasy and unconscious
material might allow one to enter more fully into a work of art and
thus lead to superior judgment. Armed with a battery of question-
naire measures, Child demonstrated that high agreement with art
experts correlated with these measures of cognitive style, and that
two of these correlations were unaffected by the amount of art
training of the subject.

In order to test the hypothesis that tolerance of complexity is
related to aesthetic judgment, subjects were asked to indicate
whether or not they agreed with pairs of statements such as: "Inso-
far as the study of philosophy makes one doubt his basic beliefs, it
should be encouraged," and "Most of our social problems would
be solved if we could somehow get rid of the immoral, crooked,
and feeble-minded people." People who agreed with the first statement and disagreed with the second tended to agree with the connoisseurs in their aesthetic evaluations, whether or not they also
had some background in art.

To test the relationship between aesthetic choice and independence of judgment, subjects were asked to indicate agreement or
disagreement with pairs of statements such as: "The happy person
tends always to be poised, courteous, outgoing, and emotionally
controlled," and "The unfinished and the imperfect often have
greater appeal for me than the completed and polished." People
who disagreed with the first but agreed with the second tended
also to agree with the art experts, again whether or not they had
any background in the arts. Thus, agreement with expert judgment
seems to grow out of independent thinking.

To test the possibility that access to fantasy and primary-process thinking—the ability to regress to infantile, primitive modes of thought—is related to aesthetic judgment, subjects were asked about pairs of statements such as: "I get little pleasure or fun out of playing with words or language—as by talking nonsense, baby talk, or in a foreign accent—and seldom do that sort of thing," and "I sometimes have daydreams in which I become a heroic type of figure—either all-powerful, all-knowing, and successful, or someone who has sunk to the lowest depths of depravity, weakness, and suffering." Those who disagreed with the first statement and agreed with the second also agreed with the aesthetic judgment of the experts. However, when the contribution of art background was statistically removed, the correlation was no longer significant. Thus, the ability to regress cognitively appears to be associated in some way with background in the arts; by itself, it does not necessarily lead to superior aesthetic judgment.

These are some of the most important correlations between aesthetic judgment and cognitive style. These relationships can be found as early as the high school years. They also extend across cultures, such as Japan (Child and Iwao, 1968), Pakistan (Anwar and Child, 1972), and Greece (Haritos-Fatouros and Child, 1977).

If the kinds of paper-and-pencil tests used in these studies in fact reveal stable inner characteristics—an issue on which there is disagreement—then the findings indicate that those whose judgment accords with experts are characterized by a particular cognitive style or orientation toward experience. These people possess an active, inquiring, independent mind, with a high tolerance for complexity. Such a temperament would lead them to seek out experiences that are challenging because of their novelty and complexity. The aesthetic value of a work of art thus can be argued to be a function of its aptness for engaging the attention of an active mind.

This position gains support from a number of studies demonstrating that artists prefer more complex patterns than do nonartists (e.g. Munsinger and Kessen, 1964). That this is due to cognitive style rather than simply to greater experience in looking at patterns is suggested by studies showing that people who prefer works of greater complexity are characterized by original, dissident, and eccentric personality traits, whereas those who prefer simpler works tend to be low in originality, conservative, and conventional (Barron, 1952, 1953; Barron and Welsh, 1952; MacKinnon, 1962). People with active minds may seek out more complex art because it engages their attention and poses a greater challenge. Perhaps for such people art serves an epistemic function, satisfying perceptual curiosity and the need to explore, whereas for others art serves primarily a diversive need.

What one likes in art may also be determined by one's personality. Such an influence could work in two opposing ways. On the one hand, people might prefer works of art that are congruent with their overt personality traits. On the other hand, perhaps they prefer works that express feelings or attitudes that they sense are lacking in their own personality.

Following from Freudian theory, people should like in art that which is lacking in their lives. Freud believed that people find in art what they are forbidden to enjoy in reality. Art compensates for the deficits of life. Thus, to the extent that there are individual differences in people's response to art—an issue on which Freud had little to say—people should be expected to seek out works of art possessing properties that contrast with their overt personality but which resonate with all that is repressed. Thus, a person with a great deal of repressed sexuality or aggression, who appears highly controlled on the surface, should like art that is uncontrolled, violent, or erotic.

There is considerable evidence to suggest that Freud was wrong. Instead of preferring art that compensates for their lacks, people often prefer art that mirrors their overt personalities. For example, in addition to a high level of aesthetic agreement among individuals, known as the "general factor," Eysenck (1940, 1940–1941, 1941a) also found a "bipolar factor" related to temperament. Using colors, paintings, lines of poetry, polygons, and odors, this study demonstrated that extroverts preferred simple, obvious stimuli, whereas introverts preferred subtle, complex, diverse stimuli. Extroverts, who are presumably more expressive, preferred paintings that were themselves more expressive; introverts, presumably more controlled, preferred paintings that were also more somber and controlled. Similarly, emotionally stable people preferred calm subjects, and unstable individuals liked the dramatic in art (Burt, 1939). And people with a high need for achievement preferred cool colors, choosing green and blue plaids in preference to red and yellow ones (Knapp, 1957; Knapp, McElroy, and Vaughn, 1962). Those with low achievement motivation preferred warm, exciting colors, choosing the red and yellow plaids. Because those with a high achievement motivation are probably more emotionally controlled, these aesthetic preferences are consistent with the subjects' level of emotional expressiveness: uncontrolled people liked stimulating colors; controlled people preferred restrained colors. Although these findings appear to contradict Freud's theory, they can be framed in psychoanalytic terms. Instead of seeking in art that which they have repressed, people perhaps seek in art those qualities that help to buttress their defenses and keep what they have repressed safely buried.

These studies were based on a correlational method in which subjects' scores on a standard personality test were correlated with their preferences. One psychoanalytically oriented researcher, Pavel Machotka (1979), objected to the superficiality of such an approach, arguing instead for the necessity of in-depth clinical interviews with each person. Machotka carried out such a clinical study to test the two competing models of the relation between aesthetic preference and personality—the view that people seek in art what they have repressed in their lives, and the view that they seek in art those qualities that may help to buttress their defenses and keep what they have repressed safely buried.

The study focused on individual differences in people's preferences for nudes represented in paintings, drawings, and sculptures, which differed in a number of respects. The dimensions on which the nudes varied included male versus female, exhibitionist versus shy, sentimental versus direct, calm versus passionate, and physically perfect versus flawed. Unaware of the dimensions on which the nudes had been rated, subjects were asked to indicate their liking for each work on a scale of one to seven. Those who revealed consistent preferences for one or the other pole of a particular dimension, such as giving high ratings to all of the calm nudes or to all of the passionate ones, were selected for further analysis. These persons were the atypical ones. Out of an initial group of two hundred subjects, three groups of twenty each were selected. It was assumed that any extreme and stable preference betrays the fulfillment of a psychological need, and that any dynamics uncovered in these extreme cases would obtain in attenuated form in more typical cases.

In an effort to uncover deep personality traits, these participants were then subjected to detailed clinical interviews. The interviewer, unaware of the particular preferences of the interviewees, probed issues such as love, intimacy, sex, aggression, childhood, and relation to parents. The personality traits of high scorers at each pole of a particular dimension were compared. For example, those people who preferred nudes embodying calmness and control were contrasted to those who preferred nudes expressing drama and passion, whether aggression, pain, or ecstasy (Fig. 2.4).

Those who preferred calm nudes, referred to as the "calm subjects," presented a constellation of personality traits quite different from that shown by the dramatic subjects.

The calm subjects were extremely controlled in the expression of their drives, imposing strict restraints on aggression, sexuality, and alcohol use. They feared disorder in their lives, recalled strict upbringings, and tended to lack intimate relationships. One subject was repelled by St. Bartholomew, a figure expressing agony (Fig. 2.5). "It's like hanging a picture of a baby that's been napalmed," he said (pp. 197, 212). Another denied the evidence of his senses when viewing this nude, suggesting that St. Bartholomew was being helped down rather than hoisted up. Clearly, for these subjects aesthetic choice served as a support for their defenses against arousal. They did not want disorder or arousal in their lives, and they did not like art that might threaten their defenses against disorder.

The dramatic subjects were similar in many ways. They also kept a strict check on their drives and lacked intimate relationships. But there was one key difference between these two groups. The dramatic subjects valued their emotions and enjoyed them. Rather than fearing arousal and passion, they simply had difficulty

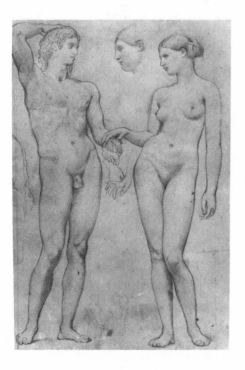

2.4 *Ingres*, Studies of a Man and a Woman for "The Golden Age," *and Montorsoli*, Bozzetto for a Fountain Figure. *The calm nudes are preferred by people who avoid arousal in their lives, in contrast to the more passionate nude, which is preferred by people who long for the arousal felt to be lacking in their lives.*

2.5 *Ribera*, The Martyrdom of St. Bartholomew. *The violence in this painting repels people who avoid arousal in their lives.*

experiencing them in real life. For these people, then, art was compensatory: they sought in art what was not granted to them in life.

A similar trait distinguished subjects who liked nudes in art from those who rejected nudes. People who wished for intimacy in their lives but failed to attain it liked nudes. Those who feared intimacy expressed a distaste for nudes. Thus, on a number of dimensions, Machotka found that people who value the expression of emotion tend to use art to gratify unconscious needs that cannot be fulfilled in reality; those who are repressed, possessing strong inhibitions, seek in art qualities that function to support these inhibitions and to keep arousal low. These findings challenge the arousal theory, which maintains that arousal is universally sought in art.

The study showed that art serves different needs for different people, and the aesthetic choices of individuals extend and support their normal method of coping with the world. For some, as Freud believed, art is a compensation, replenishing life's lacks, supplying nourishment to desires that have been repressed. For others, art nourishes not the repressed but rather the guardians of repressed material: extremely inhibited people experience a greater need to diminish anxiety about forbidden wishes than to play out such wishes.

Of course, the study only included people whose preferences departed radically from those of the average responder. By treating the variations as the phenomena of interest and ignoring the mean, it took the opposite road from the typical preference study. Thus, as Machotka himself admits, whether the findings can be generalized to more typical people is not known. It is probable that extreme preferences are indeed evidence that either a need or a defense is being supported. However, for more typical preferences which cut across those dimensions isolated by Machotka, it seems less likely that art would so directly and consistently serve a need or a defense. Instead, preferences may depend on a greater variety of factors, such as one's mood at a given time, or the need for exploration and the pleasure in coming to understand a complex work of art. Moreover, whether the findings would be relevant to nonrepresentational art, or to art that does not represent people (on whom one can project one's needs and defenses) is not known. Nonetheless, this clinical research is the first work that has shown, at least for certain types of individuals and certain types of material, that art may serve radically different psychological needs for different people.

The issues of aesthetic evaluation and preference contribute to an understanding of the function served by art. Yet there is more to the aesthetic experience than making decisions about either value or preference. What is critical is reading the work of art, and this involves powers of discrimination, intellect, and feeling.

The art critic Jakob Rosenberg (1964) made detailed comparisons between pairs of works which on the surface look very similar. Through these comparisons, Rosenberg demonstrated the way in which extremely subtle differences between works, such as quality of line, coherence of organization, or clarity of form, render one work inferior to the other. Perhaps, then, what is of real importance for the perceiver is the ability to perform these subtle discriminations; less important is the attachment of a label of "better" or "worse," or "like" or "dislike," to each member. If a person is able to see the fine differences between a Picasso and a Dufy line drawing of a reclining woman, it matters not at all which drawing is preferred or judged to be superior.

The ability to make fine discriminations is intertwined with the ability to make value judgments. Finer discriminations make it possible to reach a value judgment. If one is able to see more properties of a work, one has more to judge. But the relationship also works the other way. If viewers are shown two similar paintings apparently signed by Rembrandt but feel that one is in fact a fake, they will begin to look more closely at the two works and will come to notice fine differences to which they were previously blind. Thus, more subtle discrimination leads to more skillful evaluation, and superior evaluation leads to more powerful discrimination (Goodman, 1968).

Reading and making sense of a work of art, perceiving subtle differences and making fine discriminations, are what give pleasure to the aesthetic experience. And the satisfaction granted by gaining an understanding of a work of art is independent of whether or not a work is considered pleasing. The ability to make relevant discriminations does not unfold automatically; rather, it may well hinge on familiarity with the arts, on motivation, and perhaps even on cognitive style.

Freud's attraction to Michelangelo's *Moses* can best be understood in these terms. Whether the sculpture represented all that Freud had repressed or whether it served to buttress his defenses, it undeniably challenged Freud's powers of understanding. The sculpture was not immediately understandable. Making sense of the *Moses* required hours of careful scrutiny and hypothesis testing. It was this process of "reading" the work and making subtle discriminations that engendered Freud's strong emotional response to the *Moses*, just as his emotional response led to further efforts at reading and understanding the work.

TWO *Painting*

3 What's in a Picture?

Painting is a science and should be pursued as an inquiry into the laws of nature. Why, then, may not landscape painting be considered as a branch of natural philosophy, of which pictures are but the experiments?

—John Constable

How we make sense of pictures has puzzled and intrigued philosophers and artists for centuries. To see why, try an experiment. Find a fairly realistic painting, such as John Constable's *Wivenhoe Park* (Fig. 3.1). Place yourself two inches away from the painting and look at it. You see a flat surface covered with different colored

3.1 Constable, Wivenhoe Park, Essex, *perceived as a window on a three-dimensional space.*

3.2 Severini, Dynamic Hieroglyphic of Bal Tabarin, *which expresses frenzy, noise, and heat.*

daubs of paint. Now step back a few feet and look again. The colored plane has been transformed into a window on a three-dimensional world: instead of flat patches of paint, you see solid objects located in depth. How it is that we can "read" a flat surface as a three-dimensional space is a challenging problem posed by representational pictures.

As you step back from *Wivenhoe Park,* not only do you see the three-dimensional scene that is represented, but you also perceive the wistful mood of serenity and calm that is expressed. As you look at the painting *Dynamic Hieroglyphic of Bal Tabarin* by Gino Severini (Fig. 3.2), you see a quite different mood, one of excitement and frenzy, as well as a quality of loudness and perhaps even heat. Pictures are as likely to be loud or quiet, calm or anxious, as they are to be blue or green. How we come to grant pictures such suspiciously human states as serenity or frenzy, and such nonvisual properties as heat or loudness, is a second question raised by the visual arts.

Reading Pictorial Representation

Perception has always proved problematical to philosophers and psychologists because it operates at a distance. A visual perception of a tree is made possible by light rays from that tree which often travel considerable distances from the tree to our eyes. Whether these light rays unambiguously specify that they come from the tree, or whether by themselves they provide ambiguous information which must be supplemented or transformed in some way by the perceiver, is one of the fundamental questions that perceptual theorists have tried to answer.

The perception of pictures presents a special problem for perceptual psychology. First of all, the representational information carried by pictures is more impoverished than information available in the ordinary environment. For instance, the cows in Constable's painting carry much less information than "real" cows. We cannot see the eyes, the hoofs, or the texture of their hides, nor can we walk around them to see their other side, yet we have no trouble reading the images as cows. Black and white pictures are also impoverished: they render the world in grays, but we do not take them as depictions of a gray world. And while line drawings depict only the edges of objects, we do not read such drawings as representations of a wire world.

Pictorial information is not only impoverished but also contradictory. Certain depth cues declare the surface of *Wivenhoe Park* to be flat, while other depth cues suggest that the objects in the picture are located in three-dimensional space. One depth cue that declares the surface to be flat is given by the fact that we have two eyes. Our eyes converge on an object that we are looking at. If the object is near, the angle of convergence is greater than if the object is distant. This angle of convergence is interpreted by the brain as information about distance. Because it depends on our two eyes, this is called a binocular cue. When we look at *Wivenhoe Park*, the angle of convergence is identical for each image in the picture, revealing that each image is the same distance from us.

Another depth cue, motion parallax, is yielded by moving our head as we view a scene. As we do this, nearer objects are displaced faster and farther than more distant objects. When we move our head in front of *Wivenhoe Park*, all of the pictured objects are displaced at an equal rate, thereby revealing that they all lie on the same plane and are equidistant from us.

Although both binocular and motion parallax cues inform us that Constable's painting is flat, pictorial cues such as linear and atmospheric perspective push us toward a three-dimensional perception of the picture. The laws of linear perspective dictate that distant objects be made smaller in size than closer ones, and that the receding parallel edges of an object be depicted as converging. By the rules of atmospheric perspective, also called aerial perspective, colors of objects in the distance appear hazier and blurrier than those in the foreground.

How the artist manages to make us reject the two-dimensional truth given by binocular and motion parallax, and accept the three-dimensional lie given by pictorial depth cues, is a complicated story. Of course, we are not actually fooled by pictures. Even when we read a two-dimensional picture as depicting a three-dimensional scene, we never lose the awareness that we are looking at the illusion of depth rather than at a real three-dimensional scene. But the question remains how the artist achieves this illusion. Three competing solutions have been proposed, each based on a different theory of how perception operates in the ordinary, non-pictorial environment.

Direct Registration Theory

Perhaps the most common sense theory of perception is the registration theory, formulated by James J. Gibson (1950, 1966, 1979). According to this theory, perception is unproblematical because the information available to our senses is rich and unambiguous. The light traveling from the environment to our eyes preserves information about the structure of its source, information such as the texture, contrasts, and edges of objects in the environment. Given a moving, two-eyed observer, this information is automatically picked up and registered by the nervous system, resulting in veridical perception of the environment. Visual perception is thus effortless and direct, requiring no interpretation or guesswork.

According to Gibson, the perception of a picture is almost as effortless and veridical as the perception of the ordinary environment. A picture is a rich source of information: despite the fact that binocular and motion parallax cues declare its surface to be flat, there are enough pictorial depth cues for the perceiver effortlessly to perceive it as a representation of solid objects located in three-dimensional space. The information received by the retina is automatically picked up by the nervous system to yield our perceptual experience of a three-dimensional representation.

Gibson (1954) proposed that a realistic picture looks realistic because the picture gives off light rays identical in wave length and intensity to the light rays emitted from the actual depicted scene. Given a perfect fit, a picture can even deceive the observer into thinking that it is the real thing. The view that pictures can, in principle, emit the same light rays as the objects that they represent has a venerable tradition, originating in the Renaissance. Leonardo da Vinci advised artists to use a simple but clever device in order to create perfect surrogates of nature (Richter, 1970). Leonardo knew that because light rays converge, the light from an object to the eye forms a pyramid. If a glass plane intersected this pyramid, one could look through this window with one eye in a fixed position and trace the scene viewed on the glass (Fig. 3.3).

3.3 *Dürer,* Draftsman Drawing a Portrait, *showing a typical Leonardo window. Looking through it with one eye and tracing the scene on the glass yields an accurate perspectival copy.*

This should yield a perfect perspectival copy. Such a device came to be called "Leonardo's window." If artists then mastered the laws of color mixing, Leonardo believed, they could produce a picture yielding the same pattern of light rays as the scene itself.

Gibson conducted an experiment which attempted to demonstrate that a picture could in fact fool the eye (1960). A life-size photograph of a dimly lit hall was arranged so that it could be viewed with one eye through a peephole. Looking through the peephole, observers would find themselves in the same position, or station point, with respect to the hall, as the camera was when the photograph was taken. Behind a second peephole observers could view the actual hall, again from the same relative stance as when viewing the photograph. Subjects were asked to decide when they were looking at the photograph and when they were looking at the actual hall. One-third of the subjects were fooled by the photograph and thought it was the real hall. An even more dramatic finding was reported by two other researchers: viewing a photograph of a room through a peephole, subjects unanimously believed they were looking at an actual room (Smith and Smith, 1961).

Gibson used such results as evidence that information from pictures can correspond, point for point, to information from the nonpictorial world. The problem with this conclusion is that the viewing conditions were abnormal. First, the photograph was viewed with only one eye. When two eyes are used, binocular cues help to distinguish between pictures and three-dimensional objects. Second, because of the peephole, observers could not move their heads. Had they been able to, motion parallax cues would also have revealed the fact that all parts of the hall lay on the same plane. Finally, the peephole was positioned so that the observer stood at the same position at which the camera stood when the scene was captured on film. But ordinarily pictures are viewed from a variety of angles, not necessarily the one corresponding to the position of the camera's lens or the painter's eye. And viewing a picture from a different angle from that of the photographer or painter causes a perspectival distortion which can serve as a cue that one is looking at a picture rather than a three-dimensional scene (Fig. 3.4).

Other problems include the fact that evidence from photographs cannot necessarily be generalized to paintings, the photographs were life-size, and the hall was dimly lit. All of these factors make this situation a special one. Normally there is no mistaking a representational picture for the real thing: we see it

3.4 Drawing seen from the correct station-point and from the side. Viewing a picture from the wrong angle causes a distortion in perspective.

with two eyes and we move around it, looking at it from various angles. And yet, even though our eyes are not fooled, we see a three-dimensional scene. Clearly this cannot be due to any identity of light rays between the picture and the scene.

Given these problems, the claim that pictures and nonpictorial objects can give off the same light to the eyes is untenable. Even if pictures were usually seen under Gibson's special viewing conditions, this theory of pictures could never account for our perception of black and white line drawings. A line drawing of a face does not give off the same light as an actual face: it lacks color, its surfaces are blank, and although its lines correspond to edges of the face, the light from a line is different from the light from an edge of the face itself. Yet black and white line drawings are instantly recognizable. Nor could this theory account for our recognition of caricatures, which sometimes is even more immediate than our recognition of photographs, shaded drawings, and outline drawings (Ryan and Schwartz, 1956). Although there may be a direct correspondence between the edges of a real face and the lines in a line drawing of this face, even this degree of correspondence is lost in a caricature, because its lines are deliberately distorted.

Recognizing these problems, Gibson (1971) revised his theory. The notion of "point-for-point correspondence" between picture and scene was replaced with the concept of "higher order correspondence." According to the new theory, a representational picture preserves higher order information from the represented scene. This information consists of invariant features, such as textures, contrasts, and edges. These features are invariant because they are unaffected by superficial changes, such as alterations in illumination, changes of viewing angle, or the stretching of forms involved in caricature.

This theory of the information captured by pictures can now handle black and white shaded and line drawings and even caricature. A black and white shaded sketch of landscape preserves the color relationships in the real scene by its various shades of gray: the lightest gray corresponds to the brightest parts of the actual scene. A line drawing of a room yields the same higher order information as the room itself because the lines of the picture correspond to the edges of the surfaces in the room. And a caricature of a person yields the same information as a real life view because the caricature preserves the relationships among the features: if the face has a protruding nose, this protrusion may be exaggerated in the caricature, but the relationship between the protrusion of the nose and its length is preserved.

Pictures also preserve what Gibson called "texture gradients." Surfaces in the environment tend to have regular, homogeneous textures: a lawn is textured by blades of grass of constant size, a floor may be textured by black and white tiles of equal size, and a fence is textured by equally spaced posts. Because light rays converge, forms take up less space in the visual field as they recede: textures, thus, appear denser the more distant the surface.

In *Wivenhoe Park*, the posts of the fence become increasingly closely packed from left to right. This texture gradient allows us to perceive the fence as a structure of even height receding into depth, rather than as an uneven structure parallel to the plane of the picture. Were we looking at the actual scene rather than at a picture of it, binocular and motion cues would also tell us that the fence was regular but receding. In the absence of such cues, texture gradients alone guide our perception.

In sum, according to direct registration theory, light is lawfully related to its origins and is automatically picked up from the retina by the nervous system. Perceivers therefore need not supplement the information that reaches their senses. This information, by itself, is sufficient for veridical perception to occur.

3.5 *Figures illustrating the phenomenon of size constancy. Although the distant figure forms a smaller image on the retina, the two men are perceived as the same size.*

Constructivist Theory

In contrast to direct registration theory, constructivist theory holds that the information supplied to our senses is fundamentally ambiguous and thus must be supplemented by the beholder. Whereas for registration theory perception is a matter of detection, for constructivist theory perception is a matter of construction.

Constructivist theory can be traced to Hermann von Helmholtz, a nineteenth century German physicist and physiologist who put forth a surprising claim. Although perception may seem effortless and direct, Helmholtz (1867) argued that this feeling is illusory. The information available to our senses, taken by itself, provides ambiguous and misleading information about its source; perceptions are the product of constant, unconscious, supplementation on the part of the perceiver. And because the information that must be supplemented is inherently ambiguous, perception is essentially a matter of guesswork.

The classic example from constructivist theory is a scene composed of two people, one standing close by, the other far away (Fig. 3.5). The light rays from the figures converge on the retina of each eye, forming retinal images. The rays from the nearby person take up a larger area on the retina than do the rays from the distant person. Since the retinal images are two-dimensional, if we read these images literally, we would perceive two people on the same plane, one person much smaller than the other. Fortunately, however, we are not limited to the information on our retina. We go beyond the information given on the retina, and Helmholtz argued that we do this by the mechanism of "unconscious inference." Because of our knowledge that people are roughly the same size, we infer that the tiny person is not a midget on the same plane as the larger person but a person of normal size at a greater distance. According to Helmholtz, this inference is made possible by our knowledge of the world, gained from experience. While most constructivists agree that perceptual inference depends on learning, some have suggested that learning is unnecessary. Instead, inferences are made automatically as the perceiver integrates information on the retina with nonvisual cues such as ocular muscle movements (Festinger, Burnham, Ono, and Bamber, 1967).

Because perceptual inferences are made unconsciously, we feel as if perception is immediate and effortless, given directly by the information in the light. But if we did not go beyond the information given, the world would look very different indeed. A distant elephant would appear smaller than a nearby person. And as the elephant approached, it would seem to expand in size, like a stationary balloon filling with air.

The art historian E. H. Gombrich applied constructivist principles to the problem of picture perception. Gombrich (1960) set out to show that pictures would be perceived as flat, nonrepresentational arrangements of color and line were it not for the "beholder's share" in the task of picture perception. The beholder must actively read into the picture in order both to recognize the objects depicted and to perceive depth. A painting, according to Gombrich, is like an inkblot in a Rorschach test: both are vaguely suggestive of objects in the world, and both invite projection. *Wivenhoe Park* may appear highly realistic, but no painting of an object can contain all of the detailed information that nature gives about that object. *Wivenhoe Park* only supplies hints of the actual park. Look at a close-up of one of the painted trees, and all that is seen are daubs of paint; move back, and through the mechanism of projection, the imagination transforms these daubs into leaves. The perceiver takes the artist's hints and reads in the rest.

The perceiver does not read in at random. Projections are guided by our knowledge of what objects tend to be like. We see what we expect to see. When listening to an unclear radio station, we understand the words better if the program is familiar, because expectation usually guides our guesses correctly. So also, when we are looking at a painting, our guesses are molded by the expectations created by context. A vague shape next to a cluster of trees in Constable's painting is likely to be read as another tree; that same shape next to a group of cows in the distance is likely to be read as another cow. This phenomenon occurs in our perception of the ordinary environment as well: we have all had the discomfiting experience of "recognizing" something in the distance, only to realize, on approaching closer, that we had entertained the wrong hypothesis.

The claim that knowledge guides the recognition of objects in a painting has a logical extension. If we have no knowledge of the object represented, there is some information that we ought to, but will not, read in. Thus, the picture will be misperceived. Gombrich offered the example of a painting of fur trim on a piece of clothing. No matter how realistic the picture, it cannot adequately convey tactile information. Thus, the fur's texture must be read in by the perceiver. But the perceiver who has never touched fur will not know what to read in. Just such a problem was faced by someone who had never seen snow. Upon seeing a painting of snow, this person imagined it to have a waxy texture. The same problem occurs even in the perception of the texture of real objects, if the viewer has never had the opportunity to touch them.

The mechanism of projection also accounts for the operation of what Gombrich dubbed "the etc. principle." When painters set out to depict an object, they cannot possibly capture all of the details of that object: there are only a finite number of marks that can be made on a canvas, but there is an infinite amount of information that painters are trying to depict. Thus, when painters are rendering a head of hair, for example, they paint in a few strands of hair very realistically and leave the rest blurred. But observers project onto the blurred parts and actually imagine that they see all of the tiny strands of hair. It is as if the painters had painted a few strands and had then said "etc., etc."

Perceivers do not actually hallucinate strands of hair that are not there. If brought to their attention, perceivers can surely see that only a few strands are painted in. However, people are not ordinarily reflective about the problem of picture perception and thus do not usually become aware of how little the painted scene matches the real one.

For Gombrich, the perception of depth in pictures is also based on the mechanism of projection guided by knowledge. All configurations on a two-dimensional surface that are meant to conjure up a three-dimensional world are ambiguous. There are an infinite number of shapes in space of which a particular two-dimensional image is the correct perspective view. A picture of an oval, for example, could be a representation of an oval lying in the same vertical plane as the picture, or it could represent a circular form

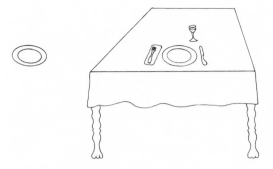

3.6 Oval shape, perceived in isolation as an oval placed parallel to the picture plane, but perceived in context as a circular form receding horizontally.

viewed obliquely, receding into space (Fig. 3.6). The fence as depicted by Constable could be either perpendicular to the observer's line of sight, with converging rails and posts placed increasingly close together, or receding from the observer, with parallel rails and evenly spaced posts. In the real world, these ambiguities could be resolved through the use of binocular and motion depth cues. Because such cues are useless in the case of pictures, we must rely on educated guesswork. The actual shape of the fence that we see depends on what we expect to see, based on our knowledge of fences. Given that we know that fences tend to be parallel, with evenly spaced posts, we read this image as a regular fence that appears irregular because it is receding in space.

Paradoxically, according to Gombrich, the more illusionistic the picture, the richer the inferences required of the reader in order to complete the illusion. A comparison of the Constable painting with a copy of this painting by a child illustrates the point (Fig. 3.7). In Constable's landscape, the grass ranges in color from light brown to rich green. Yet the beholder must decode it as a uniform color in and out of the sun and at different distances from the eye, since distant objects look duller in color. In the child's version, no such decoding is necessary, because the grass is painted all one color. A similar point can be made about the fence. In Constable's version, the perceiver must decode the converging lines as parallel but receding. In the child's flatter version there is no need to translate converging lines into parallel lines since the lines are, in fact, parallel. There is no perspectival distortion.

In sum, the apparent effortlessness of the recognition of objects receding into space in the Constable picture is illusory. Veridical perception of pictures requires a great deal of unconscious guesswork, which is empirically guided by previous experience, knowledge, and expectations.

Whereas direct registration theory maintains that pictures succeed as representations because they capture the same information as is contained by what they depict, constructivist theory places more distance between the picture and the pictured object. A picture captures only a fragment of the information contained in the real thing. All the rest is read in, whether correctly or incorrectly. Pictures do not objectively resemble what they represent. Rather, the resemblance that observers experience is imposed.

A view even more divergent from registration theory was proposed by Nelson Goodman (1968). Also a constructivist, Goodman argued that pictures bear an arbitrary relation to what they represent. The criteria for realism are relative, determined by the system of representation in the culture. To say that a picture looks like nature is to say that it "looks the way nature is usually painted" (p. 39). Recognizing what a picture represents is entirely a matter of learning how to read the conventions used by the culture. If we do not know the conventions, it does not matter how much we know about the objects depicted. Pictures can be read correctly only if we are versed in the language of pictorial representation adopted by our culture.

3.7 *Child's copy of Constable's* Wivenhoe Park, Essex, *painted not as the image is formed on the retina but as the scene is experienced. Note the lack of perspectival distortion and the uniformly colored grass.*

3.8 *Building drawn in perspective, with horizontal lines converging as they recede from the eye but vertical lines remaining parallel. The laws of perspective in this picture do not conform to the laws of optics.*

Even linear perspective, which seems to create the illusion of reality so convincingly, is said to be a convention that we must learn to read. For instance, the laws of perspective state that the edges of objects appear to converge as they recede in distance from the eye. But in pictorial perspective, this rule is only partially applied: horizontal surfaces are depicted by lines that converge in the distance, but vertical surfaces are depicted by parallel lines.

Nonetheless, we read both sets of lines as receding in distance from our eyes. Take the case of the drawing of a building (Fig. 3.8). Although the top of the building is further from the observer's eye than the bottom, the vertical edges remain parallel in a drawing.

Even if the artist follows the rules dictated by geometry more consistently, and thus makes the vertical edges of the building converge, the ambiguity in the picture remains. If the building is drawn so that only the front wall is visible, we cannot know if the configuration is a floor receding along a horizontal plane, a wall extending along the vertical axis, or a wall leaning away from us (Fig. 3.9). All we can do is establish conventions that dictate one reading or another. Thus, whereas classical constructivist theory has us understand pictures because of what we know about the objects depicted, the conventionalist view has us understand pictures because of what we know about other pictures.

Gestalt Theory

The gestalt theory of perception, as formulated by psychologists such as Kurt Koffka (1935), Wolfgang Köhler (1929), and Max Wertheimer (1945), lies midway between the registration and constructivist accounts of perception. Like direct registration theory, gestalt theory maintains that perception involves no inferences or guesswork; but like constructivist theory, gestalt psychology assumes that the perceiver transforms the information reaching the senses. The incoming information is transformed not by knowledge, as constructivists hold, but by the operation of a perceptual principle called the "simplicity principle." Each pattern of light

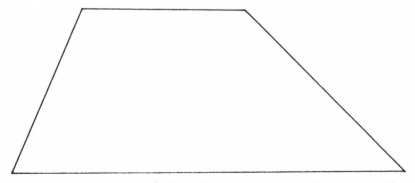

3.9 *Ambiguous shape, which could represent a rectangle or trapezoid receding horizontally, vertically, or at any angle in between.*

that hits the retina is said to produce a pattern in the brain called a "brain field." The brain field organizes itself in the simplest, most economical way. And this determines how the world is perceived.

Thus, both the gestalt and constructivist schools claim that the perceiver goes beyond the information that reaches the retina. But here agreement ends. Constructivist theory holds that we go beyond the retinal image by using our learned and thus potentially idiosyncratic knowledge of the world to infer what is out there. Gestalt theory holds that we go beyond the retinal information because of universal, inherent, and innate organizing principles of the brain.

Rudolf Arnheim (1972, 1974) extended gestalt theory to the domain of picture perception by demonstrating the way in which pictorial information is transformed by the observer through the operation of the simplicity principle. Arnheim made clear that "simplicity" is not measured by counting the number of elements in a pattern. For example, a pattern with six dots can be simpler than one with only four dots (Fig. 3.10). Moreover, the same number of elements can form a simple or a complex pattern, depending on how the elements are related. Thus, a pattern with asymmetrically overlapping triangles is more complex than one with adjacent triangles (Fig. 3.11). Simple patterns, rather than being characterized quantitatively in terms of number of elements, are characterized by order, regularity, balance, and clearly defined structures. Other gestalt theorists have been still more specific about which principles constitute simplicity. Simple gestalts are defined as having high redundancy of information, high economy of encoding,

3.10 Dot patterns, in which six evenly spaced dots, though containing more elements, form a simpler arrangement than four irregularly spaced dots.

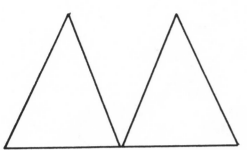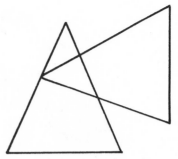

3.11 *Triangles, which arranged symmetrically form a simpler pattern than the same number of triangles intersecting asymmetrically.*

low uncertainty, and low randomness (e.g. Attneave, 1954; Hochberg and McAlister, 1953; Perkins and Cooper, 1980).

The simplicity principle was used by Arnheim to account for pictorial depth perception. Recall the problem of the converging fence in *Wivenhoe Park.* According to gestalt theory, we see the fence as receding into space and constructed of parallel rails and evenly spaced posts because the pattern created by parallel lines and regular posts is simpler than that created by converging lines and irregularly spaced posts.

There are many other examples of how the deformation created by perspective creates depth through the operation of the simplicity principle. Consider a trapezoidal checkered shape (Fig. 3.12). How are we to decide if this form is an irregular trapezoid standing vertically in the plane of the picture or a rectangular tile floor receding into space? According to direct registration theory, the texture gradient created by the tiles tells us that it is a floor receding horizontally. According to constructivist theory, if the context of the picture leads us to expect a floor, we see it as a floor. The irregularly sized and shaped tiles also help: because we know that tiles tend to be of uniform size and shape, we read the floor as composed of regular tiles that look irregular only because they are receding. In contrast to both of these theories, gestalt theory holds that we unconsciously select the simplest reading. Even if we had no knowledge of tiles, we would read this image as a receding rectangle because this is the simpler reading. A receding rectangle is simpler than an upright irregular trapezoid, because the rectangle is the more regular geometrical form; a wall of receding uniform tiles is simpler than a vertical wall of tiles of different shapes and sizes, because uniformity is simpler than variation. Thus, wherever a simpler—namely more symmetrical, balanced, and redundant—pattern is yielded by reading a configuration as three- rather than

3.12 Ambiguous shape, which could represent either a trapezoid checkered by forms of different shapes and sizes, extending vertically, or a rectangle with regular tiles receding horizontally.

two-dimensional, depth will be perceived (see also Attneave, 1972; Hochberg and McAlister, 1953; Hochberg and Brooks, 1960).

Evaluating Theories of Representation

The three theories of pictorial representation can be classified into two categories: registration theory, on the one hand, claims that no information need be added by the observer, and constructivist and gestalt theories, on the other, postulate some form of transformation of pictorial information by the observer. The available evidence reveals problems with direct registration theory and supports the claim that the perceiver intervenes and transforms the information in some way.

Central to the registration theory of picture perception is the claim that in some way texture gradients unambiguously convey depth. But there are at least two problems with this view. First, texture gradients do not, by themselves, clearly disambiguate. Consider a trapezoid whose texture is denser at the top (Fig. 3.13). The texture gradient in this picture cannot tell us which of three readings to choose: a rectangle receding horizontally; a rectangle extending vertically, with correct perspective so that the lines converge and the texture becomes denser as the object increases in distance vertically; or a rectangle or a trapezoid receding at any one of a number of oblique angles (Goodman, 1968). The unavoidable conclusion is that the selection of a reading must be based on something given by the perceivers themselves: either their expectations determine their choice, as constructivist theory holds, or the simplicity principle does so, as gestalt theory holds. Moreover, the very assumption of textural homogenity would be viewed by a constructivist as a piece of real-world knowledge, gained by noticing that textures in the world tend to be regular, and by a gestaltist as a simplicity assumption, since regular textures are simpler than irregular ones. For these reasons, constructivist and gestalt theorists do not feel that texture gradients alone, without the intervention of either real world knowledge or the simplicity principle, can reveal depth.

Not only are texture gradients by themselves insufficient to reveal depth, but they are also unnecessary. There are no texture gradients in outline drawings. There is only linear perspective and foreshortening. And this by itself, even according to registration theory, is potentially ambiguous (Kennedy, 1974). An outline in the form of an oval could just as easily be an oval parallel to the picture plane as a circle receding into the distance (Fig. 3.6). Yet we have no trouble recognizing depth in line drawings. There are only two possible explanations for this: either we read in what we expect to see (if the oval is on a dinner table, we see it as a circle because we expect plates to be round), or we choose the simplest reading (a circle is simpler than an oval because every point on its circumference is equidistant from its center.)

That texture gradients are neither necessary nor sufficient to disambiguate is not the only evidence against registration theory. Another piece of evidence is the fact that we perceive the size of an object as constant despite variations in the amount of space that it takes up on the retina as its distance from us varies. The phenomenon of size constancy is demonstrated by holding one's left hand far away and one's right hand close up. The two hands appear to be the same size. But if the hands are made to overlap in one's visual field, a striking size difference becomes apparent. The left hand now appears shrunken. This is evidence that we do not normally experience our retinal images; we have to engage in tricks and strategies in order to do so. The fact that we normally

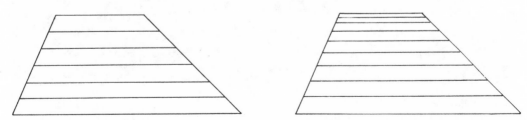

3.13 *Trapezoids, one with a uniform texture, indicating that it is a vertical trapezoid, the other with a texture that becomes denser at the top, suggesting that it is a receding rectangle.*

experience the distant hand as the same size as the close one tells us that we are unconsciously scaling up the distant object. It is as if we say to ourselves that the left hand is far away, and thus perspective causes it to appear shrunken in size; we know that it is not shrunken, so we will correct for this and actually see it as bigger.

The same kind of unconscious supplementation on the part of the perceiver occurs with pictures. Whenever pictorial depth cues such as perspective or overlap alert us that an object is meant to be read as distant, we unconsciously scale that object up in size. Gombrich demonstrated this by a slight alteration of the elements of Constable's *Wivenhoe Park*. He superimposed the house on the far side of the lake onto the lawn in the right hand foreground of the picture, in front of the lake; and he superimposed the last right-hand section of the fence on top of the first section in the left foreground (Fig. 3.14). The effect is striking. Both the house and the fence section appear much smaller when they are interpreted as near to, rather than distant from, the point of observation. But their sizes have not been altered. This is good evidence that we cannot help but actively read into a picture. If the perceiver did not intrude in this way, the reductions in size caused by perspec-

3.14 *Montage of Constable's* Wivenhoe Park, Essex, *with house and fence superimposed (arrows). They appear much smaller when interpreted as near rather than far away, because distant objects are unconsciously scaled up in size to compensate for the reduction dictated by perspective.*

tive would appear much more extreme and thus, perhaps, disquieting.

The existence of visual illusions in the perception of the real as well as the pictorial world is also damaging to registration theory. That visual illusions occur is evidence that perceptions can go wrong. Perceptions are likely to go wrong if the information to the senses is impoverished, requiring supplementation or transformation. Reading into a picture incorrectly leads to error. If all the information were out there simply to be registered, there should be no reason for perceptions to go astray.

These are only a few pieces of evidence that the perception of pictures involves more than simply the pickup and registry of information. The information reaching our senses is transformed in some way. The task is thus to seek evidence to decide whether this transformation occurs by means of the perceiver's knowledge of the world, as constructivist theory claims, or by means of the operation of the simplicity principle, as gestalt theory holds.

Such evidence is not easy to find. In many cases, constructivist and gestalt theories make identical predictions, rendering a test between them impossible. For example, consider the tile floor (Fig. 3.12). Both theories predict that this form will be read as a rectangular surface of tiles receding in depth. Reading the tiles as uniform is necessary for the floor to be seen as receding. And the interpretation of the tiles as uniform is predicted both by the observer's prior experience with tiles (the constructivist explanation) and by the simplicity principle (the gestalt explanation).

To choose between constructivist and gestalt accounts of pictorial depth perception, cases are needed in which only one principle—knowledge or simplicity—is operating. Better yet would be cases in which these two principles make opposing predictions. One case in which recognition can be explained by the simplicity principle, without the intervention of knowledge, is that of unfamiliar geometrical shapes (Fig. 3.15). These configurations could be read as two-dimensional. Yet they are immediately read as three-dimensional, even though such forms have probably never been encountered in the real world (Perkins, 1979). And just as a drawing of an oval could represent an oval, a circle or any number of shapes in between, so also there are an infinite number of three-dimensional forms that these drawings could depict. Yet the observer assumes that the forms are made up of right angles and parallel edges. This assumption is made because right angles and parallel edges are simpler than oblique angles and nonparallel edges. There is no way that this assumption can derive from knowledge of such forms, since these forms are unfamiliar to the

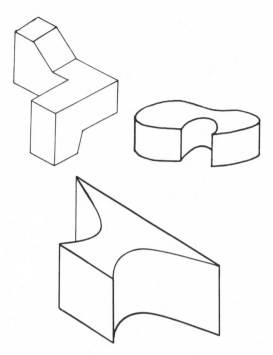

3.15 Unfamiliar forms, which are instantly read as possessing right angles and parallel edges, in contrast to the greater complexity of oblique angles and non-parallel edges.

observer. In this case, then, the simplicity principle alone accounts for what is perceived.

When simplicity is not relevant, and prior experience or knowledge are all that one can rely on, pictures can still be read correctly. Consider the case of seeing probable rather than improbable objects. A daub of paint next to a group of trees will be read as another tree; that same daub next to a group of cows will be read as a cow. There is nothing simpler about either reading: the only possible explanation seems to be that we have projected an image into the picture on the basis of expectation.

Another example in which knowledge operates successfully without the simplicity principle is the case of the depiction of fur, mentioned earlier. Knowing the texture of fur allows us to read the picture correctly. But never having touched fur before, we have no way of discovering its texture from the picture. Here, recognition is achieved through the application of prior knowledge alone. It is not simpler to recognize the fur's texture, but it is more correct.

There are some cases in which the simplicity and knowledge principles make rival predictions. Consider two drawings of cubes from different angles, the first of which is most easily seen as a three-dimensional cube, the second as a two-dimensional design (Fig. 3.16). Although we may be able to see the second as three-dimensional, we have to work at maintaining this reading. No such work, however, is required of the first. In each case, the form is read in the simplest way. A three-dimensional reading of the first form is simpler than a two-dimensional one, because the latter would yield an irregular shape. But a two-dimensional interpretation of the second form yields a regular pattern. Thus, it is simpler to perceive the second form as two-dimensional than as a regular three-dimensional cube, since adding a third dimension increases the level of complexity. Now, suppose that we are told that the second form is a cube. Suppose further that it is situated next to many forms like the first. This still does not help us to see it as a cube. We cannot maintain a view of it as a cube, for it keeps slipping back to its more comfortable, and simpler, two-dimensional configuration. Greater familiarity with cubes than with hexagonal designs, and even explicit directions to see it as a cube, are to no avail. It appears that the tendency to reduce a pattern to the simplest form that it allows can override the tendency to see what we expect to see.

The same dominance of simplicity over knowledge may occur when, in photographs, there are unfortunate juxtapositions, such as a person waving at the camera with her arm behind another person's head. In such cases, the arm sometimes appears to be emerging from the top of the other person's head. In terms of familiarity, such a reading makes no sense. We know that arms do not grow out of heads. However, in terms of simplicity, this reading becomes explicable. Reading it as an arm growing out of a head allows us to see one continuous contour defining both head and arm. This is an illustration of an aspect of the simplicity principle called the principle of good continuation, and it demonstrates again how simplicity may override knowledge (Perkins, personal communication). A similar instance of the dominance of simplicity over familiarity occurs when letters are embedded in a complex pattern. Familiar as we are with the alphabet, we often find it very difficult to see the letters. Instead, we see the larger pattern.

But just the opposite may also occur: familiarity sometimes overrides simplicity. Consider the finding that an irregularly

3.16 Cubes drawn from different angles, one readily perceived as a three dimensional cube, the other more readily perceived as a two-dimensional design. Here, simplicity dominates knowledge.

shaped room, when viewed through a peephole positioned at a certain angle, appeared to observers to be rectangular (Ames, 1955; Ittelson, 1952). But when subjects were exposed at length to this room, and allowed to manipulate objects within it in various ways, such as by poking with a stick while looking through the peephole, they eventually learned to see the room correctly (Kilpatrick, 1954; Weiner, 1956). Here is a case, outside the domain of pictures, in which knowledge comes to dominate simplicity.

In conclusion, both knowledge and simplicity by themselves can succeed in achieving a correct pictorial reading. When pitted against each other, in some cases the simplicity principle predominates, while in other cases, familiarity may take over. Depending on the degree of simplicity and familiarity involved, it is sometimes easier to see a simple figure than a familiar one; in other situations, it may be easier to see a familiar one than a simple one. Overall, however, simplicity is a more powerful principle for explaining depth perception, while knowledge is usually more helpful in explaining object identification.

Reading Pictorial Expression

There is more to a work of pictorial art than what it represents. If it is to function aesthetically for us, we also must perceive the moods and nonvisual sensory properties that it expresses. Full appreciation of Constable's *Wivenhoe Park* requires more than a recognition of a three-dimensional scene; the perceiver must also apprehend the mood of serenity expressed. Appreciation of Severini's painting *Dynamic Hieroglyphic of Bal Tabarin* (Fig. 3.2) requires that one perceive the mood of frenzy and excitement, and the qualities of noise and heat.

When an inanimate object such as a picture is characterized as serene or frenzied, sad or happy, loud or hot, these terms are applied metaphorically. While *Wivenhoe Park* is literally a rectangular painted surface dominated by muted colors, it is only metaphorically serene. And while Severini's work is literally a surface of bright colors and diagonal, intersecting lines, it is only metaphorically frenzied, noisy, and hot.

A picture can express both psychological properties, such as sadness, serenity, or anxiety, and nonvisual sensory properties, such as loudness, heat, or sharpness. The properties that a work expresses are independent of the emotional or physical state of the artist or the perceiver. A cheery artist can make a sad painting. And a sad painting need not make us feel sad in order for us to perceive it as sad. The properties that a picture expresses are also independent of what it represents: a picture of a serene person may be frenzied; a picture of a winter landscape can be warm. Moreover, abstract works, which do not represent, certainly do express. The American painter Mark Rothko, whose canvasses are entirely abstract fields of color, insisted that he was not interested in the relationships of color and form; rather, he was interested in expressing human emotions—"tragedy, ecstasy, doom" (Lark-Horowitz, Lewis, and Luca, 1973, p. 229). In the words of the philosopher Ernst Cassirer, no visual experience is composed simply of sensory data, of brightness and color: "We can consider . . . a simple line . . . according to its purely expressive meaning . . . A peculiar mood is expressed in the purely spatial determination: the up and down of the lines in space embraces an inner mobility, a dynamic rise and fall" (1957, III, 200). And Rudolf Arnheim argued that there is no such thing as "pure" form, since even the simplest line expresses a feeling or mood and is therefore symbolic (1974, p. 461).

If the properties expressed are conveyed neither by the mental state of the artist or perceiver, nor by what is represented, to what are they due? Gestalt and constructivist psychologists give opposing answers to this question.

The Iconic View

Gestalt psychologists such as Arnheim (1949) have argued that formal properties, such as color, form, and line, bear an iconic relation to nonvisual properties, that is, a relationship of resemblance. For instance, certain colors and forms in some structural way actually resemble sadness; others resemble anxiety. Thus, we can tell what a picture expresses because it actually looks like what it expresses.

This position has its history in the earlier gestalt interest in "physiognomic" perception (the perception of moods in inanimate objects) as opposed to "geometrical-technical" perception (the perception of literal properties) (Köhler, 1929, 1937; Werner, 1961; Werner and Kaplan, 1963). According to gestalt theory, physiognomic perception allows us to see a mood in a pattern because the pattern possesses the same structure as the mood (see also Langer, 1953). This view is based on the principle of isomorphism: moods are said to be similar to perceptual patterns in their underlying structural organizations. Thus, the columns of a temple express striving because they seem to be pushing upward against the heavy weight of the roof, just as a striving person must struggle forward against obstacles. A weeping willow expresses sadness because it is structurally similar to the psychological property of sadness: both the structure of the tree and the mood are passive and lacking in energy. Similarly, a painting with lines inclined in an upward direction expresses animation because upwardly inclined lines are structurally similar to the buoyancy felt when one is animated.

According to the iconic view, expressive properties are not limited to works of art but are universally perceived in inanimate natural objects. A boulder, for example, expresses strength; a weeping willow expresses sadness. Expressive properties are also universally perceived in the human body: upturned lips express gladness; a furrowed brow expresses worry; a slow, dragging gait expresses passivity or sorrow. Thus, expressive properties are inherent in the perceptual patterns of nature as well as art.

Because perceptual patterns are structurally similar to what they express, the perception of expression is deemed to be an elementary, direct, and unlearned process. Moreover, expressive properties may be noticed before and remembered longer than the formal patterns that make expression possible. According to iconic theory, it is more natural to perceive a fire as expressing violence than to perceive it as having particular colors and shapes as it flickers. And we may well remember the expression of an object after having forgotten its precise color and shape. We are more likely to recall that a twisted blanket thrown in a heap over a chair looked "tired" than to recall its color (Arnheim, 1949). Similarly, we often remember the mood of a painting, novel, or film long after we have forgotten the subject or the plot.

Of course, formal properties do not possess an inherent meaning independent of the context in which they are found. Thus, a dark watercolor painting may express gloom, while a dark pen and ink sketch need not, since colors are not an option in this picture. Similarly, Mondrian's *Broadway Boogie Woogie* expresses liveliness to the perceiver who knows that Mondrian's paintings are typically much more formal and severe (Fig. 3.17). If we were told that *Broadway Boogie Woogie* had been painted by Severini, whose paintings are rhythmic, brilliantly colored, and free (Fig. 3.2), *Broadway Boogie Woogie* would seem, by constrast, to express formal restraint (Gombrich, 1960). Arnheim pointed out a similar example to show that context can affect our recognition of what is expressed. To twentieth century ears, a Mozart concerto expresses serenity and cheer; but to Mozart's contemporaries, the same concerto expressed violent passion. Arnheim ascribed this difference to the vivid contrast between Mozart's concerto and the music of his time.

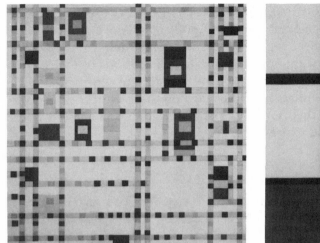

3.17 Mondrian, Broadway Boogie Woogie, *expressing liveliness and gaiety in contrast to his usual style, shown here in* Composition with Red, Blue, and Yellow, *but expressing restraint in contrast to Severini's painting in Fig. 3.2.*

The Constructivist-Conventional View

In direct contrast to the iconic position is the extreme constructivist claim that pictures express by means of arbitrary conventions (Goodman, 1968). The difference between an iconic and a conventional relation has to do with resemblance and lack of resemblance. A picture of a dog is usually considered to resemble an actual dog. The word *dog*, however, neither looks nor sounds like an actual dog and is arbitrarily paired with its referent. It is because of the arbitrary relationship between word and referent that a Westerner hearing Chinese for the first time cannot understand what is being said. And it is because of the iconic relationship between picture and referent that a Westerner has no trouble recognizing the objects represented in a Chinese painting.

The claim that pictures express by means of conventions amounts to saying that the formal means of expressing sadness or cheer are arbitrarily determined by the culture. A dark-toned painting does not resemble gloom in any inherent way. Depending on the perceiver's culture, this same dark painting may express gloom or cheer.

The difference between the gestalt and the constructivist views parallels the different ways that these theories handle the problem of representation. For gestalt theory, perception of what a picture represents is immediate, owing to the operation of the simplicity principle, and unlearned. For constructivist theory, perception of what a picture represents depends upon cognitive construction: perceivers must piece together the cues, using their knowledge of either the world or the representational conventions of their culture. Thus, for gestalt theory, accurate reading of representation and expression requires no knowledge on the part of the observer; for constructivist theory, the role of knowledge is crucial for both representation and expression:

	Perceiving representation	Perceiving expression
Constructivist theory	Constructed through knowledge of world or knowledge of cultural conventions of representation	Constructed through knowlege of cultural conventions of expression
Gestalt theory	Immediately given by the operation of the simplicity principle	Immediately given by the isomorphism between perceptual patterns and nonvisual states

In its account of the perception of expression, gestalt theory sounds very much like the registration account of the perception of pictorial representation: according to both views, the perception is direct and unmediated, requiring no supplementation by the observer.

Evaluating Theories of Expression

If the iconic view is correct, there should be considerable agreement about what a picture expresses. Moreover, it should not be necessary to learn to read what is expressed, since it is not necessary to learn to recognize similarity. If the constructivist-conventional view is correct, there should be disagreement across cultures in determining what a picture expresses. The conventional view also predicts that the conventions of expression must be learned by exposure to the norms of one's culture.

Unfortunately, there is only meager evidence with which to choose between the iconic and the conventional view of expression. The evidence falls into three categories: studies that have investigated whether individuals within a culture agree on what properties a pattern expresses, studies that have investigated the possibility of agreement across cultures, and studies investigating how children judge what is expressed.

Studies that have examined how people within a culture perceive expression demonstrate high agreement among people (Arnheim, 1949). For example, when asked to draw lines expressing various emotions, people respond quite predictably. In one study, only straight lines and angles were used to express "exciting," "furious," "hard," and "powerful"; only curved lines were used to express "sad," "quiet," "lazy," and "merry." Upward lines were used to express "strength," "energy," and "force"; downward lines were used to express "weakness" and "depression" (Lundholm, 1921; see also Hochberg, 1978; Kreitler and Kreitler, 1972; Murray and Deabler, 1957; Peters and Merrifield, 1958; Poffenberger and Barrows, 1924; Springbett, 1960; Werner and Kaplan, 1963; Wexner, 1954).

On the basis of several studies yielding such results, it is reasonable to conclude that people within a culture agree about what properties are metaphorically expressed by perceived patterns. But despite common belief, such evidence does not provide strong support for the iconic position. Since the people were in the same culture, and since they were all adults, they could have learned the culture's conventions for expression. The only critical test of the iconic position is to administer such tasks cross-culturally or to study children who are too young to have learned these conventions.

The cross-cultural evidence is mixed. On the one hand, some agreement across cultures was found when subjects were asked to judge the properties expressed by simple patterns (Werner and Kaplan, 1963; see also Osgood, 1960; Jakobits, 1969). On the other hand, all cultures clearly do not agree on how particular moods are to be expressed. For instance, in Western culture, black expresses evil or gloom and white expresses purity, innocence, and lightheartedness. But in the Peking Opera, actors paint their faces black to indicate a sound, honest, upright character; white faces express craftiness and cunning.

Studies of children's abilities to perceive expressive properties have revealed that, when confronted with a picture, children do not show sensitivity to the mood expressed until the elementary school years (Carothers and Gardner, 1979). However, when shown an isolated line or color swatch, even preschoolers are able to perceive certain expressed properties (Gardner, 1974a). This suggests that the perception of expression is not entirely a matter of mastering arbitrary conventions.

Given the mixed cross-cultural evidence, perhaps the most reasonable conclusion is that we are born with the ability to perceive certain connections between perceptual patterns in different sensory modalities, such as brightness and loudness, and between perceptual patterns and psychological states, such as brightness and positive affect. What is given at birth accounts for the agreement that has been found across cultures and for the ability of young children to perceive expression in the same way as adults. But culture writes on top of what is given at birth, and the particular culture into which a person is born may reinforce as well as override these innately given connections. In cases where a culture overrides them, disagreement across cultures, as well as between child and adult, will be found.

Reading pictures may appear effortless. Nevertheless, making sense of a work of pictorial art requires an intelligent and inquisitive eye. This is especially true in the case of representation. Apprehending a two-dimensional surface as a three-dimensional space requires that perceivers go beyond the information given. This feat is accomplished by one or more means: the two-dimensional representation is enriched by what perceivers know about the world, by what they know about the conventions of representation, or by the organizing influence of the simplicity principle. Each of these mechanisms may operate on its own, or they may operate in conjunction with one another. When two or more of these principles dictate competing readings, depending on the context, any one of them may predominate.

If the perceiver is only able to see what a picture represents, then the picture is not functioning aesthetically. Nonaesthetic pictures, such as maps and diagrams, symbolize by representation, but only works of art symbolize by expression. It would be odd indeed to describe a map as serene, a diagram as sad. Reading expression is essential if a picture is to be apprehended in an aesthetic mode.

An aesthetic attitude requires a willingness to suspend the temptation to look right through a picture and instead to notice the picture's surface properties: its use of line, color, and texture to express moods or nonvisual sensory properties; its arrangement of forms on the picture plane; and its style. This operation is carried out effortlessly by people versed in the arts. People with no special familiarity with the arts certainly have the capacity to notice these surface properties, but are less likely to do so spontaneously.

All that artists have to work with is the surface; yet through surface manipulations, they allow us to see beyond the surface to a three-dimensional space or an expressed mood. Aesthetic vision requires that the perceiver step back and see the surface as well as its relation to the properties expressed and the illusory three-dimensional level. Perhaps this is what it means to be an expert in other domains as well. For instance, in the case of language, the ordinary person listens right through a sentence to its meaning: surface aspects, such as sound properties or precise wording, are ignored. The reader of poetry or the linguist, in contrast, listens to the surface of a sentence and tries to understand the relation of the surface level to the deeper level of meaning. And so also the connoisseur of pictorial art focuses on the surface of a picture in order to apprehend its relation to the illusory third dimension, or to the nonvisual properties that are expressed.

4 The Untutored Eye

Conversation between an adult and a five-year-old:
Adult: *"Which is prettier, a flower or a picture of a flower?"*
Child: *"A flower."*
Adult: *"Always?"*
Child: *"Yes."*
Adult: *"Why?"*
Child: *"Because artists sometimes mess up."*

No one places books in front of two-year-olds and expects them to understand the written text. Reading words, everyone agrees, is a skill that must be *learned.* But pictures are another matter. It is commonly believed that pictures are not read at all; rather, they are seen, and seeing entails immediate understanding.

Such an assumption is not entirely justified. The untutored eye apprehends a picture quite differently from an experienced one. This is because seeing by itself is not enough. Just as in the case of the written word, some aspects of a picture must be read as well as seen.

Six-month-olds confronted with Constable's *Wivenhoe Park* (Fig. 3.1) may well recognize the familiar depicted objects. Certainly if they have previously had the opportunity to see cows, they will recognize the cows in the painting. But they will be unable to perceive the illusion of depth that any adult would immediately notice. For infants, the cows and the house do not appear to lie on different planes.

Three-year-olds will have no problem reading the depth cues in *Wivenhoe Park.* For them, the cows graze unambiguously in front of the house. However, so dominated are they by what the picture represents that its aesthetic aspects—its expression, composition, and style—go entirely unnoticed. They are not aware of its expressed serenity and calm. They fail to notice the balanced play of forms on the picture plane. And they are insensitive to the style in which Constable painted. For these children, *Wivenhoe Park* is simply a picture of cows; thus, it looks more like a painting of cows by a different painter than another Constable painting without cows. Not until the age of six or seven are children able to perceive the nonrepresentational, aesthetic components of a picture. Even so, a fully developed and conscious sensitivity to these aspects of a picture—expression, composition, and style—may not be acquired until the adolescent years.

In short, different aspects of a picture are perceived and understood at different ages and levels of experience. Because children perceive pictures so differently from adults, and because there is more to a picture than meets the eye of the average adult, what is considered aesthetically pleasing also differs from one developmental level to the next, and from the typical adult to the connoisseur. A person's familiarity with the pictorial arts often determines what is actually seen in a picture; and what is seen determines, in turn, the kinds of pictures found to be appealing.

Recognizing Depicted Objects

Adults who look at a still life with fruit recognize that the round red forms on the flat surface of the canvas are apples. They also realize that the apples are not real but are just representations. In short, they see the similarity between the red disks and real apples, but they also see the difference. Did they have to learn to see representational pictures in this way, or is this ability inborn?

Adults in Western culture have had many opportunities to look at pictures of apples. They may well have seen someone point out other pictured apples and label them "apples." And they have had the opportunity to touch the surface of the picture and thereby ascertain that the red circles are not apples that they could actually eat. Thus, it is not unreasonable to suppose that the ability to recognize the content of the picture as a representation of apples is a product of learning. But an experiment by two psychologists called this common-sense assumption into question (Hochberg and Brooks, 1962).

In order to determine whether recognizing objects in pictures is an unlearned skill or a product of learning through exposure to pictures, the researchers raised a child in a world without pictures. Labels were removed from cans, no pictures hung on the walls, and the child's books were devoid of pictures. Thus, the child received neither training in labeling pictures nor mere exposure to pictures. Just before his second birthday, a critical test was performed. He was presented first with line drawings and then with black and white photographs of familiar objects, such as a shoe or a key, and was asked to name what he saw. Surprisingly, almost every picture was correctly labeled—even the simplest outline drawings with minimal interior detail. And not only did the child instantly see the similarity between a picture of a shoe and his own shoe, but he also saw the difference and thus did not try to put the pictured shoe on his foot. This study showed that the recognition of depicted objects is a skill which does not depend on exposure to pictures (see also Daehler, Perlmutter, and Myers, 1976; Jahoda, Deregowski, Ampene, and Williams, 1977).

Since no tuition is required to recognize pictured objects, this ability may well be present not only at two years of age but also in infancy. Recent research confirms this expectation. To demonstrate picture perception skills in infancy, researchers have used what is called the "novelty-preference" paradigm (Fagan, 1970). This paradigm exploits the fact that infants are engaged by novelty. Given a choice between looking at something familiar and something novel, they choose to look at the novel stimulus. In the novelty-preference paradigm, infants are presented with a stimulus until they have become familiar with it. They are then presented with two stimuli simultaneously: the original stimulus, and a novel one. If they recognize the original stimulus, it appears familiar to them and thus holds little interest for them. They prefer to look instead at the novel stimulus.

In one study of pictorial perception in infants, five-month-olds were seated in the lap of a parent and exposed to two identical three-dimensional dolls presented simultaneously for a minute (DeLoache, Strauss, and Maynard, 1979). They were then shown three different pairings: the familiar doll and a novel doll; color photographs of the familiar and the novel dolls; and black and white photographs of the familiar and novel dolls. These pairings were presented for ten seconds, while observers recorded the amount of time the infants looked at each stimulus.

As expected, given a choice between the original and a new three-dimensional doll, infants looked longer at the novel one. Surprisingly, the same findings occurred with both color and black and white photographs. Given a choice between a photograph of the original doll and of a new doll, infants preferred the picture of the new doll. This demonstrates that the infants perceived the similarity between the original doll and its photograph.

In the same study, infants were also shown to be able to see a similarity between a color photograph of a face and a line drawing of that same face. This is indeed impressive, because the similarity between a line drawing and a photograph of a face is not based on individual features but occurs at a more abstract level. What is similar about a color photograph and a black and white sketch of a face is not the way the eyes or mouth are depicted but rather the overall pattern or orientation of the faces.

To determine whether infants' success on these tests resulted from an inability to discriminate between pictures and objects or from an ability to see the similarity as well as the difference between the two, a "visual-preference" paradigm can be used. In this paradigm, infants are presented with two stimuli. If they look longer at one of the stimuli, the conclusion is made that they can tell the difference between the two. If they look equally at each, however, no conclusion can be drawn, since infants may see the difference yet have no preference.

Using such a paradigm, the investigators presented five-month-olds with four different pairs of stimuli: the three-dimensional doll and its color photograph; the doll and its black and white photograph; the color photograph of a face and the line drawing of the same face; and the color photograph of a face and the black and white photograph of the same face (DeLoache et al., 1979). In all cases, looking time was significantly different between the two members of a pair, a result which revealed that the infants could tell the difference between a three-dimensional object and its two-dimensional representation, and between different kinds of two-dimensional representations of an object. In all cases, infants preferred the more realistic stimulus, looking longer at the three-dimensional stimulus than the photograph, and looking longer at the color photograph than either the black and white photograph or the line drawing (see also Dirks and Gibson, 1977; Fantz, Fagan, and Miranda, 1975; Field, 1976; Rose, 1977; Ruff, Kohler, and Haupt, 1976).

Although the findings unambiguously reveal that infants can match pictures to objects and can also discriminate between them, this does not permit the conclusion that pictures function as representations for the infant. Indeed, given the lack of symbolic capacities during the first year of life (Piaget, 1963), it would be highly unlikely for infants to recognize that a picture stands for something else. A further piece of evidence that pictures do not function as representations for infants is the fact that infants often treat pictures in the same way as objects. For instance, infants have been observed to smile and interact socially with pictures of faces (DeLoache et al., 1979) and to reach for both solid objects and their pictures (Field, 1976; but see Bower, 1972). Thus, whereas infants can see the similarity and the difference between a picture and an object, for them the picture is just another interesting object to look at, one with no symbolic representational status.

Not only is recognition of pictured objects present in infants, but it also appears to be present in monkeys, chimpanzees, and even pigeons (Cabe, 1976; Davenport and Rogers, 1971; Hayes, 1951; Patterson, 1977; Zimmerman and Hochberg, 1963, 1971; but see Winner and Ettlinger, 1979, who failed to demonstrate picture recognition in chimpanzees). But, like human infants, nonhuman primates appear to confuse objects and their representations. Monkeys sometimes reach for pictured objects and, upon seeing a picture of a wristwatch, they have been known to put their ear to the page to listen for the tick (Kennedy, 1974). These same behaviors have been observed in a chimpanzee (Hayes and Hayes, 1953).

All these studies considered recognition of rather simple, realistic pictures. More complicated pictures require more active strategies on the part of the viewer. In these cases, recognition may well depend on either maturation or learning.

Confronted with a picture of an object depicted with only the barest of hints, young children do not effortlessly read its representational content. For example, recognition improves with age in the case of line drawings with incomplete outlines (Gollin, 1960, 1961), geometric figures with dashed lines (Piaget and Inhelder, 1967), and out-of-focus photographs (Potter, 1966). Thus, while we seem to be "wired" to see the resemblance between certain abstract stimulus arrangements, such as schematic outline drawings, and real objects, we are not neurologically prepared to read extremely impoverished pictures. Instead, recognition of such pictures appears to require a considerable amount of guesswork and inference, strategies that are not found in the newborn.

Ambiguous pictures which can be read in more than one way also pose problems for young children, who have difficulty ignoring the irrelevant information in such pictures. In one study, children were shown pictures in which an object, such as a person, was made up out of separate complete objects, such as pieces of fruit (Elkind, 1970; Elkind, Anagnostopoulou, and Malone, 1970). Thus, one of the pictures was a representation of a person made up out of an apple for the head, bananas for the legs, and so on. Children under seven did not see the contours as part of both the man and the fruit. Instead, they reported either that they saw a man or that they saw pieces of fruit. Adults, however, saw both a man and fruit, and they could describe the relationship between them. A similar study showed that children perform poorly on an embedded figures task in which one element is a part of two different wholes (Ghent, 1956).

Other kinds of pictures that pose problems for young children are those that make use of cultural conventions, such as "path of movement" lines to suggest that the depicted object is in motion, as in lines drawn behind a speeding car (Friedman and Stevenson, 1980). Clearly, making sense of such pictures requires learning how the culture has chosen to depict figures in motion.

Children's difficulties with impoverished or ambiguous figures may be a result of their lack of systematic scanning strategies. When viewing a picture, six-year-olds use many small eye movements rather than a few broad ones and thus fail to sample the picture as fully or systematically as do adults. And while adults focus on a particular feature and then attempt to identify this feature by moving around to neighboring areas, children under four or five focus on a dominant feature and then scan downward (Braine, 1972). Thus, if a nondominant feature is at the top of a picture, it may never be noticed. Given such scanning strategies, young children often fail to notice informative aspects of pictures. This may explain why they fail to recognize impoverished or ambiguous representation.

Since children do not have to learn to recognize unambiguous pictures as representations of objects, adults who have lived in a world without pictures should also have no difficulty with such recognition upon seeing a picture for the first time. Yet in the early decades of the twentieth century, anthropologists studying cultures without pictures often reported the contrary (Kennedy, 1974; Segall, Campbell, and Herskovits, 1966). It was frequently noted that adults, when shown a picture for the first time, were puzzled by it, turning it over and over in order to figure out what it was. The conclusion was drawn that picture recognition requires learning through exposure to pictures.

However, the fact that people unused to pictures are at first puzzled by them does not necessarily mean that they cannot recognize pictorial representations. Perhaps they are simply treating the picture as they would any novel object, turning it over and over in wonderment. In fact, more controlled cross-cultural research has demonstrated that adults shown a picture for the first time can recognize the objects represented (Hudson, 1960; Hagen and Jones, 1978). In the presence of detailed colored slides and photographs, recognition appears to be effortless. When people from cultures without pictures are shown black and white photographs and black and white shaded drawings, recognition is still successful, with one qualification. People often seem to go through a process of "catching on" to what a picture is. They may not at first realize that the forms on the paper have any meaning. When they do catch on that the forms are representations of objects in their world, such as a familiar animal, they often need to piece together an interpretation, labeling each part of the depicted object—such as "legs," "tail," "eye"—before recognizing the whole (Deregowski, Muldrow, and Muldrow, 1972). Or they may need to be told what the depicted object is. Once they have this information, they are able to identify its component parts (Kennedy and Ross, 1975). The raw ability to perceive seems to be there, but it sometimes needs a little prodding to reveal itself.

Thus, there is a contradiction between developmental and cross-cultural research: children recognize unambiguous pictures immediately, but adults shown a picture for the first time are initially confused. There are several ways to explain this conflict of results. For one, the pictures shown to children have been much simpler than those shown to adults in cultures without pictures. This by itself could cause the discrepancy, especially since children do experience some difficulty in recognizing certain kinds of complex pictures, such as impoverished or ambiguous ones, and even Western adults have difficulty reading atypical pictures, such as aerial photographs (Cockrell and Sadacca, 1971; Powers, Brainard, Abrams, and Sadacca, 1973). Another way to explain the contradiction is that the adults studied had had many years of experience in a world without pictures. Presumably they had developed a set of strategies which they customarily used when confronted with a novel object, and these strategies did not include reading the object as a picture. A picture seen for the first time must seem stranger to adults than it does to children who are learning new things about their world everyday.

Reading Depth in Pictures

The ability to recognize an object in a picture appears to require neither learning nor development. But the ability to recognize depth in pictures is not such a simple matter. Although infants have been shown to be able to pick up depth cues in the ordinary environment, the ability to read depth in pictures is not given at birth.

The lack of pictorial depth perception in infants was demonstrated in an experiment with six- to eight-week-olds (Bower, 1966). A white cube twelve inches on a side was placed one meter from the infants' eyes (Fig. 4.1). Infants were trained to turn their

CONDITIONED STIMULUS	TEST STIMULI 1	2	3
TRUE SIZE			
TRUE DISTANCE 1	3	1	3
RETINAL SIZE			
RETINAL DISTANCE CUES	DIFFERENT	SAME	DIFFERENT

4.1 *Forms used to test infants' depth perception. Infants were trained to respond to a twelve-inch cube one meter away (the conditioned stimulus). Test stimuli were, from left, a twelve-inch cube three meters away, a thirty-six-inch cube one meter away, and a thirty-six-inch cube three meters away. When real objects were used, infants perceived the distance cues, but when pictures were used, they reponded to the retinal size of the cubes, ignoring the pictorial depth cues.*

head slightly to either side whenever this cube was presented. This cube, presented one meter from the infant, thus became the conditioned stimulus. The training was effected by rewarding the infants with a peek-a-boo when they turned their head in the presence of the conditioned stimulus. They were then shown one of the following four stimuli: the twelve-inch cube three meters away, a thirty-six inch cube one meter away, a thirty-six inch cube three meters away, or the conditioned stimulus itself. The number of times that the infants turned their heads to each stimulus, presumably in the hopes of getting a peek-a-boo, was recorded. During this testing period, no peek-a-boos were given.

The conditioned stimulus can be expected to elicit the highest number of head turns. The stimulus eliciting the next highest number of turns ought to be the one that is perceived by the infants as most like the conditioned stimulus. Results showed that, after the conditioned stimulus, the twelve-inch cube three meters away received the highest number of responses, followed closely by the thirty-six-inch cube one meter away. The thirty-six-inch cube three meters away, which differs in both size and distance from the conditioned stimulus, but which yields a retinal image identical to the conditioned stimulus, received the lowest number of responses. This pattern of results showed that infants were responding to the actual size as well as the actual distance of the conditioned stimulus, rather than to the size of the retinal image created by the conditioned stimulus. The fact that they responded to the actual distance of the conditioned stimulus, turning their heads to the larger cube one meter away even though it yielded a larger retinal image, showed that infants can perceive depth in the three-dimensional environment. But when infants were shown slides of the cubes instead of the solid cubes, they performed quite differently. Now the thirty-six-inch cube three meters away elicited the same number of head turns as the conditioned stimulus. Thus, in the pictorial condition, infants responded to retinal size cues, turning to the pictorial cube that created the same retinal image as the conditioned stimulus. The pictorial distance cues in the slides, such as linear perspective and shading, apparently went undetected.

Both binocular and motion parallax cues declare a picture to be a flat surface. To recognize depth in a picture, the perceiver must overlook these cues and rely instead on other cues, such as linear perspective or texture gradients, which must in turn be supplemented with a considerable amount of "reading in" or by the operation of the simplicity principle. Since pictorial depth cues are more impoverished and ambiguous than cues available in the ordinary environment, and since the information they provide conflicts with that provided by binocular and motion parallax, it is not surprising that infants cannot perceive depth in pictures.

Although pictorial depth perception is absent at birth, it is present in children at least as young as three. In one study, children three years and older were asked to judge which of two houses in a picture was farther away (Olson, 1975). The distance cues included height on the picture plane (one of the houses was sometimes placed higher up), occlusion (one house was sometimes partially occluded by the closer one), and linear perspective (a grid of converging lines was drawn in some of the pictures). Three-year-olds responded almost perfectly when the depth cues were height and occlusion, either separately or in combination, but the addition of linear perspective cues yielded no significant improvement (see also Olson, Pearl, Mayfield, and Millar, 1976; Wohlwill, 1965; Yonas, 1979; Yonas, Goldsmith, and Hallstrom, 1978).

Although a number of studies have demonstrated the ability to respond to pictorial depth in the preschool years, under certain conditions children are less accurate depth readers than are adults. One such condition occurs when a picture is viewed from the wrong position or station-point. Viewing a picture from the wrong station-point usually causes some perspectival distortion to occur (Fig. 3.4). While adults seem to correct for this distortion unconsciously (Rosinski, Mulholland, Degelman, and Farber, 1980), children who are asked to judge pictorial depth perform significantly less accurately when the picture is viewed from the wrong station-point (Cooper, 1977; Hagen, 1978).

While the ability to perceive relative depth in pictures seems to be present as early as the age of three, children have much greater difficulty determining precisely how far away a pictured object is meant to be relative to other objects in the picture. This ability is known as absolute depth judgment. For example, while three-year-olds perform as well as adults when asked to judge the size of actual objects placed at various distances from them in an alley, when the same judgments must be made from a picture, children as old as seven are less accurate than adults (Yonas and Hagen, 1973).

Even adults, however, have difficulty making precise metric judgments in pictures (Hagen, 1978; Perkins, 1979). They tend to read pictures as flatter than they actually should be read, given the perspective. The tendency to perceive less depth than is specified by the perspective cues may be due to the fact that binocular and motion parallax declare the picture plane to be flat, yielding information which competes with the perspective cues.

To determine whether pictorial depth perception depends upon repeated exposure to pictures containing depth cues, or whether the ability develops independently of such experience, researchers have studied adults in cultures without pictures. As with investigations of object recognition in cultures without pictures, studies of depth perception in these cultures at first suggested that depth cues could not be read without extensive exposure to pictures. The classic study in which such an argument was made was conducted in South Africa (Hudson, 1960). Bantu adults and children who were unfamiliar with pictures were shown various pictures representing depth. In one picture, a hunter in the foreground stood poised to spear an antelope (Fig. 4.2). In the distance, an elephant stood on a hill. The depth cues in this picture were overlap (one hill was partly obscured by another hill closer to the viewer) and familiar size (although elephants are larger than antelopes, the elephant was rendered smaller in order to indicate that it was farther away). After identifying the objects in each picture, subjects were asked about the relation between the man and the two animals: "What is the man doing? What is closer to the man?" Correct reading of these depth cues should indicate that the hunter is trying to spear

4.2 *Drawing used to test pictorial depth perception. Adults who had never seen pictures failed to perceive the depth in this drawing and thought the hunter was trying to spear the elephant.*

the antelope; if the picture is read without depth, it appears that the hunter is trying to spear the elephant. Bantu adults and children frequently saw the hunter as aiming his spear at the elephant. Thus, they perceived the picture two-dimensionally. This finding suggests that exposure to pictures is a necessary condition for depth perception.

But this conclusion is open to question. The major problem seems to be that the drawings used were ambiguous: the distant objects, such as the elephant, were too big (Hagen and Jones, 1978). When these pictures are shown to Western adults, the depth is often read incorrectly. For instance, Scottish adults scored only 69 percent correct (Jahoda and McGurk, 1974). When these pictures were shown to American college students, many could not decide whether the hunter was attacking the elephant or the antelope (Kennedy, 1974; Winner, 1980).

Studies using less ambiguous pictures have shown that depth cues are accurately read by adults with no prior exposure to pictures (Hagen and Jones, 1978). Although many of the studies report that performance among people unfamiliar with pictures is somewhat lower than among Westerners, these small differences may well be due to the difficulties encountered in conveying the nature of the task, a problem in all cross-cultural research (Cole and Scribner, 1974). The finding that adults in nonpictorial cultures can read pictures as representations of three-dimensional scenes leads to the conclusion that exposure to pictures is not a necessary condition for pictorial depth perception. The ability to perceive depth in a picture must, then, be due either to maturation or to the perceptual learning that takes place in negotiating the three-dimensional but not the pictorial world. This finding challenges the extreme constructivist claim that perspective is a conventional cue rather than a faithful representation of optical information (Goodman, 1968).

Reading Pictorial Expression

The ability to read pictorial representation is partially present at birth and fully present within the space of a few years, except for certain kinds of atypical pictures. But what about a picture's other mode of symbolization? Pictures can express nonvisual sensory properties by means of color and line, such as heat, noise, or quiet, and they can also express psychological states, such as sadness, gaiety, or anxiety. Must the ability to perceive what a picture expresses be learned through exposure to pictures, or is it, like pictorial object recognition, present at birth?

Several studies have addressed this question. Some of these have examined children's abilities to appreciate the expressiveness of simple abstract stimuli, such as color patches and lines; others have investigated whether children can perceive expression in actual works of art. These two types of studies have yielded different results.

In one study, subjects ranging in age from three years to adulthood were given pairs of nonverbal stimuli, such as two color swatches or two lines, and were asked to match each pair to sets of polar adjectives, such as *happy-sad, loud-quiet,* or *hard-soft* (Gardner, 1974a). By age eleven and a half, children proved as successful as adults at mapping polar adjectives onto diverse sensory domains. Thus, straight lines were "hard," rounded lines were "soft"; thick lines were "loud," thin ones were "quiet"; yellow was "happy," violet was "sad." Seven-year-olds were almost as successful, and even preschoolers performed at a level above chance, although they were unable to offer an explanation for their matches. Thus, when explicitly asked to select the happy or the sad line or color, and when given a forced choice task in which success on matching one member of the pair automatically means success with the other member, preschoolers demonstrate sensitivity to expressive properties of visual stimuli (see also Lawler and Lawler, 1965; Walton, 1936).

Whether the ability to perceive expressive properties in visual patterns is a result of a learned association, such as having heard adults call bright colors "happy," or whether the ability is given by the nervous system, cannot be determined by these studies, since the youngest children were already three years old. However, recent studies with infants suggest that this ability may be inborn. One set of studies demonstrated that infants as young as six months can perceive the similarity between visual and auditory stimuli, such as a dotted line and a pulsing tone, or a continuous line and a continuous tone (Wagner, Winner, Cicchetti, and Gardner, 1981). For instance, infants prefer to look at a dotted line when hearing a pulsing tone, but switch their preference to a continuous line when listening to continuous tone. Another study demonstrated that three-week-olds can perceive the similarity between bright colors and loud sounds (Lewkowicz, 1980). Thus, at a very rudimentary, nonreflective level, the ability to perceive resemblances between visual and auditory properties may be present even at birth. These resemblances are as abstract as those between visual patterns and psychological states. Thus, perhaps infants will also be shown to be able to perceive psychological properties expressed by visual patterns. This problem is extremely difficult to investigate, but the field of infant research is progressing at such a rapid rate that the answers to these questions may well appear within the next decade.

Research into the question of whether children notice expressive properties in actual works of art, particularly in representational works in which what is expressed must compete for attention with what is represented, has shown that children do not spontaneously describe expressive properties of pictures until preadolescence. For instance, not until this age do children talk about a painting as "warm" or "sad" (Machotka, 1966). However, children can see properties that are expressed before such properties are mentioned spontaneously. This was demonstrated when children were asked to complete pairs of pictures identical in all respects except the mood expressed (Carothers and Gardner, 1979). One of the paired pictures represented a happy person, the other a sad person. Children were asked to add a tree and flowers to each picture (a production task) and then to select from two pictures of trees and flowers the one that would best complete each picture. The expressively appropriate picture completion for the happy picture was a tree and flowers in full bloom; for the sad picture the appropriate choice was a bare tree with wilting flowers (Fig. 4.3).

While ten-year-olds had no trouble selecting the completion that expressed the mood of the depicted person, seven-year-olds proved unable to do so. Thus, it appears that sensitivity to the mood expressed by a picture is a rather late developing skill. However, if a more direct method had been used, and children had been asked which tree was sad and which happy, earlier success could be predicted. In contrast, poorer performance might also be

4.3 *Happy and sad pictures used to test children's sensitivity to expression (left), with a completion for each: blooming tree and flower for happy picture, droopy tree and wilted flower for sad picture.*

expected if the contrast between moods were subtler than that between happy and sad, as between the two negatively tinged moods of sadness and anger.

The few studies of the child's ability to perceive expression suggest that with respect to simple, nonrepresentational auditory and visual patterns, this ability is given by the nervous system in a very rudimentary form at birth. A more generalized version of this ability is present within a few years of life. But children do not on their own notice such properties in works of art until the middle years of childhood, and they do not spontaneously talk about such characteristics in paintings until early adolescence. Thus, despite the fact that, for an adult, what a painting expresses is sometimes the aspect first noticed and the one best remembered (Arnheim, 1949), children seem to acquire the ability to read representation in a work of pictorial art prior to the ability to read what is expressed.

Sensitivity to Composition and Style

In Vincent Van Gogh's *Starry Night* (Fig. 4.4), the forms are not arranged symmetrically but are more heavily weighted to the left side of the picture plane. Yet the painting does not feel off-

4.4 *Van Gogh,* Starry Night, *demonstrates how a painting can be asymmetrical yet balanced.*

balance. The brightness and isolation of the moon on the right lend this small circular form added weight, which offsets the weight of the trees on the left. In a successful pictorial composition, no form is positioned at random, and any rearrangement of the forms alters the often delicate balance achieved.

Sensitivity to the composition of a painting requires, first of all, that one scan the entire picture plane. Perceivers must also be able to overlook subject matter and attend to the geometry of the relationships among the forms. For instance, they must be able to tell the difference between a symmetrically organized picture and an asymmetrically organized one such as *Starry Night.* And for *Starry Night* to appear balanced, the observer must perceive the small form of the moon as having added weight owing to its brightness and isolation (Arnheim, 1974).

Relatively little is known about the ability to perceive the composition of pictorial art, either among adults or among children. Several studies have revealed that young children fail to attend to the composition of abstract visual patterns. Studies of infant perception show that infants are highly sensitive to the contour of a pattern but not to the structure and organization of its parts (Bond, 1972). Sensitivity to the internal structure of a pattern is a skill that is not fully developed until the middle elementary school years (Chipman and Mendelson, 1975). This was demonstrated when children were asked to decide which of two patterns was simpler (Fig. 4.5). The two patterns possessed the same amount of external contour but varied in internal structure. When the patterns possessed a low level of contour, even the youngest subjects, four-and-a-half to five-and-a-half years old, could detect the internal structure. But the ability to notice composition in patterns with high contour improved only gradually between the ages of four and eight. This study suggests that the development of sensitivity to composition is not complete until at least the middle elementary school years (see also Boswell, 1974; Paraskevopoulas, 1968).

The ability to perceive composition in actual works of art has been the subject of surprisingly little study. However, the results of one such study mirror the results of research using abstract patterns (Gardner and Gardner, 1973). Children were presented with sets of four pictures and asked to group the pictures into two piles, putting together the ones that were "most alike." The sets were de-

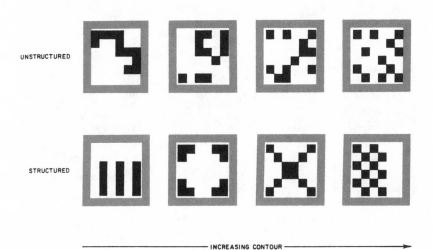

UNSTRUCTURED

STRUCTURED

INCREASING CONTOUR

4.5 *Patterns used to test sensitivity to structure. Preschoolers could detect the internal structure only in the patterns with low contour.*

vised so that they could be divided on the basis of either subject matter or "dominant form," that is, composition. In a typical set (Fig. 4.6), one painting contains two boats, one on the left and the other on the right; a second consists of a row of boats extending from upper left to lower right; a third consists of a row of people also extending from the upper left to the lower right corner; and a fourth consists of two people, again placed to the left and the right. The paintings can be sorted by subject matter (boats versus people) or by composition (horizontal pairs versus diagonal series).

Subjects in this study ranged in age from five to nineteen. Classification by subject matter decreased with age, with the main drop occurring between eleven and fourteen years; and classification by composition increased with age, with the main spurt occurring between seven and eleven years. By nineteen, subjects sorted consistently by composition yet demonstrated the ability to sort either way.

4.6 Paintings used to test sensitivity to composition: (top) Monet, Boats Leaving the Harbor; Brueghel, The Blind Leading the Blind; *(bottom) Homer,* Fishing Boats, Keywest; *and Cézanne,* Paul Alexis Reading to Emile Zola. *They can be sorted by subject matter (boats versus people) or by composition (two dominant elements versus row of elements receding into the distance at an angle).*

Sorting by composition in the face of competing subject matter cues is a rather difficult task. When a simpler measure is used, there is evidence that young children are quite able to perceive some compositional structure. Shown several pictures containing identical elements but balanced in different ways, and asked to indicate a preference, children as young as six demonstrate a preference for the symmetrical ones (Winner, Mendelsohn, Garfunkel, Arangio, and Stevens, 1981). Similar results have been obtained with three-dimensional constructions (Daniels, 1933–34).

Despite the fact that young children have the raw ability to perceive composition, composition is at first a transparent property of a picture, something that is simply "looked through" in order to perceive what the picture represents (Gardner and Gardner, 1973). The attention of the young child is drawn entirely to a picture's representational content. And to see only what a picture represents is to fail to perceive the picture as a work of art.

The representational content of a picture blinds children not only to its composition but also to its style. Compare Constable's *Wivenhoe Park* (Fig. 3.1) to Van Gogh's *The Starry Night* (Fig. 4.4). Both represent a landscape. Yet the two paintings are characterized by very different styles: they diverge in line quality, the texture with which the paint is applied, the character of the forms, color usage, and the like.

Discerning style is an integral part of understanding a picture as a work of art. Recognizing the style in which a work is painted informs us how to read the work and allows us to notice subtle aspects of the picture which would otherwise go undetected (Goodman, 1975; Wollheim, 1979). Once we notice that a particular painting is a Constable, we begin to discern more Constable-like properties. And in the case of nonrealistic styles, such as cubism, an inability to read the style can even interfere with our perception of what is represented: it is only upon mastery of the stylistic rules of cubism that a cubist picture can be seen as a coherent representation of objects. In more than one way, then, the perception of style stimulates our powers of insight and discovery.

Philosophers and art critics have long wrestled with the meaning of this elusive yet important property called style. (Ackerman, 1962; Goodman, 1975; Meyer, 1979; Schapiro, 1962b; Wollheim, 1979). It is difficult to specify the precise features that constitute style; at least, no fixed list of stylistic properties can be compiled (Goodman, 1975; Gombrich 1960). One empirical study demonstrated the role of color and texture in the recognition of style (Gardner, 1974b), but many other features may also be a part of an artist's style. (Berlyne and Ogilvie 1974; O'Hare and Gordon,

1976). In brief, stylistic features are at a highly abstract level; two works in the same style may possess extremely different individual features, and two works in very different styles may be composed of similar elements.

Because the same elements can constitute different styles, attempts to discover who painted a particular painting by studying its minute details often lead to failure. Such a method was proposed by Giovanni Morelli, an Italian physician who tried to apply principles of handwriting analysis to the study of pictorial style (Gombrich, 1960). Morelli's method consisted of looking at the minute details of a picture—how the fingernails were painted, or the shape of the earlobes. But by focusing on details, one may misidentify the painter, since style is in fact a global property of a work. Connoisseurs have usually rejected Morelli's rational, scientific approach in favor of intuition nurtured by years of experience in looking at paintings.

We mean two things when we talk about recognizing style. At the highest level, sensitivity to style means looking at a painting and knowing that it was painted by Rembrandt or Constable. This kind of style sensitivity is not possible for the casual spectator and is limited to those who have developed a knowing eye through familiarization with the arts. But there is a lower level of style sensitivity which may be achieved by the typical individual. At this level, style perception means simply the ability to perceive enough properties of works to sense the similarity, say, between two paintings by Van Gogh, or the difference between a Constable and a Van Gogh, even without having heard of Van Gogh or Constable. This ability ought to make it possible to see such family resemblances even if the two Van Gogh paintings differ in obvious ways, such as their dominant colors, layout on the canvas, or subject matter.

While adults demonstrate the raw perceptual ability to notice stylistic family resemblances even when such resemblances cut across works of very different content, children appear to lack this skill. In a typical study probing the development of the ability to detect a picture's style, children ranging from six to fourteen years of age were shown arrays of six reproductions of paintings (Gardner, 1970). In a typical array, two landscape paintings by Cézanne, used as standards, were on the left (Fig. 4.7). On the right side of the array, divided from the two Cézannes by a heavy line, were four other paintings, the test items. Of these four, one was also by Cézanne but depicted a different subject matter (a still life), and another had the same content as the two standards (a landscape). The remaining two paintings were unrelated in style or content.

Subjects were told that the two paintings on the left were by the same painter. They were instructed to pay close attention to these and to select the one of the four test pictures that was painted by the same person. Selecting on the basis of subject matter would yield an incorrect choice. The arrays were also constructed so that selecting on the basis of some very obvious property, such as dominant color, would also fail to yield a correct choice. Only the ability to perceive the style of the two works on the left would lead to the correct selection.

The results demonstrated that as long as it is possible to classify paintings by subject matter rather than style, children below about fourteen years of age fail to sort by style. So taken are they by what a picture represents that they are blind to the style in which it represents.

The study also dealt with whether children are actually incapable of perceiving style in pictures, or whether they simply fail to attend to this property. When the subject matters were homogeneous, such as when all six painting were still lifes, or when all six paintings were nonrepresentational, even six year olds were able to classify on the basis of style. The fact that the youngest children performed as well as adolescents when the distraction of content was removed indicates that the ability to perceive style develops long before style becomes more noticeable than subject matter, and long before the child is aware that what characterizes the works of an individual painter is a consistent style rather than a uniform content.

The poor performance of children in the face of the competing cue of content and their successful performance when this misleading cue is removed are highly similar to performance in a very different domain—the conservation of quantity (Piaget, 1952). Preschool children fail to conserve quantity when confronted with misleading perceptual cues. For instance, when water from a short wide glass is poured into a tall narrow breaker and thus rises to a higher level, children insist that the narrow container has more water in it, because the water is higher. But when the misleading perceptual cue is removed, as when the water levels are screened from view, even the preschooler will admit that the two containers have the same amount (Bruner, 1966).

Further evidence that the underlying ability to detect style exists long before it manifests itself is gained from two successful efforts to train children to overlook content in favor of style. In

4.7 *Paintings which can be sorted by subject matter or by style, used to test children's sensitivity to style. (This page, from top)* Cézanne, The Arc Valley and Mont-Sainte-Victoire *and* Auvers: Village Panorama (*standards*); (*opposite page, top*) Vermeer, The Concert (*unrelated in both style and content*); Cézanne, Still Life with Onions (*same style but different content*); (*bottom*) Rembrandt, The Obelisk (*same content as standard but different style*); *and* Goya, Ascensio Julia (*unrelated in both style and content*).

one of these studies, ten-year-olds were given seven half-hour training sessions, over the course of seven weeks, in which they were consistently reinforced for sorting by style but not by subject matter (Gardner, 1972). Comments by the children suggested that the two most successful strategies were to make a global, intuitive judgment of the overall similarity of two pictures or to imagine how the original painting would feel if touched. The later strategy led children to match pictures because they looked "rough" or "smooth" or "pasty." Since texture is a critical cue for style (Gardner, 1974b), this strategy proved highly successful. The study also determined that the ability to sort by style is not dependent on level of cognitive development as indicated by Piaget's tests. Rather, style sensitivity reflects an ability to detect recurrent pat-

terns or textures. These abilities develop both as a function of increasing perceptual differentiation—the ability to detect finer and finer details (Gibson, 1969) and as a function of increasing skill in the deployment of perceptual strategies—knowing which features count in style detection and which can be ignored.

Another study was carried out with ten-year-olds to investigate the relative effectiveness of different training methods (Silverman, Winner, Rosenstiel, and Gardner, 1975). This study showed that intensive exposure to only a few painting styles is somewhat more effective in facilitating fine discriminations than exposure to a wide variety of styles; and training in pattern recognition in the scientific domain (in this case classification of birds and fishes by species) has a positive effect on style discrimination in the arts. Training in style was also shown to have an effect on children's own drawings, yielding pictures with more varied textures and increased blending of colors. This is one of the few findings demonstrating a direct effect of perception on production, thus indicating a connection between the two realms.

These studies in style sensitivity demonstrate that young children are capable of discerning stylistic features but simply do not think to look for them or know how to do so. Once they catch on to the task, they are able to make fine differentiations among closely related styles. Such a finding provides support for claims made by perceptual psychologists that, with enough experience in a particular domain, people come to differentiate features that previously were indistinguishable (Gibson, 1969).

Developing Aesthetic Judgment

The domain of art is value-laden. We cannot look at a work of art without wondering if we like it or if it is "good." But our aesthetic judgment is restricted by what we attend to. Adults with some familiarity with the arts make aesthetic judgments on the basis of such aspects as style and composition, or the way in which a mood is expressed. Children who are blind to these aspects of a painting are able to make judgments only on the basis of more obvious properties, such as representational content and dominant color. As children begin to attend to other aspects of a painting, the basis of their value judgments begins to shift.

Because children attend to different aspects of works of art than do connoisseurs, they often prefer works other than those deemed of value by the connoisseurs. This was demonstrated in a simple test devised to assess aesthetic preferences (Child, 1964). The test consisted of pairs of pictures. Members of each pair were similar in style and subject matter, but one member of each had been judged aesthetically superior to the other by at least twelve out of fourteen judges familiar with the arts (Fig. 2.3). Subjects ranging in age from around six to seventeen or eighteen were seen in groups, shown the picture pairs, and asked to select the preferred member of each pair.

Children between six and eleven chose the picture considered better by the experts only about 35 percent of the time. Agreement with experts began to rise at around twelve years, and it peaked at about 50 percent by seventeen or eighteen. The fact that agreement never rose above 50 percent reveals that adults (the eighteen-year-olds) who are not particularly familiar with the arts do not respond to paintings as do those who are very familiar with the arts, such as art students and artists. Although a score of 50 percent on a two-choice measure may appear to reflect chance responding, in this case subjects were probably not choosing randomly. First of all, the younger children agreed with the experts at a level well below 50 percent, which indicates that they were not responding at random. The older subjects' score of 50 percent was achieved by a steady rise from the nonrandom level of 35 percent. Second, an item analysis revealed that for some pictures there was consistent agreement with experts, whereas for others there was consistent disagreement. Thus, it appears as if there are certain properties of art works that experts like but that children and typical adults dislike.

Subjects in this study were asked to pick the picture that they liked the best. They were not asked to select the one they thought was better. Apparently the question asked makes no difference to children under twelve, for when they were asked either to select their preferred work or to judge which work was beter, they responded identically (Child, 1965). College students, however, were more likely to agree with experts if asked for a judgment (50.2 percent agreement) rather than a preference (40.5 percent agreement). This suggests that for the child, taste determines judgment, whereas for the connoisseur, judgment probably determines taste.

These studies used an explicit measure of preference, requiring the child to make a conscious and deliberate choice. If a more covert measure of preference were used, such as the amount of time spent looking at each member of a pair, the relation between preference and attention could be probed. Children and adults may look longer at the pictures that they say they prefer. Or their attention may be drawn more to works that they consciously claim to dislike. A developmental study of the effect of preference on attention, using actual works of art, has not been undertaken.

The divergence between the preferences of connoisseurs, on the one hand, and children and typical adults, on the other, can be explained in at least two possible ways. First, the expert has had much more exposure to and training in the arts and has spent more time thinking about what makes a work of art good. Second, those who gravitate to the arts may be characterized by a special constellation of personality traits. The role of the first factor was determined by exposing children and typical adults to the arts and engaging them in discussion about aesthetic merit. The role of personality was probed by comparing the personalities of people whose preferences were close to connoisseurs' with people whose preferences fell at the other end of the spectrum.

That education makes a difference in aesthetic preference was shown in a study of college students (Child, 1962). When the students were exposed to pairs of pictures differing in aesthetic merit and given feedback as to which was considered best by experts, their preferences began to accord more with those of connoisseurs. When elementary and high-school age children were shown pairs of pictures and were engaged in a discussion about why one was better than the other, their performance also improved significantly (Child, 1964). After the training, they altered their opinions on a number of the pictures in the direction of the opinion of the experts. Similarly, when elementary school children were shown pairs of pictures containing one "good" composition and one with compositional faults, such as a picture with two conflicting focuses of interest, the "better" works were not consistently preferred (Voss, 1936). However, when the experimenter also pointed out the compositional principles that were violated and discussed why one picture was superior, children began to prefer works considered better by experts. However, after six months the trained children had reverted to their original level of aesthetic judgment (see also Wilson, 1966).

It is not only familiarity with the arts that affects aesthetic preferences, but also, perhaps, one's personality. A comparison of the personality traits of adults who demonstrated high aesthetic agreement with connoisseurs to those of adults who showed high disagreement revealed that their personalities could be reliably distinguished (Child, 1965). In comparison to low scorers, high scorers displayed more independence of judgment, tolerated greater complexity, and scored higher on a scale assessing "regression in the service of the ego," that is, the tendency to welcome playful and childlike forms of thought and fantasy. Although these characteristics have not been causally related to aesthetic choices, the correlational evidence is suggestive.

Extending this research downward on the age spectrum to high-scoring versus low-scoring high school students produced similar results, except for the measure of regression in the service of the ego (Child, 1964). No such correlations were found for children between six and eleven. Failure to demonstrate these correlations among younger children may have resulted from the fact that a more indirect measure of personality was used: whereas older subjects were given personality tests, younger children were interviewed by their teachers. But a more intriguing explanation for the lack of correlation in young children is also possible. Perhaps personality variables are differently related to preference in the early years. If so, those who as ten-year-olds agree highly with experts may not be among those who agree highly as adolescents. Only a longitudinal study could determine the accuracy of this suggestion.

Criteria Determining Aesthetic Preferences

The degree of concordance with experts tells little about the criteria on which children base their aesthetic preferences. It is possible to choose the same work as the expert but to do so for entirely different reasons (Child and Iwao, 1977). Determining the grounds of aesthetic preferences is by far the most important question to ask in trying to chart the development of aesthetic judgment. To investigate this question, researchers have examined the various types of properties of art works that are preferred by individuals ranging in age from infancy to adulthood. Such study has revealed that children of different ages have predictable and consistent aesthetic preferences.

We all begin life with the same set of visual preferences: certain kinds of patterns rivet our attention at birth. This has been determined by presenting infants with two displays simultaneously and noting which one commands the greatest amount of looking time. Studies using this paradigm have shown that for the first two to three months of life, infants' attention is governed by innate neurological structures. Irrespective of their familiarity or novelty, certain stimuli are always more attractive to look at than others. For instance, given the opportunity to gaze at either a focal color, such as red, or a peripheral color, such as magenta, infants prefer the focal one (Bornstein, 1975). Given the choice of a curved or a straight contour, infants prefer the curved form (Fantz and Miranda, 1975). And within an array, infants fixate on the points of highest contrast (Haith, 1966).

While these visual preferences do not disappear, after a few months, attention in the visual as well as auditory realms begins to be governed by a new principle. Degree of novelty now becomes a critical determinant of preference (Kagan, 1970). Visual displays that infants perceive as moderately novel, neither too familiar nor too unfamiliar, are those that rivet their attention. Thus, if infants who have become familiar with a 2×2 checkerboard pattern are given a choice of looking at the old 2×2 pattern, a new 4×4 pattern or a new 16×16 pattern, they prefer the 4×4 pattern because it is moderately discrepant from the first array. The emergence of novelty as a determinant of preference is quite probably related to the fact that infants begin to construct mental representations of patterns which allow these patterns, when re-encountered, to be recognized as familiar.

Once the degree of novelty begins to determine the appeal of a visual display, generalizations can no longer be made about the physical properties preferred by infants. What is moderately novel to one infant and thus preferred may well be familiar to another and thus not preferred. But the attractiveness of the originally compelling physical characteristics, such as high contrast or focal color, does not disappear. Given two patterns that are equally novel or familiar, older infants, like younger ones, prefer a high to a low contrast pattern. But given a familiar pattern with high contrast and a moderately novel one with low contrast, older infants prefer to look at the novel one, despite the fact that it is characterized by less contrast.

It is not difficult to find parallels between the laws of visual preference given at birth and the aesthetic preferences of adults. The degree of novelty is undeniably important in the Western artistic tradition, in which value has increasingly come to be placed on works that violate traditional norms. And artists often exploit the use of focal colors or high contrast. Yet many painters also use peripheral colors and muted contrast. Thus, no direct and determinant lines can be drawn from infancy: adult preferences are broader, and adults may come to prefer properties that do not catch the infant's attention.

No one has yet examined infant preferences for actual works of art, perhaps because those who have studied infant visual preferences have been interested in perception rather than the arts. Moreover, it is easier to determine the basis of visual preferences by presenting simple stimuli, such as geometric patterns, rather than actual paintings, which differ from each other in innumerable ways. Thus, pictures have been broken down into their components, and infants have been given a choice between arrays differing only along one dimension.

For the same reason—increased certainty over the basis of preference—an equivalent strategy has often been adopted for the study of aesthetic preferences in the years after infancy. For instance, studies of children's preferences for simple geometric figures have revealed that, with age, children prefer figures characterized by greater symmetry, such as a regular instead of an irregular circle (Brody, 1970), and by greater simplicity (Brighouse, 1939). These trends would be difficult to account for in terms of Berlyne's arousal theory, which predicts that people should prefer moderate rather than low levels of complexity. Thus, such findings pose yet another challenge to the generality of the arousal theory.

Studies of aesthetic judgment in the years following infancy have also considered the development of preferences for colors, usually presented in isolation.Early studies of the development of color preferences consistently found that young children prefer warmer hues than do adults (Beebe-Center, 1932; Valentine, 1962). However, in these studies, hue was confounded with saturation, or vividness of hue. When given a choice among colors varying only in hue, with saturation and brightness held constant, people at all ages prefered cooler hues, such as greens and blues, to warmer ones, such as reds and yellows (Child, Hansen, and Hornbeck, 1968). Where children differ from adults is in their response to saturation: irrespective of hue, children below about nine years prefer more highly saturated colors. Given a choice between a highly saturated orange (a warm hue), and a green low in saturation (a cool hue), younger children prefer orange, and older children prefer green. Thus, initially saturation overrides hue in the determination of color preference; later, hue overrides saturation.

This developmental shift is thought to reflect an increasing ability to differentiate. Degree of saturation is a global property, as it is something that cuts across hue, whereas hue is a more differentiated property. If development involves the ability to respond to increasingly differentiated properties, as gestalt and Gibsonian perceptual psychologists argue (Köhler, 1929; Gibson, 1969), then preferences should be initially based on a global and later on a more differentiated property.

Whether these findings are generalizable to the colors a person prefers in a painting is questionable. In a painting, colors exist in relation to each other, and context is known to affect the perception of color (Albers, 1963). A red square on a green background, for instance, looks brighter, because of the contrast to its complementary color green, than it does on a pink ground. Similarly, red next to yellow becomes bluish-red, and yellow next to red becomes greenish-yellow (Newhall, 1940). Moreover, color affects weight (Arnheim, 1974). Bright colors, for example, look heavier than dull ones. Thus, while a child may prefer a bright to a dull color in isolation, a particular area in a painting may look too heavy if painted bright. Color also interacts with meaning. Older children may prefer green to yellow, green being the cooler hue, but when it comes to the color of the sun in a painting, they may find a green sun unpleasantly disturbing, especially when realism becomes an important criterion during the middle childhood years.

Because it is risky to generalize from preferences for simple, isolated stimuli to the child's response to actual works of art, researchers have also studied the development of preferences for works of art in all their complexity. By presenting paintings one at a time and asking children to discuss each one, researchers have uncovered three stages of aesthetic judgment, beginning with the age of four and extending into adolescence.

During the period between about four and eight years of age, children are attracted to a painting for two reasons: they like either its color, its represented content, or both (Machotka, 1966). Of these two criteria, subject matter is dominant. Given a representational picture of a horse, children are apt to say that they like it because they like horses. If they happen to dislike horses, they will reject the picture. Children at this level think that paintings should be about pleasant, happy subjects (Parsons, Johnston, and Durham, 1978). Little awareness is demonstrated of the boundary between the world of pictures and the world of the objects represented (Francès, 1968). For the young child, a picture appears to be a transparency through which to view the represented content. As a result, expression, style, and composition go unnoticed.

When asked to choose between two nonrepresentational works, children at this stage ingeniously, and consistently still manage to base their preferences on subject matter. Fixating on a detail that reminds them of an object, they report, for example, that they like the picture because they see a horse in it, and they like horses (Francès, 1968; Gardner, Winner, and Kirchner, 1975). When the content of a picture pair is held constant, or when choosing between abstract pictures, children at this stage also often base their preference on color (Lewis, 1963). In fact, young children respond more positively to abstract paintings than do older children. Whereas a four-year-old may like such works for their color or for some imagined subject matter, a ten-year-old is apt to reject them for their very lack of representation.

Because their taste determines their judgment, children at this stage display a high degree of relativism when it comes to aesthetic standards. When asked how one decides if a work of art is good, children typically reply that it is good "if I like it" (Gardner et al., 1975; Parsons et al., 1978). Indeed, whether asked to select the picture they like best, the one others would like best, or the one that is painted the best, the response given does not vary at this age (Rosenstiel, Morison, Silverman, and Gardner, 1978). An awareness of aesthetic standards has not yet emerged, and these children are unable to "decenter" and consider how others might view a particular painting. This egocentrism in the domain of aesthetic judgment parallels the finding in the domain of moral judgment that young children justify moral choices on the basis of personal needs (Kohlberg, 1969).

By eight or thereabouts a marked shift has occurred. In this second stage, which lasts until adolescence, the degree of realism in a picture is the most important determinant of its appeal (Child and Iwao, 1977; Francès and Voillaume, 1964; Gardner et al., 1975; Lark-Horowitz, 1939; Lewis, 1963; Machotka, 1966; Parsons et al., 1978; Todd, 1943). Type of content represented, though much less important than for preschoolers, is also still a factor. While children at this level are now willing to accept subjects that are not happy and pleasant, they reject depictions of violence on the moral ground that violence is bad (Parsons et al., 1978).

The use of realism as the dominant criterion for aesthetic evaluation leads to a decline in the appeal of abstract works as well as of those that are representational but nonrealistic, such as a Matisse portrait. Realism is an all-pervasive criterion at this age. Photographs are judged superior to paintings, and "real" objects are preferred to photographs of these objects, because the real object can be touched on all sides while the picture "is flat and just a copy" (Gardner et al., 1975). Such preferences seem to be evidence for the increasing appeal of realism. In this respect infants more closely resemble ten-year-olds than preschoolers, since they too prefer the solid object to the picture, and the more realistic picture to the less faithful one (DeLoache, Strauss, and Maynard, 1979).

The insistence on the criterion of photographic realism rises steadily during the elementary school years and declines somewhat during adolescence. The importance of realism as an aesthetic criterion prior to adolescence most likely stems from a combination of two factors. It may be a result of the development of the ability to judge how realistic a picture is. Unlike older children, six-year-olds, when shown two paintings differing in degree of realism, often report that both are equally realistic (Francès and Voillaume, 1964). Even more important, however, preference for realistic paintings seems to reflect the increasing literalism and conventionalism of the elementary school years, which has been noted in many other artistic domains as well. For instance, the shift in preference from abstract to realistic paintings is accompanied by a parallel shift in preference from figurative to literal language (Geick, 1980).

It is perhaps as a function of their increased insistence on rules and conventions that children of middle childhood have abandoned the relativism that they expounded just a few years earlier. Now, when asked how one decides if a work of art is good, children reply that this is a decision best left to the experts. Such a reply is reminiscent of the law and order stage of moral reasoning in which what is right is determined by what is allowed (Kohlberg, 1969).

By the early adolescent years, the demand for realism has been dropped, except in cases in which the painting seems to require it. At this third stage, different styles and all degrees of abstraction are accepted and justified with reference to the artist's intention. Any subject matter is acceptable; moral objections to particular kinds of content are no longer voiced, which suggests that the adolescent realizes that the moral and the aesthetic spheres are separate (Parsons et al., 1978). For the first time, evaluations begin to be grounded on formal criteria, such as a painting's style, its composition, its luminosity, or its emotional impact (Machotka, 1966; Parsons et al., 1978). Only among children identified as "talented" does one encounter such sophisticated justifications at a younger age (Lark-Horowitz, 1937, 1938, 1939).

Despite the increased reliance on formal criteria in aesthetic evaluations, adolescents believe that aesthetic standards are relative. Either they are simply a matter of personal opinion (Gardner et al., 1975), or they are relative with respect to the artist's intentions—that is, any painting is good if it is painted according to the way the artist wanted it to be (Parsons et al., 1978). Thus, the adolescent has regressed to the relativism of the preschooler, although the type of relativistic reasoning in the two age groups is very different. This regression to relativism again echoes a finding in the domain of moral reasoning: college students temporarily regress to an earlier relativism in which what is morally right is wholly a matter of personal needs (Kohlberg, 1969). The parallels between reasoning in the aesthetic and moral domains suggest that reasoning about art reflects not only the increasing relevance of the aesthetic aspects of pictures but also the development of general cognitive structures of thought (Parsons et al., 1978).

The art of reading paintings depends upon a multiplicity of skills. The viewer must be able to look through the surface to what is represented. But the ability to recognize a two-dimensional arrangement of forms and colors as a representation of objects located in three-dimensional space is only the beginning of the task. Reading pictures as works of art requires that the viewer perceive far more than what is represented. Only if the seduction of the representational content is resisted can the viewer perceive style, composition, and expression. Adopting this pictorial attitude is not unlike adopting a metalinguistic attitude when reading a work of literature: one must be able to attend to the sound properties of the words rather than merely to what they denote. This aesthetic attitude toward both pictures and words appears to develop long after the ability simply to decode their referential meaning.

The general developmental pattern delineated in existing research does not necessarily reflect the intrinsic course of human development in the domain of the pictorial arts. Most of the research has been conducted in the United States and Europe. The developmental trends revealed so far may actually reflect the fact that the arts have relatively little place in technological societies, and are so little stressed in their schools. Children may have the capacity to see a great deal more in paintings, at a much younger age, than Western research suggests. Given a culture in which the arts are stressed and are accorded a central role in education, a three-year-old might have no difficulty in perceiving the calm mood of Constable's *Wivenhoe Park*, its composition, or even its style.

5 The Development of Drawing

Once I drew like Raphael, but it has taken me a whole lifetime to learn to draw like children.

—Pablo Picasso

Don't translate my works to those of children . . . They are worlds apart . . . Never forget the child knows nothing of art . . . the artist on the contrary is concerned with the conscious formal compositions of his pictures, whose representational meaning comes about with intention, through associations of the unconscious.

—Paul Klee

Enter a preschool classroom filled with three- and four-year-olds. Many of the children will be engaged in making pictures. Preschool children are typically prolific draftsmen, producing drawing after drawing without tiring of the task. The drawings that they make have long intrigued adults (Fig. 5.1). For instance, humans

5.1 *Typical preschool drawings: tadpole, with arms and legs radiating from a circular shape that represents either the head or the head and trunk fused; fold-out drawing, with buildings placed perpendicularly to the road, yielding a mix of contradictory viewpoints; X-ray drawing, showing the contents of animal's stomach.*

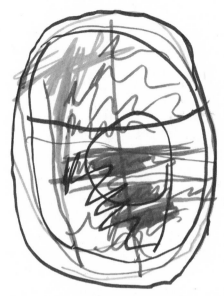

5.2   *Drawings by a five-year-old, demonstrating the free, expressive quality of early artistry, and by an eight-year-old, demonstrating the conventionality at elementary school age.*

are initially represented as "tadpoles," consisting of a circular form, with facial features, out of which arms and legs radiate. Houses lining a street are drawn perpendicularly to each side of the road, creating a kind of fold-out drawing. And objects are often drawn so that they appear transparent. These "X-ray" drawings allow one to see through an object to something behind or inside of it. Why preschool children draw such odd pictures is puzzling.

A comparison of preschool drawings with those produced by children in the middle elementary school years presents yet another puzzle (Fig. 5.2). The drawings of preschool children charm us with their balanced use of space, their expressive colors, and their originality. This age has sometimes been looked upon as the flowering of childhood artistry. The drawings of elementary school age children, on the contrary, seem to be less free and to have less power to charm. They reveal a more sophisticated level of technical skill, but they are also highly conventional and strictly representational. This apparent loss of artistic flair with age demands an explanation.

Another puzzle is posed by the drawings of children who appear to be prodigies in the visual arts. Some children have revealed an ability to draw at the level of a skilled adult. For example, a work by an autistic child prodigy bears a striking similarity to a Leonardo da Vinci sketch (Fig. 5.3). Such child prodigies may have arrived at this extraordinary height only after first negotiating all of the ordinary stages of artistic development. Or maybe they were able to skip the ordinary sequence of stages, drawing like masters from the start.

These are some of the puzzles posed by the pictures made by children. Because the solutions are not obvious, rival explanations have been proposed. On the one hand, children's drawings have been explained in terms of skills that the child lacks. Some have argued, for instance, that conceptual confusions underlie children's drawings. On this account, the tadpole reflects the child's deficient concept of the organization of the human body. Others, noting the difficult tasks posed by graphic representation, have suggested that children do not yet possess the full repertoire of strategies needed to plan and produce adult-style drawings. On this account, the oddities in children's drawings are a direct result of the difficulties of

5.3 *Drawing by an autistic child, Nadia, at age five and a half resembles Leonardo's* Study for the Sforza Monument.

representing a three-dimensional object on a two-dimensional surface.

At the opposite extreme is the argument that children's drawings are successful solutions to visual problems. Children's drawings seem odd, it is said, only when held up against the Western ideal of naturalistic representation, which occupies only a brief phase in the history of pictorial art. Children are said to be primarily interested in creating balanced forms and willing to sacrifice realism to this goal. Parallels have been drawn between children's art and the art of adults from various periods in history for the purpose of showing that children's drawings should be judged not as failed attempts at realistic representations but as successful attempts at making clear, forceful visual statements.

Despite this disagreement about the meaning of drawings by children, there is general agreement about the characteristics of such drawings at different ages. Children's drawings can be roughly classified into five stages. First is the scribbling stage, which emerges between one and two years of age. Out of the scribbles that the child constructs emerge the first designs—forms that are more controlled than scribbles, but which are not yet representational. At about the age of three or four, the first spontaneous representational drawings emerge, including the tadpole human. The early representations of the preschool years give way to more coherent representations during middle childhood. However, although the representational drawings during middle childhood are more differentiated and complex than earlier ones, they are not much more realistic. It is not until about the age of nine or ten that children begin to strive toward optical realism in their drawings.

Scribbles

During the second year of life, children in Western culture begin to make marks upon a page. These first markings take the forms of scribbles. Scribbling children concentrate intensely on the activity of marking and often produce one drawing after another in rapid succession. They are typically unconcerned with color and produce a series of scribbles using only one marker, ignoring any others available.

As children scribble, their arms move in a regular rhythmic motion around the page. One might think, therefore, that children are interested simply in the motor activity itself. Yet if their marker is replaced with one that leaves no trace, children soon lose interest in scribbling (Gibson and Yonas, 1968). Clearly, then, not only is scribbling a motorically pleasurable activity, but children are also interested in the traces that their motor activity leaves on a surface.

The scribble patterns that children produce are spontaneous inventions: no one sits down and teaches an eighteen-month-old to scribble. A detailed classification of the types of patterns yielded by early scribbles distinguished twenty scribble elements, such as dots and vertical, horizontal, curved, and zigzag lines (Kellogg, 1969; Fig. 5.4). A simpler classification, however, distinguished only two types of scribbles: whirls, loops, and circles, on the one hand, and multiple densely patterned parallel lines on the other (Golomb, 1981).

Whether or not children's first scribbles are highly differentiated, these first markings are the building blocks for later drawings. The circular loops that children discover in their scribbles later become the heads of tadpoles; the vertical lines are used for legs, and the horizontal lines for a ground line on which figures will be placed. Scribbling children are experimenting with the medium of drawing and are beginning to discover for themselves what kinds of marks can be made upon a page.

Prerepresentational Designs

Children do not pass immediately from scribbling to making representational pictures. During the second and third year of life, scribbling gives way to more controlled, nonrepresentational configurations. According to Rhoda Kellogg (1969), the emergence of these "designs" is made possible during the later stage of scribbling when children begin to place their marks so that they occupy a defined space with respect to the edges of the page. Kellogg identified seventeen of these placement patterns. In a typical placement pattern, lines are drawn so that the page is diagonally filled

5.4 Basic scribble patterns produced by children.

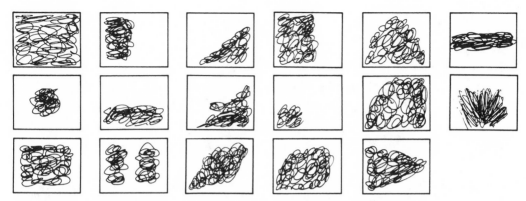

5.5 *Placement patterns that emerge late in scribbling, yielding basic geometrical forms such as triangles or rectangles.*

or so that a rectangle is formed in the middle of the page (Fig. 5.5). Careful placement of the scribbles within the borders of the page results in the emergence of a basic geometric form, such as a triangle or a rectangle. By three years of age, children begin to draw these geometric forms with a single outline instead of filling them in from the inside-out with a scribbled line. Five recurring "diagrams" were found to be constructed in this fashion: circles and ovals, squares and rectangles, triangles, crosses, and X's. Not all of children's outlined forms are regular ones, so a category was reserved for "odd" forms.

Next, according to Kellogg, children begin to combine two diagrams, yielding "combines." When a cross is combined with a circle, rectangle, or square, a "mandala" is formed (Fig. 5.6). Mandalas have often been noted in children's drawings, and they also recur in the adult art of many cultures. The Swiss psychiatrist Carl Gustav Jung (1960) was impressed by the fact that his patients often reported the appearance of mandalas in their dreams. Jung believed the mandala to be one of the archetypal images of the collective unconscious of the human race, an image that symbolizes harmony because of its perfectly balanced union of opposites: circular and straight lines. Not unlike Jung, Kellogg ascribed the emergence of the mandala to the fact that such perfect harmony is pleasing to the eye. But unlike Jung, Kellogg argued that the mandala is a direct outgrowth of the previous forms that children have discovered how to make.

The characterization of diagrams and combines as universal forms in children's art and as necessary stages along the road to

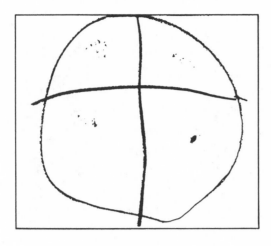

5.6 *Mandala drawn by a three-year-old.*

representation has been challenged by other findings. In one study, only four percent of the children drew diagrams (Golomb, 1981). Some children, however, drew letters from the alphabet. Although some letters might look like diagrams (the letter *O*, for instance), the children explicitly designated these forms as letters.

Doubt has also been cast on the inevitability of the diagram and combine stages by the anthropologist Alexander Alland, who studied children in cultures without drawing (Gardner, 1980). When eight- and nine-year-olds were given the opportunity to draw for the first time, they produced no evidence of these two stages. Instead, children began almost immediately to draw representationally (see also Millar, 1975). Thus, the appearance of controlled, nonrepresentational designs does not appear to be a necessary stage along the road to graphic representation.

Emergence of Representation

When children first begin to draw, they have little interest in representation. Most observers of child drawing agree that early scribbles and designs are not failed attempts to represent. Rather, children's first drawings are visual explorations of lines, shapes, and colors.

Children seem to become interested in the idea of representation before they are able to produce a recognizable representation. The evidence is that they begin to label their scribbles and designs as if they were representations. Thus, children may produce a scribble and then announce that they have drawn a picture of their mother. Because the children appear to be "wishing" their designs into representations, this phenomenon is called "romancing."

Romancing may occasionally occur almost as soon as children have begun to scribble, but not until the age of three or four do children spontaneously produce forms that are recognizably representational. Unlike children who romance, older children announce their representational intentions ahead of time. They say that they are going to draw their mother, and the result is a recognizable, though far from realistic, representation of a human figure.

Although representational drawing rarely emerges spontaneously before the age of three, children have the raw capacity to represent graphically at an earlier age. Supplied with an outline of a person and asked to draw in features such as eyes, nose, mouth, and navel, even two-year-olds succeed in mapping these features appropriately (Freeman, 1980; Gardner, 1980; Fucigna and Wolf, 1981). And asked to draw a specific object, such as a fish, children who typically scribble when left to themselves can produce a readable representation of the requested object (Golomb, 1981). Moreover, the stage of nonrepresentational drawing does not give way abruptly to representational drawing. For a while, children continue to scribble or to make geometrical designs at the same time as they are beginning to discover the possibilities of graphic representation (Golomb, 1981). Children may continue to make abstract designs even when they more typically produce only representational drawings.

Children's earliest spontaneous representations are highly unrealistic. The first representational form is typically the human figure, which is drawn as a tadpole (Fig. 5.1). The tadpole is a general purpose, formulaic representation of a person which does not resemble a specific person. Although children may identify two tadpoles as their mother and father, no differentiation between these two tadpoles is made.

Color use at this stage is also unrealistic. Children are not concerned with matching the colors of their depictions to the colors of the objects that they are depicting. Thus, people may be purple, grass may be red, and the sun may be green. Investigators have tried to relate the colors in a picture to the personality of the child (e.g. Altshuler and Hattwick, 1969). Children who painted with warm colors were said to be warm and affectionate; those who used blue were said to be emotionally controlled; and the use of black signified an absence of emotion. Such interpretations are called into question by the finding that children use colors from left to right or from right to left on their easel, regardless of the

5.7 *Drawing by a six-year-old, showing objects unattached to the ground and floating all over the page.*

color (Corcoran, 1954). This finding serves a warning to be very cautious in interpreting a child's drawing as a reflection of personality: what looks intentional and therefore significant to the adult may have been quite unintentional on the part of the child.

Not only do they create unrealistic forms and colors, but children at this stage do not try to organize the objects on the page in the way that they are related spatially in the world. Instead, objects typically float all over the page (Fig. 5.7). While these objects may not appear connected by any logic, they are often connected by a visual logic. The layout of forms on the page creates an ordered and balanced two-dimensional composition (Arnheim, 1974; Garfunkel, 1980; Winner, Mendelsohn, Garfunkel, Arangio, and Stevens, 1981).

Perhaps the most controversial aspect of children's first representations is the ubiquitous tadpole. Explanations for this form have been couched in either negative or positive terms. Typical of a negative, "deficiency" explanation is the view that the tadpole reflects the child's undifferentiated concept of how the parts of the body are organized (Piaget and Inhelder, 1967).

More positive accounts have proposed that the tadpole form is not determined by the child's concept of the organization of the body. Nor is it a failed attempt to create a visible likeness. Rather, it is determined by its structural derivation from earlier forms in the child's graphic repertoire (Arnheim, 1974; Golomb, 1973; Kellogg, 1969). Children who attempt their first representational drawings do not do so by first looking more closely at the objects that they intend to represent. Instead, they look at the abstract shapes already in their repertoire and discover in these simple forms the schemas with which to represent objects in the world. Children are trying to create balanced, ordered forms that also represent. Perhaps because it is so far beyond their ability, the idea of creating a realistic likeness of a person has not even occurred to them.

Among the earlier forms from which the tadpole is said to derive is the circle, which is the simplest of all geometrical forms and one of the first that the child produces (Arnheim, 1974). A number of steps along the way from circle to tadpole have also been proposed (Kellogg, 1969). In the combine stage, children join two diagrams. When a circle and a cross are joined, a mandala results. Soon children complicate this form by placing more than one cross inside the circle (Fig. 5.8 left). Though children may have simply intended to produce a design, this form is often labeled a "sun" by an eager parent or teacher. Children who had no intention of drawing a sun are certainly able to see the resemblance between their design and the sun. Thus, they begin to make their mandalas even more sunlike, with the lines beginning at the outside of the circle (Fig. 5.8 right). The initial attempts to represent humans are said to derive directly from this sun schema. By limiting the number of radiating lines and by adding two eyes, children can trans-

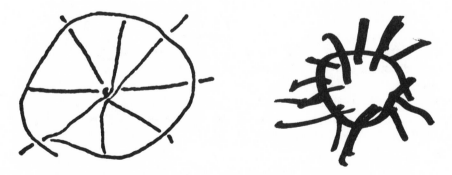

5.8 *Mandala with multiple crosses, typical of three- and four-year-olds, and sunlike mandala by a four-year-old, thought to grow out of the earlier mandala form.*

form the sun into a tadpole. The development of other representations—animals, houses—are explained similarly by pointing to their structural origins in prior invented schemas (Kellogg, 1969).

This account of the structural derivation of the tadpole is compelling, but it may be flawed. The main difficulty is that simply because the tadpole resembles earlier forms that children have mastered does not mean that it is derived from these earlier forms. The mandala, sun, and tadpole may look alike merely because they are all determined by the same principle, such as the search for regularity (Goodnow, 1977).

The circular tadpole shape may also represent either a head with limbs, or a head and trunk fused. Those prone to deficiency explanations of tadpoles believe that the circular form is simply a head. The child has thus omitted the body, wrongly allowing limbs to extend from the head (Lowenfeld and Brittain, 1970). Investigators who employ positive rather than negative terms argue that the tadpole is not simply a head without a trunk. Rather, the circular form stands for both head and body, globally fused (e.g. Arnheim, 1974). On this account, the child has not erroneously drawn the arms from the head but has quite correctly placed the arms on the form that contains the trunk.

To test whether the circular form represents head only, or head and body fused, preschool children were given a predrawn head and trunk and asked to add arms (Freeman, 1980). The reasoning was that if the tadpoles which children usually draw represent a head only, then children should add arms to the head on this task. If their tadpoles are a head and trunk fused, then children should add arms to the trunk.

When the predrawn head was smaller than, or the same size as, the trunk, children usually drew the arms correctly from the trunk. However, when the head was larger than the trunk, they were more likely to draw the arms from the head. This tendency to add arms to the biggest circle, called the "body-proportion effect," appears to override the child's knowledge that arms should come from the trunk. Nevertheless, the fact that arms were most often added to the trunk when the head was smaller than or equal in size to the trunk indicates that children know that arms come from trunks, not heads. It also suggests that tadpoles are not simply heads without trunks. Rather, they are undifferentiated head-trunk units.

Further evidence for this comes from a study of children between the ages of three and eleven who were administered a variety of tasks involving the representation of a human (Golomb, 1973). Among the tasks, children were asked to draw a person from scratch, to assemble a human out of given parts, to make a person as the experimenter dictated each part to be constructed, to dictate the parts of a person as the experimenter drew, to copy a person, and to select the best representation of a person.

The representations of humans produced by children at all ages varied significantly across tasks. On the spontaneous drawing task, the ubiquitous tadpole made its appearance. When given more directed drawing tasks, children were able to produce figures with considerably more detail and differentiated organization than is characteristic of tadpoles. For example, when asked to dictate the parts of a figure to the experimenter, who drew each part as dictated, children invariably mentioned more parts than they themselves had spontaneously drawn. And when the experimenter drew arms emanating from the head, as in the children's own tadpoles, the children often insisted that this was wrong. When asked to complete a figure given only a head, children again performed at a higher level than on the spontaneous task; in this task they made no tadpoles and instead always added a trunk. Asked to select the best representation, children rejected the tadpoles in favor of the most detailed representation of a person. And when the experimenter dictated the parts without indicating where to place each one, children were able to put each part in its correct place: only four percent of these dictated drawings were tadpoles.

This study provides a way to tease apart competence and performance and thereby interpret the widespread phenomenon of tadpoles. Children are quite capable of achieving a higher degree of realism, but they do not choose to do so. Tadpoles cannot be taken as a reflection of the child's primitive or confused concept of a person. If this were the case, alterations in task would not heighten performance, and the child's cognitive level would impose itself equally on all tasks.

Taken together, the research indicates several reasons for the ubiquitous tadpole. First, children's early drawings make use of simple, global forms, such as the circular form of the tadpole. Second, children appear to be attracted to symmetrical forms, the tadpole being an example of radial symmetry. And third, children are not interested in trying to create a realistic representation of a human. Rather, they are simply attempting to construct a representation that "stands for" a human.

Representation During Middle Childhood

The drawings produced during the years of middle childhood, from approximately six to ten years of age, are most often representational, although children also may continue to draw designs. One of the most notable new features of drawings in this period is that forms have become more differentiated and complex. For example, the global circular form of the tadpole has given way to a figure with a clearly differentiated head and trunk (Fig. 5.9).

Another notable characteristic is that the spatial organization of drawings has become more coherent. While early representational drawings consist of unanchored, floating objects that often fill up the page, children now begin to relate the objects to a groundline. Typically, a line is drawn across the bottom of the page, along which objects are placed, and a skyline is often drawn across the top of the page (Fig. 5.10). One study found that in over five thousand drawings, only one percent of those by three-year-olds had groundlines, but 96 percent of those by eight-year-olds had them (Wall, 1959). While the use of a groundline yields a more coherent representation of space, there is as yet no attempt to represent the third dimension.

Drawings are not always organized around a baseline at this age. Also found, although less frequently, are fold-out drawings

5.9 *Human figure with head and trunk differentiated, drawn by a five-year-old.*

5.10 *Drawing with a baseline and skyline, by a seven-year-old.*

(Fig. 5.1). These drawings lack a unitary point of view. Thus, in the drawing shown, where houses are placed perpendicularly to each side of the road, the houses are drawn as if the viewer were standing in various different positions with respect to the road.

Several explanations have been offered for this phenomenon. Such spatial organization may reflect children's general cognitive level (Piaget and Inhelder, 1967). At this age children are unable to adopt an overall point of reference for all of the units of a drawing, just as they are unable to coordinate viewpoints in other cognitive tasks. This phenomenon has also been explained by the fact that children try to follow a rule which specifies that they must avoid overlapping, and thus occluding, one shape by another (Goodnow, 1977). To avoid overlap, they may be compelled to draw objects from different points of view. And finally, the explanation is given that children are deliberately trying to draw each object so that it can be shown in its most characteristic way (Arnheim, 1980). To do this, they must sacrifice a unitary point of view. Distortions are thus made in the interest of the clearest display.

Not until the invention of central perspective in the Renaissance did artists begin to draw from a unitary viewpoint. Before that—and even afterward sometimes, by choice—adult artists con-

5.11 Hunting Hippopotami in the Marshes, *Egyptian tomb relief, fifth dynasty, showing the mixture of viewpoints (head and legs in profile, frontal torso) that is found in children's drawings.*

structed drawings from mixed viewpoints. For instance, in an Egyptian painting, the face is shown in profile, while the body is drawn from a frontal view (Fig. 5.11). The same phenomenon appears in the sculptures of Michelangelo and the portraits of Modigliani. Thus, the lack of a consistent viewpoint in children's drawings, it is said, should not be described as a defect (Arnheim, 1980).

This view, however, may overestimate children's abilities. While adult artists may choose to draw a picture from mixed viewpoints, they do so consciously and intentionally in order to create a strong visual statement. To assume that the child is similarly motivated seems extreme. A more conservative interpretation is that children, unlike adults, do not intend to create a particular visual effect and are simply unable to draw in a more realistic way.

Another characteristic type of drawing at this stage is the odd X-ray drawing, in which figures appear to be transparent (Clark, 1896–97). Two species of such drawings have been distinguished (Freeman, 1980). In one species, something is depicted that is always invisible to the eye in the "real" world, such as the food in an animal's stomach (Fig. 5.1). In the other species, one object partially behind another is shown through the front object (Fig. 5.12).

These two types of drawings have often been lumped together because both depict objects as transparent, yet they are most likely produced for different reasons. Children who draw the contents of a person's stomach may do so because they are more interested in the stomach contents than in creating a realistic drawing. Children who draw overlapping figures by allowing the back figure to show through the front one may do so because they do not know how to make one figure occlude another. There is evidence that children often try to avoid overlap by granting each object its own space (Goodnow, 1977). Perhaps when it is impossible to segregate each figure, children are forced to draw overlapping figures transparently. Evidence has been found that as the tendency to segregate figures declines, transparencies increase (Freeman, 1980).

As with fold-out drawings, X-ray drawings need not be indicative of some kind of inability (Arnheim, 1980). Parallels to the child's X-ray drawings can be found in primitive art and in twentieth century nonrepresentational art (Fig. 5.13). Like the adult artist, the child may be trying to make a strong visual statement.

5.12 X-ray drawing by a five-year-old, in which objects appear transparent.

5.13 *Chagall*, Pregnant Woman, *a painting similar to the child's X-ray drawing in Fig. 5.1.*

While the result is not realistic, it has its own visual logic. For instance, Arnheim notes that a necklace drawn so that the full circle of the necklace is visible through the neck is a child's attempt to make a visual equivalent for the concept "around."

Once again, however, the child and the adult artist may be differently motivated. Although the parallels between child and adult art are indisputable on the surface, the children may have no alternative but to make X-ray drawings. And they may not intend the strong visual effect that they create.

The Emergence of Realism

By the age of nine or ten, children's drawings become less free and hence less striking to the adult eye. Children now begin to adopt their culture's conventions of graphic representation. The emergence of conventionalism can be seen in children's growing fascination with cartoons. Children of this age often make drawings of comic strip figures, copying those that are produced by adults (Wilson and Wilson, 1977). The emergence of conventionalism also results in more realistic drawings. The X-ray and fold-out drawings produced just a year or two ago are now rejected as incorrect. Children no longer draw a simple groundline and skyline with blank space in between, but allow the ground to meet the sky, thus creating more of a sense of depth (Lowenfeld and Brittain, 1970).

During the adolescent years, children begin to use perspective. The way in which children come to discover the laws of perspective makes a fascinating story, which has been documented in a study (Willats, 1977). Children between five and seventeen years of age were seated in front of a table with objects on it and were asked to draw what they saw (Fig. 5.14a). The children used six different strategies to represent space, and these strategies formed a developmental sequence.

The youngest children, five and six years old, drew a rectangular box for the table top and let the objects float above it (Fig. 5.14b). No attempts at representing depth were made at this stage. At the next stage, seven- and eight-year-olds drew the table top as a straight line with little or no surface, resembling a groundline, and placed the objects on that line (Fig. 5.14c). Thus, like the younger children, they depicted the scene in an entirely two-dimensional manner.

Only during the third stage, beginning at about nine, did children attempt to depict the third dimension. In the first such attempts, the table top was drawn as a rectangle. The lines of the table were therefore parallel and did not converge (Fig. 5.14d). Children may do this either because they know that a table top is rectangular and they wish to show this, or because the only way that they know to represent back-front relations is by mapping them onto top-bottom relations. According to the second explanation, children have no choice but to represent the back of the table by the top of the rectangle, and the front by the bottom of the rectangle.

The next stage of representing the third dimension, peaking at about age fourteen, yielded a parallelogram for the table top. Here the lines are again parallel, as in the previous stage. But now, instead of running from top to bottom, the lines run obliquely across the page (Fig. 5.14e).

In the last two stages, adolescents were able to draw in perspective, making the far side of the table top smaller than the near side. Some adolescents drew the table top with lines that con-

5.14 (a) Correct perspective drawing of table, showing angle size and six points of overlap. (b) Stage one drawing, with no depth or overlap and objects floating above the table top. (c) Stage two drawing, with no depth or overlap; table top shown from the side so that only the edge is visible. (d) Stage three drawing, with back-front relations represented by top-bottom relations (asterisks indicate overlap). (e) Stage four drawing, with table top drawn as a parallelogram. (f) Stage five drawing, with naive perspective, lines converging only slightly. (g) Stage six drawing, with correct perspective, lines converging according to the laws of optics.

verged only slightly (Fig. 5.14f). They seemed to realize that lines receding into the distance appear to converge, but they had not learned to apply this rule so that an optically realistic representation could be achieved. Thus, their perspective was geometrically inaccurate and naive. Other adolescents achieved a geometrically correct perspective, in which the lines converged at the appropriate angles (Fig. 5.14g). These final stages extend through adulthood, since without training the typical adult draws in the same way as the typical adolescent.

According to Willats, this stage sequence cannot be explained by an increasing desire or ability to draw what one sees. One reason is that children's drawings get less realistic before they get more realistic. Whereas one may well see a table top as an edge (stage two, Fig. 5.14c) when looking at it at eye level, one only sees it as a rectangle (stage three, Fig. 5.14d) from a bird's-eye view, which is hardly a common viewpoint, and one never sees a table top as a parallelogram (stage four, Fig. 5.14e). Nor can the development of perspective be explained entirely by the incorporation of the culture's way of depicting perspective. Children never see a table top drawn as a rectangle, and they would encounter it as a parallelogram only in a mechanical drawing class. But the parallelogram solution appears before the age at which mechanical drawing is introduced in schools.

Instead of reflecting the ability to draw what one sees or to incorporate how the culture depicts depth, these stages, Willats argued, reflect children's cognitive ability to solve a problem. The problem that they are faced with is the task of representing a three-dimensional scene on a two-dimensional surface. The solutions at each stage reflect children's best efforts to solve this problem. With age, children spontaneously invent increasingly complex and abstract rule systems for the representation of space.

However, not all cultural influences can be excluded in explaining the emergence of perspective drawings. If children naturally invented perspective on their own, then perspective would have been invented long before the Renaissance. The opportunity to view perspective drawings produced by adults must be a factor in the discovery of perspective, even if perspective need not be formally taught in school. The parallelograms that children draw, for instance, may reflect their simplified interpretation of correct perspectival drawings that they have seen.

At least in Western culture, the adolescent years are a time when children become extremely critical of their drawings (Brittain, 1968; Lowenfeld and Brittain, 1970). While drawing is a central aspect of the life of most preschoolers, it occupies a far less important place in the life of an adolescent. Many adolescents simply stop drawing. Without further training and practice, no further development will occur. This decline, however, is very likely a phenomenon of modern, industrialized societies. In cultures such as Bali, in which the arts are accorded a central role in the society, such decline may not occur.

Gestalt Theory of Drawing

The effort to explain the hallmarks of drawings characteristically produced by children has been pushed to its limits by theorists in the gestalt tradition. They have tried to account for the evolution of drawing by one overarching principle. Just as Freud attempted to explain the motivation of the artist, the dreamer, and the child at play by one principle, gestalt psychologists have posited one principle that is supposed to underlie the development of drawings from infant to adult.

According to Rudolf Arnheim (1974), for example, drawings proceed from simple, global forms to complex, differentiated ones. This one principle is said to account for the entire developmental course of drawing. One reason given for the lesser differentiation of children's drawings is that all psychological development proceeds from global to differentiated structures. Another reason has to do with the different function that drawings serve for the child. Unlike adults, children are not interested in making drawings appear naturalistic. The very idea of trying to be naturalistic has not occurred to them. Indeed, the desire to make illusionistic drawings is a late development in Western history as well as in childhood (see also Gombrich, 1960). Thus, children draw tadpoles because that is all that is necessary to represent a human. As far as is possible to determine, children never actually believe that their drawings look like the objects they represent.

There is much evidence to support this theory that the development of drawing proceeds from global to more differentiated schemas, or from the simple to the more complex. In the domain of shape, for example, the first form to emerge from the scribble is the circle. According to gestalt theory, this is because the circle is the simplest visual pattern, symmetrical in all directions. Before other shapes have been invented by children, the circle is used simply to represent "thingness" rather than roundness. Thus, children may draw the teeth of a saw as circles (Fig. 5.15), even though they know that the teeth are sharp. Although initially the circle is the child's only shape, eventually this form gets differentiated into other shapes. It is only when other, more angular shapes become

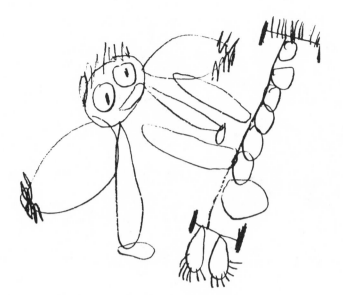

5.15 *Drawing of a saw with circular teeth, suggesting that circular forms stand for all kinds of shapes, including angular ones.*

available that children can be said to use circular shapes to represent roundness.

The same phenomenon is found in the domain of line, angle, and size (Arnheim, 1974). When children draw lines rather than enclosed forms, they first use only straight lines, since these are visually simpler than curved ones. At first, straight lines stand for all elongated shapes, whether curved or rigid. Only after children have differentiated lines available to them do they have the option of using curved lines to represent curved shapes. Similarly, the simplest angle is one of 90°, since it combines a vertical and a horizontal line, and this is the first angle found in children's drawings. Initially, therefore, right angles stand for all angular relations; only later is obliqueness differentiated from right angularity. And at first all objects are drawn the same size, no matter what their relative size in actuality. Thus, when a child draws a parent as tall as a tree, it is unwise to interpret this psychoanalytically as evidence that the child feels overpowered. Rather, the child has simply not yet differentiated size and thus does not vary the size of shapes in order to encode objects of varying size. Only when size has become differentiated does the option to draw things of different sizes exist.

This developmental course of artistry—proceeding from global to differentiated forms, from states of maximal contrast to subtler, weaker contrasts—is said to be a universal pattern that unfolds autonomously, independent of culture or education. The gestalt psychologist Henry Schaefer-Simmern (1948) even argued that this de-

5.16 *Drawing without overlap (top), by a teenager at the start of a drawing course, and drawing after five months in the course, demonstrating overlap in the horse's legs and the placement of the horse in front of the bush.*

velopmental pattern is so inevitable that it reveals itself in all beginning attempts at drawing, no matter what a person's age or IQ. To test this view, a wide range of people including normal and retarded children, normal, retarded, and psychotic adults, and delinquent teenagers, were asked to draw. The teenagers and adults had presumably drawn before, but only as children, and thus had not drawn for some years.

All of the participants began to draw very simple outlined figures. Gradually, their figures developed complexity, as more parts were added and as contrasts became subtler (Fig. 5.16). The findings were taken to show that any individual, when provided with drawing materials and left alone, will pass through the same graphic sequence.

This developmental sequence was also found in the history of art in different cultures. There are numerous parallels between each stage of artistic unfolding in the individual and in paintings, drawings, sculptures, and tapestries from various periods of history (Schaefer-Simmern, 1948). Thus, both child art and "naive" adult art display a structural unfolding similar to that exemplified over the centuries by sophisticated works of art (see also Gablick, 1976).

Any theory that attempts to account for a wide range of phenomena by one principle is likely to be vulnerable in many respects. One piece of evidence challenging Schaefer-Simmern's theory comes from the work of the anthropologist Alexander Alland (Gardner, 1980). When drawing materials were given to children who had never drawn before, within the space of a half-hour some children had passed through numerous "stages" and were soon producing quite differentiated drawings. Drawings produced by eight- nine- and ten-year-old children of Tibetan refugees in Nepal proved the same point. These drawings were collected by David Brown while teaching school in a tiny mountain village in Nepal. The children in this village had never drawn before. Yet when they were given crayons and paper, the very first drawings that they produced were extraordinarily complex (Fig. 5.17).

It is easy to poke holes in grand schemes. Where Schaefer-Simmern found parallels between the works of various populations, one can also note differences. Nonetheless, there may well be some truth to Schaefer-Simmern's theory. Although differences between the drawings of different populations can surely be found, underlying resemblances also exist. There are undeniable and intriguing similarities between the pictorial works of recognized artists and those by children, untrained adults, and even retardates. This suggests that the ability to produce aesthetically pleasing

5.17 *Complex painting by a twelve-year-old Tibetan child who had never painted before.*

drawings is the capacity of all humans, whether trained or untrained, including those of below average intelligence.

Children's Drawings as Art

Schaefer-Simmern and Arnheim illuminated resemblances between the art of the child and the art of the sophisticated artist. In my view, the strongest resemblances are those between the adult artist and the young child under the age of nine or ten (see also Gardner, 1980; Lowenfeld and Brittain, 1970). The drawings of the preschool and early elementary school child are unrealistic, free, balanced, and beautifully colored. The resemblance of young children's art to that of modern masters can readily be seen in the works of two preschoolers (Fig. 5.18). The drawings of older children, however, are aesthetically less interesting. A ten-year-old's drawing is tight and constrained, striving toward conventional forms of realistic representation. Lines are carefully drawn, sometimes with a ruler; and children of this age use steretyped forms

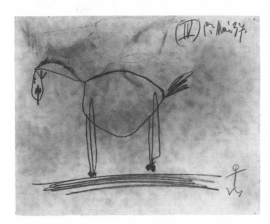

5.18   Klee, Inside the Body's Cavern (*top left*), *and similar drawing of a human figure by a preschool child;* Picasso, Study for Guernica (*bottom left*), *and similar drawing of a horse by a five-year-old.*

handed down by the culture to depict such objects as houses, trees, and flowers (Fig. 5.2 right). While a five-year-old's drawings could conceivably be passed off as works by an adult artist, one could hardly do the same with an eight- or nine-year-old's drawings.

A resemblance between child and adult art would not have been noted a few centuries ago, when the Western artistic ideal was one of realism. However, with the reemergence of non-naturalistic and nonrepresentational art in the twentieth century, as well as the discovery of the art of primitive cultures, the works that entered twentieth century museums began to bear intriguing resemblances to child art. Twentieth century artists have often noted the resemblance between their art and that of the young child. The child is seen as a genius, the early years of life as a golden period in artistic development that will soon fade, and the freedom and originality of early childhood as gifts to be regained only by those few individuals who go on to become artists.

A less romantic view of the early years of child art has also been articulated. While children's drawings possess undoubted aesthetic appeal for the adult and may resemble great works of art, these drawings may mean something very different for the child. It is possible, for example, that the child is intensely involved in putting marks on paper, but has little interest in the final product. Perhaps the drawings that so please adults are only happy accidents that the child had no intention to create and could not even recreate if asked. The final product, no matter how pleasing, ought not to be taken as evidence that the child is in control of the effects produced. Only if such control can be demonstrated can the conclusion be reached that the process by which the child creates is the same as that underlying mature creation.

Of the few attempts to test whether children are in control of the aesthetic effects that they produce, one study investigated the development of control over two aspects regarded as "symptoms" of the aesthetic: repleteness and expression (Carothers and Gardner, 1979). Repleteness refers to the fact that in a work of art, relatively more aspects of the symbol "count" than in a nonart object. And expression refers to the psychological states and sensory qualities metaphorically conveyed by a work of art (Goodman, 1968). While children's drawings appear replete and expressive to adults, it is possible that the children themselves are unaware of these aesthetic symptoms. The quality of the line, for example, may have been produced quite accidentally, perhaps as a result of the pressure they enjoy exerting with their arm. Similarly, a painting that strikes adults as expressing joy, such as a brightly colored picture with yellow daubs of paint, may express this mood unintentionally. The child in question may make all pictures this way, or the painting may simply reflect the colors that were at hand.

Whether children's drawings possess repleteness or expression cannot be determined simply by examining works produced spontaneously. All works of art, even those produced by children and chimpanzees, or by accident, possess these two properties for perceivers if the perceivers attend to all physical aspects of the works and apprehend a mood expressed. The issue is to determine whether these properties were intentionally or accidentally produced.

In the study, six-, nine-, and eleven-year-olds were given pairs of incomplete drawings and asked to complete the drawings—the production task—and to select the best completion from a given array—the perception task. Each pair of incomplete drawings varied along the dimension of repleteness or expression. To investigate sensitivity to repleteness, one set of pairs was identical in all respects but line quality. For example, one member of a pair contained lines of uniform thickness, while the other member contained lines of varied thickness (Fig. 5.19). Children were asked to add another person in a blank space in the picture and to make the addition in the way that the artist would have done it. If children are sensitive to repleteness—that is, if they realize that the properties of the line other than its contour, such as its thickness, are relevant to a drawing—then they should attend to these properties and complete these drawings using the same line quality. The same should hold for the completions that they select.

To investigate sensitivity to expression, the investigators constructed another pair of incomplete drawings identical in all respects except the mood of the person represented and certain features of the environment. For instance, a person in one picture was sad, and there were clouds in the sky; in the other picture, the person looked happy and the sun was out (Fig. 4.3). Children were asked to complete the pictures by adding trees and flowers. They were not asked to add a person, because this would undoubtedly have elicited sad or happy people, which would be an indication of representational rather than expressive skill. If children are sensitive to expression and realize that the mood expressed by a picture is as important as what the picture represents, then they should attend to this property and complete the drawings "in the same mood." Again, the same prediction holds for the multiple-choice perception task.

Six-year-olds failed on both the repleteness and expression

5.19 *Drawings with different qualities of line, used to test children's sensitivity to repleteness.*

tasks. In the repleteness task, they completed both members of a pair using the same line quality (Fig. 5.20 left); and for the most part, they selected completions at random. Similarly, in the expression task, they completed the happy and the sad picture in the same way (Fig. 5.21 top) and selected completions at random. Nine-year-olds succeeded on both tasks when given the multiple-choice version but performed less well in the production version. By the age of eleven, children succeeded on both versions of both tasks. They completed and selected the drawings using the appropriate type of line (Fig. 5.20 right). They also completed and selected the pictures in the appropriate mood. For example, the happy picture was often completed with a tree with apples and flowers in full bloom, while the sad picture was completed with drooping flowers and a gnarled tree without leaves (Fig. 5.21 bottom).

This test revealed something of a paradox. During the same years that children produce art works that are most pleasing to adult eyes, they display little sensitivity to aesthetic properties of pictorial art. And during the years when children's drawings become highly conventionalized and therefore less pleasing to adults,

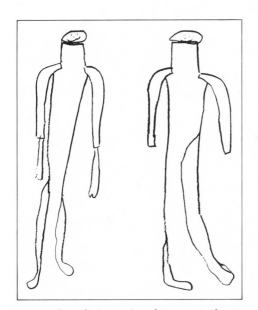

5.20 *Completions of repleteness task: six-year-old makes no distinction in line quality; twelve-year-old uses different kind of line in each picture.*

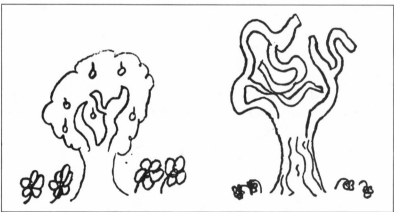

5.21 *Completions of expression task in Fig. 4.3: seven-year-old makes no distinction in expressive quality (top); twelve-year-old draws a blooming tree and healthy flowers for the happy picture, a tree without leaves and wilted flowers for the sad picture.*

children display a heightened sensitivity to these same aesthetic properties.

A painting by a four-year-old may please adults as much as one by Miró or Picasso; indeed, the two works may even look strikingly alike. But the findings of Carothers and Gardner call into question the conclusion that this four-year-old is an artist in the same sense as Miró or Picasso. While children's drawings may appear aesthetically pleasing to adult perceivers, this does not lead to the conclusion that these drawings are functioning in the same way for the child. The mature artist is aware that all of the variations in the physical surface of a painting count, not only those necessary for accurate representation. The child appears blissfully unaware of this fact. And the adult artist is able deliberately to use color and line to express a particular mood, which again is a skill that young children seem to lack.

The evidence suggests that the romantic view of the child as an artistic genius must be tempered. While the end products of child and adult artist may be similar, the means are different. If children see no alternatives in how to draw, and if their products are to a certain extent accidentally produced, then the child artist is very different from the mature artist who intentionally chooses to use lines in certain ways and convey particular moods.

Despite the crucial differences between the artistic process in the child and the adult, there are important similarities. If children were entirely oblivious to alternatives, and if their works were entirely random, then their drawings would undoubtedly fail to charm adults so regularly. In the intensity of their emotional involvement with drawing and in their willingness to explore and experiment, regardless of the dictates of convention, preschool children resemble the adult artist (Gardner, 1980).

The developmental course of graphic artistry appears to follow a "U-shaped curve" (Gardner and Winner, 1982). The drawings of the very young resemble those of the adult artist and are prized by adults; those of the middle childhood years possess no such resemblance and seem to be less appealing. U-shaped curves have been found in many cognitive domains (Strauss, 1982). In these U-shaped phenomena, the returned capacity is often superficially similar to its early form but is quite different in its underlying properties, as the study by Carothers and Gardner testifies in the case of drawing. Moreover, the dip in the U need not represent a true loss but may rather be diagnostic of an ongoing reorganization that is necessary for the later, mature reemergence of this capacity. Thus, the decline of originality and freedom during the school years may be a necessary cost when children are learning to master the conventional use of the graphic symbol system. Only when children have fully mastered the conventional rules of picturing can they expect to break them with full effectiveness.

The works of preschoolers, while bearing undeniable resemblances to those of mature artists, can be seen as preconventional.

Although they appear to violate norms and thus seem original, the children themselves are unaware of the norms that are violated. The years of school age are best seen as a conventional period, in which the norms are carefully mastered. Evidence of a concern for rule mastery and an avoidance of rule violation can also be seen in other aesthetic domains, such as the realm of figurative language. This period is then followed by the postconventionalism of the mature artist, who is able to break the previously mastered rules and achieve originality once again. Although the mature artist's products may resemble those of the preconventional child, these products are achieved by a very different process.

The Phylogeny of Drawing

The resemblances among early child art and the art of the sophisticated artist show that the ability to produce visual art is not the province of a few geniuses but is a capacity possessed in some degree by all humans. There is also reason to believe that it is not only humans who have this ability, but also nonhuman primates—chimpanzees, orangutans, and gorillas.

Left alone in the wild, apes have never been reported to engage in any form of what might be called art. However, psychologists have provided laboratory chimpanzees with paints, paintbrushes, and paper. While they fail to engage in artistic behavior on their own, when supplied with materials, they have been known to paint with a brush and to finger-paint.

But paint applied to paper is not necessarily a work of art. What is needed is some indication of pleasure and engagement on the part of the chimpanzee, as well as a certain measure of control and intentionality. And such evidence is forthcoming. Chimpanzees do become extremely involved in the act of painting, display a high level of concentration, and although never rewarded for painting, continue the activity for long stretches of time, often preferring to paint than eat and throwing a tantrum if their materials are taken away. The marks that they make are not random. And the end product has undeniable aesthetic appeal. In fact, art experts, shown paintings by chimpanzees, have sometimes assumed them to be of human origin and have praised them for their dynamism, rhythm, and sense of balance.

In an amusing study, subjects were shown paintings by a child, a chimpanzee, and two adult painters (Hussain, 1965). The subjects were not told that the paintings included ones by children and chimpanzees but were simply asked which they preferred. On the average, subjects preferred the chimpanzee paintings to those by one of the adult artists.

The most extensive investigation of primate painting reviewed the evidence on the artistic behavior of gorillas, orangutans, and monkeys as well as chimpanzees (Morris, 1967). Congo, a chimpanzee at the London Zoo, began to paint at the age of one and a half years; by the age of four, he had produced 384 paintings. Each painting was made in only a few minutes; sometimes a painting was completed in seconds. During the process, Congo was seated in a chair and handed brushes, one at a time, loaded with paint. Colors were proffered in random order, and Congo had no choice of colors. This procedure was necessary because otherwise Congo mixed all of his paints together—a trait that clearly distinguished him from a human child. Another difference between Congo and a human child was that the experimenter had to keep handing him fresh paper. This was because, once a page was filled, he began to paint on top of the already painted surface. Congo exhibited less interest in the finished product than in the process. Nevertheless, Congo stopped painting if his paintbrush ran out of paint, thus revealing that he was not only interested in the motor activity itself.

The resemblances between paintings of Congo and the drawings of children produced during the scribble stage are striking. Both chimpanzee and child produce vertical, horizontal, and curved lines, as well as dots. However, it was not until a year after Congo had begun to paint, at age two and a half, that he progressed to multiline scribbles (Fig. 5.22). And although he advanced to the diagram stage, in which simple geometric shapes are outlined, at this point the paths of human child and young chimpanzee begin to diverge. To begin with, Congo produced only two of the six diagrams found among human children—the circle and the cross. He never produced a square. Most importantly, he never began to draw representationally. Thus, he appeared unable to discover on his own that marks on paper may symbolize three-dimensional objects in the world.

The conclusion cannot be drawn, however, that graphic representation is beyond the ken of nonhuman primates. According to two reports, one chimpanzee named Moja and one gorilla named Koko, both of whom had been trained in sign language, have created representational drawings (Gardner and Gardner, 1978; Patterson, 1977). For instance, the chimpanzee Moja drew a picture which was very different from her typical scribbles (Fig. 5.23). Because so few lines had been made, her companion, Tom Turney, put the chalk back in Moja's hand and signed to her to "Try

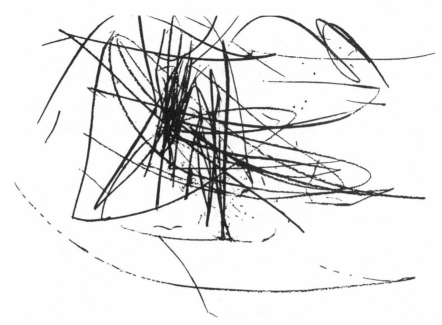

5.22 *Multiline scribble with fan pattern by the chimpanzee Congo, who never produced a representational drawing.*

more," but she dropped the chalk and signed "Finish." This reply was unusual, and the drawing also was unusual, as it contained many fewer lines than Moja's typical scribbles. Turney then asked Moja, "What that?" She replied, "Bird." Subsequently, Moja labeled other drawings that she produced, and these labels appear to be related in a comprehensible way to the form taken by the drawing. For instance, radial shapes were called "flower," round shapes were called "berry." She also replied appropriately to questions asking her to name the artist. When asked, "Who draw this?" she answered "Moja."

A key feature distinguished these two primates, Moja and Koko, from other primates studied. Moja and Koko had both been taught the rudiments of sign language. Thus, they had extensive experience in symbolizing through the medium of gesture. Perhaps these primates had grasped the idea of representation through their training in the use of gesture as a symbolic medium. The notion that something can be used to stand for something else—a by no means trivial concept—may have allowed these animals to symbolize in the graphic medium. At this point, it is possible to conclude that, at least without explicit training in symbolization through gesture, nonhuman primates do not draw representationally.

Although chimpanzees display little penchant for pictorial representation, they do resemble children in their remarkable sense of visual balance. Congo's lines did not go off the page, which demonstrated a sensitivity to the space of the paper. His most common motif was a fan shape, and the size of the fan was always adjusted to the size of the paper. He concentrated on the center of the page, often making a fan motif with radiating lines. The fan was usually in the center of the page, but once when the fan was placed too far to the right, Congo corrected the imbalance by stretching out the lines to the left (Fig. 5.24). Thus, chimpanzee paintings are in no way a compilation of random marks; instead, they display a sense of spatial relations and balance. The existence of such sensitivity to two-dimensional spatial organization is further supported by studies demonstrating that monkeys, given the choice between a symmetrical and an asymmetrical pattern, select the symmetrical pattern (Morris, 1967).

In order to provide a more controlled test of the ape's sense of balance, chimpanzees were given a piece of paper with a small figure on it in an off-center position (Schiller, 1951). Often the chimpanzees added marks in a location on the page that would balance the previous marks. And given a page with marks on three of the corners, the chimpanzees added a mark to the fourth corner, thus producing a more symmetrical effect. Surprisingly, when these same tests were given to young children, their products were less balanced. These children seemed more interested in exploring lines than in achieving symmetry.

One may conclude that nonhuman primates, given the opportunity, can create pictures of striking visual balance. But while the

5.23 *Nonrepresentational drawing by the chimpanzee Moja, and Moja's drawing of a bird, for which she produced the sign "bird."*

5.24 *Painting by the chimpanzee Congo, with lines stretched out on the left in a lopsided fan pattern, perhaps to correct the imbalance.*

child is sometimes fascinated more by exploring the properties of the medium than in achieving perfect symmetry, and while the child progresses to a representational stage within a few years, the chimp remains locked in at a nonrepresentational level. The finding that chimps engage in aesthetic behavior provides evidence that the "explosion" of cave paintings in the Upper Paleolithic may not have been so sudden but may have developed gradually, beginning at least with the ancestors of Homo sapiens. Nonetheless, there does appear to be a sharp break between the nonrepresentational capacities of the chimpanzee and the representational art of the cave people. With the exception of those chimpanzees taught sign language, it appears that only humans are able to create representational pictures. This suggests that pictorial representation is a high level skill, and thus the emergence of representation in the child is a significant cognitive milestone.

Autistic Drawing Development

An examination of the drawings of normal children invites sweeping generalizations across ages and even across cultures. Children's initial graphic attempts yield scribbles; out of these scribbles, a vocabulary of simple geometrical forms emerges; by combining these basic geometrical forms, children construct their first schematic representations. The preschooler's figures are composed of simple geometric shapes: a person is constructed by drawing a circle for head and trunk, from which four straight lines emanate to represent arms and legs; a tree consists of a circular top and a rectangular trunk; a house is a square plus a triangle. These schematic figures continue into the school years and become increasingly rigid and conventionalized.

Such is the typical course of drawing development. And although there is a small amount of cross-cultural evidence that some of these stages can be skipped or passed through quickly, the view has generally been held that a child cannot begin to draw in a highly naturalistic manner without first following this route. At least one child, however, diagnosed as autistic, appears to have reached an extraordinary level of artistry through an entirely different route. With the astonishing discovery of Nadia, an autistic child who began to draw at the age of three and a half, all of the generalizations previously made about the necessary stages of artistic development were opened to challenge (Selfe, 1977).

Nadia was born in England in 1967, to Ukrainian émigré parents. Although her two siblings were normal children in all respects, Nadia presented a remarkably abnormal profile. Although she had mastered a few words by the age of nine months, this meager vocabulary soon disappeared. Nadia was unable to produce or understand language. She was, in effect, mute. Nadia's parents placed her in a school for retarded children. Because she appeared to be making no progress there, her mother brought her, at age six and a half, to a clinic, where she was diagnosed as autistic.

Autism is a rare disorder of early onset, usually diagnosed before thirty months of age, with a number of severe accompanying symptoms: language is often extremely impaired; such children are socially withdrawn, show more interest in objects than in people, avoid eye contact, remain unreachable within their private world, and often display compulsive, ritualistic behavior. The cause of this condition has not been firmly established. Whether autism is a neurological disorder (Rimland, 1964), or a response to a certain pattern of family interaction (Bettleheim, 1967), remains in dispute.

Autistic children often possess one or two preserved "islands" of exceptional skill (Kanner, 1943; De Myer, 1976). Some autistic children are able to perform astonishing feats of mathematics. Others possess photographic memories, such as the child who was able, after a visit to an ice cream store, to write out all thirty–one flavors seen posted on the wall (de Villiers and de Villiers, 1978). Still others can sing back an opera perfectly after hearing it only once, or read aloud at two years of age, although with no understanding of the meaning of what they are reading.

To the psychologists who observed Nadia at the clinic, she appeared lethargic, clumsy, and slow in her movements. She possessed only a handful of single-word utterances, suggesting a stage in language acquisition that normally occurs briefly at one year of age. When given a thick yellow crayon with which to draw, Nadia resembled a two-year-old: she scrubbed a piece of paper with the crayon, producing a formless scribble.

During this first visit to the clinic, Nadia's mother showed one of the psychologists, Lorna Selfe, a few of Nadia's drawings, rendered with a ball-point pen (Fig. 5.25). The drawings were astonishing. With fluid contour line, Nadia had executed highly naturalistic drawings of complicated subjects, such as a horse and rider, a reindeer, a pelican, and a pair of crossed legs. They were reminis-

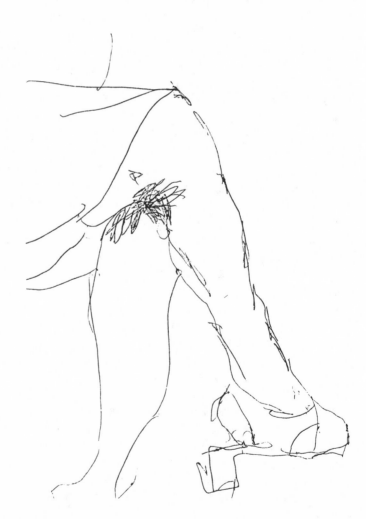

5.25 Naturalistic drawing
by the autistic child Nadia
at age six years, eight
months.

cent of sketches made by Renaissance artists (Fig. 5.3; Dennis, 1978; Gardner, 1979, 1980; Gregory, 1977; Pariser, 1979). In Nadia's drawings, the perspective and foreshortening—which are not normally mastered until early adolescence—and the effortless tracing of highly articulated contours made it at first seem impossible that the drawings could have been produced by such a young child.

Only after witnessing the six-year-old Nadia actually engaged in drawing were the psychologists willing to believe what still seemed impossible. To strain credulity even further, Nadia's mother said that her daughter had begun to draw at three and a half. Remarkably, the drawings from that age were nearly as sophisticated as those of the six-year-old.

Nadia also drew with great rapidity. But despite her speed, she could extend one line to meet another and then stop it at the exact point where it met the other line, with no overlap or near miss. Thus, she showed fine motor control, even though appearing quite clumsy on nondrawing tasks. Moreover, when she first drew something she had never drawn before, such as a pair of crossed human legs, she did not show any need to practice the rendering to get it right. Her initial drawings of a new subject were as faithful as her later ones.

From all available evidence, drawing was one of the few meaningful experiences in Nadia's isolated existence. If she had been given a ball-point pen instead of a thick crayon on her initial visit to the clinic, she would in all likelihood have produced one of her extremely sophisticated drawings rather than a formless scribble. But the psychologists did not know at the time that Nadia, in an obsessional manner typical of autistic children, would draw in only one medium. The fineness of a pen's line was what enabled her to execute her subject matter with such a high degree of detail. Probably because of her fascination with capturing complicated flowing contours with line, she showed no interest in the medium of paint or clay. She also showed no interest in the use of color. Nadia seemed concerned with one thing only: faithful rendering of contour. Clearly, Nadia's drawings have little in common with those of other children her age. They seem much closer to the works of accomplished artists. Yet there are a number of unusual features, particularly with respect to the process by which she drew, that set Nadia's work apart from that of the mature artist.

To begin with, although her drawings were always inspired by a model, usually by another picture, she never referred to the model when she drew but looked only at her drawing. Nadia typically studied a picture closely. Then days, months, or even years later, she reproduced the picture. [This is reminiscent of the delayed audition of autistic children, whereby phrases or melodies are recalled exactly long after they were heard (Park, 1978; Rimland, 1964).]

The order in which Nadia drew the parts of a figure was irrelevant to the end product. She could place one detail on the left, another far over on the right, and then join them at a later point with an intermediate form. And they always fit. Drawing a horse, for example, she first drew the neck, followed by the ears, and only then did she trace the outline of the head, fitting it in perfectly and fluidly joining ears and neck.

A further difference between Nadia and an adult artist is that she seemed more interested in the process of drawing than in the final product. She frequently drew a figure right off the page, displaying no sense of the space of the page itself. Sometimes she even began to make a drawing on top of an earlier one, reminiscent of the chimpanzees, who also displayed little interest in the finished product. What both Nadia and the chimpanzees seemed to lack was any sense of the communicative or display value of a picture.

Another unique aspect of her style was the slavishness with which she copied reality. To be sure, she often altered proportion and size or reversed the image's orientation. But in her compulsive, photographically exact rendition of detail, Nadia differed from the adult artist who adds, distorts, alters, or invents. Further evidence for this slavish copying comes from a test in which Nadia was given squares and circles with gaps in them and was asked to copy them from memory. Normal persons often remember and reproduce these figures without the gaps, thereby creating a better gestalt, or more regular form. Nadia, however, reproduced these incomplete forms exactly. This finding suggests that Nadia's need to reproduce with utter faithfulness predominated over any aesthetic considerations of good gestalts. It is probably because of her ability to reproduce so faithfully that, when she was given the Goodenough draw-a-woman test, an IQ test in which higher scores are achieved for inclusion of greater amounts of detail, Nadia achieved a score of 28, which gave her an IQ of 160.

After Nadia's autism was diagnosed, she was given intensive therapy and was taught to use language. For a while, as Nadia's language skills increased, her drawings declined both in quantity and in quality. But by her early adolescent years, Nadia again began to produce extraordinarily fluid and realistic drawings.

Nadia's drawings not only are unlike those of normal children but also are wholly unlike those of other atypical children, such as children who are psychotic, deaf, or retarded. The drawings of psychotic children are bizarre and are not highly realistic. The drawings of deaf children appear to resemble those of normal children, although deaf children develop graphically at a somewhat slower rate than normal (Thiel, 1927). And the drawings of retarded children appear to follow the normal sequence, although this sequence is passed through at a very slow rate (Lark-Horowitz et al., 1973; Selfe, 1977).

Nadia's drawings cast doubt on the claim that a regular series of stages must be passed through before a person can begin to draw realistically. Nadia appears to have skipped all of the stages that precede the emergence of naturalistic drawing during the adolescent years, and her drawings are also well in advance of those of the typical adolescent. She did not begin with simple, undifferentiated forms but appeared from the start to draw highly differentiated, complex forms. Of course, it is possible that Nadia passed through all of the early stages in a few days and that her drawings from that time were simply not preserved. But since her mother never reported such information, it is safe to assume that these stages were skipped. Moreover, even if the stages were passed through in a few days, such a rapid emergence of talent, apparently on a par with mature artistry, would still require explanation.

The presence of such extraordinary skill in a child without language, who performs at a subnormal level on other cognitive tasks, is in fact extremely difficult to explain. The drawings of Nadia have not yet been fully demystified, although several explanations have been offered. It may be that until science can explain the phenomenon of the child prodigy in any domain, to say nothing of the co-occurrence of autism and prodigious capacity, a satisfactory explanation of Nadia will not be forthcoming.

One possible explanation rests on the fact that Nadia was socially isolated. Cut off from the world, possessing little language and social skills, she turned to drawing as an avenue of communication. The problem with this explanation, however, is that children who are retarded or psychotic, and thus equally cut off from the world, do not draw like Nadia. Moreover, since Nadia often drew right over her drawings, she did not appear to be using drawing in a communicative way.

It has also been suggested that Nadia's skill resulted from the possession of eidetic imagery, the ability to remember every tiny detail of a visually perceived array. There is evidence that she did have such a photographic memory. For example, she could pass an eidetic imagery test. When shown two pictures, one at a time, she was able to juxtapose the pictures in her mind and select a third image that combined the forms of the first two pictures. Perhaps it was her vivid and exact visual memory that enabled her to draw so realistically. With a photographic image in her mind, she could have simply copied the form in her mind's eye. This would explain why she never needed to refer to the model drawn.

But again, this explanation is not convincing. To begin with, if the possession of a completely accurate image is sufficient to capture that image realistically on paper, then normal children ought to be able to draw equally accurately when they are drawing from a model. After all, a model has all of the details of the photographic image. Moreover, although eight percent of children have eidetic imagery (Haber and Haber, 1964), none draw like Nadia. Finally, Nadia's drawings often contained alterations in size, proportion, or orientation, which render it increasingly implausible to claim that she was simply tracing an eidetic image seen in her mind's eye.

A more promising explanation rests on Nadia's extremely limited ability to generalize, to form abstractions, and to classify objects into categories (Selfe, 1977). One test revealed that while Nadia could match objects to pictures of those objects, she could not match two pictures of the same object unless both pictures represented the object in the same orientation. She also appeared unable to recognize relationships among pictures of different objects belonging to the same class. For example, Nadia failed to match pictures of different types of chairs. This difficulty in forming concepts is not unlike the finding that autistic children cannot acquire the rules of language. Thus, those who do speak sometimes do so by dipping into a repertoire of memorized sentences, and they are unable to form new sentences because they have failed to extract the general rules governing sentence formation (Brown and Herrnstein, 1975).

The lack of a rich conceptual system may be related to highly naturalistic drawing skill (Pariser, 1979). The simple schemas invented by normal children reflect their ability to form generalizations. The use of a circle for a head, for example, is an abstraction in that it is somewhat like all heads and overlooks all the individual variations in head shape. The fact that Nadia did not use such simplified schemas but instead transcribed the optical image in all of its particularity suggests that she was unable to form visual concepts. She had no choice but to render every detail of a figure, since she was unable to grasp its general form. She was, in brief, unable to go beyond the optical information given.

Perhaps because Nadia's conceptual development was so limited, knowledge of the object seen did not interfere with her attempt to represent the object. Studies of normal children have shown that knowledge may interfere with optical realism. For instance, young children were shown to draw objects in their canonical, or typical, orientation, regardless of how the model was positioned (Freeman and Janikoun, 1972). Thus, a cup was always drawn in profile, with its handle showing. Children's copies of representational images such as cubes or rectangular solids were much less accurate than their copies of nonrepresentational, flat geometrical designs (Phillips, Hobbs, and Pratt, 1978). Presumably the familiarity of the cube caused subjects to emphasize what they knew about the object. For instance, many drew the cube's sides as squares, even though this violated the laws of perspective as well as their retinal image of the cube. And when copying a drawing, adults were shown to be much more accurate if they were forced to copy the model upside down (Edwards, 1979). In this orientation, they did not know what they were copying. Thus, their knowledge of the object did not interfere, and they could attend only to the contour of the lines.

It may be that Nadia's conceptual deficiency left her free to see and record objects with a naked eye. Nadia drew in a way that Arnheim (1974) thought impossible, precisely because people's visual concepts interfere with their photographic transcriptions: "We cannot hope to understand the nature of visual representation if we try to derive it directly from optical projections of the physical objects that constitute our world . . . If we assumed that the point of departure for visual experience was the optical projections supplied by the lenses of the eyes, we would expect that the earliest attempts at imagery would cleave most closely to these projections" (p. 163).

Although Nadia is the most famous, she is not the only autistic child to have shown exceptional drawing abilities. Most autistic prodigies have demonstrated special skills in mathematics, music, or memory, but there are several such children whose talent, like Nadia's, appears to be in the visual arts (Park, 1978). These autistic children also scored way above average on perceptual motor tasks, and way below average in linguistic tasks and on IQ tests. Like Nadia, they drew extremely faithful line drawings, capturing complex objects with fluid, finely articulated lines. But none of these children produced drawings quite as astonishing as those of Nadia. None captured with the same extreme fidelity the forms of such complicated figures as prancing horses. Moreover, not one of them began to demonstrate their drawing skill at Nadia's early age of three and a half, first showing it instead around the age of seven or eight. In the exceptional photographic realism of Nadia's drawings, and in the extremely young age at which she began to produce them, she remains unique.

Thus, Nadia's genius cannot be explained entirely by her autism. It may well be that Nadia possessed an innate, probably neurological proclivity in the domain of the visual arts. The possession of such talent, along with the lack of interference from conceptual knowledge, might have allowed her to create astonishing works of visual art before the age at which even gifted children—those who become artists as adults—are able to begin to draw so realistically.

Gifted Drawing Development

Gifted children, like autistic prodigies, have been noted much more often in music and mathematics than in the visual arts, and they have never been noted in the literary arts. Yet Picasso produced extraordinary drawings at the age of nine, demonstrating highly sophisticated draftsmanship (Fig. 5.26). Klee drew astonishingly well at six, and by nine was producing drawings with accurate perspective and foreshortening (Fig. 5.27). Vasari's *Lives of the*

5.26 *Picasso,* Bullfight Scene and Doves, *painted when he was only nine and already showing skilled draftsmanship.*

5.27 *Klee,* Country Home in Bern in the Länggasse, *drawn when he was nine but showing stage four perspective, which is attained by few children under eleven and is typically not reached until thirteen or fourteen.*

Most Eminent Painters, Sculptors, and Architects (1912–1914) yields a number of Renaissance artists who were said to be skilled draftsmen by the age of seven or eight. And exceptional drawings can be found today by gifted children at least as early as the age of eight or nine (Fig. 5.28).

An understanding of the graphic development of nonautistic prodigies may provide an instructive contrast to both the typical course of development and the atypical route of autism. Unfortunately, little systematic information has been gathered on this issue. But in 1979, when an exhibit of the childhood works of Israeli artists was put together by Ayala Gordon at the Israel Museum in Jerusalem, a wide range of well-known Israeli artists submitted samples of their childhood and adult work. At the same time, drawings produced by children who had come to see the exhibit were put on display. It was thus possible to make immediate comparisons between the drawings of normal and gifted children.

5.28 Black Christ,
*sophisticated drawing
by a nine-year-old.*

The drawings of the gifted children bore interesting resemblances to those of normal children, but were also different in intriguing ways. Like the normal preschool child, the gifted children passed through a preconventional phase in which their drawings were free, expressive, and harmoniously composed. Yet here the similarity to the typical preschool child ended. The gifted children drew much more naturalistically than the typical preschooler, already using fluid contour lines rather than schematic geometrical shapes.

During the elementary school years the gifted children passed through a conventional phase, in which objects were represented by rigid and conventionalized schemas and drawings were less "aesthetically" composed, although to a lesser extent than normal children. Gone was their fluid line as well as their previous sense of balance and composition. In place of the fluid line could be seen more rigid schematic renderings. And in place of their previous overall sense of balance was an intense concentration on certain details, resulting in a loss of overall structure. In brief, like drawings of average school-age children, the childhood drawings of artists seemed to pass through a more rigid, conventional phase, concomitant with a decrease in aesthetic appeal.

But this conventional stage was passed much sooner than in the case of the normal child, who usually never emerges from this stage. By the age of ten, the gifted children had developed a personal style that could be seen in their adult works. And they reached artistic maturity at early adolescence.

Thus, the course of graphic development in a gifted child is not qualitatively different from the normal progression. The same initial stages are passed through, albeit with some differences and at a much faster rate. What distinguishes normal from gifted is that only the gifted emerge from the conventional stage.

These gifted children resembled normal children to a far greater extent than they resembled autistic prodigies. They did not draw at a highly naturalistic level at a very young age, nor did their drawings achieve the heights of Nadia's skill in any way. While Nadia shared with these artists a strong inborn talent, her conceptual impairment allowed her to do immediately what it takes normal artists years to learn how to do (cf. Gombrich, 1960).

Different paths of graphic development are taken by the typical child, the nonhuman primate, the autistic child with a genius in the visual arts, and the gifted child who may go on to become an artist in adulthood. The chimpanzee shares a sense of visual balance with the average child but is left behind when the child discovers that drawings can represent. The average child passes through the same stages as the gifted child, but the gifted one travels this route more quickly and leaves the normal child behind at the end of the conventional stage. The austistic child prodigy seems to be on a different road altogether, yet, shares some characteristics with the end state of mature artistry: a sensitivity to contour, a keen visual memory, and the ability to harness this memory to motor patterns so as to "read off" an image in the mind's eye, converting it effortlessly and faithfully into a visual pattern on the page. But while the mature artist is free to choose whether to draw naturalistically or not, the autistic child prodigy appears to have no choice but to represent in an optically realistic style. In lacking the freedom not to draw naturalistically, and in thus lacking full control of the artistic product, the autistic child prodigy never reaches the end state of artistic development.

THREE Music

6 The Sounds of Music

The theme of my symphony is the stabilization of a personality. In the center of this composition . . . I saw a man with all his experiences. The finale resolves the tragically tense impulses of the earlier movement into optimism and the joy of living.

—Dmitri Shostakovich

I consider music by its very essence powerless to express anything whatsoever: a sentiment, a phenomenon of nature, or the like.

—Igor Stravinsky

Wagner's opera *Tristan und Isolde* concludes with a section of approximately ten minutes called *Der Liebestod*, a title that is translated as "The Love Death." In this finale, the music gradually gains in loudness and breadth, refusing to settle in any one key. The music achieves a feverish height of intensity and then becomes calm, muted, and peaceful: a point of repose is finally reached as the music comes to rest in a single key.

With a few exceptions, music is entirely nonreferential: musical pitches do not denote anything. Yet a piece of music is commonly said to have meaning. The *Liebestod*, for instance, is often perceived to express sexual passion. Wagner described it as "one long ecstasy" (1924, p. 710). The question for psychology is how a nonrepresentational sequence of sounds is able to express a particular human experience.

Not only is it common to speak of musical meaning, but it is also customary to think of music as able to evoke an emotional response. Most listeners admit to being powerfully affected by the *Liebestod*, experiencing a gradual build-up of tension, followed ultimately by relief. This too is a psychological issue, to discover how a series of sounds with no referential content is able to touch the emotions.

Both the meaning of music and its emotional effect are based on the kinds of sounds, and relations among sounds, that people actually hear when listening to a piece of music. The elements of music that have received most psychological study are tonality, pitch, and melody. Rhythm and meter, though also fundamental to music, have been relatively little explored.

The Perception of Tonality

Sounds are the raw material of music. The sensation of sound is a function of the vibration of air molecules which have been set in motion by the source of the sound. Not all sounds are musical. Musical sounds are produced by regular vibrations; the noise of a metal trash can falling over, or the sound of a racking cough, are produced by irregular, chaotic vibrations (see Lowery, 1966).

The pitch of a musical sound is determined by the frequency of vibration of the source of the sound. The greater the number of vibrations per second, the higher the pitch. The range of pitches that the human ear can hear is extremely wide, varying from frequencies of 20 to 20,000 vibrations per second, and within this range, many fine discriminations can be made. However, music does not make use of all of these pitches: out of this large continuum, a subset of discrete pitches is selected for use. The domain of color contrasts instructively to pitch. The painter is not restricted to a fixed subset of possible hues but can use colors separated from each other by the finest of gradations. The composer, however, can use only those discrete pitches selected by the culture for use in music.

In Western music, the range of pitches selected for use is divided into repeating octaves, each of which consists of twelve notes separated from each other by one semitone, or half-step, as shown on the keyboard of the piano. Beginning with the note C and playing each black and white note until the next C is reached yields the chromatic scale. Music of most cultures does not use the chromatic scale but is based instead on the diatonic scale. This scale consists of only seven of the twelve semitones in the octave, separated from each other by either a whole- or a half-step.

Almost all of the music that Westerners are familar with, including rock and roll, jazz, and folk songs, is written within a particular key. What this means is that, at any given point in time, a piece consists primarily of the notes that comprise a particular scale. Thus, a piece in the key of C major consists primarily of the notes of the C-major scale. The notes in a given key can be thought of as the members of an immediate family. They are perceived as closely related, and in the context of a particular key, tones outside of this key sound like distant cousins.

The notes within a key do not all have the same function. One of the most important roles is played by the first note of the scale, called the tonic. In the key of C, the tonic is the note C; in the key of G, the tonic is G. The tonic is perceived as the most stable sounding note in a melody and is heard as the central tone toward which all the others gravitate. The existence of a tonal center gives a melody a feeling of stability: as the melody moves away from the tonic, a sense of tension is generated; with the return to the tonic, listeners feel that they have arrived back home, and the tension is resolved.

Because the tonic sounds most stable, melodies usually end on this note, thereby achieving a feeling of completeness. If a melody ends on the tonic, it feels "right." But if the tune ends on a note such as the second note of the scale, the melody feels as if it were hanging in midair and seems to cry out for further resolution. There is an anecdote that Mozart, as a child, heard a piece of music that felt unfinished because it did not return to the tonic. Mozart was unable to let the piece end without resolution and finished the piece himself by playing the tonic chord. A similar story is told about Bach.

Western music rarely remains entirely within one key but instead modulates from one key to another. As a piece changes key, the tonic, or tonal center, also changes. Such shifting of tonal centers creates a sense of movement and instability. Remaining in one key, and thus maintaining the same tonal center, yields a sense of calm and stability. In the twentieth century, key and tonal center were rejected altogether in the composition of atonal music. Because such music lacks the organizing framework provided by a key, it makes greater processing demands on the listener. In the words of the anthropologist Claude Lévi-Strauss (1970, p. 25), atonal music "is like a sailless ship, driven out to sea by its captain."

The importance of tonality in organizing the listener's perception of music has been demonstrated in a number of psychological studies. Musically trained listeners can hear the difference between tonal and atonal melodies (Dowling, in press), and it is easier to recognize a melody heard previously if the melody is tonal rather than atonal (Francès, 1958). Tonality does not just facilitate recall of a melody; it also facilitates recall of single pitches. Single pitches are more accurately recalled if first heard within a tonal rather than an atonal context (Dewar, Cuddy, and Mewhort, 1977).

Even listeners who are untrained in music perceive tonality and find tonal melodies more coherent than atonal ones, as shown in a study of tune construction (Bamberger, Duckworth, and Lampert, 1981). Adults with no particular knowledge of music were given a set of five bells, each with a different pitch, and were asked to construct a tune. The five pitches were C, D, E-flat, F-sharp, and G. These pitches do not unambiguously define a single key and thus do not generate a tonal center, because no one scale contains all five of these notes, and in fact no more than three of the notes belong to any one scale. Faced with the task of constructing a coherent tune with a set of pitches that did not define a single key, the participants in the study had considerable difficulty. The solution eventually achieved was to treat C, D, and G, three pitches that belong to the same scale, as the stable pitches, and to emphasize these through repetition. The other two bells, which fell outside of the scale defined by C, D, and G, were treated as embellishments to the more stable pitches. In this way, the tune builders succeeded in generating a melody with a tonal center. This study demonstrates that the organizing effect of tonality exists for the untrained as well as the trained listener. However, the facilitation is usually stronger for those who have some formal instruction in music (Dowling, in press; Francès, 1954, 1958, 1968).

It is difficult to interpret the role of learning and experience with respect to the organizing effect of tonality. The fact that people lacking formal musical training can perceive the organizing effect of tonality does not mean that experience is unimportant for the perception of tonality. The untrained listeners in the tune construction study had undoubtedly heard a great deal more tonal than atonal music, since the former is the predominant music of Western culture. The fact that Westerners have come to internalize the "grammar" of tonality is most probably the result of listening to countless pieces of tonal music. But only if studies were carried out in a culture with different scalar systems could the role of experience in the perception of tonality be assessed.

Although it is not known with certainty whether tonality is a natural category or is constructed from listening and formal training, tonality has been shown to be a psychologically real category for the Western listener. We use tonality as an organizing framework in processing the music that we hear all around us. Just as, in a painting composed primarily of blues and grays, a daub of orange is experienced as something of an outsider, so also in a melody composed in the key of C, notes from a distant key make their intrusion felt. This sense of intrusion need not be unpleasant. In fact, the establishment of this sense may be important in maintaining the interest and attention of the listener.

The Perception of Pitch Relations

While even those without musical training can perceive the organizing framework of tonality, listeners with formal training in music are able to go beyond this and perceive other relationships among various tones within a key. Pitches are related to each other in a number of ways. They are related by their frequency distance from one another. For instance, C is closer to D than to E, since D is one whole-step away and E is two whole-steps away. Pitches are also related by the framework of key. In the context of the key of C, for example, C sounds more related to D than to B-flat, because D is in the key of C but B-flat is not.

Finally, pitches are related by their overtones. The tones of most instruments are made up of a combination of sounds—a fundamental sound, whose pitch names the note, and a series of sounds of higher pitch, called overtones. The overtones are more faint than the fundamental, but without them the note would sound impoverished.

The sequence of fundamental and overtones is called the harmonic series. The frequency of an overtone is related to the frequency of the fundamental by a regular ratio. For instance, high C, the first overtone of the fundamental middle C, vibrates at two times the frequency of the fundamental. The first overtone is usually the loudest. The next overtone of middle C is G above high C, the fifth note of the scale of C. On most instruments, this is usually the next loudest overtone of C. The fifth note of any scale is called the dominant. Because of its close relationship to the tonic, the dominant plays a role similar to the tonic.

The quality or timbre of a sound is due to the number of overtones present and to the relative intensities of the overtones. Instruments differ in these respects. It is because of overtones that the sounds of the different instruments are clearly distinguishable from one another.

The measurement of pitch by frequency distance versus overtones yields different predictions about pitch perception. For instance, by the measure of frequency distance, middle C should sound more like its adjacent note, C-sharp, than a C one octave higher. But according to the overtone measurement, middle C and high C should sound more alike, since the loudest overtone of middle C is the C one octave higher. Similarly, by frequency distance, C and D should sound more like each other than C and G, since C and D are separated by the smaller interval difference. But by the measure of overtones, C and G should sound more alike, since the second loudest overtone of C is G.

The kinds of tonal relations that listeners can perceive are determined by their level of formal training. This has been demonstrated in an experiment where subjects with two to five years of musical instruction were asked to judge the degree of similarity between two tones presented in the tonal context of the key of C major (Krumhansl, 1979). To establish the tonal context, subjects were first played either the C-major scale or the C-major triad (C-E-G-C). Immediately following, subjects heard two tones and were required to rate the similarity of the first tone to the second. The pairs to be rated varied in three ways: the size of the interval between pitches (A-B versus A-D), their presence in the scale of C major (D-E versus D-D-sharp), and their presence in the C-major triad (C-G versus C-D). In addition, the direction of comparison was systematically varied. In some cases, the first tone was either a note from the major triad chord or some other note from the C-major scale, while in other cases such tones were presented second.

Subjects with musical training perceived a complex pattern of pitch relationships. Tones in the C-major scale were judged to be more similar to other tones within the scale of C than to tones outside of that scale. For instance, D was judged more similar to E than to D-sharp, even though D and D-sharp are closer in frequency. Tones an octave apart were perceived as very similar, despite the fact that they are many half-steps apart. The tones of the C-major triad were judged to be particularly closely related. Thus, C and G were rated more alike than C and D, even though C and D are closer to each other in frequency. These relations found among tones demonstrate that, when trained listeners hear pitches within a tonal context, they relate these pitches by membership within a key and by overtones rather than by sheer frequency difference.

The similarity judgments for pairs of tones often proved asymmetrical. That is, ratings differed depending on the order in which the two tones were presented. Recall that subjects heard an initial tone and were asked to judge its similarity to a second tone. When the second tone was the one most closely related to the tonal context, similarity ratings were higher than when the tones were heard in the opposite order. For instance, asked to compare B to a tone from the C-major triad, such as E, subjects reported greater similarity than when the comparison was made in the reverse direction, from E to B. Similarly, judging the similarity of a tone outside the established key of C, such as G-sharp, to a tone within C, such as E, yielded higher ratings than when the comparison was made from E to G-sharp. Thus, tones unrelated to the tonal structure were heard as more similar to tones related to the tonal structure than the reverse.

What these asymmetries suggest is that, in a given context, certain tones are more central or prototypical than others. In the context of the key of C, the actual tones of the C scale feel more central and stable than tones outside of this scale; and tones comprising the C-major triad feel more central than tones that are in the scale of C but not in the C-major triad. Thus, the findings fit with the experience of the tonic as the most stable note of any scale.

Research in other domains has shown that prototypicality yields asymmetrical effects in comparison tasks (Rosch, 1977; Tversky, 1977). For instance, most people would consider China to be a better, more prototypical example of an Asian communist nation than North Korea. Thus North Korea seems more like China than China seems like North Korea. The more prototypical instance—China—is the stable standard of reference against which more peripheral instances are judged. In the same way, certain tones in a given context are central, stable reference points against which more peripheral tones are judged. Nonprototypical tones are less stable and tend to drift toward the central ones. The claim that certain tones are the prototypical ones against which others are measured gained support from an experiment demonstrating that nondiatonic tones, tones outside a given scale, are more easily confused with diatonic tones than the reverse (Krumhansl, 1979). The fact that some notes sound more stable than others is an important issue in the emotional response to music.

Naive listeners perceive pitch in a considerably less structured manner than listeners who are trained. To demonstrate this, the listening abilities of people with extensive training, averaging 7.9 years of instruction and 5.6 years of performance, were compared with people having little or no training (Krumhansl and Shepard, 1979). Subjects heard the seven tones of an ascending or descending C-major scale. The eighth note, an octave from the first, which normally completes this sequence, was omitted. Subjects then heard a single tone from somewhere in the octave. This tone was drawn from the entire set of thirteen chromatic notes, ranging from the omitted tonic note that constitutes the normal ending to the note one octave beyond the tonic. Listeners were asked to rate how well the final tone fit with, or completed, the preceding sequence.

Several factors might influence such judgments. If sheer frequency distance is important, listeners should prefer the tonic one octave from the first note of the sequence, followed by tones close in frequency to this tonic. But if tonal relations are important, listeners should demonstrate a hierarchy of preferences: the best ending should be the tonic at either end of the octave; followed by the other most stable tones, the tones of the C-major triad; followed by the other C-major scale tones; and followed last by the tones outside the scale of C.

Musical training determined which of these criteria were used. For those with no training, frequency distance proved much more important than it did for trained listeners. Those with training demonstrated a hierarchy of relations within the diatonic scale. Preferred first, and equally, were the tonics at either end of the octave; these were followed, in descending order of preference, by the fifth note of the scale, the third note of the scale, other tones within the scale of C, and finally, by tones outside the C scale. This study demonstrated that the structural relations extracted from tonal sequences of notes depend to a great extent on one's level of training and skill.

Categorical Perception of Pitch

Surprisingly, formal training may actually reduce the accuracy with which listeners perceive pitches. Trained listeners appear to perceive musical tones in a categorical mode. That is, given a tone that is slightly out of tune, the trained ear hears it as if it were in tune.

Categorical perception has been established in the domain of speech (Eimas, Siqueland, Jusczyk, and Vigorito, 1971; Liberman, Cooper, Shankweiler, and Studdert-Kennedy, 1967). For instance, speech sounds such as "pah" and "bah" differ from each other in terms of "voice onset time," or the amount of time between the opening of the lips and the vibration of the larynx. To utter the sound "pah," the lips must open before the larynx begins to vibrate, while in the case of "bah," the lips open almost simultaneously with the buzzing of the larynx. Using a machine that synthesizes speech sounds, researchers can make pronunciations of "pah" gradually shade into "bah" by steadily narrowing the voice onset time. However, we do not hear all of these subtle shifts. Instead, we hear two discrete categories: different variants of "pah" are all heard as "pah" until a certain voice onset time is reached, at which point we hear different variants as "bah."

While speech sounds are perceived categorically, studies have shown that subjects without formal musical training perceive pitch continuously (Burns and Ward, 1974; Vinegrad, 1972). That is, untrained listeners appear to perceive minute changes in frequency, even those that result in a pitch between two semitones. Trained listeners are less sensitive than untrained listeners to such tiny frequency changes. Because of their extensive experience in listening to the semitones of Western music, musicians transform continuous variations in pitch into the discrete categories of the culture's semitones. Just as in speech perception we perceive only those differences that make a difference in meaning, such as "bin" versus "pin" but not two different varieties of "bin," musicians notice only those intervals that signal a change of note in their culture.

Categorical perception was demonstrated in a study of musicians with excellent relative pitch (Siegel and Siegel, 1977a). Relative pitch refers to the ability to recognize a note when given a reference point. For example, given C and told that it is C, the listener can identify other notes. Relative pitch is a different and more common ability than perfect pitch, in which no reference point is needed to identify a note.

Subjects were asked to judge the size of various intervals. First they heard a standard interval consisting of two successive tones, C and F-sharp. This interval is called an augmented fourth, or tritone. Subjects were asked to assign to the perceived distance between the tones any number over 100. They then heard thirteen intervals, each consisting of two successive tones. Most of these intervals were just slightly out of tune, ranging from a flat fourth one-fifth of a semitone below a perfect fourth to a sharp fifth one-fifth of a semitone above a perfect fifth. For each interval, subjects were asked to judge the distance between the two tones as they compared to the distance in the standard interval. Thus, if subjects thought an interval was half as large as the standard, they were instructed to assign it a number half as large as that given to the standard. If they thought an interval was one and a half times larger than the standard, they were instructed to assign it a number one and a half times as large. To avoid a possible response bias of simply rounding off numbers to the value corresponding to the nearest accurate interval, subjects were instructed to make their judgments as fine-grained as possible.

On this magnitude estimation task, the musicians demonstrated categorical perception of pitch. Although all thirteen intervals were acoustically different from one another, subjects used only a few numerical responses. In other words, an interval just a fraction larger than a true fifth tended to be judged as if it were a true fifth. Thus, subjects did not appear to hear thirteen slightly different intervals but instead heard the thirteen intervals as instances of three accurate intervals.

To rule out the possibility that subjects had detected the fine, within-category acoustic variations but had rounded off their responses to the value corresponding to the nearest accurate interval, subjects were subsequently told that some of the intervals had been out of tune. They were then asked to judge the proportion of out-of-tune intervals that they had heard. On the average, subjects judged 37 percent of the intervals to be out of tune, although 77 percent were in fact out of tune.

Thus, it appears that while nonmusicians may not categorize pitches, musicians are subject to the illusion of categorical perception. Variations of less than a semitone are not perceived by Western musicians because such differences are not meaningful in Western music. This perceptual illusion is fortunate, since music is often slightly out of tune, and categorical perception allows the trained ear to ignore minor inaccuracies. Acoustic studies by Carl Seashore (1967) demonstrated that well-known performers deviated quite often from the precisely correct pitch. "It is shockingly evident," concluded Seashore, "that the musical ear which hears the tones indicated in the conventional notes is extremely generous and operates in the interpretive mood . . . The hearing of pitch is largely a matter of conceptual hearing in terms of conventional intervals" (p. 269). Thus, the perception of music, at least by the musical listener, may be more a matter of interpretation than hearing.

What a listener ordinarily perceives and what a listener is able to discriminate may be two different matters. That is, a skilled listener may tend spontaneously to perceive categorically. However, this same listener may be able to detect deviations if explicitly "set" to listen for them. Although this does not occur in the domain of speech perception—no matter how hard we try, we cannot hear differences between different varieties of "pah"—it seems to be a logical possibility in the case of music. There is even some evidence for this. For instance, whether or not people perceive musical intervals categorically depends on the precise task used (Burns and Ward, 1978). The tasks used by the Siegels in the categorical perception study were not designed to assess the limits of listeners' discrimination abilities. If musicians were played pairs of intervals consisting of one interval in tune and one out of tune and asked to identify the one out of tune, they might well be able to detect the one that was slightly "off." Nonetheless, when not prepared to expect deviations, the trained ear appears to perceive in a categorical mode.

Some cross-cultural observations lend further support to the claim that training in music leads to categorical perception (Siegel, 1981). Not every culture defines the basic interval as the semitone. Music from India, for example, is based on microtones, which are smaller intervals than the semitone. If Western musicians noticed only those variations with musical significance in their culture, then they would probably be unable to perceive the microtone interval in Indian music. That is, two tones separated by less than one semitone should sound the same. Although there is no evidence for this, there is evidence for the reverse, in the case of an Indian musician who made finer discriminations in Western music than Western musicians do (Rao, 1923). The Indian musician described what he heard when listening to a Western vibrato, which consists of a slight fluctuation of pitch often less than a semitone. The Western listener interprets the vibrato as a constant pitch with a rich sound. But because he was sensitive to the microtone interval, the Indian musician interpreted the sound as a fluctuating rather than a constant pitch. He also interpreted the variation as significant and believed that it was meant to express agitation.

A similar case involves a Western ethnomusicologist who studied the music of the Australian aborigines. The music of the aborigines is one of the few in which the octave relationship is relatively unimportant. This music also does not use other standard Western intervals. The ethnomusicologist apparently became so immersed in aborigine music that she lost the ability to recognize standard Western intervals, including the octave. Thus, it appears as if the ability to hear the similarity between tones separated by an octave can be lost without sufficient exposure to this interval. This is a striking finding, since the ability to hear the octave relationship is a basic and primitive skill that can be found in the untrained human listener (Dowling, 1978a; Humphreys, 1939). This ability has also been demonstrated in rats, who were trained to run across a grid to food when a certain tone was sounded. When a tone one octave away was sounded, but not when other tones were sounded, the rats responded as if they had heard the original tone and ran across the grid to food (Blackwell and Schlosberg, 1943). Thus, we appear to be naturally predisposed to hear the octave relationship; but given sufficient immersion in a music that does not make use of this relationship, we cease perceiving it.

The Perception of Melody

The perception of tonal relations among pitches affects how larger units of music—melodies—are perceived and remembered. We can all recognize familiar tunes. To do this requires that we store something of the tune in our memory so that when we hear it again, we know that we have heard it and we know what to expect. But just what it is that is stored is not immediately obvious. The simplest explanation would be that we store the individual notes. But this cannot be the case, for everyone can recognize a melody when it is transposed to a new key, that is, when all of the notes are altered but the relationship among the notes is preserved. The fact that we typically hear no difference between various transpositions of a melody is one of the classic examples offered by gestalt psychologists to prove their claim that what we perceive are not the individual elements of a stimulus but rather the *relations* among the elements.

Another solution would be that we store the individual notes along with a set of transposition rules. But if so, the original notes would retain a special status relative to transposed notes. And it has been shown that no such special status exists (Dowling, 1981). Two successive melodies were played and subjects were asked to decide whether the second melody was the same as or different from the original. When the second melody was a transposition of the first, people were just as likely to say it was the same as the first as they were when the second melody was an exact copy of the first.

Or perhaps we store the actual notes, the "chromas," independently of the octave in which they are played. Thus, we might hear the "A-ness" or "C-ness" of a note and store this alone, irrespective of the octave in which it is heard. To test this hypothesis, the familiar tune of *Yankee Doodle* was distorted by selecting each note randomly from one of three octaves (Deutsch, 1972). Thus, every note in the sequence was in its correct position on the scale—that is, it had the right name—but the notes were not in the correct octaves with respect to each other. Despite the fact that the notes remain correct, this type of distortion destroys the contour of the melody. The contour is the pattern of ups and downs formed by the notes, which can be represented as a sequence of plusses for ups and minuses for downs. Musically untrained subjects proved unable to recognize the contour-distorted tune. To their surprise, even professional musicians were unable to identify the tune. Thus, chroma information appears to be insufficient for recognizing even a very famliar melody, and contour appears to play an important role.

Studies have shown that what we perceive and remember is either the precise interval sizes between notes or the contour of the melody. In the case of familiar melodies, we store precise intervals between notes. Thus, a familiar melody is stored in terms of its exact intervals, such as +4, −3, +2. This has been demonstrated in experiments in which people were asked to detect small changes in melodies in which the intervals but not the contour were altered. When the tunes used were well known, even musically untrained listeners could detect small interval changes that preserved contour (Attneave and Olson, 1971; Dowling, 1978b).

While we can detect interval distortions of familiar tunes, even severe distortions do not prohibit us from recognizing a familiar tune (Dowling, 1972; Dowling and Hollombe, 1977). Thus, if we hear *Happy Birthday* sung with the intervals distorted but the contour preserved, we can identify it even though we realize that it has been played incorrectly. This tells us that we store both the interval sizes and the contours of the familiar tunes, and that contour can be used independently of interval size to recognize such tunes.

Further support for the role of contour in the storage of a melody came from a variation of Deutch's (1972) *Yankee Doodle* experiment in which chromas were taken randomly from different octaves. It was found that preserving the contour of the melody along with the chromas improved performance (Dowling and Hollombe, 1977). While the importance of contour was thus demonstrated, another study showed that chromas are important also. In a further twist on the *Yankee Doodle* study, the contour was preserved and the chromas were again picked randomly from different octaves (Kallman and Massaro, 1979). However, the chromas were altered by one or two semitones. The distorted melody that resulted was just as difficult to recognize as the melody in which the contour was changed but chromas preserved. Thus, recognition of melodies depends on both contour and chroma information. Whereas chroma information is not sufficient for recognition, it appears to be necessary.

While we store both contour and precise interval size in the case of familiar tunes, we recall new melodies by their contour but not their intervals (Dowling and Fujitani, 1971). A new tune is stored in terms of a pattern such as + + − + −, rather than by + 5 + 4 − 3 + 2 − 4. Consequently, melodies with the same contours but different interval sizes are easily confused with each other.

Contour is not the only dimension that is stored when we hear a new melody. When we hear tonal melodies, we also store some information about the key in which the melody is played. In one study, a brief, unfamiliar tonal melody was played, followed by various contour-preserving transformations of that melody, and subjects were asked to indicate when the second melody was the same as the first (Bartlett and Dowling, 1980). When the transformation remained within the same key, subjects tended to confuse the transformation with the original melody. But when the transformation was in a distant key—that is one which shared relatively few notes with the key of the first melody—less confusion occurred. The likelihood of confusion varied with the distance between the original and the new key: the more remote the new key, the less the chance of confusion. If the melody was transformed into an atonal tune, even fewer confusions occurred. This was called the "key distance effect": the greater the distance between the two keys, the greater the ease of discrimination between two same-contour melodies. With familiar tunes, however, the key distance effect was not demonstrated, as listeners failed to discriminate between familiar melodies in two distantly related keys. This fits with a well-known phenomenon: one can listen to versions of *Happy Birthday* in two distantly related keys yet hear no difference between the two.

All of these findings hold for musically trained as well as naive listeners, although the effects are stronger among those with training. Formal training appears to be most important in cases in which difficult, subtle discriminations are necessary. Thus, listeners are able to hear and store a considerable amount of information when they hear a melody. If the tune is familiar, they can perceive and recall its precise pattern of interval sizes. If the tune is heard for the first time, they can perceive and recall its contour and even, to some extent, the key in which it is played.

The Embodied Meaning of Music

How the elements of music are perceived governs the issues raised by Wagner's *Liebstod:* the meaning of music, the response to music, and the means by which both of these are achieved. Composers disagree about whether music conveys any meaning at all. Philosophers and music theorists, however, have distinguished two ways in which music conveys meaning. Some have proposed that the meaning of a piece lies entirely within the work, in the perception of the relationships that formally define the piece. Others have maintained that the meaning lies outside of the work, in that music refers to, or expresses, emotional states, scenes from nature, or abstract concepts such as courage or transience. The music theorist Leonard Meyer (1956) called the former group "absolutists" and the latter group "referentialists." Absolutists posit an embodied meaning, one entirely intramusical; referentialists posit an extramusical or expressive meaning. It is not necessary to choose between these two types of meaning. Any piece of music conveys meaning in both of these ways. One listener may derive meaning from the *Liebestod* by expectantly waiting for the piece to come to rest in one key; the ending finally confirms that long-held expectation. Another listener, or even the same listener, may hear the *Liebestod* as expressing the course of sexual passion.

Intramusical meaning is said to exist because music embodies implicative relationships (Meyer, 1956). Musical meaning of this sort is a matter of internal reference; that is, a musical event arouses expectations in the listener because it points to, or implies, other musical events that are likely to follow. Our expectations are built on gestalt laws of perceptual organization. For example, the law of good continuation leads us to expect a pattern to continue in its initial mode of operation. The law of closure leads us to expect a piece to end with a feeling of completeness and stability.

Composers often deliberately create and then violate expectations. The law of good continuation is exploited in Chopin's *Prelude* op. 28 no. 2: a certain continuity of notes is established, into which in the fourteenth measure an unexpected note intrudes. The same law is exploited in Bach's *Well-Tempered Clavier*, when a piece which has been entirely in the minor mode ends on a major chord. The law of closure is exploited by the *Liebestod*, which refuses to come to rest in a single key, contrary to our expectations. When a piece deviates from a traditional framework, the expectations of trained listeners are frustrated, and they feel surprised. Such listeners are also made self-consciously aware of what they were expecting, and that it did not, in fact, occur.

Because embodied meaning is a function of expectation, such meaning is dependent upon the knowledge that we bring to the musical experience. For instance, while the law of continuation may lead trained listeners to expect a piece by Handel to move through a limited range of keys, they should have no such expectation when listening to Wagner, Liszt, or Debussy. Instead, they should expect the piece to modulate constantly to different keys, since a wider range of modulation is the norm, rather than the exception, for these composers. When a given style is known to have a great deal of change, then change comes to be seen as the norm. Without such knowledge, however, listeners experience the change as unexpected.

What is experienced and expected as an ending is thus also dependent on knowledge of the style in question. For instance, the same cadential formulas that in Renaissance music convey closure are inadequate to convey closure in eighteenth and nineteenth century music. In later music, the Renaissance ending fails to constitute a real completion. Listeners who are familiar with later music but not with Renaissance music will hear a Renaissance piece as incomplete. They will expect more. But listeners who are familiar with the Renaissance style will experience the cadential formula as complete.

Embodied meaning is therefore a function of both our knowledge of a style and our expectations that are highlighted by the composer's deviations from the norms of the style. Because of the importance of knowledge of the style in question, it is primarily the trained listener who perceives embodied meaning. Because embodied meaning is a function of expectation, which depends on understanding the style, music in a wholly unfamiliar style has less embodied meaning for the listener. Unfamiliar music cannot arouse powerful expectations. On hearing Indian music for the first time, we do not know what to expect because we do not know the rules by which it is constructed. However, this does not mean that the music will be meaningless for us. It is possible that this music will have at least some extramusical expressive meaning. For instance, if it is composed of low notes played slowly, we may read the piece as expressing sadness. If it is fast and staccato, we may perceive it as cheerful. It is also possible that this music, even though strange to our ears, will evoke an emotional response.

The Expressive Meaning of Music

More than any other art form, music has often been said to be the language of the emotions. This statement has a great deal of truth to it. But the claim has also been misinterpreted. It is sometimes taken to mean that music is a vehicle for the expression of the composer's emotions. Overcome by joy, composers write a sprightly symphony; bowed by grief, they compose a funeral march. But a piece of music can express many contrasting moods in rapid succession. The composer's moods could hardly be so mercurial (Langer, 1953). Moreover, composers can create a work expressing sadness while in a happy mood. Thus, to claim that music is the language of the emotions should not be taken to mean that music is the direct expression of composers' emotional states.

This claim is more often misinterpreted to mean that music elicits emotion. While music in fact elicits emotion, perhaps more powerfully than any other art form, this claim is very different from saying that music expresses emotion. A piece may express sadness without eliciting sadness in the listener.

The philospher Susanne Langer (1953) has analyzed how music

expresses emotion (see also Meyer, 1956; Pratt, 1931). According to Langer, while music may well elicit emotion, its main function consists in being about emotion. This is made possible by the kind of symbols used by artists. Scientists make use of discursive symbols, such as literal language and numbers, which have fixed definitions and are thus readily translatable. Artists use presentational symbols which are untranslatable, and which are understandable only through their relations within the total structure of a work. Presentational symbols capture the flux of sensations and emotions that we experience. Ordinary language cannot do this. We can speak about why we feel a certain way, but we cannot use words actually to convey the quality of our feelings. Music, however, is a form of presentational symbolism that is peculiarly well adapted to expressing the character and quality of the inner life.

The reason for music's expressivity is the fact that the structure of music mirrors the structure of emotional life. Music sounds the way moods feel. Music is structured in terms of tension and release, motion and rest, fulfillment and change. These subtle and swift alterations mirror precisely the subtle fluctuations of mood to which we are subject. Thus, the structure of Wagner's *Liebestod*—its suspenseful crescendo and final return to calm—mirrors the emotional experience of passion and release.

By expressing the realm of feeling, music provides a cognitive experience for the listener. Music mirrors the structure of the emotions, and thus it helps to make the emotions conceivable. In brief, we cannot reflect about the world of inner experience through discursive symbols. We can do so only through presentational symbols.

Psychological studies have attempted to test the claim that music expresses emotion by determining whether there is any consensus about the emotions a piece of music expresses. Most such studies have demonstrated a respectable degree of agreement among individuals with and without formal musical training. In one study, musically trained and untrained adults were asked to listen either to short fragments of music (8–12 measures) or to entire movements (Hevner, 1936, 1937). Subjects were given a checklist of adjectives referring to emotions, such as *happy, sad*, and *playful*, and were asked to indicate which adjectives applied in each case. Considerable agreement was found. In general, happy, playful moods were said to be expressed by music in the major mode; sad, dreamy moods by music in the minor mode. Firm rhythms were heard as vigorous and dignified; flowing rhythms as graceful, dreamy, and tender. Dissonant chords, in which the tones sound harsh and jarring, were felt to express moods like excitement, agitation, or sorrow, while consonant chords, in which the notes seem almost to fuse together, were felt to express happiness and serenity. The saddest effect was determined by a combination of factors: the minor mode, a low pitch, a slow tempo, and dissonance (see also Francès, 1958; Pratt, 1931; Rigg, 1940).

Another study confirmed these findings and fleshed out the picture (Brown, 1981). A tape was constructed of twelve selections from nineteenth century music. The tape contained six pairs of selections which differed in genre and composer, but which were thought to express similar emotions. The range of moods that the selections were judged to express was wide: "elegiac gentle sorrow," "tender and hushed," "rustic good humor," and so forth.

Three kinds of subjects participated. One group consisted of nonmusicians who were unfamiliar with classical music. A second group was composed of instrumentalists who had had extensive musical training but did not particularly like nineteenth century music. A third group consisted of musicians who were well versed in nineteenth century music. Thus, subjects varied in terms of both musical training and liking for—and thus presumably familiarity with—the type of music whose moods they were to judge.

The subjects were asked to group the twelve selections into six pairs, based on the mood expressed. The results demonstrated high agreement among all groups with Brown's classifications by mood, whether or not subjects were trained in music, and whether or not they were knowledgeable about the kind of music in question. It may be concluded that music possesses an expressive meaning, and that one need not be familiar with the music in question to identify these meanings. It also appears that people can agree about a nontechnical, metaphorical language of emotional expression to describe musical meaning. Thus, the claim that music is the language of the emotions gains empirical support. But the extent to which this is due to a structural parallel between music and the emotions remains to be determined.

The Emotional Response to Music

Not only is the *Liebestod* expressive of a certain range of emotions, but it also arouses emotion in the listener. Music is associated with certain physiological responses: it affects pulse, respiration, blood pressure, and the electrical resistance of the skin, and it delays the onset of muscular fatigue (Mursell, 1937). All of these changes are ones that also occur during emotional experiences. For instance, changes in the skin's electrical resistance occur in response to heightened arousal and are the clues used in lie detector tests. These physiological changes are more likely to be produced by music if the listener is a musician; for nonmusicians, these responses occur more randomly (Francès, 1958).

There may well be an especially intimate link between sound and emotion. Some people who become deaf report a consequent draining of feeling (Heider and Heider, 1941). People can watch the suffering of an animal if the suffering is silent; but once they hear cries of pain, they cannot escape an intense emotional response (Brown, 1981). Thus, sound may bear more of a relation to emotion than do visual stimuli.

Verbal reports of composers and critics suggest how the formal aspects of music elicit the affective reactions of tension and relief (Meyer, 1956). The same processes that give rise to embodied meaning—the creation and violation of expectation—give rise as well to the affective responses to music. Composers deliberately create and then violate expectations in the listener. By delaying the fulfillment of expectation, the composer creates suspense. The greater the suspense, the more the tension, and thus the more the relief at the eventual resolution.

While a listener with some formal knowledge of music responds to the frustration of an expectation by consciously waiting for the formal device that will fulfill the expectation, the untrained listener responds to such frustration by simply experiencing a sense of tension. And when the expectation is finally fulfilled, the untrained listener simply feels a sense of relief. Whereas the trained listener consciously waits for the *Liebestod* to come to rest in a key, the untrained listener simply feels tension followed by relief when it comes to rest within a key at the end.

Thus, the frustration of expectation is the basis of both the intellectual and the affective response to music. While untrained listeners may lack the technical knowledge and the labels, and while their responses are somewhat less differentiated than those of trained listeners, it is basically the same process that occurs in both types of people. However, trained listeners are able to experience both responses, while untrained listeners experience only the affective response.

Because music in an entirely unfamiliar style elicits fewer powerful expectations than does familiar music, unfamiliar music cannot arouse the kind of emotion caused by the violation and confirmation of anticipations. However, some emotional responses may well be universal. Frenetic, fast music and slow, regular music, for example, may evoke consistently different affective responses in all cultures. But subtle sequences of feelings of tension and relief are probably available only to listeners who know at least vaguely what to expect.

The view that our response to music is based on our expectations can explain a number of phenomena. For instance, it explains why Mozart insisted on playing the final notes on the piano so that the tune would end on the tonic. Ending on the wrong note had violated his expectations and created tension, and he sought the emotional release of resolution. The same argument may account for the emotional response to dissonance (Meyer, 1956). Consonance is the norm, and dissonance is the deviation. Through deviation, dissonance derives all of its affective power: a dissonant chord delays the arrival of the expected consonance and thus arouses tension.

The thesis that the affective response to music is grounded in the violation of expectations has not been tested systematically. It is possible that listeners hear less than is claimed. Many listeners who lack formal training in music probably do not feel tension when, for example, a piece in *The Well-Tempered Clavier* ends on a major chord. Not only may such listeners be reflectively unaware of what has occurred, but they may also fail to perceive the shift from minor to major at any level. Only by testing listeners' expectations using both musically naive and sophisticated listeners can one determine the degree to which the emotional response to music is a function of expectations.

The successive feelings of tension and relief as expectations are violated and confirmed is not the only kind of emotion aroused by music. Another very common and powerful way in which music arouses emotion is through association. Often the listener has an association, whether conscious or unconscious, to something that arouses affect. A piece of music might, by association, remind the listener of a painful event that occurred in the past. The listener then begins to feel sad. Organ music is most often heard in church; thus, it elicits feelings associated with religion. These kinds of associations are extramusical, and they bear no necessary connection to the structure of the music. Yet they are extremely powerful, and they probably occur more often among untrained listeners who are less preoccupied with listening to the formal structure and thus more responsive to extramusical associations.

Music both expresses and induces emotions, and these two functions should be sharply distinguished. A piece of music may express sadness and also make listeners sad. But it is also possible for a piece not to make listeners feel sad at all, even though they perceive the piece as expressing sorrow.

However, while expressing and inducing emotions are logically different processes, essentially the same principles may be at work in both. The crescendos, tensions and resolutions in music are recognized as expressing emotions, and it is just these aspects that are responded to emotionally. Listening to a piece expressing sadness, we may hear the sadness so clearly that we become sad ourselves. Likewise, when we see a friendly face, we can both recognize it as friendly and feel a corresponding surge of friendliness. Thus, although expressed and induced emotions are logically different and do not always correspond with one another, our emotional response to music may well be, in part, the product of perceiving what is expressed.

Music consists of highly structured sound. Much of the structure is built on the physical, acoustic properties of music, such as the relations among pitches based on overtones. But while music itself is highly organized, the amount of structure that is perceived depends on the listener's level of musical training and experience. Simply through the informal experience of listening to Western tonal music, the listener becomes able to perceive some of the tonal relations used by Western culture. And through formal musical training, listeners come to impose even more structure. They can recognize when a piece modulates from one key to another; hearing only a few notes, they can infer the key in which the notes were played; hearing only the opening of a piece, they are able to predict that certain structures are likely to follow; and hearing an interval a fraction out of tune, they may well perceive the interval as one that is in tune.

The listener's response to the *Liebestod* now becomes more understandable. In this finale, the music does not settle into any one key. Thus, no tonal center is generated. Psychological studies have shown that tonality is a psychologically real category even for the listener who lacks formal training in music. Melodies that do not have a tonal center are difficult to assimilate and recall; they are experienced as unstable; and they create a sense of tension in the listener. Tension is also created by the deliberate violation of expectations: listeners expect a piece to achieve closure by coming to rest in one key, but the *Liebestod* refuses to do this until the very end. When the finale ultimately does achieve closure, the tension is dissipated and a sense of relief is experienced. It is because listeners can perceive this movement from a state of tension, instability, and intensity to one of calm and resolution that they are able both to perceive meaning in the *Liebestod* and to react emotionally to it.

7 The Innocent Ear

Listening is a talent, and like any other talent or gift, we possess it in varying degrees.

—Aaron Copland

To look at a picture is not necessarily to see it. One can look at a painting and yet remain blind to some of its most important aspects. So also with music: listening is no guarantee of hearing or understanding.

To understand music means, in one sense, what the formally trained musician can do: label important musical events, such as recapitulations and cadences, or label musical forms, such as the fugue and the sonata. But there is another, more everyday sense of understanding music. Ignorant of the technical jargon of music, the ordinary listener understands it by responding to the important musical events in the piece. For example, knowing nothing about cadences, the listener may still hear their quality of musical closure.

Several abilities go into being a good listener. According to the composer Aaron Copland (1939), the most important requirement is to be able to store a melody in memory so that when it is heard again, it is recognized. "If there is such a thing as being tone-deaf," Copland remarked, "then it suggests the inability to recognize a tune" (p. 6).

Most musicians believe that several other abilities also go into being a good listener. To begin with, the listener must perceive the relative stability of the tonic, in order to experience the tension produced by failing to return to the tonic and the relief when the melody eventually comes to the rest on this note. While the listener need not be able to identify the mode, major or minor, in which a piece is played, it is essential to sense a shift from one mode to the other. Similarly, while the listener need not be able to identify the key in which a piece is played, it is necessary to recognize a shift from one key to another, to distinguish between shifts to a near key and to a distant one, and to distinguish between tonal and atonal music. And while attending to the surface rhythm of a piece, the listener ought to be able to hear, in the mind's ear, the underlying, fixed background beat or pulse against which the surface rhythm is measured.

Some of these skills are present at birth, while others emerge only after experience in listening to music or after formal musical training. While it seems implausible to think that the ability to respond to painting or literature is present at birth, such a claim seems less outrageous when it comes to music. After all, as parents have always known, infants respond readily and spontaneously to the rhythms and melodies of music. The infant who cannot be calmed by food or physical contact may well relax if rocked to the music of a lullaby.

The Infant Ear

In some respects, infants are remarkably good music listeners. They have what Copland believes to be the most important ingredient for the listener: the ability to recognize a melody. They are also able to recognize simple rhythmic patterns. However, sensitivity to more complex aspects of music, such as tonality, is entirely absent at birth.

Infants as young as five months have been shown to recognize melodic contour (Chang and Trehub, 1977a). In this study, infants heard six-note atonal melodies played thirty times over a five-and-a-half-minute period. During this time, the infants became bored with the tune, and their heart rate habituated to the stimulus. Subsequently, they heard either an exact transposition of the melody to a new key or a transposition of the melody along with an alteration in contour. Thus, in both cases the second stimulus contained all new notes, but in the exact transposition the contour was unchanged. If the second stimulus is perceived as different from the first, the infant's heart rate will change; if it is perceived as simply a continuation of the first stimulus, heart rate will not change. Infants in this study continued to habituate to the transposed tune with preserved contour—that is, their heart rate did not change— but they dishabituated to the tune with altered contour—that is, their heart rate slowed, indicating renewed interest in the stimulus. What this reveals is that the transposition without contour alteration was heard as the same as the initial stimulus. Since the only thing shared by the initial and the transposed tune was melodic contour, the infants must have been able to recognize melody. This study clearly demonstrates that infants can hear the similarity between a tune and its transposition, and that they can notice the difference between two tunes of different contours (See also Melson and McCall, 1970).

The ability to detect simple rhythmic patterns is also present as early as the ability to store and recognize melody. In another study, infants as young as five months were shown to be able to perceive the difference between a rhythm divided into groups of two and three (—— ———) and one divided into groups of four and two (———— ——) (Chang and Trehub, 1977b).

Thus, the infant is able to apprehend simple musical gestalts, whether these be melodic contours or rhythmic groupings. Sensitivity to more subtle aspects of music, such as mode and tonality, and the ability to hear an underlying pulse given a surface rhythm, are skills that do not emerge until the early and middle years of childhood.

The Development of Listening Skills

By the time children have reached their eighth or ninth birthday, they have achieved the level of musical competence of untrained adults. They possess melodic recognition skills, they are now sensitive to mode and tonality, and they are able to hear an underlying pulse when given a surface rhythm. But in at least one sense they have lost something possessed a few years earlier. With their increased ability to abstract melodic, tonal, and rhythmic structures, they have lost the ability to store individual pitches with precision.

While even infants can recognize simple melodies, the ability to recognize a melody when other aspects of the music have been altered does not develop until five to eight years of age. For instance, most five-year-olds are unable to identify a melody if its rhythm or its harmonic accompaniments are altered, but by eight, most can do so quite easily (Pflederer, 1964). Studies of this sort, in which children are asked to recognize an invariant structure despite alterations in other sound properties, have been likened to Piaget's studies of conservation, in which children were asked to conserve an invariant amount of a particular substance despite changes in its perceptual appearance (Piaget, 1952). Studies of music conservation have examined the ability to conserve, that is, to recognize a melody despite alterations in its rhythm. In other such studies, children were asked to conserve meter despite a change in the duration of notes or to conserve rhythm despite a change in pitch (Pflederer, 1964). In all of these studies, children did not demonstrate musical conservation skills until the age of five to eight. The ability to recognize an underlying structure despite superficial transformations is clearly important in music, in which melodic themes are frequently repeated in different keys or by different instruments (see also Botvin, 1974; Serafine, 1979).

Although the ability to store a simple tune is present in infancy, and the ability to conserve melody despite changes in other properties emerges without educational intervention, formal training exerts a powerful effect on melody recognition (Dowling, in press). The ability to recognize a tune was studied in two groups of children: six- and eight-year-olds who had been in an instrumental music program for about half a year, and six- and eight-year-olds on the waiting list who had not yet entered this program. The children were given two recognition tasks: they heard a brief, unfamiliar tonal melody, followed by either an exact repetition or a melody different in both contour and pitches; and on a more difficult task, they heard a melody, followed by either an exact repetition or a melody different in contour but containing the same pitches in a different order. On the first task, six-year-olds without training achieved scores of 75 percent correct, when chance performance would have yielded 50 percent. Those six-year-olds who had taken music lessons performed at a much higher level, achieving 90 percent correct. Thus, six-year-olds are able to learn to detect contour and pitch. Eight-year-olds had no difficulty with this task: untrained children scored a little under 90 percent; for children with training, scores increased slightly to a little over 90 percent.

On the second task, in which subjects were asked to recognize changes in contour when all of the notes, although reordered, remained the same, training exerted less of an effect on the youngest children. Untrained six-year-olds performed at a 65 percent level, while those who had taken lessons achieved scores of about 70 percent. More important, trained six-year-olds performed at about the same level as did children two years older without training. Thus, unlike the first task, performance on the second task did not improve simply as a function of age. However, with formal musical training, eight-year-olds did very well, achieving 80 percent correct. Thus, on this more difficult task, training appears to have more of an effect on older than younger children.

A word of caution is in order. It is possible that the training was not responsible for improving performance in this study. Rather, the children who were most gifted to begin with were perhaps those who were admitted to the music program, while less gifted children were placed on the waiting list. Only by randomly assigning children to a training group could the contribution of giftedness be ruled out.

Sensitivity to tonality has been demonstrated in children as young as five (Bartlett and Dowling, 1980). In this study, five-year-olds heard the first part of *Twinkle Twinkle Little Star* played in the key of C. They then heard either a transposition or a tonal imitation of this tune. In a tonal imitation, the contour is preserved but the interval sizes are altered; that is, the pattern of ups and downs remains the same, but the precise distance between any two notes is either widened or narrowed. In a transposition, both contour and intervals are unchanged. The transpositions and imitations were played either in a key near to that of the original melody or in a distant key.

Children and nonmusician adults were asked to decide whether the first and second melodies heard were the same or different. The transposition ought to be heard as the same melody, and the tonal imitation ought to be heard as different. The adults had no difficulty on this task. They heard both near and far key transpositions as the same as the original melody, and they heard the tonal imitations as different. When the imitations were in the same or in a near key, their ability to distinguish them from the original melody was only a little bit worse than when they were in a far key. This pattern of results shows that adults can detect changes in interval size, since they heard the difference between a melody and its imitation, and that they can detect gross changes in key, since they distinguished somewhat more accurately when the imitation was in a distant key.

Five-year-olds responded very differently from the adults. They could not distinguish between the original melody and either near (or same) key imitations or the near key transpositions. They could, however, distinguish the original melody from both transpositions and imitations in a distant key. Thus, five-year-olds, like adults, can distinguish near from far keys. But their failure to distinguish between the target melody and tonal imitations in the same or in a near key shows that they cannot detect changes in interval size. By eight, however, children begin to look more like adults, since near key imitations were accepted as the same as the original less often than far key transpositions. Thus the eight-year-old can detect changes in interval size as well as gross changes in key.

Other studies have also demonstrated the emergence of sensitivity to tonality around the age of six, seven, or eight. For instance, by seven, children can detect sudden changes in key in the middle of familiar tunes (Imberty, 1969). A preference for tonal over atonal melodies increases with age; and for six-year-olds, but not for younger children, the use of tonal melodies rather than atonal ones facilitates performance on a task in which individual notes within a melody must be recognized (Zenatti, 1969). The age at which sensitivity to tonality has been found varies from study to study, most probably as a result of the different tasks used. No study has yet demonstrated tonal sensitivity before age five.

Unfortunately, the evidence does not show whether such sensitivity to the tonal structures of Western music is due to universal maturational processes or to acculturation. Only with studies of children developing in cultures with different tonal systems can this be answered. Such studies would most probably show that there is nothing special about Western scales. Thus, children growing up in the Orient ought to develop an ability to perceive the scale structure of their culture but be unable to grasp the corresponding Western structure. If this turns out to be the case, it will show that perceiving tonality is much like acquiring a first language. While the acquisition of any particular language depends on the language to which the child happens to be exposed, the capacity to master language at all is a maturational one that does not depend on formal training. So also the capacity to master tonal structures may well depend on the general ability to organize hierarchically an incoming flood of sensations, while mastery of any particular scale structure may reflect the tonal system to which the child has been exposed.

Within one to three years after a sensitivity to tonality has emerged, children become aware of the typical structure of a melody. In particular, they begin to recognize that a melody feels right when it ends on the tonic. For instance, eight-year-olds can tell the difference between a completed melody and one left unfinished without a stable final note such as the tonic (Teplov, 1966). One year later, children are able to select the tonic as the most appropriate final note (Reimers, 1927). This was demonstrated by playing melodies to children ranging from seven to fourteen years. Each of the melodies had a different ending, and only one ended on the tonic. Children were asked to select the tune with the best ending. Seven-year-olds never chose the one that came to rest on the tonic, and eight-year-olds chose this one 11 percent of the time, which is below a chance score, since chance alone would yield a score of 25 percent. Nine-year-olds chose the tonic half the time, and this choice increased steadily with age until, by thirteen to fourteen it was chosen 96 percent of the time. Only a sensitivity to tonal structure and a corresponding awareness of the hierarchy of notes within a scale could enable children to succeed on this task.

Another study was able to demonstrate a sensitivity to the tonic as a musical ending in children as young as six (Brehmer, 1925). Children were played a brief melody that ended on the tonic triad, a chord that makes a particularly stable ending because it includes both the tonic and the dominant, the fifth note of a scale. They were then played the same melody with one alteration. Sometimes the tonic triad was altered, thus affecting the "goodness" of the ending. The study revealed that those alterations which affected the tonic triad were easiest to detect at all ages, including the youngest age of six.

The most probable reason for the age difference in the findings of these studies is that the tasks assigned differed in difficulty. In the study with the nine-year-old finding, children had to decide consciously on what constituted the best ending. In the study with the six-year-old finding, endings were manipulated in order to test their effect on the children's recognition of an alteration. The children who succeeded at this task and thus recognized alterations in the tonic may well have done so without realizing that ending on the tonic actually constitutes the most appropriate completion.

While the ability to recognize a melody and organize it in terms of its tonal structure develops in all children, another ability emerges in only a few individuals. This is the ability called absolute pitch or perfect pitch. Absolute pitch is best understood in comparison to the much more common ability, relative pitch. With absolute pitch, one can identify a note without anchoring it to another known note. Absolute pitch enables the listener to identify correctly any note heard in isolation. Although it has commonly been held that the possession of absolute pitch is related to giftedness in music, there appears to be no necessary correlation between the two (Shuter, 1968).

Whether absolute pitch is hereditary or is a product of training has been the subject of controversy. It has been shown that absolute pitch can be fostered at any age by training (Crozier, 1980). However, absolute pitch may be more common among younger than older children. One piece of evidence supporting such a view comes from a study in which children between three and six years were taught to sing three tunes (Sergeant and Roche, 1973). Each child was given six training sessions over the course of three weeks. One week after the last lesson, they were asked to sing back the three tunes. Surprisingly, while older children proved better able to retain and sing back the overall pattern of the song—its contour and even its precise intervals—it was the younger children who sang back the pitches most accurately. Thus, the ability to perceive and store pitches precisely may be more strongly represented in the very young. With age, this ability may give way to the ability to grasp and retain the overall pattern or gestalt of a tune. This same kind of developmental process may be at work in the case of eidetic imagery, the ability to store images that are photographically accurate. While about eight percent of young children possess eidetic imagery, this capacity appears to decline with age, giving way to more schematic, generalized memories faithful to the structure of a scene or object but not to its precise details (Haber and Haber, 1964).

The ability to recognize clear alterations in rhythmic patterns is present in infancy, and even young children can accurately imitate simple rhythms by clapping or beating on a drum (Bamberger, 1982). Thus, it might seem that sensitivity to this basic and universal aspect of music is a skill that does not undergo development. However, when children of different ages and levels of training were asked to invent written notations to represent a rhythmic pattern, these representations differed in intriguing ways (Bamberger, 1982). To the extent that a graphic representation can be considered an accurate reflection of one's mental representation of a rhythm, this finding suggests that the aspects of rhythm that are apprehended are determined both by age and by level of formal musical training.

Consider the clapped rhythm of the familiar nursery rhyme, "One, two, buckle my shoe; three, four, shut the door." The standard method of notating rhythm captures two aspects of this pattern of claps: its underlying pulse and surface rhythm (Fig. 7.1 top). Pulse refers to the meter, or the regular underlying time intervals, and rhythm refers to the variable pattern of actual beats within those time intervals. Although there are ten claps, standard notation indicates that there are only eight underlying pulses, since claps three, four, eight, and nine are performed twice as fast as the other claps. Standard notation shows that there are two kinds of claps here: ones followed by a brief duration of silence before the onset of the next clap (claps three, four, eight, and nine) and ones followed by a longer duration of silence (all the other claps).

There is, however, another way of organizing this rhythm. Many people claim to hear two slow beats followed by three fast beats. This pattern is then repeated. On formal analysis, this is puzzling, since the duration of the unit of clap five—its sound and the silence following it—is longer than the unit of claps three and four. It is possible to hear these three claps as the same only by overlooking the underlying pulse and attending to the surface pat-

Standard Notation

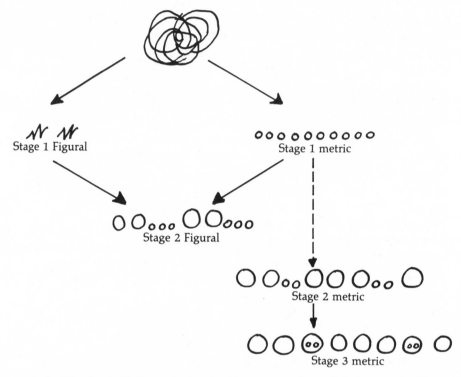

7.1 *Standard rhythm notation for the nursery rhyme "One, two, buckle my shoe; three, four, shut the door," and notations invented by children to capture this rhythm.*

tern in which the fifth clap is heard. When the listener attends to the context immediately preceding clap five, instead of to the duration between claps five and six, clap five sounds as brief as the two claps preceding it. By hearing the fifth clap within the context of claps three and four, the listener can pull the fifth clap into the package formed by claps three and four. These two ways of organizing rhythm are called metric and figural. In the metric mode, listeners attend to the duration from each clap to the next. In the figural mode, they attend to the figure, or phrase, in which a clap is heard. In the latter mode, the immediate context of a beat affects how it is heard, while in the metric mode, context is irrelevant.

Children were asked to listen to this pattern of claps and to draw a picture of the rhythm so that they could remember it or so that someone else could clap it (Bamberger, 1982). The children produced six types of drawings (Fig. 7.1 bottom). The drawings by the youngest children, aged four to five, reflected neither a figural nor a metric perception of rhythm. Children of this age repeated the continuous swinging motion of their clapping in their drawings, yielding scribbles. They did not extract the discrete claps from the continuous action of clapping. The result is one long, pulsing, cyclic line.

Six- and seven-year-olds produced stage one figural and metric drawings. These drawings were more advanced than those by younger children, because they captured the correct number of events in the rhythm. However, these early figural and metric drawings differed significantly from each other, and both types underwent development with age. In stage one figural drawings, children captured the two repeated figures of the rhythm by drawing two discrete zigzag lines. These drawings were actually played on the paper. As the lines were drawn, the child's arm moved in the rhythm of the claps. But once the marks were made, no visual record of the rhythm remained except for the boundary between the two phrases. These drawings were classified as figural because they showed the child's effort to capture the two repeated figural phrases.

Whereas early figural drawings focused on the two repeated rhythmic figures, stage one metric drawings focused on the number of discrete claps. These first metric drawings revealed the child's effort to extract each separate clap from the continuous motion of clapping. Concentrating only on this aspect, children produced a row of discrete but undifferentiated forms, such as circles. These drawings were classified as metric because they showed the child's effort to count up the precise number of units in a rhythm.

Eight- to ten-year-olds typically produced stage two figural drawings, while eleven to twelve-year-olds produced these and stage two metric drawings as well. Stage two figural drawings were clearly more advanced than earlier ones, since each event was now separated from the continuous motion of clapping. Figural drawings at this stage contained a row of shapes, such as circles, one for each clap. The two repeated figures were separated by a space, and events within each figure were differentiated to show faster and slower action. Larger circles stood for actions of longer duration, smaller ones for briefer actions. As one child said, "You can see that there are two and then three claps. The three little circles get faster and they go together." She then gestured with her arm to indicate that "go together" meant as in one bodily movement (p. 200).

In stage two figural drawings, the relation between the size of each form and the actual rate of claps was not consistent. In the rhythm that the children heard, clap five was performed as an event of longer duration, just like claps one, two, six, and seven. However, the fifth clap was represented by a small shape. The children who drew these drawings insisted that they were accurate representations of the rhythm that they had heard and performed. Musically untrained adults agreed (Bamberger and Hildebrandt, 1979). These drawings seem intuitively to be correct, even though a formal analysis of the rhythm reveals them to be inconsistent.

It may well be because of the motoric experience of clapping that claps three, four, and five are perceived as the same. When this pattern is clapped, these three claps feel like part of one bounded gesture. Moreover, clap five functions as the ending of the figure of claps three, four, and five, while clap six functions as the beginning of the figure formed by claps six and seven. Thus, while the fifth and sixth claps are followed by the same duration of silence, they have different figural functions. The figural children were intent on capturing the functions of claps within the rhythm and were unaware of the similarities in duration among claps. Although the stage two figural drawings were more distanced from the experience of clapping than the first figural drawings, the child at this stage was still trying to capture on paper the way it feels to clap this rhythm.

Stage two metric drawings differed fundamentally from figural ones. While stage two figural drawings focused on the function of claps within figures, stage two metric drawings attempted to capture the relative duration of the different kinds of claps independent of their function within a figure. Claps of longer duration were consistently drawn with larger shapes, those of shorter duration with smaller shapes. Thus, children who produced this type of notation were able to distance themselves from the experience of clapping the rhythm, to reflect upon it, and to classify each clap solely by virtue of its duration, ignoring its position within a figural phrase. But while stage two metric drawings captured something that stage two figural drawings ignored, the metric drawings also failed to capture the boundaries between the two repeated rhythmic figures. It may be for this reason that these metric drawings seemed so "wrong" to figural perceivers.

Fully developed stage three metric drawings were produced only by children and adults who had learned to read standard rhythm notation. While stage two metric drawings captured the relative duration of claps, stage three metric drawings captured their exact duration with reference to an unchanging metric, the background beat. Stage three metric drawings were in fact quite similar to standard rhythm notation. The empty circles represented the background beat. When the performed event was equal in duration to the underlying beat, only the beat was shown, as a circle. When the performed event was faster than the background beat, the surface rhythm was shown against the background by placing dots inside the circle. Fully developed metric drawings showed that claps three and four go precisely twice as fast as the background beat. Such drawings are possible only if one steps back from the felt experience of clapping and extracts the underlying beat from the heard surface rhythm.

Metric and figural drawings are fundamentally different. While figural drawings focused on the function of claps within a figure, metric drawings captured either the relative or the exact duration of the different kinds of claps. In their objective focus on measuring, metric children failed to represent the boundary between the two large figures and the different functions of claps five and six. Thus, metric drawings, like standard notation, leave the problem of interpretation, or finding the figures, to the performer. Musicians call this "phrasing." For instance, to perform the phrasing of the nursery rhyme, "One, two, buckle my shoe" might involve clapping the third, fourth, and fifth claps louder or softer than the first two claps, thus indicating that in some sense these three claps form a unit. Phrase markings in a musical score indicate figural groups, but these markings often do not appear in scores. Instead, phrasing is usually considered a matter of the performer's interpretation.

In sum, neither the metric nor the figural drawings captured the two aspects of a fully apprehended rhythm—its discrete, measured events and its continuous, bounded figures or phrases. To children who drew figural drawings, metric drawings seemed wrong, while to those who drew metric drawings, figural ones seemed equally wrong. The ability to perceive figurally appears to be erased after one has learned to read standard notation. Many of the children in this study perceived figurally, as reflected in their spontaneous figural drawings. But once they had mastered the adult symbol system for notating music, this sensitivity appeared to vanish. The person trained in reading standard rhythm notation simply cannot see figural features of the rhythm. Too often, metric notations are considered to be the "right answer," and figural ones are considered less developed. This is unfortunate since figural drawings capture something that is extremely important for musical expression, that is, for "playing musically" and achieving a kind of musical coherence (Bamberger, 1982). Without the figural phrases, a piece has little feeling. But these rules are not notated because they are considered intuitive. Thus, the child's earliest, intuitive understanding of rhythm represents a way of knowing that remains important and ought to be retained even after more formal modes of understanding have been achieved.

Infants come equipped with some basic capacities to perceive music, but also with severe restrictions as compared to what eight-year-olds can perceive. What distinguishes infants' music perception from that of older children is the degree of abstraction entailed. To store a melody or a rhythm, all that the listener must do is attend to the organization of a surface pattern. But to hear mode, tonality, or underlying pulse requires hearing an inferred structure in the mind's ear. Infants cannot go far beyond the musical information given. Nevertheless, despite the inability of infants to go beyond the musical information given, music retains its capacity to exert a powerful emotional effect on them, as testified by the calming effect of lullabies and rhythmic rocking on newborns.

During the years of middle childhood, a sensitivity to more subtle aspects of music develops. Now children can go beyond the information given to infer an underlying structure. Children become able to perceive the organizing effect of tonality and develop an awareness of how a melody ought to sound, preferring tunes that end on the tonic rather than on some other note. They also become able to hear as well as represent the underlying pulse against which the surface rhythm is played.

With age and with training, children appear to lose two important listening skills. The ability to store pitches with precision declines, most probably simply as a result of age; and the ability to perceive figurally declines, as a result of formal training in music notation. Careful intervention may be necessary in order for these skills, so important for musical sensitivity, to be retained.

8 The Birth of Song

As neither the enjoyment nor the capacity of producing musical notes are faculties of the least use to man in reference to his daily habits of life, they must be ranked among the most mysterious with which he is endowed.

—Charles Darwin

Music has no apparent survival value. And yet music has persisted since the time of our first human ancestors. Even infants respond to music, and within a few years they begin to produce music on their own by humming bits and pieces of melodies.

Studies of the ability to produce music have addressed three issues. Investigators have sought to discover whether there is a universal song invented by children no matter what the tonal system of their culture. Researchers have sought to document the stages through which children pass as they come to master their culture's tonal system. And the intriguing issues raised by the existence of musical prodigies have been explored.

A Universal Chant

The drawings of a small Japanese child cannot be reliably distinguished from those of a French child of the same age. Despite the graphic tradition of the culture, children's earliest drawings are based on a small set of schemas which appear to be universal (Kellogg, 1969). Given the fact that tonal systems differ across cultures much more than do graphic systems, one might not expect such striking uniformity in music. Yet there is anecdotal evidence to suggest that the first musical inventions of children are the same in all cultures.

While there is no systematic body of research on similarities and differences among children's songs of different cultures, a number of suggestive observations have been offered. The composer and conductor Leonard Bernstein (1976), for example, in his search for the universal in music, argued that children in different cultures tend to tease each other by singing a repetitive minor third (Fig. 8.1 top). This same descending minor third is used by children when they call to one another (Fig. 8.1 middle). Often children elaborate it by an additional step of a fourth in their singing games (Fig. 8.1 bottom).

Bernstein argued for the existence of a universal chant composed of just these intervals. The reason he gave for the universality of this chant has to do with a universal acoustic aspect of music: the harmonic series. When the note played is C, the first overtone is C one octave higher. The next three overtones, in order of increasing ascendancy, are G, C, and E (Fig. 8.2). The fifth overtone falls in between A and B-flat and was dubbed by Bernstein a "sort-of-A." It is not itself a pitch that is used in Western tonal music, nor are any of the remaining overtones.

The child's chants are composed of either two or three of these different overtones. The fundamental and first overtone are always omitted, left to be "inferred" by the listener, and the next three overtones are sung. If the fundamental is C, therefore, notes G, E, and sometimes a "sort-of-A" are sung. In other words, the universal child's chant is composed of the three new overtones of a note, the ones that are actually different notes from the note itself.

Music of all cultures is inescapably rooted in the acoustic phenomenon of the harmonic series. Thus, it would not be surprising if what is universal in children's songs—the pattern of intervals sung—is based upon this acoustic phenomenon. "Those three uni-

8.1 Children's chants (from top): teasing, based on the interval of a minor third; calling, based on the interval of a minor third; and game, based on the intervals of a minor third and fourth.

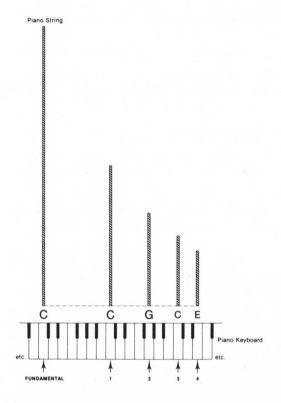

8.2 *First four overtones of the fundamental C.*

versal notes," Bernstein writes, "are handed to us by Nature on a silver platter" (p. 27).

Bernstein has taken a few examples of spontaneous chants and has woven a story that is appealing in its simplicity as well as its explanatory power. But because it is based on anecdotal evidence, this story can only be considered hypothetical. Systematic evidence must be gathered from a number of different tonal cultures in order to determine whether children indeed first invent chants based on such interval relations.

Mastery of the Tonal System

Only a few studies of early musical development have been carried out, and these have all been based on Western children. With these studies, it is possible to begin to chart the stages through which children pass en route to mastery of the Western tonal system. Studies must now be conducted in other cultures in order to discover whether, as in the case of language acquisition, children's musical development passes through a universal series of stages. However, the earlier the stages reported in Western culture, the more likely they are to be maturationally rather than culturally determined.

Song, like language, begins in the crib. Just as infants babble the phonemes of language, they also display an ability to produce the rudiments of music. Infants explore a wide range of pitches (Otswald, 1973), and they can imitate some of the pitches that they hear (Revesz, 1954).

Three-month-olds in one study could repeat the last note of a piece at the correct pitch (Platt, 1933). They were also able to add a subsequent note, usually a quarter-tone lower, thus achieving a kind of ending. One seven-month-old crooned the octave when happy, uttering the upper note with indrawn breath and the lower note with outgoing breath. Another four-month-old imitated a dog's bark to the tune of G-G-C, the dominant and tonic of the C-major scale.

In a more controlled study, infants below six months learned to imitate pitches after a few short training sessions (Kessen, Levine, and Wendrich, 1979). Infants heard pitches from the minor triad D-F-A. They were able to sing back the pitches that they heard about two-thirds of the time, and these imitations were often almost perfectly in tune. Not only did the infants demonstrate the ability to discriminate pitches and match what they produced to what they heard, but they also appeared to enjoy the task and work hard at it.

Thus, there is both anecdotal and experimental evidence that infants possess the rudimentary abilities necessary to make music: they vocalize, they vary pitch, they correctly imitate pitch, and in general they seem fascinated with the sounds of their own voices. Much as two-year-olds scribble, enchanted with both the motoric activity and the marks that their scribbles leave, and much as six-month-olds babble the phonemes of language, infants also produce the rudiments of song. But the ability to create what could be considered a melody, and the ability to confine this melody to one key, develop much later, except in the case of highly gifted children, who can often sing in key even at one year of age.

By the time children reach their first birthday, they begin to construct rudimentary melodies. And by the age of six, children have, on their own, attained the competence level of the untrained adult. During this five-year progression, three hurdles are overcome: pitch comes to be discrete rather than continuous, interval repertoire is increased to include wider intervals, and melodies acquire a tonal organization.

Since the child's earliest spontaneous efforts to make music are in the vocal realm rather than the instrumental, the focus of research has been on the tunes that children sing rather than on their mastery of instruments. Studies of early musical development have often yielded the predictable result that children's performance improves with age. For example, as children get older, the ability to carry a tune increases (Drexler, 1938). Some investigations, however, have sought a more fine-grained view of the stages through which children pass and the strategies that they adopt as they try to produce a melody. In one study, nine first-born middle-class children were intensively observed for five years, beginning at the age of eighteen months (Davidson, McKernon, and Gardner, 1981; McKernon, 1979). This investigation yielded rich information about the development of children's spontaneous songs as well as their acquisition of standard songs.

During the first half of the second year, children sing in continuous rather than discrete pitches. In this sense, children's earliest musical vocalizations are very different from adult music, which is almost always based on discrete pitches. This type of early song does not reflect an inability to sing discrete pitches, for even infants can imitate discrete pitches. Nevertheless, left to their own devices, children first produce melodies that are undulating, continuous blends of pitches. Children typically glide over several pitches in a single breath, allowing no single pitch to be distinguished (Fig. 8.3).

The first milestone in musical development occurs at about eighteen months, when children begin to produce discrete pitches. The intervals present in the songs at this age are extremely narrow. One study found that the earliest intervals produced are minor thirds (Werner, 1961). But another study reported that, while the third is one of the most common early intervals, the very first intervals produced are even smaller (McKernon, 1979). In this study, 43 percent of the intervals sung between seventeen and twenty-three months were seconds. Thus, the pitches of these early intervals are close to each other in register, such as C-B, rather than in

ca. 5 seconds

8.3 Song without discrete pitches, produced by a fifteen-month-old.

8.4 *Song with irregular rhythm, produced by a nineteen-month-old.*

harmonic or key relationships, such as C-G. This finding contrasts with the data on older children's production.

Between the ages of one and a half to two and a half, the most common intervals observed are major seconds, minor thirds, and unisons, followed by minor seconds and major thirds (McKernon, 1979). The most common intervals in songs in all cultures are seconds and minor thirds (Nettl, 1956b). Thus, the very first intervals acquired by children are among those most commonly sung by adults. By the age of two and a half, larger intervals, such as fourths, begin to be heard. Thus, development is characterized by a gradual expansion of interval size (Jersild and Bienstock, 1934; McKernon, 1979; Nettl, 1956a; Werner, 1961).

The contour of the child's first melodies is undulating, rather than primarily ascending or descending (McKernon, 1979). Since undulating melodies are the most common types in adult songs as well (Nettl, 1956b), in this respect too, as with the most common intervals produced, early songs resemble adult songs. However, with respect to rhythm and tonal organization, first songs are very different from those produced by adults.

Early songs lack a consistent rhythmic organization (McKernon, 1979; Moorhead and Pond, 1941). At times, children sing with no underlying beat at all. At other times, small groups of notes possess an underlying beat, but the pattern of beats varies randomly from one group of notes to another (Fig. 8.4).

Long after children have mastered discrete pitches and expanded intervals, their melodies remain atonal. Invented tunes are often chromatic rather than diatonic, that is, they are based on any or all of the notes in an octave rather than on the notes of a particular scale.

One of the earliest signs of incipient tonal sensitivity is found at about three and a half years of age, when for the first time children distinguish between the beginning and ending of a phrase. Their phrases tend to begin on a relatively high note and then descend to, and end on, a lower note. Moreover, when asked to complete a melody, children of this age can end it on the tonic. Thus, some of the rules of tonal melody construction are beginning to be mastered (Davidson, personal communication).

Although children do not reliably sing songs in one key until about six, most are able to do so by the age of three, four, or five (McKernon, 1979). It seems likely that, lacking the adult's years of experience in listening to tonal music, children simply do not consider tonality important. Even the average adult, when humming a familiar tune, does not always sing to a tonal framework. Just as adults, while concentrating on a telephone conversation, create doodles that seem to have little overall integration and thus resemble the drawings of schizophrenics, they also unintentionally create melodies lacking an overall tonal organization.

The child's first spontaneous songs can be characterized as rambling atonal groups of pitches which lack a coherent underlying pulse. Thus, first songs are held together neither by tonal nor by rhythmic organization. As a result, these songs are highly unpredictable and difficult to recall. Moreover, lacking the two musical conventions of tonality and rhythmic organization, invented songs are very different from the songs passed down by Western culture.

In mastering standard songs, children are first able to reproduce only the melody's lyrics. Following this, rhythm is mastered, which is then followed by contour. Only later are children able to produce the correct intervals and to remain within a key (Davidson et al., 1981; Gesell and Ilg, 1946; McKernon, 1979; Revesz, 1954; Teplov, 1966). Adults pass through a similar sequence when learning a new song (Davidson et al., 1981).

A study of one child's acquisition of the alphabet song *ABC* over a number of months showed the child's gradual incorporation of a regular rhythm into the song (Fig. 8.5; McKernon, 1979). In the first rendition of *ABC* at nineteen months, the intervals were narrow and the contour undulating. The rhythmic structure was loose and governed by pauses for breath. This initial version of a standard song was just like the child's spontaneous songs at this age. By twenty-three months, the rhythmic organization of the song had matured: the child now recognized that there must be a longer note at the end of each block of A-B-C, and that the letters L-M-N-O must be sung more quickly. And by twenty-eight months, the child produced the correct rhythmic organization.

Development in the two domains of spontaneous and standard songs is roughly parallel. Structures that appear in children's standard tunes are usually the ones that have appeared in their spontaneous tunes. However, as children get older, their ability to render standard tunes begins to outstrip their spontaneous performance (McKernon, 1979). Although small pieces of the spontaneous tunes of three- and four-year-olds may be tonally organized, spontaneous tunes at this age lack a clear underlying tonal structure. And

8.5 *Rendition of the alphabet song (from top) at nineteen months, twenty-three months, and twenty-eight months.*

children do not yet attempt to repeat their invented songs or teach them to others. However, in their standard tunes, preschool-aged children become able to master a tonal organization which makes their songs both repeatable and memorable.

Thus, mastery of the culture's tonal system is a gradual process. Children must first learn to produce discrete rather than continuous pitches. Next, they must become able to sing wider intervals than those first produced. Finally and perhaps most difficult of all, they must become able to invent or copy tunes that possess a tonal organization.

The Musical Prodigy

All normal children pass through this gradual development sequence. Some children, however, follow another route. In the case of children with exceptional musical talent, these stages may be skipped altogether.

The anthropologist Claude Lévi-Strauss once commented on the astonishing, almost incomprehensible difference between those few geniuses who can compose music and the rest of mankind: "We do not understand the difference between the very few minds that secrete music and the vast numbers in which the phenomenon does not take place, although they are usually sensitive to music ... Theoretically, if not in fact, any adequately educated man could write poems, good or bad; whereas musical invention depends on special gifts, which can be developed only where they are innate" (1970, p. 18). The average adult can, if pressed, write simple poems and stories and draw passable pictures. And like the child, all adults can construct simple melodies in their spontaneous song. However, Lévi-Strauss suggests, the gulf separating the average from the gifted individual is far greater in music than in other artistic domains.

Whether the gulf separating ordinary adults from Shakespeare or Leonardo da Vinci is narrower than that separating them from Mozart is debatable. Whatever the answer, the musical prodigy is clearly differentiated from the rest of the crowd. Without any formal instruction, humans universally master the highly complex structure of language, enabling them to produce an infinite number of novel, grammatical sentences. But only a tiny minority are able to master the structure of music in order to generate novel melodies that exert a mysterious power over the rest of humanity.

Some have suggested that the source of this difference is inborn and neurological. That is, while training and practice may well be important—even necessary—to the development of a musician, these are to little avail if hereditary aptitude is lacking. There is a variety of evidence that musical talent is innate. Most well-known musicians revealed their gift at an extremely early age— often at two or three years of age, and almost always before six. Many sang before they could speak and composed and performed astonishingly well at a tender age. Mozart improvised at four and performed his own music at five. Mendelssohn was even more of a child virtuoso than Mozart. And the violinist Yehudi Menuhin was performing with symphony orchestras at the age of seven.

Another piece of evidence for the claim that musical talent is innate is that early musical talent has appeared in children growing up in families with little or no interest in music (Gardner, 1973a). Moreover, differences among individual children are enormous, and these remain despite training, as Arnold Gesell and Frances Ilg noted: "Individual differences are perhaps more marked in aesthetic expression than in any other field of behavior. Greatest variation is shown in musical ability. A child of 21 months may sing songs accurately while some adults may never attain this ability. Lack of ability, unless dependent upon physical handicaps, may not show itself during the pre-school years, but giftedness in artistic expression may be detected very early" (1946, p. 258).

Exceptional musical ability has often been noted in children who are very deficient in other capacities. Severely retarded children have sometimes been reported to excel in music. One teenager with an IQ of 55 was able to play seven instruments, could compose pieces of high quality, and possessed a repertory of over a thousand songs which he could sing from memory (Gardner, 1973a). Even more frequently, exceptional musical skill has been observed in autistic children, some of whom lack language and all of whom exhibit severe emotional disturbances and avoid social contact (Rimland, 1964). One such child did not begin to acquire language until three but at eighteen months was able to sing entire operatic arias.

The coincidence of extraordinary musical skill and strong cognitive and emotional disturbance suggests that musical ability is a separate and innate neurological capacity requiring comparatively little external stimulation in order to emerge. In this sense, musical ability may be much like the physical ability to walk, or the ability to master the syntax of language. In all these cases, the capacity appears simply to evolve on its own, independent of other abilities. The difference is that the capacity to walk or to speak is possessed by the average human; only the exceptional human possesses the capacity to make music. While both retarded and autistic children often display musical precocity, children such as these do not go on to become great composers and performers as adults. The autistic child able to sing back an operatic aria at a year and a half is thus a far cry from a child prodigy such as Mozart, even though at an early age their talents appear indistinguishable.

There are numerous anecdotal reports about the childhoods of great musicians. One mother of a prodigy reported that at ten months, her child sang to himself on key. The pianist Lorin Hollander, after hearing a Haydn quartet at age three and a half, was able to sing back the entire piece perfectly later that day. And at three, the pianist Arthur Rubinstein listened to his older sister playing the piano and surprised his family by faultlessly playing the pieces she had been practicing (Winn, 1979). Another child at three surprised his parents by singing back an entire symphony after only one hearing (Marshall, 1981).

Despite many anecdotal reports about the childhoods of great musicians, there exist few careful studies of these prodigies. One exception is a psychological study of the Hungarian musical prodigy Erwin Nyireguhàzi (Revesz, 1925). Although Nyireguhàzi did not speak until he was three years old, before the age of one he was able to sing back songs that he heard. At four, before he had any formal lessons, he was able to play on the piano any melody that he happened to hear. By seven, he could transpose pieces to a new key, sight-read difficult pieces, and remember complex Beethoven sonatas. He began to compose at six, and by adolescence his compositions were said to show creative genius. Nor did this early talent wither away, for he went on to become a renowned pianist.

While prodigious musical talent appears very early, it does not mature without strong discipline and formal training. Almost all child prodigies who go on to become great as adults are both nurtured and pushed by their parents and teachers. The gift is never fully developed when it is first observed, and it must be nourished through daily training. Those who continue with music as adults all report having had at least one parent or teacher who cared deeply about their musical talent and who worked with them daily, sitting with them as they practiced and establishing a structure of discipline. The violinist Isaac Stern remarked: "There *has* to be someone pushing, a parent or a teacher. Every one of the kids I've guided has someone like that in their lives, pushing them, sometimes gently, sometimes horribly, sometimes, unfortunately, to the point of driving the child away from music. It's the quality of parental pushing that helps determine the eventual outcome of the prodigy" (Winn, 1979, p. 40).

Musical prodigies are often as hard on themselves as are their parents and teachers (Marshall, 1981). For example, one child refused to go to sleep each night until he had mastered the passage that he had set for himself that day. These children usually have an extraordinary amount of energy. One mother of a prodigy recalled that as a baby, her child seemed never to need a nap.

Thus, extensive work in childhood appears to be necessary in order to become a great musician. Louise Behrend, a music teacher, suggested that this is why so many great musicians have been Oriental or have emerged from the early twentieth century Jewish population of the Russian city of Odessa. Because these two cultural groups are extremely disciplined, they would tend to foster musical ability (Winn, 1979).

But training at any age will not do. The training of a future musician must be initiated at a very young age. Most great performers began taking lessons in their early years. "A string player," the violinist Alexander Schneider stated, "should begin at five years old. Later is too late" (Winn, 1979, p. 40).

Parental discipline is not all that is necessary to the maturation of early talent. A certain personality structure may also be important (Winn, 1979). Children who are rebellious and independent often react negatively to the parental pressure, refusing to practice and thus never going on to become great composers or performers. Those who succeed may well be those who are more compliant.

Exceptional aptitude at a very early age, a parent who nurtures and trains this ability, and a willingness to accept the harsh rigors of hours of daily practice are thus crucial ingredients for becoming a great composer or performer as an adult. In addition, it is necessary to be deeply moved by music. Isaac Stern put this well: "The child must become possessed by music . . . It can happen at any time between the ages of ten or so and fourteen. Suddenly the child begins to sense something happening and he really begins to work . . . At this point the prodigy begins to flower. It happened to me when I was eleven." And the violinist Nathan Milstein remarked: "I didn't like to play the violin when I was a child. I didn't love music. Few children do. But suddenly I changed because I started to love what I play, not just the playing" (Winn, 1979, pp. 40–41).

This deep emotional involvement in music appears not to emerge until adolescence. At that age, musical prodigies undergo a critical period of transition—a shift from a stage of precocious talent to one of more mature, seasoned artistry. Here, according to Menuhin, is where many flounder, unable to make the bridge between sheer mechanical skill and personal expressive style (Winn, 1979). It is at this age that a "midlife" crisis occurs (Bamberger, personal communication). At about fifteen, prodigies begin to ask themselves why they are so involved in music, whether they are simply fulfilling their parents' dreams, or whether this is what they themselves want to do with their lives. Few prodigies escape this crisis, and it is here that many give it all up.

Why more child prodigies are found in the domain of music than in the visual or verbal arts has intrigued and puzzled psychologists. An explanation may be drawn from a comparison with the other areas in which prodigies are most often reported—mathematics and chess. What music, mathematics, and chess all appear to have in common is that they are built upon a highly complex system of formal rules. Mastery of these rules is independent of the knowledge gained from the experience of human relationships. It is difficult to imagine how one could write a good poem, short story, or novel without having weathered important experiences. It is less difficult to imagine how, lacking life's experiences, a young child could compose a sonata.

But perhaps even a child prodigy cannot compose a great piece of music. Great music is not only technically complex but also deeply expressive of human experience. Emotional expressiveness, of course, plays no role in mathematics or chess. The danger for child prodigies in music is that they may acquire technical skill, mastering the formal rules of music, and yet never attain emotional depth. This emotional depth can come only with time and experience and thus will never be found in even the most prodigious child genius. The violin teacher who taught Itzak Perlman, Dorothy Delay, demythologized the child prodigy by insisting: "Children are *never that good*. No matter what you say, a child can never play the way a 45-year-old musician can" (Winn, 1979, p. 41).

The musical skill of the young child who will go on to become a great musician differs from the exceptional musical skill that emerges spontaneously in children who are extremely deficient in other intellectual and emotional capacities. The musical genius of a retarded or autistic child is a preserved island of skill, emerging full-blown entirely independent of general intelligence, normal personality development, training, and other environmental support. In the case of the child destined for musical greatness, the early talent is not fixed and is capable of extensive growth as a result of rigorous training. But it is commonly believed that the most rigorous of training programs will not produce a genius unless the seeds of genius are there to begin with.

This traditional belief that only the talented few can benefit from extensive training to become great as adults has been challenged by the Japanese violinist Shinichi Suzuki (1969). Through a carefully designed method, Suzuki has taught thousands of ordinary Japanese children to play the violin in a manner comparable to that of child prodigies. Suzuki's pupils begin their training as early as the age of two. The first stage of training involves the mothers more than the children. All mothers are given violin lessons, and they practice the violin daily in the presence of the children. The violin is treated as a special object that the children are not yet ready to use or even to touch. As a result, the children naturally begin to yearn to play the violin themselves.

Once it is clear that the children are internally motivated to begin to play, they are given a small violin and are allowed to begin taking lessons. But taking lessons does not mean learning to play from sheet music. The children are never exposed to formal notation. Instead, they are taught to play by ear. Constantly exposed to violin music, even to the extent of wearing tape cassettes in their knapsacks, the children learn to play the music back directly on the violin. Thus, they learn through sheer imitation, and they learn only after they have been "manipulated" or seduced into wanting to learn. The results of this teaching are astonishing: listening to preschool-age Suzuki-trained children playing Mozart, famous musicians have been moved to tears.

Suzuki demonstrated that by clever and rigorous training beginning at an early age, the average child can perform skillfully in music. Most of his students, however, do not go on to become great musicians. And it is entirely possible that those who do are the ones who were exceptionally gifted to begin with. Suzuki himself has not been concerned about this failure to produce a generation of adult Mozarts, because the ultimate goal of his training is the instillation of discipline and the building of character.

Suzuki's pupils can be seen in some sense as the mirror image of autistic and retarded musical prodigies. Both groups of children are superficially indistinguishable in their musical ability, but for Suzuki children, the musical ability is the product of rigorous early training, while for autistic or retarded children, it is an inborn mental ability that emerges on its own without benefit of training. In neither group is there a population of future Mozarts. The genius of an adult Mozart appears to be a productive blend of what is possessed by the Suzuki pupil and the autistic child: inborn giftedness along with grueling training initiated at a very early age. And even this blend is not sufficient: musical genius must await the emotional tie to music that develops only in some, and which does not usually emerge until the adolescent years.

Data from different cultures are not yet sufficient to determine whether there is some natural form of music invented by all children apart from the tonal systems of their cultures. If there is such a universal, it may well be built upon the harmonic series, as Bernstein suggested. The harmonic series is a physical, acoustical phenomenon by which musical notes are related, rather than an organization imposed solely by the mind of the listener. Thus, this acoustical phenomenon could form the basis of the chants that children invent regardless of the tonal system of their culture. But such a possibility cannot be verified until more evidence is amassed about children's early musical inventions in cultures with very different scalar systems.

Much more information is available on how children master the music of Western culture, which makes it possible to chart how the average child becomes able to sing a tune that is held together both tonally and rhythmically. Children begin by singing continuous pitches in very narrow ranges. When they become able to produce discrete pitches, the intervals created are at first extremely restricted, and they expand only gradually. Children progress from producing songs with neither tonal nor rhythmic organization to ones, both invented and learned, that possess such structure.

Comparatively little is known about the musical child prodigy and about what differentiates the prodigy from the average child. Although exceptional musical development is the product of both rigorous training and inborn talent, there is no information on the nature of this inborn talent. Quite probably the brain of the prodigy is neurologically different from that of the average child. But just how different is a question that neuroanatomists are at present unable to answer.

Perhaps the most useful way to think about the problem of musical precocity is by comparing music and language. Both music and language are based upon complex systems of rules. The rule system of language is probably even more complex than that of music. Yet within the space of just a few years, every child in every culture masters a first language. Thus, all children are, by right, linguistic geniuses.

The ability to perform music, either vocally or on an instrument, and the ability to compose music both entail the capacity to master a symbol system. In this sense, music is like language. But while everyone is able rapidly to master the symbol system of language, only the rare individual can accomplish this feat with respect to music. Musical genius seems an awesome capacity precisely because the kind of skill needed to master music is so rarely represented in the human population, whereas the same skill is taken for granted when it comes to language.

FOUR Literature

9 The Literary Experience

My principal idea was to write a book in which the reader would not be reading the text of a novel but a description of the act of reading per se.

—Italo Calvino

In reality, each reader reads only what is already within himself. The book is only a sort of optical instrument which the writer offers to the reader to enable the latter to discover in himself what he would not have found but for the aid of the book.

—Marcel Proust

Imagine a reader who is deeply engrossed in reading Shakespeare's tragedy *Macbeth*. Toward the end of the play, the reader will encounter Macbeth's response to the news of his wife's death:

> Tomorrow, and tomorrow, and tomorrow
> Creeps in this petty pace from day to day,
> To the last syllable of recorded time;
> And all our yesterdays have lighted fools
> The way to dusty death. Out, out, brief candle!
> Life's but a walking shadow, a poor player
> That struts and frets his hour upon the stage
> And then is heard no more. It is a tale
> Told by an idiot, full of sound and fury
> Signifying nothing.

These lines present at least three challenges to readers' understanding. Readers must attend to the sound properties of the words in order to determine their contribution to the meaning of the passage. They must notice when words are used metaphorically, such as "syllable," "candle," and "stage," and try to make sense of these metaphors. Finally, they must achieve some sort of unified understanding of Macbeth's entire speech and, subsequently, of the play as a whole. These tasks are interdependent. For example, sometimes a particular sound quality underscores the sense of a metaphor, or a pattern of sound helps to unify the text. At the same time that readers attempt to understand the text, they also experience an emotional response to what they read—feelings of tension, sorrow, suspense, excitement. These affective responses are elicited by the readers' growing understanding of the lines, and they in turn stimulate further understanding.

Readers must also confront many other aspects of literature. For instance, competent readers are sensitive to the author's style, the mood expressed, the setting, character development, and point of view. However, the sound properties, metaphors, and structure of a literary test are three central components in the experience of reading.

The Sounds of Literature

A literary work is far more difficult to translate than a nonliterary text, such as a newspaper article, book review, or political speech. And of all forms of literature, poetry poses the greatest challenge to translation. One of the reasons that literature always loses something in translation is the near impossibility of preserving the sound properties of a text when it is translated. Yet the sound properties in a work of literature are rarely arbitrary: they are deliberately constructed by the writer to contribute to the meaning expressed by the text. As Pope wrote in *An Essay on Criticism*, "The sound must seem an echo to the sense" (line 365).

Macbeth's speech illustrates how sound can be made to echo sense. The vowel sounds of "tomorrow and tomorrow and tomorrow" express a sense of largeness and thus suggest the endlessness of time. The brevity of the words "struts" and "frets" suggests the brevity of an individual life. And the use of alliteration enhances the memorability of the lines. The phrase "*dusty death*" is much more memorable than the nonalliterative "*musty death*."

The study of the effect of phonetic properties in literary works was pioneered by the linguist Roman Jakobson. For instance, Jakobson (1960) pointed out how sound echoes sense in Edgar Allan Poe's poem "The Raven":

> And the Raven, never flitting, still is sitting, *still* is sitting
> On the pallid bust of Pallas just above my chamber door;
> And his eyes have all the seeming of a demon's that is
> dreaming,

And the lamp-light o'er him streaming throws his shadow
>   on the floor;
And my soul from out that shadow that lies floating on the
>   floor
>>>   Shall be lifted—nevermore!

In this last verse of the poem, some of the words are "chained together" by their sound. For instance, "raven" and "never" are mirror images of each other: the consonantal structure of "raven" is r-v-n; that of "never" is n-v-r. And in the phrase "still is sitting, still is sitting," the sounds *sti* are immediately followed by the same sounds rearranged as *sit*. This type of sound play has effects which extend outside the domain of sound and into the domain of meaning. One of the things this poem is about is the never-ending stay of the raven, and Poe writes about this unending visit with words chained together in sound. Just as the bird is inextricable from the poet's room, so the words are inextricable from each other. Thus, the sense of unendingness is expressed on two levels: on the level of word meaning and on the level of sound. The use of sound properties parallel to the meaning of a line of verse serves to enhance the line's referential meaning.

The use of sound to enhance meaning exists outside of literature as well. One such nonliterary example of these effects is the political slogan "I like Ike" (Jakobson, 1960). This slogan is memorable because the sound of the third word (*Ike*) is totally contained in that of the second word (*like*). This suggests a feeling (*liking*) that totally envelopes its object (*Ike*). Similarly, the first word (*I*) is fully included in the third word (*Ike*), suggesting that the subject (*I*) is enveloped by the beloved object (*Ike*).

Another of Jakobson's examples is the line "I'd walk a mile for a Camel." This is one of the most successful advertising jingles ever invented. The consonantal sounds k-m-l are first formed by "Walk a *mile*" and are then repeated in *"camel."* It is surely for this reason that the phrase has survived long after the advertisement was replaced by new ones. To erase any doubts, consider how much less memorable is the phrase "I'd go a mile for a Kent!" There are other remarkable parallels between the sound effects of poetry and those of the lines invented by Madison Avenue copywriters (Keyser, in press). The most successful and memorable advertising slogans exploit just those kinds of phonetic tricks that poets use.

Meaning in literature is enhanced not only by the interrelationships of sounds but also by the inherent properties of sounds.

Some sounds have large, bright, sharp, penetrating, or glittering qualities; others have small, drab, dull, or soft qualities. When such sounds constitute words that actually refer to things which are bright or sharp or penetrating, they produce a sense of "aptness" in the relationship between the word and what it designates. For instance, consider the Spanish word for pigeon, *paloma*. This word has a gentle, melodic, harmonious sound. Its English equivalent, *pigeon*, has a much more abrupt, prosaic sound. Each name suits its referent well, since the pigeons in Puerto Rico are beautiful, softly colored birds, while most in Boston are drab and gray.

This phenomenon is called phonetic symbolism. Experimental evidence attests to the psychological reality of this phenomenon (Brown, 1958). For instance, English speakers were asked to match two nonsense syllables contrasting in sound, such as *mal* and *mil*, with two objects contrasting along a single dimension, such as a large and small table (Sapir, 1929). The task was to decide which syllable formed the most appropriate name for each table. There was surprising agreement among subjects ranging from eleven years of age to adults. For instance, given *mal* and *mil*, approximately 80 percent of subjects at all ages matched *mal* to the larger table.

One explanation for the consensus that certain sounds are large and others small is physical (Newman, 1933). The experienced "size" of a vowel is related to both the acoustics of the vowel and the articulatory apparatus that produces the vowel. First, vowels have been found to express increasing size in the order: i (as in $\overline{ee}$), e (as in the French *été*), E (as in *pet*), *æ* (as in *pat*), and a (as in German *Mann*). That is, i tends to be associated with the smaller objects, while a is linked with the larger ones. The vowels in this sequence have certain physical properties. They decrease linearly in frequency, which is an acoustic property. Moreover, when uttering each of these vowels in the order of increasing size, the tongue is positioned further and further back in the mouth, and the mouth opens wider and wider. These are physical properties of the speaker's articulatory apparatus. Thus, vowels sound larger to the extent that their frequency is lower, they are produced with the tongue farther toward the back of the mouth, and the mouth is opened wider. Similar physical sources have been found for relationships between consonant and size, and between vowel sound and brightness.

The associations between sound, on the one hand, and size or brightness, on the other, may be rooted in more than physical properties. Another possible explanation is that people learn to associate certain sounds with certain dimensions. Perhaps it is just accidental that in English, most words referring to small objects contain vowels such as *i* (little), while words referring to large objects contain vowels such as *æ* (grand). Studies carried out only with native speakers of English cannot answer this question. To determine whether the link between *æ* and large and *i* and small is natural or arbitrary requires a look at other languages.

In one such study, a list was constructed of antonymic pairs of adjectives, such as *warm-cool* and *heavy-light* (Brown, Black, and Horowitz, 1955). The list was then translated into three unrelated languages: Chinese, Czech, and Hindi. Eighty-five English-speaking adults with no knowledge of these three languages were shown a pair of Chinese words, such as *ch'ung-ch'ing*, along with the equivalent pair in English, such as *heavy-light*. The task was to decide which of the two foreign words, *ch'ung* and *ch'ing*, ought to be translated as "heavy" and which as "light." Given no natural similarities between sound and meaning, people should respond at chance level, correctly translating only about 50 percent of the pairs. In fact, however, for most of the pairs, subjects agreed among themselves on the translation at a level somewhat above chance. That is, they agreed on which of two meanings best fit a certain sound. Moreover, subjects were twice as likely to select the correct as the incorrect meaning. For instance, *ch'ung* was usually correctly paired with *heavy*, and *ch'ing* with *light*. Thus, there seem to be sound-meaning correspondences that cut across historically unrelated languages and which may be natural to the human brain.

The extent to which a universal phonetic symbolism exists should not be overestimated. The subjects agreed with each other at a level only slightly above chance. And when Chinese-Americans who knew little English were asked to match the Czech and Hindi pairs to Chinese pairs, they failed to agree among themselves at a level above chance on the meaning of the foreign words. Yet this extension of the study should perhaps not be used to draw too strong a conclusion, since it included only nineteen subjects. When all the evidence is in, the finding will likely be that some associations of sound and meaning are indeed universal, while others are arbitrarily imposed by a language community (Brown, 1958).

Thus, there may be at least some sound-meaning resemblances that cut across all human languages; and within any given language there is quite a strong consensus about the meanings expressed by certain sounds. These sound-meaning correspondences are not often exploited in ordinary language, where speakers and listeners expect the primary function of words to be referential. But in literature, sound is deliberately made to echo sense. And the evidence indicates that readers have the capacity to recognize the sound-meaning resemblances of literature.

All of the psychological studies of the ability to perceive sound-meaning correspondences have been carried out with words presented out of any literary context. All these studies have used forced-choice tasks to elicit a response. Such studies do not prove that readers, left to their own devices, actually use their ability to perceive sound-meaning links. To answer such a question, it would be necessary to look at readers reading literature. For example, do readers engrossed in *Macbeth* ever notice that the vowel sounds in "tomorrow" express a sense of largeness and thus of unending time? The psychological experiments conducted so far show that readers have the ability to see such a link. But whether they use this ability, or whether perhaps only readers well-versed in literature do so, is not known.

It may well be that such sound-meaning correspondences have an effect even if readers remain unaware of the link. The use of a word with a particular sound may strike readers as apt even if they do not know why. By carefully altering the sounds of a text, substituting "the next day" for "tomorrow," for example, and exploring readers' responses to the original and the altered text, one could begin to determine the impact and appeal of sound-meaning correspondences.

The Nature of Metaphor

Upon learning of the death of his wife, Macbeth says some things that he does not literally mean. He calls for a candle to be put out when he is not referring to a candle but to a human life. And he talks about a stage when he is actually referring to the world. The reader must recognize these usages as metaphorical. If they are taken literally, the text will be misunderstood.

Although associated with literature, metaphors are not limited to literature but also pervade ordinary language (Lakoff and Johnson, 1980). One need only glance at the newspaper to find metaphorical uses of language. Agreements between nations are "cemented," negotiations are "severed," and tensions reach the "boiling point." Consider the *New York Times* quotation of the day for February 7, 1981, delivered by Senator William L. Armstrong: "The inmates have taken over the asylum. The Democrats, who have been telling us that it's all right to raise the national debt, are going to vote against it. And the Republicans, who have told us that it was morally wrong to raise the national debt, are voting for it."

Metaphors are used in everyday conversation to characterize psychological traits. People are described as cold, brittle, or crooked. Auditory adjectives are used to describe colors (*loud, quiet*), and tactile terms are used to describe sounds (*velvety, scratchy*). Metaphors sometimes play an important role in theory building in science (Gruber, 1978; Kuhn, 1979; Turbayne, 1962). For instance, among cognitive psychologists today, the mind is metaphorically characterized as a computer. Conceiving of the mind as a computer may play an important part in furthering understanding of how the mind works (Boyd, 1979).

While metaphors pervade ordinary discourse, they occupy a special role in literature. First of all, though writers vary greatly in the extent to which they make use of metaphor, the sheer frequency of metaphorical usage is greater in literature, especially poetry, than in ordinary language. More important than simple frequency is the fact that the metaphors of ordinary language are for the most part "frozen"; that is, they have been used so much that we know their metaphorical meaning automatically, without ever thinking about their literal sense. Thus, we can know that a "loud color" is a bright color without having to reflect on the relationship between auditory loudness and visual brightness. The metaphors of literature, however, tend to be "novel." To call life a "brief candle" is not part of everyday speech, but a formulation encountered for the first time. Novel metaphors make far more demands on the reader than frozen ones, whose meanings can simply be learned as independent lexical entries.

A metaphor is not simply an ornamental use of language. Nor is it simply a way of saying something that could just as easily have been said literally, for in most cases, paraphrasing a metaphor into literal language alters its meaning. Metaphors serve important and indispensable functions in language and in thought. If people were limited to strictly literal language, communication would be severely curtailed, if not terminated.

Aristotle suggested that we need metaphors to express new insights: "Strange words simply puzzle us; ordinary words convey only what we know already; it is from metaphor that we can best get hold of something fresh. When the poet calls old age 'a withered stalk,' he conveys a new idea, a new fact, to us by means of the general notion of 'lost bloom,' which is common to both things" (*Rhetoric* 1410b, lines 13–18). The literary critic Phillip Wheelwright observed that, "in order to speak as precisely as possible about the vague, shifting, problematical and often paradoxical phenomena that are an essential part of the world, language must adapt itself somehow to these characteristics" (1954, p. 43). It would be impossible to speak of new ideas or insights if language had only fixed, literal meanings. Thus, one function of metaphor is to allow communication of things that cannot be literally expressed. If "brief candle" were paraphrased as "short life," the sense of beauty, intensity, and fragility that is conveyed by likening life to a candle would be lost.

Metaphors serve other functions as well. They are a more vivid and memorable way of capturing meaning than is literal language. The memorability of a metaphor may come about because of a "surprise" factor. As Aristotle noted: "Liveliness if specially conveyed by metaphor, and by the further power of surprising the hearer; because the hearer expected something different, his acquisition of the new idea impresses him all the more. His mind seems to say 'Yes, to be sure; I never thought of that' " (Rhetoric 1412a, lines 19–23).

Metaphors are compact, condensed ways of expressing an idea (Ortony, 1975). Even to begin to capture literally what Macbeth means by referring to life as a "brief candle" would require the use of many more words: life is brief, vulnerable, sputtering, intense, heated, burning, beautiful, and so forth. Thus, metaphors serve important and indispensable functions in language and in thought.

To make a metaphor, words must be used in novel ways. In a metaphor, a word or larger unit of language is used to refer to something that it does not literally denote. By means of this, two elements are equated—the literal referent of the word and the referent to which it is metaphorically applied.

Metaphors link elements that are quite different from each other but are also similar in certain nontrivial respects. When Macbeth calls life a "candle," he joins together two things—human lives and candles—that are different, as they belong to different categories, but also alike, as they are both fragile and transient. These twin criteria of similarity and difference were first described by Aristotle, who observed that "Metaphors must be drawn . . . from things that are related to the original thing, and yet not obviously so related—just as in philosophy also an acute mind will perceive resemblances even in things far apart (Rhetoric 1412a, lines 9–12).

Metaphors can be placed somewhere along a continuum between literal uses of language, on the one hand, and anomalous uses, on the other. To attempt to make a metaphor by linking elements that are "obviously related," to use Aristotle's words, would produce not a metaphor but a statement grounded in literal similarity. Consider two statements taken from one analysis (Ortony, 1979a, 1979b):

(1) Sores are like warts.
(2) Billboards are like warts.

Common sense suggests that there is a difference between these two statements: sores really are like warts, but billboards are not really like warts. The first statement is grounded in literal similarity; the second is grounded in metaphorical similarity.

The difference between these two statements has to do with the relative salience of the properties linking the two terms. In statement 1, highly salient properties of "warts" are also of high salience to "sores." That is, when subjects were asked to list properties of sores and also of warts, they commonly placed "ugly protrusions" high on each list. In statement 2, highly salient properties of "warts" are of low salience for "billboards." When asked to list properties of billboards, subjects most frequently cited "used for advertising," "found by the roadside," and "large." The property "ugly protrusions," which was high on subjects' lists for "warts," was much lower on their list for "billboards."

Thus, when a statement links two elements that share properties important to both, it is generally not a metaphor but a statement of literal similarity. Had Macbeth likened a candle to a torch, it would not have been a metaphor. When statements link elements that share properties of high salience to the second term but of low salience to the first term, a metaphor is born. To return to Macbeth, two salient properties of candles are their impermanence and their fragility. These properties characterize lives also, but they are not the first thing that occurs to someone when thinking about life.

This salience imbalance criterion for metaphor does not apply to all metaphors. Consider the statement "Clouds are cottonballs." Most people would count this as a metaphor, although the properties white, soft, and fluffy are highly salient to the referents of both terms, rather than salient to one and of low importance for the other. Nevertheless, the criterion applies to a large enough body of metaphors to serve as a useful way of beginning to distinguish metaphors from literal similarity statements.

If the salience imbalance is reversed, so that a highly salient property of the first term is matched with a low salient property of the second term, an anomaly results. To say that warts are billboards makes little sense. An anomaly also results if the two terms of a statement share properties of low salience to both. Had Macbeth called life a chair, he would have uttered an anomalous statement. Although both lives and chairs can be said to be sturdy, this property is of low salience to each term. To be sure, it is always possible to come up with some meaning for an anomaly, because any two things are alike in some respects (Fraser, 1979; Goodman, 1972; Pollio and Burns, 1977). However, since the shared properties of the two terms of an anomaly are of low salience for each, the interpretations that subjects come up with often appear contrived. Moreover, while some agreement can be expected as to the meaning of a metaphor, wide disagreement is to be expected given an anomaly, since any two things share many trivial properties.

Similes and metaphors can be considered fundamentally the same, for both are based on nonliteral similarity; their only formal difference is the presence or absence of the word "like." When a metaphor is in the form of "An X is a Y," the first and second terms are called the topic and vehicle, respectively. The set of shared properties between the two terms is called the ground (Richard, 1936). When Macbeth says, "Life's but a walking shadow," he utters a metaphor in such a form. When Macbeth says, "Out out, brief candle," he utters the vehicle and leaves the topic to be inferred; this is called a topicless metaphor. When he says "It is a tale told by an idiot," he creates a whole sentence metaphor, which can be taken either literally or metaphorically (Ortony, 1980). While this sentence has both a topic ("it") and a vehicle ("tale told by an idiot"), "it" is an unspecified term. Thus, if this sentence were in a different context, such as a discussion of a story, it could have an entirely literal meaning. Unlike whole sentence metaphors, metaphors with specified topics and vehicles yield clear falsehoods if taken literally. There are exceptions, such as the statement "That murderer must be an animal," which has both a true metaphorical sense (the murderer is wild and dangerous) and a true literal sense (he is biologically an animal). However, most metaphors with specified topics and vehicles are false if taken literally.

How metaphors convey meaning has been the subject of much dispute. The traditional, common-sense view is that a metaphor is a comparison between two elements, and thus its meaning is yielded by a comparison of its topic and vehicle. Most contemporary theories of metaphor however, adopt an interactionist view (Black, 1962, 1979; Richards, 1936; Wheelwright, 1954). To say that life is a shadow is not simply to compare these two things. Rather, this metaphor invites us to see life as if it were a shadow. While comparison may well be part of the process that we go through in interpreting a metaphor, the meaning of metaphor is quite different from a comparison between two things (Searle, 1979).

According to the interactionist position, topic and vehicle interact to yield a meaning greater than the sum of its two parts: topic and vehicle fuse to form a new whole. This interaction is assumed to occur asymmetrically: that is, the vehicle reorganizes our view of the topic, rather than the reverse. The vehicle selects, emphasizes, and suppresses features of the topic by implying statements about it that normally apply only to the vehicle.

The view that metaphors are not simply comparisons and that the topic and vehicle play different roles has been supported by a number of studies. One piece of evidence that a metaphor invites us to see the topic as the vehicle is that when the positions of topic and vehicle are reversed, a very different statement—either an anomaly or an entirely different metaphor—results (Ortony, 1979a, 1979b). Consider the statements:

(1) Sermons are like sleeping pills.
(2) Sleeping pills are like sermons.

Statement 1 is a perfectly sensible metaphor: a highly salient aspect of sleeping pills, "induces sleep," is applied to sermons, to show that sermons are so boring that they put one to sleep. Statement 2 is an anomaly: the shared property is of low salience to the vehicle, as the sleep-inducing property of sermons is not their most important characteristic, and it is of high salience to the topic.

Consider two other examples:

(1) Surgeons are like butchers.
(2) Butchers are like surgeons.

These statements show that a reversal need not yield an anomaly but may result in a new metaphor. In statement 1, important characteristics of butchers are applied to surgeons, yielding the meaning that surgeons are violent and clumsy. In statement 2, salient properties of surgeons are applied to butchers, yielding the meaning that butchers are precise and skillful. If topic and vehicle played symmetrical roles, as implied by the comparison view, such reversals ought not to alter meaning.

Further evidence for the asymmetrical role of topic and vehicle comes from other studies. People rarely reverse the positions of these two terms in recall (Verbrugge and McCarrell, 1977). After hearing a metaphor such as "Skyscrapers are giraffes," people tend to imagine skyscrapers turning into giraffes; but after hearing "Giraffes are skyscrapers," people imagine giraffes turning into skyscrapers (Verbrugge, 1980). And the rated similarity of the two elements of a metaphor is affected by which one is placed first as the topic and which is placed second as the vehicle. For instance, the rated similarity of rabbits to children differed depending on whether subjects had heard "Children skipping rope are like rabbits" or "Rabbits are like children skipping rope" (Harwood and Verbrugge, 1977).

The asymmetry of metaphoric statements obtains in nonmetaphoric comparisons as well (Tversky, 1977). Normally people place in the first position the term that refers to the most important or prototypical element. Thus, it is customary to say "China is like North Korea" rather than "North Korea is like China." Because China is the most important communist nation of the Orient, it thus becomes the standard against which smaller communist nations are compared.

Importance is not all that determines which term is placed first. In certain cases, the degree to which the term refers to something close to "human" is also a determinant (Connor and Kogan, 1980). In one study, subjects were shown paired pictures of objects and asked to construct metaphorical sentences in which the two depicted objects were equated. For example, shown a picture of an old man along with one of a withered tree, subjects could respond by saying "The old man is a withered tree" or "The withered tree is an old man." Most subjects preferred the former order. There may be a tendency to make the object that is more like us the topic rather than the vehicle. Animate things are more like humans than inanimate objects; other humans are more like us than other animals. Thus, the asymmetry of metaphors may derive from the way we view the objects under comparison. Those with more importance, or those felt to be more like ourselves, are the focus of the comparison. The lesser term is used as a way of subtly reshaping our view of the dominant term. Paradoxically, however, while the topic is the focus of attention, the vehicle does the bulk of the work.

Processing and Remembering Metaphors

Whether metaphorical language requires a special kind of processing has been the subject of much controversy. The claim that metaphors make special processing demands stems from the assumption that when we hear a sentence, we initially try out a strictly literal interpretation. We then check this interpretation to see if it makes sense within the context in which it is heard. If it does, we stick with it; if it does not, we go on to try out a metaphorical interpretation. According to such a model, there are three stages in the processing of a metaphor: literal interpretation, recognition that it makes no sense in the context, and rejection of it in favor of a metaphorical interpretation. These stages are allegedly passed through in a matter of milliseconds. Moreover, these steps are not accessible to conscious awareness.

According to this three-stage model of metaphoric processing, the reader of Shakespeare momentarily takes *Macbeth* to be saying that life is, quite literally, a shadow. This interpretation is rejected because it is absurd: life is a very different order of thing from a shadow caused by an obstruction in front of a light source. The reader then attempts a metaphorical solution and comes up with something that makes sense.

If this model is correct, metaphors ought to require more processing time than nonmetaphors. This claim was put to the test in a study using pairs of vignettes ending with the same sentence (Ortony, Schallert, Reynolds, and Antos, 1978). The final sentences in each pair made sense according to either a literal or a metaphorical reading. In one case, the paragraph called for a literal reading of the final sentence; in the other case, the metaphorical meaning made sense. In half of the items, the target sentences were preceded by only one sentence; in the other half, they were preceded by several sentences.

If it is natural to adopt a literal interpretation first and to arrive at a metaphorical interpretation only as a second step, then those sentences whose contexts required a metaphorical reading should have taken longer to understand. This was indeed the case when the target sentences followed 1-sentence contexts. However, in longer contexts, no difference was found in terms of speed of understanding. Thus, when metaphors are encountered in sufficient context, which is how they are encountered in both literature and ordinary language, they seem to be interpreted directly. The listener or reader does not have to attempt and then discard a literal interpretation but may go straight for a metaphorical reading. This study counts as evidence against the three-stage model, which suggests that we always process a metaphorical sentence literally before we process it metaphorically.

The three-stage model also suggests that arriving at literal interpretations is automatic, whereas moving to a nonliteral reading is a matter of choice. Another study, however, found that we can no more inhibit a metaphorical interpretation than we can a literal one (Glucksberg, Gildea, and Bookin, in press). Subjects had to listen to a series of sentences and decide for each sentence whether it was literally true or false. Of the false sentences, some were false both literally and metaphorically, such as "Some roads are birds." Others were literally false but metaphorically true. For instance, the sentence "Some jobs are jails," while literally false, is metaphorically true, since some people are trapped in their jobs.

The question was to determine how long it took to decide that these sentences were false. The three-stage model predicts no difference in speed of deciding that both sentences were literally false. According to this model, the subjects should have tried out a literal interpretation, seen that it was false, and responded "false." They need never have considered the metaphorical reading of the sentences, because they were not trying to make sense of the sentences but were simply deciding on their literal truth. In fact, however, when a metaphorical interpretation of a literally false sentence was available, subjects took longer to decide that the sentence was false. This showed that they must have accessed the metaphorical interpretation. The truth of the metaphorical reading interfered with the conclusion that the sentences were literally false. Thus, subjects were unable to ignore a metaphorical interpretation even when such an interpretation was irrelevant to, and interfered with, the task at hand.

Both of these studies failed to support the three-stage model of metaphor processing and suggested instead that arriving at nonliteral meanings requires no more effort than arriving at literal meanings. Studies of how people process idioms, such as "kick the bucket," and indirect requests, such as "Can you tell me what time you close?" have further supported this view. Idioms are processed as fast as comparable nonidiomatic phrases (Swinney and Cutler, 1979). And the literal and contextually anomalous meanings of indirect requests are often not accessed at all (Clark, 1979).

One possible reason why there is no difference in the speed of processing metaphorical and literal language is that even literal language requires going beyond the information given (Rumelhart, 1979; Saddock, 1979). The reading selected depends upon the context in which the sentence occurs. To illustrate the similarity between metaphorical and ordinary language, consider the sentences:

(1) Here is the bank.
(2) Would you mind passing the salt?
(3) Don't wear your red sweater.
(4) It went under that one.
(5) This is a dog (pointing to a black and white cartoon of a dog).

None of these sentences is metaphorical. Yet each requires a certain amount of active construction and inference in order to be understood. In sentence 1, we must decide, given the context, whether the reference is to a river bank or a money bank. In sentence 2, we must ignore the literal sense of the question and recognize that we are being asked to do something. In sentence 3, the listener has the choice of taking the request literally by doing nothing, or inferring that it means to wear something besides the red sweater (Eson and Shapiro, 1980). In sentence 4, the listener must determine the referents of "it" and "that," which have an infinite range of possibilities in both cases. Only context can disambiguate the statement. And in sentence 5, the listener must realize that the referent is not a real dog.

These examples all require going beyond what is literally stated and constructing the speaker's meaning and intention by attending to the linguistic and extralinguistic context. Thus, one might conclude that there is no fundamental difference between metaphorical and literal language. But so extreme a conclusion would be unwarranted. When metaphors occur in a rich context, and when these metaphors are fairly simple, they may well be understood as quickly and automatically as are literal statements. But when metaphors occur out of context, so that it is not immediately clear whether a literal or a metaphorical reading is called for, they require harder work. And when metaphors are complex, such as those found in poetry, they undoubtedly require a great deal more work. This is attested to by the fact that experts in literature are so often stymied by a metaphor, write pages about its possible meaning, and heatedly disagree with each others' interpretations (Vayo, 1977). Although some kinds of literal language, such as dense philosophical passages, can be as difficult to interpret as obscure metaphors, there is little doubt that complex metaphorical language requires a great deal more work than ordinary literal prose.

When we store a metaphor in memory, we do not store it verbatim. Nor do we store the topic and vehicle alone. Rather, we appear also to store the ground of the metaphor.

This was demonstrated by a study in which subjects were given a series of metaphors to recall, such as "Billboards are warts on the landscape" (Verbrugge and McCarrell, 1977). Subjects were then given one of three types of memory prompts: a topic (billboard), a vehicle (wart), or a ground (ugly protrusion on a surface). Not only did the first two types of prompts prove effective, but of more interest is the fact that the ground facilitated recall. Yet the ground contained no words that appeared in the original sentence. The ground specifies a relationship in which both billboards and warts engage: both protrude unattractively from some kind of surface. The fact that stating this relationship facilitates recall demonstrates that metaphor understanding involves the extraction and storage of an abstract relation between topic and vehicle.

Even stronger evidence that metaphors are stored abstractly came from the finding that nonlinguistic representations of the ground are effective memorial aids (Verbrugge, 1974). A metaphor about a tyrant squashing a victim was recalled by looking at an abstract diagram of a large shape on top of a small one. Even musical representations of grounds proved effective. Thus, at least some kinds of metaphors are stored in a highly abstract, modality-free language. The fact that metaphors are stored in this way suggests that linguistic metaphors are only one form of a metaphorical process that cuts across modalities of communication.

The Quality of a Metaphor

When Macbeth calls life a "brief candle," he has uttered an apt and appealing metaphor. Suppose that instead of likening life to a candle, Macbeth had called it a "brief story." Such a usage would also be metaphorical. And it even captures some of the same meaning—that life is transient. Nevertheless, it is much less appealing.

Whether there are rule-governed differences between "good" and "bad" metaphors is an extremely difficult question to answer. Many investigators feel that the laws which determine the quality of a metaphor, or of any work of art, can never be discovered. Because metaphors vary along innumerable dimensions, a particular metaphor may be good, or bad, for any one of many reasons. Each case, therefore must be judged on its own.

Some researchers disagree, however, and have sought to discover what determines quality in a metaphor. One study attempted to determine just how much and what kind of difference between topic and vehicle results in a good metaphor (Tourangeau and Sternberg, 1981). It did so by examining two ways in which topic and vehicle differ. First, there is the distance between the topic and the vehicle, called "between subspace distance." In "A wildcat is a hawk among mammals," the between subspace distance is small: a wildcat and a hawk are "close" in distance because both are animals. In "A wildcat is an ICBM among mammals," however, the between subspace distance is large, since a wildcat and an ICBM are two very different things: one is an animal and the other is a machine. Second, there is the distance between the two terms' relative positions within their respective domains, called "within sub-space distance." In both of the previous metaphors, within sub-space distance is small: hawks are aggressive predators among birds, wildcats are aggressive predators among mammals, and ICBM's occupy the same position with respect to machines. However, in the metaphor "A wildcat is a robin among mammals," the within subspace distance is large: wildcats are predators among mammals; robins are not predators among birds.

One hypothesis of the study was that good metaphors have large between subspace distances but small within subspace distances. In other words, the topic and vehicle ought to be drawn from very different domains, but they should play a similar role within their domains. Another hypothesis was that the aptness or appeal of a metaphor differs from its comprehensibility: unlike apt metaphors, a metaphor is comprehensible to the extent that both within and between subspace distances are small.

To test these hypotheses, sets of four metaphors were constructed, with the metaphors varying according to these two types of distance, as in the set:

(1) A wildcat is a hawk among mammals (between subspace distance small, within subspace distance small).

(2) A wildcat is a robin among mammals (between subspace distance small, within subspace distance large).

(3) A wildcat is an ICBM among mammals (between subspace distance large, within subspace distance small).

(4) A wildcat is a blimp among mammals (between subspace distance large, within subspace distance large).

Subjects were asked to rank the metaphors on scales of both comprehensibility and aptness. The results supported the hypotheses. Metaphor 1 was rated the most comprehensible (both distances are small), and metaphor 4 was rated the least comprehensible (both distances are large). The most apt or appealing image was metaphor 3, since wildcats and ICBM's come from very different domains but play similar roles within each domain.

This study was only a first stab at understanding what makes a metaphor appealing. The metaphors tested are quite distant from the great metaphors of literature. And the items used seem more like analogies than metaphors. It is not known whether the findings can be extended to different kinds of metaphors, such as ones that involve the metaphorical use of verbs or adjectives. Moreover, what effect different types of context have on the judged quality of metaphors is not known. Nevertheless, this study offered a glimpse of one way to go about the difficult task of analyzing quality in a work of art.

While the distance between topic and vehicle in this study was varied, the ground linking them was held constant. Another study of metaphoric appeal varied this factor by examining preferences for different types of ground (Silberstein, Gardner, Phelps, and Winner, in press). Subjects were given a topic and a choice of several vehicles with which to link the topic. Each topic-vehicle link was based on a different type of ground. The vehicles were linked to the topic on the basis of a static, perceptual property (shape or color), a dynamic perceptual property (movement or sound), an abstract, nonperceptual property (harshness, explosiveness, impermanence), or some combination of two properties. For instance, in one item, the topic "volcano" could be linked to the vehicles "a bright fire truck" (color), "a roaring lion" (sound), "a whale spouting water" (movement), "a very angry man" (nonperceptual, as both are exploding, out of control), and "tomato sauce boiling over a pot" (combination of color and nonperceptual grounds). The nonperceptual links were, by their nature, less immediately obvious than the perceptual ones.

Adults found the combination grounds more appealing than those based on only one property. This proved true even though combination grounds included all possible kinds of grounds. Of the single grounds, nonperceptual links were preferred above all perceptual links. And of the perceptual links, dynamic ones (movement and sound) were preferred over static ones (color and shape). These findings suggest that good metaphors are based on more than one link between a topic and a vehicle. Moreover, good metaphors are likely to be based on links that are subtle and not immediately obvious, since nonperceptual grounds were preferred. Finally, good metaphors are more apt to be based on dynamic, changing properties of two elements, such as the way they move or the sound they make, rather than on fixed properties, such as their shape and color.

Interpreting the Text

The central problem facing readers when they encounter a literary metaphor is to resolve the tension created by the incompatibility of the topic and vehicle. Once the metaphor is understood, the incompatibility and resultant tension dissolve. A similar problem faces readers when they encounter the text as a whole. As readers begin *Macbeth*, they do not yet have a sense of its structure. Nor do they yet have a fully formed interpretation of the play. The text can be thought of as a puzzle that must be solved. As readers move through the play, they begin to grasp its structure, and they begin to achieve a sense of the text as a whole. Once they arrive at some kind of understanding of the text, the tension created by the text-as-puzzle dissipates.

Just how readers go about interpreting the text is a subject of controversy. Most investigators, however, agree about one thing: the evidence from different kinds of studies consistently supports a view of readers as extremely active. The text is not a vessel of meaning which readers receive. Rather, readers construct the text (Iser, 1978; Rosenblatt, 1978). In order to experience a comprehensible, unified text, readers must bring a number of assumptions to the text. As soon as they begin to read, they must make hypotheses and inferences about the meaning of the sentences. And they must often discard initial hypotheses in favor of new ones as they read on.

The literary critic Louise Rosenblatt (1978), in an investigation of how readers make sense of texts, gave her graduate students in literature a number of texts to read. The students were not told who the texts were by, and they were asked to write down their responses as soon as possible after they began to read. One of the texts was a quatrain by Robert Frost, "It Bids Pretty Fair":

> The play seems out for an almost infinite run.
> Don't mind a little thing like the actors fighting.
> The only thing I worry about is the sun.
> We'll be all right if nothing goes wrong with the lighting.

Readers initially hypothesized that the poem was about making a movie or a play, in such comments as: "This seems to me to be bits of conversation between people who are interested in movie making," or "Perhaps the director is writing to the producer." For most readers, the third line, with its reference to the sun, forced a rejection of this initial hypothesis. This word led readers to question what kind of a play would have sun for lighting and to have second thoughts, such as: "The third line seems most confusing. If I stick to my theory of producer talking to backers, it really makes no sense." As readers became aware of the need for a new hypothesis, some began to read the stage as a metaphor for the world and the actors as a metaphor for humankind. They then proceeded to try to find a metaphorical meaning for "sun." Some concluded that it referred to moral and spiritual guidance. One thought that it might stand for the atomic bomb.

These responses are not finished interpretations but rather initial stages in the readers' attempts to construct finished interpretations. The hundreds of such protocols collected by Rosenblatt support a view of readers as active. Readers do not passively register a readily accessible meaning. Rather, they actively build up the meaning of the text for themselves. Doing this requires that they draw upon their general knowledge about the world and their past experience with literature. They use the text as a source of hypotheses and then as a check against these hypotheses. Constructing the meaning of a text is a self-corrective process. Rather than taking a linear route from the beginning to the end of a text, readers shuttle back and forth, often starting over entirely, and rejecting hypotheses about an early line in light of a later line.

This view of the constructive role played by readers is one of the few points of agreement among those who have studied how readers make sense of texts. Disagreements arise on two issues: whether the readers' task is to grasp the structure of the text or the structure of their own moment-to-moment experiences as they read the text, and whether all readers experience a text in the same way or differently.

Grasping the Text

Investigations of readers' grasp of a text have, for the most part, been carried out by literary critics. In one domain, however, psychologists have taken the lead. During the past decade, experimental psychologists of a cognitive stripe have turned their attention to how readers process and store simple stories.

While stories vary widely in style and content, often they share the same kind of internal structure. Aristotle maintained that a narrative plot should have for its subject "a single action, one that is a complete whole in itself, with a beginning, middle, and end" (*Poetics*, 23, 1459a, 18–20). Jakobson (1945), comparing the structural regularity of folk stories with the universality of laws that cut across human languages, concluded that literature, like language, is a system that is ordered and governed by universal laws.

As a result, literary critics known as structuralists have analyzed the common structure shared by a wide variety of stories (e.g. Prince, 1973; Propp, 1968; Todorov, 1971). Typically, a story or a traditional novel begins as the protagonists face some sort of problem or challenge. For example, Hansel and Gretel are thrown out of their home into the forest and get lost; Macbeth encounters the three witches who prophesy that he will become king. As a result of this event, the protagonist forms a goal: Hansel and Gretel's goal is to return home; Macbeth's goal is to become king. The rest of the narrative relates the protagonists' attempts to achieve this goal. The narrative concludes with some kind of resolution of the problem with which the story began: Hansel and Gretel return home; Macbeth becomes king but must pay for it with his life. This narrative structure is not exclusive to literature. It is also found in television dramas, comic strips, and movies, as well as outside the fictional domain altogether, in journalism, history, and biography. What distinguishes fictional from nonfictional narratives is not necessarily their structure but rather the various devices by which fictional narratives signal the reader that the narrative is imaginary.

Psychologists have attempted to formalize the structure of typical narratives by writing "story grammars" (Mandler and Johnson, 1977; Thorndyke, 1977), just as linguists have done with sentences. Story grammars are meant to capture the regularities of structure that cut across a wide range of stories. The grammars formulated by different psychologists differ slightly among themselves, but they all share the same basic structure. One of the first story grammars, devised by David Rumelhart (1977), specified that a story has a three-part internal structure: an initiating event that causes the protagonist to formulate a goal, an attempt by the protagonist to achieve the goal, and an outcome of the attempt. The second part of a story, the attempt to achieve a goal, can be further broken down into four parts: the protagonist selects a strategy that might lead to the goal; the strategy has certain preconditions that the protagonist must fulfill; the protagonist then applies the strategy; and a consequence results. This structure can become increasingly complicated, because to achieve the main goal the protagonist may need first to fulfill many preconditions. And the preconditions can themselves have preconditions. For instance, to become king, Macbeth must first commit murder. But to achieve this outcome, he must first meet still another condition, to convince someone to carry out the murders. Thus, a story may involve a large set of embedded goals which guide the protagonist's actions. For each subgoal, the attempt to meet it breaks down into the same four parts. Thus, the structure of a story can have many levels.

In a diagram of this structure, the major parts of a story are shown at the top, and the parts of lesser importance are located lower down, showing that the protagonist's main goal is more central to the story than any of the subgoals set up in order eventually to achieve the main goal. Consider the text of a story that Rumelhart wrote, "The Old Farmer and His Stubborn Donkey," based on an English folktale:

(1) There was once an old farmer who owned a very stubborn donkey.
(2) One evening the farmer wanted to put his donkey in its shed.
(3) First, the farmer pulled the donkey,
(4) but the donkey wouldn't move.
(5) Then the farmer pushed the donkey,
(6) but still the donkey wouldn't move.
(7) Finally, the farmer asked his dog to bark loudly at the donkey and thereby frighten him into the shed.
(8) But the dog refused.
(9) So then, the farmer asked the cat to scratch the dog so the dog would bark loudly and thereby frighten the donkey into the shed.
(10) But the cat replied, "I would gladly scratch the dog if only you would give me some milk."
(11) So the farmer went to his cow
(12) and asked for some milk to give to the cat.
(13) But the cow replied, "I would gladly give you some milk if only you would give me some hay."
(14) Thus, the farmer went to the haystack
(15) and got some hay.
(16) As soon as he gave the hay to the cow,
(17) the cow gave the farmer some milk.
(18) Then the farmer went to the cat
(19) and gave the milk to the cat.
(20) As soon as the cat got the milk it began to scratch the dog.
(21) As soon as the cat scratched the dog, the dog began to bark loudly.
(22) The barking so frightened the donkey that
(23) it jumped immediately into its shed.

The story begins as the farmer formulates a goal: to get the donkey into the shed. The rest of the story describes his attempt to attain that goal. The attainment of this goal requires that a subgoal be achieved: to make the dog bark. To get the dog to bark, the farmer must achieve another goal: to get the cat to scratch the dog. And so on. A tree structure diagram of this story can be constructed to reveal how all of the story components are related to each other, and which parts of the story are central (those higher up in the tree) and which are subsidiary (those lower down; Fig. 9.1). Such a tree structure specifies each logical part of the story, including parts that are not stated but which can be inferred.

Story grammar theorists have investigated whether such a skeletal structure has any psychological reality . Do we experience stories that fit this structure as "well-formed," and ones that violate it as "deviant"? If a story does not involve a goal to be achieved, do we still call it a story? And if we have some sense of the structure of a well-formed story, do we use this structure to make sense of and recall a story?

One of the methods used to answer these questions is to read a story to subjects and then ask them either to summarize it or to recall it later. If the tree structure grammar of the story is psychologically real, then people should be more likely to omit lower-level than higher-level branches of the tree. For instance, they ought to be more likely to forget one of the farmer's subgoals, such as getting milk for the cat, than his main goal, getting the donkey in the shed.

Another way to determine the psychological status of a story grammar derives from tests of the psychological reality of sentence grammar. Researchers read people "ungrammatical" stories, whose parts have been scrambled so that they do not adhere to the rules of the story grammar. If the grammar is psychologically real, listeners ought to feel that there is something wrong with the incomplete or scrambled story. Moreover, they may inadvertently reorder it correctly as they retell the story. Thus, just as people find a sentence such as "The boy ball the hits" ungrammatical and difficult to recall verbatim, people also ought to find a scrambled story "wrong" and difficult to recall precisely.

Studies testing these predictions with Rumelhart's story grammar show that when people are asked to summarize and recall well-formed stories, they forget or omit lower-order but not higher-order information. When asked to remember "The Old Farmer and His Donkey," for example, subjects always recalled sentences 2 and 23, which are at the top level in the diagram, while sentences 14 and 15 at the bottom level appeared in only half of the remembered stories. Eighty percent of the sentences at level 3 or above on the tree were recalled, while only 57 percent of those below level 3 were recalled. The deletion of lower-order information occurs even when memory is controlled (Bower, 1976). When two statements were remembered with equal frequency as measured by recall, the statement appearing at the higher level was more likely to appear in a summary.

When stories were read in scrambled order, people retold the

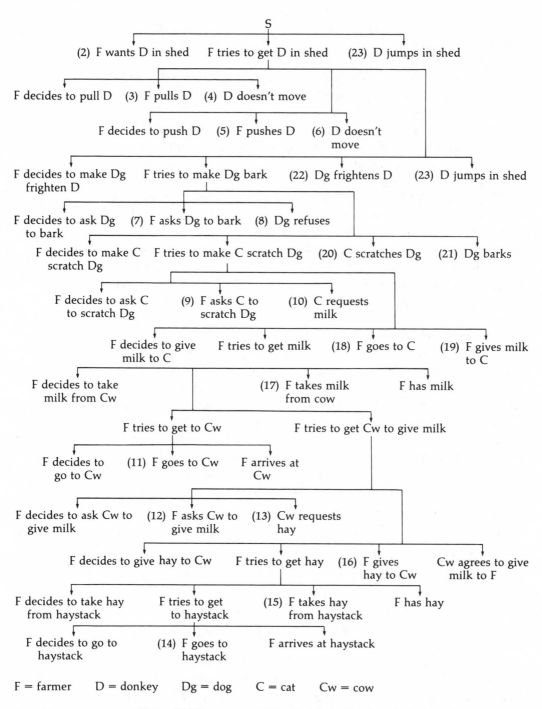

S

(2) F wants D in shed   F tries to get D in shed   (23) D jumps in shed

F decides to pull D   (3) F pulls D   (4) D doesn't move

F decides to push D   (5) F pushes D   (6) D doesn't move

F decides to make Dg frighten D   F tries to make Dg bark   (22) Dg frightens D   (23) D jumps in shed

F decides to ask Dg to bark   (7) F asks Dg to bark   (8) Dg refuses

F decides to make C scratch Dg   F tries to make C scratch Dg   (20) C scratches Dg   (21) Dg barks

F decides to ask C to scratch Dg   (9) F asks C to scratch Dg   (10) C requests milk

F decides to give milk to C   F tries to get milk   (18) F goes to C   (19) F gives milk to C

F decides to take milk from Cw   (17) F takes milk from cow   F has milk

F tries to get to Cw   F tries to get Cw to give milk

F decides to go to Cw   (11) F goes to Cw   F arrives at Cw

F decides to ask Cw to give milk   (12) F asks Cw to give milk   (13) Cw requests hay

F decides to give hay to Cw   F tries to get hay   (16) F gives hay to Cw   Cw agrees to give milk to F

F decides to take hay from haystack   F tries to get to haystack   (15) F takes hay from haystack   F has hay

F decides to go to haystack   (14) F goes to haystack   F arrives at haystack

F = farmer   D = donkey   Dg = dog   C = cat   Cw = cow

9.1 *Tree structure of "The Old Farmer and His Stubborn Donkey," showing how the parts of the story are related. Numbers refer to sentences in the story; unnumbered phrases refer to aspects of the story that are logically implied.*

story "correctly," both when summarizing the story immediately after hearing it and when recalling it later. That is, their summaries and retellings were more "grammatical" than the story that they heard. For instance, in one experiment "The Old Farmer" was told in "ungrammatical" form. Sentence 21, "As soon as the cat scratched the dog, the dog began to bark loudly," was changed to read "The dog began to bark loudly." This line was then placed between sentences 15 and 16, which describe the farmer getting the hay. Thus, the key element was moved from its position as the climax of the story to an earlier point. When asked to recall the story in this form, eight out of nine people restored sentence 21 to its proper location. Reorganizing the story was most likely inadvertent, since people were probably motivated to recall accurately.

In similar findings, when a story contained a sentence inconsistent with the grammar, that sentence was often deleted in recall (Bransford and Johnson, 1973). When stories had surprise endings, they were distorted by both deletion and addition in order to render the ending more probable (Spiro, 1977). And when the overriding goal of "The Old Farmer" was deleted so that it lacked a theme, the story was rendered less comprehensible and proved more difficult to recall: while 80 percent of the propositions of the original story were recalled, only 58 percent of the propositions in the themeless story were recalled (Bower, 1976). In the original story, each action is sensibly connected to all of the other actions, and all are connected to the protagonist's main goal of getting the stubborn donkey into its shed. In the themeless story, however, the reader is confronted with a series of arbitrary actions. Just as it proves easier to recall a ten-word sentence than ten disconnected words, it is also easier to recall a set of propositions united by a theme than a set of disconnected statements.

These studies of story understanding suggest that people have internalized the typical structure of a story. This internalized grammar is then used to understand and remember stories. Stories are distorted in comprehension and recall to fit the internalized story grammar: aspects of a story that do not fit the grammar are modified or deleted so that a good fit will be attained.

This internal representation is probably the result of having read many stories and extracted their common structure. Whether the human brain is innately predisposed to extract the kind of conflict-resolution structure that characterizes the typical story, or whether it could just as easily extract an entirely different kind of structure, is not known. However, the fact that humans have always invented stories which begin with a problem that is ultimately resolved, whether successfully or unsuccessfully, suggests that there is something natural about this structure.

The fact that we use an internalized story grammar in order to understand stories means that we use what is called "top-down" processing in order to make sense of stories. That is, our generalized story grammar allows us to generate hypotheses about what will happen next in any specific story. Thus, if we hear the beginning of a story in which a problem is introduced, we expect that the protagonist will attempt to solve the problem. And if the story does not explicitly say that the hero is trying to solve the problem, we infer that his actions are attempts at a solution. Of course, we also use other kinds of knowledge in order to make sense of a story. For example, we use our real world knowledge, especially our knowledge of what people are like. Thus, if someone does something aggressive to a character, we expect the character to react angrily.

A story grammar should be appreciated for what it is and no more. While it captures the plot structure of a story, it embodies little else. For instance, it tells nothing about the point of view from which the story is written. Yet stories differ in this respect, since they can, for instance, be told through the eyes of an omniscient author, or through the biased and limited perspective of one of the characters, and a story grammar is not able to capture this difference. Similarly, a story grammar does not capture differences in setting or mood, nor does it tell us much about character development. Because these aspects of a narrative are also important to understanding a story, other methods will have to be used to assess their effect on the reader's response.

Studies so far have employed only brief, simple stories with relatively undeveloped characters, constructed upon a problem-solving motif. Thus, the specific findings cannot be generalized to other forms of literature, to texts built upon different structures, or even to modern forms of stories that reject the traditional problem-solving structure. The findings tell nothing about understanding a poem, although they may be relevant to the understanding of traditional plays, novels, and short stories.

The story grammar approach, however, can be applied to any class of texts which share a general structure. Thus, the approach could even be applied to sonnets. What is necessary is to analyze the structure of the text and then determine whether this structure is psychologically real and whether the reader uses it to generate hypotheses about what is coming next and to integrate the text.

One fundamental problem with the story grammar paradigm is that one might well be able to predict and explain the results from the various studies of story recall without the use of a grammar at all. All the findings boil down to the claim that, after listening to many stories, we extract a prototypical story structure. We use this structure as we encounter each new story, and we filter a new story through this structure. Those aspects of the new story that do not fit the prototypical structure are likely to be forgotten by us, just as we are likely to forget the details and remember only the skeletal outlines of a narrative. This much seems true. But we could probably arrive at this conclusion by writing very general story grammars—such as problem leads to goal, which leads to subgoals, which lead to resolution—rather than the highly elaborate tree structures that have been constructed.

Grasping the Reading Experience

Story grammar theory assumes that in understanding a text, the reader's most important task is to grasp its overall grammar or structure. The structure is in the text; readers internalize this structure as a result of reading or hearing countless stories, and they go on to use this structure in order to organize and unify new stories that they encounter. The view that the text contains a structure which the reader must ferret out is shared by formalist schools of literary criticism, which regard the meaning of a text as embedded in the text, where it remains for the clever reader to discover.

In direct opposition to this view is the claim that the meaning of a text resides not in the text but in the reader's moment-to-moment experience of the text. The text acquires significance only in the context of being read. The reader is thus granted more of a center-stage role in constructing the meaning of a text.

This radical view has been championed by the literary critic Stanley Fish (1980), who argued from his own experience of reading, on the assumption that his own experience was not idiosyncratic but was representative of how any "informed reader" reads. Fish (p. 25) cited the following line from Milton's *Paradise Lost*: "Nor did they not perceive the evil plight." This sentence, with its double negative, is difficult to understand. The experience of reading it is halting. "Did they or did they not perceive the evil plight?" we ask. Because we cannot decide with certainty, our confidence in our powers of understanding is shaken. Later in the poem we come to discover that the answer is that they did and they did not perceive the evil plight: they perceived it physically but were blind to the moral significance of what they perceived.

Our temporary inability to decide on the meaning of this line is part of the line's meaning, according to Fish. *Paradise Lost* is difficult to read, and it is about the weakness of human powers. By forcing readers to become aware of the limitations of their powers of interpretation, Milton is expressing part of the meaning of his poem. Milton might instead have written the line "They did perceive the evil plight," paraphrasing the original line so that the two negatives cancel each other out. But even assuming that this line is an accurate paraphrase, it has a different meaning, because the experience of reading it is not problematical. Since part of the meaning of a text lies in the reader's subjective experience in reading it, these two lines cannot mean the same thing.

Another example of the experience of reading comes from Milton's companion poems *L'Allegro* and *Il Penseroso*. *L'Allegro* is about the carefree life, and *Il Penseroso* is about the thoughtful life. Fish argues that the experience of reading each of these poems is different, and the different experiences actually produce the meaning of each poem. In *L'Allegro*, certain lines are deliberately ambiguous. These lines are constructed so that readers cannot possibly come to a firm interpretation of their meaning. Readers are thus freed of the responsibility of having to decide on an interpretation. They are allowed to feel the availability of alternative readings. Because the poem protects readers from the arduous task of interpretation, they experience a freedom from care. And this is precisely what the poem is about: the life that is free of care. *Il Penseroso*, however, which follows *L'Allegro*, is about the serious, pensive life. Reading this poem calls for strenuous mental effort. But because the poem is not finally ambiguous, readers feel called upon to achieve a unified interpretation.

Fish notes the important aftereffects of the reader's initial interpretations which must be revised in the face of later parts of a text. The experience of having entertained a wrong hypothesis is itself part of the text's meaning. Consider these lines from *Paradise Lost* (IV, 9–12):

> Satan, now first inflam'd with rage came down,
> The Tempter ere th'Accuser of man-kind,
> To wreck on innocent frail man his loss
> Of that first Battle, and his flight to Hell.

When readers first encounter the words "his loss," they assume that this is a reference to our loss of innocence in the Garden of Eden. Read in this way, the lines are experienced as meaning that an angry Satan inflicted the loss of Eden on our innocent and vulnerable first parents. However, when readers come to the next line, they are abruptly forced to reject this reading. The final line tells them that the referent of "loss" is Satan's loss of heaven. Readers now realize that the lines do not refer to our inherent innocence; they simply describe humans as innocent of Satan's loss of heaven.

Although readers reject the hypothesis that Milton is referring to the loss of Eden, the effect of this rejected hypothesis is never fully erased. Readers are forced to abandon a hypothesis that is very attractive to them, because it asserts the innocence of their first parents and thus maintains their own virtue. By first encouraging and then correcting this interpretation, Milton makes readers aware of their tendency to reach for self-serving interpretations. And such human frailty is part of the subject of *Paradise Lost*.

Readers' experience of a text is thus part of its meaning. To understand a work of literature, readers should not ask the traditional question, "What does this mean?" Rather, they should ask a phenomenological question, "What does this do to me when I read it?" The text is not an object; it is an event that happens to readers with their participation.

While this reader response theory has been successfully taught to some students, it has not yet been systematically tested. There is no information on how uniform people's moment-to-moment experiences in reading a particular text really are. Where one reader may experience a stumbling block, another may not. If the structure of each of their experiences is thus different, and if they recognize that the structure of their response is part of the text's meaning, each may arrive at a different final interpretation. Moreover, it is not known whether the method is equally appropriate for all works of literature, or whether it is appropriate only for a limited number of literary texts in which the authors have attempted to create a parallel between the reader's experience and the meaning of the text.

Constructing Different Texts

Literary criticism has traditionally assumed that readers experience a literary text in a fairly similar way and has not sought to uncover major individual differences in readers' responses. Aristotle wrote about the cathartic effect of tragedy on "the audience member." Plato wrote about the debilitating effect of poetry on "the reader." And Freud assumed, given the common psychological structures shared by humanity, that any reader experiences a work of literature in roughly the same way. Freud believed that works of art exert power over us because we find in them the fulfillment of our deepest and most forbidden wishes. These unconscious wishes are universal ones, possessed simply by virtue of being human. Thus, every audience member attending Sophocles' *Oedipus Rex* would interpret the play, at least unconsciously, as about the primal Oedipal dilemma. Freud wrote: "I have found love of the mother and jealousy of the father in my own case too, and now believe it to be a general phenomenon of early childhood . . . If that is the case, the gripping power of *Oedipus Rex*, in spite of all the rational objections to the inexorable fate that the story presupposes, becomes intelligible . . . Every member of the audience was once a budding Oedipus in phantasy, and this dream-fulfillment played out in reality causes everyone to recoil in horror, with the full measure of repression which separates his infantile from his present state" (Bonaparte, Freud, and Kris, 1954).

Fish places himself squarely in this tradition by assuming uniformity among readers, even if he narrows this claim to informed readers within a community. Psychological studies of story understanding can also be located in this tradition, and story grammar theorists actually demonstrated uniformity. But the uniformity that they reported was in response to extremely simple tasks, such as recalling the kind of brief, pared-down stories written by psychologists to use in the laboratory. As soon as readers' responses to complex works of literature are investigated, the assumption of uniformity begins to break down.

One of the first pieces of systematic evidence of differences among readers came from the literary critic I.A. Richards (1929). Richards distributed poems to his students, with the author's names deleted. The students were asked to keep the poems for one week, to read them as often as they wished, and to record their interpretations. The students differed widely in the interpretations that they offered. Moreover, they often misread the poems, offering interpretations that were incorrect, despite the fact that the students were highly educated undergraduates at a prestigious school.

The biggest problem that the students had was in making out "the plain sense" of a poem (Richards, 1960). Consider these lines from Shakespeare's sixty-sixth sonnet:

> Tir'd with all these, for restful death I cry:
> As to behold desert a beggar born.

One reader paraphrased this to mean:

> Weary of these sights, for reposeful death I implore:
> As I see desolate one born a beggar.

This reader interpreted the word *desert* as "desolate," perhaps through a chain of associations from *desert* to *deserted* to *desolate*. But this reading is simply wrong. The word *desert* here is a noun, not an adjective, and it means "merit." According to Richards, the second line conveys the idea that even a person of merit may be thought of as no better than a beggar. While Richards did not maintain that there is only one correct reading of a text, he did insist that this reader's paraphrase is incorrect.

The students also often failed to grasp the tone expressed by a poem. They responded in terms of idiosyncratic associations and images which led them astray. And they tended to let doctrines get in the way: instead of responding to the meaning of the poem, they became involved in defending or attacking the truth value of the poet's statements.

In exposing the various ways in which readers misread literature, this study undermined the view that all readers read in the same way. This finding does not pose a problem for Fish's theory, since the readers, as undergraduates, had not been highly trained in the close reading of literature and thus probably would not qualify as informed. Other investigations, however, have found that even highly trained readers specializing in literature interpret texts in different ways. For instance, one study found differences in the strategies used to interpret a poem (Kintgen, 1980). The participants were graduate students and professors of English literature. They were asked to think aloud into a tape recorder as they read a poem, and their interpretive strategies were analyzed. The approaches of readers to the same poem were very different. One reader began by analyzing the syntactic structure of the poem, trying to identify the subject of each verb. For this reader, grasping the syntactic structure of the poem was a prerequisite for achieving a unified interpretation. Another reader, however, began by focusing on the images and their connections to each other. While these two approaches could, in principle, lead to the same final interpretation, the experience of getting there differed for each reader.

While this study uncovered differences in interpretive strategies, another study found differences in the experience and interpretation of a poem stemming from readers' personal associations to key words (Rosenblatt, 1978). Observations were made of many students, including graduate students in English, as they encountered a poem by Emily Dickinson:

> I heard a Fly buzz—when I died—
> The Stillness in the Room
> Was like the Stillness in the Air—
> Between the Heaves of Storm—

The Eyes around—had wrung them dry—
And Breaths were gathering firm
For the last Onset—when the King
Be witnessed—in the Room—

I willed my Keepsakes—Signed away
What portion of me be
Assignable—and then it was
There interposed a Fly—

With Blue—uncertain stumbling Buzz—
Between the light—and me—
And then the Windows failed—and then
I could not see to see—

In the first line of this poem, the reader is confronted with a juxta-position of two images: death and a fly. The students brought to this poem different associations to the word "fly," and this affected the reading of the poem. Some readers associated weakness and insignificance to a fly. Thus, the first stanza was interpreted as de-scribing an intense quiet in which the only thing that could be heard was the buzzing of a fly. Readers thus expected something thunderous to occur. But nothing did happen. The only event was captured in the lines "There interposed a fly." This tiny event was therefore experienced by the readers as an anticlimax. Other read-ers brought an association of filth, germs, and decay to the word "fly." Since they began with an image of a loathsome creature buzzing around a deathbed, the last stanza was experienced not as an anticlimax but as a crescendo, a final intensification of a dis-turbing image. Because of these different associations, two very different poems were experienced. Although Dickinson may have had one or the other in mind when she wrote the poem, this is of no consequence for understanding the experience of reading.

Although Rosenblatt showed that one text can be experienced in two equally valid ways by two different readers, she did not go so far as to suggest that all experiences of a poem are equally valid. An interpretation is not valid if it is contradicted by the text, or if no verbal basis exists for its interpretation. Although these criteria are vague, and readers may not be able to agree about whether an interpretation is contradicted by the text, the text, in principle, places some constraints on the reader's interpretation. The study also did not show that interpretations of one text by dif-ferent individuals are totally different. There is, in fact, a core of similarity uniting different readers' responses to particular lines in a text (Fairley, 1977). Nevertheless, beyond this core, individual differences seem to be the rule rather than the exception.

These differences have been attributed to different levels of training: because untrained readers do not know how to go about the business of reading, they come up with idiosyncratic responses (Richards, 1929). The differences have also been attributed to readers' personal associations to words and the referents of those words in a literary text (Rosenblatt, 1978). But these explanations do not constitute a comprehensive theory of individual response to literature that makes it possible to predict how different readers will read a text. The only such theory, which has been worked out by the psychoanalytically oriented literary critic Norman Holland (1968), accounts for individual differences in terms of the personalities of individual readers.

Psychoanalytic study of the literary response traditionally focused on the text and assumed a response (e.g. Freud, 1913; Jones, 1976). Holland, however, developed and tested a psychoanalytic theory of individual differences in response to texts. This approach is similar in many respects to Pavel Machotka's study of individual differences in the response to nudes in the visual arts (1979).

The theory begins with the premise that we perceive all experiences subjectively. We interpret experiences in terms of our characteristic way of dealing with the world, that is, in terms of our identity. The experience of a work of literature is no exception. In many ways a literary text is a Rorschach onto which we project our own subjective view of the world.

Four principles account for the relationship between the identity of the reader and the text. The overarching principle is that we try to find ourselves, our identity style, in the characters of a literary text. To the extent that we can experience the characters as similar to ourselves, we can enjoy the text. In an effort to find similarity, we interpret the characters as being as much like ourselves as possible.

Second, we filter the story through our defense mechanisms. We recreate the characters so that their defenses match ours. Thus we can only cope with characters who share our modes of defending against anxiety. To perceive them otherwise is too threatening.

Third, once we have filtered in and recreated those aspects of the story that we can cope with, we project our characteristic fantasies onto the text. These fantasies are often unconscious wishes that we cannot carry out in reality. The wishes and desires that we perceive the characters to have are our own projections. There is no fixed fantasy content in the text.

And fourth, after we have perceived the work through our unconscious fantasies, we transform the fantasy content into a literary interpretation. That is, we are able to think of the abstract meaning of the text. But even this final intellectualized interpretation reflects our characteristic identity style.

Evidence for this model came from readers' different views of a story by William Faulkner called "A Rose for Emily" (Holland, 1975). This story begins with the death of the main character, Miss Emily, and then slowly unfolds the history of her life. When she was young, her father had isolated her, chasing away any suitors with a horsewhip. When he died, she refused for three days to admit that he was dead or to allow the body to be removed. Later, she formed a relationship with a man named Homer Barron. She was supposed to marry him, but one day he disappeared. Miss Emily became a recluse, never leaving her house. The townspeople noticed a peculiar smell emanating from the house, but no one dared to ask Miss Emily about this. Everyone was afraid to confront her. She resisted all attempts to make her obey ordinary laws, such as paying her taxes, and no one dared force her to comply. After her death, a shocking discovery was made: a bedroom in her house was decked out as if for a wedding night, and there on the bed lay the rotting corpse of Homer Barron, whom, it was learned, Miss Emily had poisoned with arsenic. On the indented pillow next to him lay a strand of Miss Emily's gray hair.

Readers experience a great deal more than this simple recounting of events. They form an impression of what motivates each character, and they react affectively to the different characters as if they were encountered in flesh and blood. Holland studied five readers' interpretations of this story, as well as his own, and came up with six different readings.

For Holland, Miss Emily was a character deeply concerned with control. She was hiding something grotesque inside herself and keeping her dark secret under control. The story elicited fascination with, and fear of, the chaos hidden within. For the students' different interpretations, based on their own fantasies and defenses, compare the readings offered by Sam and Saul. As established through lengthy interviews and projective personality tests, Sam's dominant fantasies concerned the need for power as well as for love and admiration. He protected himself against threats to his masculine power by the defense mechanism of denial. Saul was very different. His dominant concern was the need to be in control. He feared people overpowering him and forcing him to do things against his will.

Both students were asked how they experienced a particular

description by Faulkner of Miss Emily as a young girl: "We had long thought of them as a tableau, Miss Emily a slender figure in white in the background, her father a spraddled silhouette in the foreground, his back to her and clutching a horsewhip, the two of them framed by the back-flung front door." Sam described this as "one of the most striking images in the book," in which the towns-folk are "looking through the door as her father stands there with a horsewhip in his hands, feet spread apart and between or through him you see a picture of Emily standing in the back-ground, and that pretty much sums up exactly the kind of relation-ship they had" (p 1). Sam stressed the father's dominance, and he incorrectly recalled that the townsfolk viewed Emily between her father's legs. Saul, on the contrary, saw the father in this descrip-tion as powerless. Focusing on the word "spraddled," he saw the father as sprawled across the door, an impotent figure, no longer stern and erect. Because of his fear of being overpowered, Saul perceived the father as weak and harmless.

Sam's responses to the story can be accounted for by psycho-analytic principles. First, he found his own defense mechanisms in the characters. One of his defenses was to deny threats to himself. And one of the things that captured his interest was the sadistic power that the Southern whites in this story exerted over the blacks. Once he recognized that he shared with the characters a defensive style of denial of threats to oneself, but not to others, he could project his fantasies onto the story. His fantasy was to be all powerful. He projected this wish onto the father and saw him as domineering; and he projected this wish onto Miss Emily and saw her as fierce and strong. This view of Miss Emily is markedly dif-ferent from that of Holland, who saw her as retentive.

Sam ultimately worked out an intellectual interpretation of the story. He decided that it was about keeping what is valuable from one's past yet not living in the past. This final intellectualized in-terpretation was also a product of Sam's personality, for he had longed for a nurturing mother from his childhood, the past, from whom he could draw strength to be virile in the present.

Saul's responses can also be accounted for by psychoanalytic principles. Saul's dominant concern was the need for control. He thus responded positively to characters who shared this need, such as Emily, whom he saw as withholding and contained. He reacted negatively to characters who were perceived as uncontained and who showed overwhelming power, such as the father. Like Sam, Saul's final intellectual interpretation of the work reflected his dominant drives and defenses: he viewed the theme of the story as the attempt to hold on to tradition. Thus, Faulkner's theme was perceived as one of control—holding on rather than letting go.

The different readings of Sam and Saul show that readers' responses to literature are to some extent shaped by their personalities. Readers' unconscious drives and defenses determine what they like and what they allow themselves to respond to and identify with. They even determine the final intellectualized conception of the theme of a literary work.

The various views of how readers grasp an entire text are not mutually exclusive. All theories agree that readers take an active role as they read. Readers must continually predict, infer, and revise their hypotheses about what is going on. If they fail to do this, they will not make sense of the text.

Story grammar theory goes on to argue that what is crucial for readers is to grasp the structure of the text. Once readers have internalized the structure of a typical story, for instance, they can then use this structure to organize their experience of a newly encountered story. A contrasting theory, which grants a central role to the experience of reading a text, maintains that the structure of a text does not exist "out there" on the printed page. Rather, it exists in the moment-to-moment experience of readers as they interact with the words on the page. Only if readers are alert to this experience can a text be fully understood.

Theories based on the structure of a text and those based on the structure of the reading experience represent two sides of one problem and thus may not be mutually exclusive. It may well be that readers must both apprehend the structure of the text and attend to the pattern of their experience of the text. The structure of the text influences the structure of the readers' experience. Thus, one cannot talk about the latter without the former.

Another area of disagreement is the extent to which there is uniformity among readers, and the extent to which individual readers construct their own text. Most empirical investigations of this issue have revealed considerable individual differences among readers, although these different responses are not wholly unrelated to each other or to the text. Some individual variations entail the use of different interpretive strategies; others entail personal and idiosyncratic associations to the words of the text; and still others involve projection of the readers' unconscious fantasies and fears.

Return, for a moment, to the story of *Macbeth*. As readers begin to read *Macbeth*, they face three challenges. To make sense of the play, they have to be alert to two central components of literature: sound properties and metaphors. They have to be sensitive to the ways in which sound properties enhance the meaning of Macbeth's lines; and they have to distinguish the metaphors from the nonmetaphors and process the figurative uses of language in a sensible way. Finally, they have to achieve an overall understanding of the entire play, grasping the structure of the text and perhaps the structure of their own experience of reading it as well.

These three tasks cannot be carried out independently of one another. The sound properties of a text can underscore a metaphorical meaning in the lines. For instance, Macbeth uses words that are extremely truncated ("struts and frets"), just after he metaphorically likens life to a brief candle. And achieving a grasp of the whole text cannot be accomplished if the components of a text—its sound properties and its metaphors—are not understood. Moreover, a metaphor can be extended and played upon throughout an entire text, such as the whale in *Moby Dick*. Grasping this extended metaphor can help readers to unify the text. Finally, readers' emotional response may stimulate them to understand the text, just as their growing understanding shapes their affective reactions. Moreover, their emotional response constitutes information about the work and thus helps readers to make sense of the work. This is in effect what happens in the arts when the emotions function cognitively.

If readers rise to the challenge of these tasks, they will arrive at a coherent understanding of *Macbeth*. Different readers, however, may reach different interpretations, depending upon their experience in reading literature as well as their personalities. Perhaps more than any other art form, literature makes room for projection. Because literature deals with human experiences, readers cannot help but project upon the depicted characters their own conceptions of human nature and their own fantasies and fears. In this sense, literature stands apart from music, which is not about anything at all, as well as from painting or sculpture, which may depict humans but cannot tell an extended story about human experiences.

There is no substitute for the experience of reading *Macbeth*. The reader's final goal is not to arrive at some kind of abstract interpretation of the play. If this were the final effect of reading a work of literature, one could just as well read a brief paragraph stating an abstract interpretation of the work. Tolstoy was once asked what his novel *Anna Karenina* "meant." The only way that he could answer that question, he replied, was to write the novel again, from its first word to its last.

10 Once Upon a Time

Like all great art, fairy tales both delight and instruct; their special genius is that they do so in terms which speak directly to children.

—Bruno Bettelheim

"Once upon a time, there was a land full of tiny beautiful flowers and lovely birds with golden feathers. In this land, there lived a king and a queen. They had one daughter who was both beautiful and clever. Her cheeks were rosy apples, and her hair was made out of silk.

"One sad day, the queen died. The king and his daughter were heartbroken. As the empty years passed, the beautiful birds began to leave the land, and the flowers disappeared. In place of the lovely golden birds came big black birds with sharp and fearsome beaks. The land began to look very different from the way that it used to look.

"When the princess turned sixteen, her father married a new queen. This new queen was jealous of the king's love for his daughter. She had eyes of ice and a heart made out of stone. One day . . ."

As any reader knows, these lines are the beginning of a typical fairy tale. Children encounter many stories like this—in story books, in comic strips, and on television. At least in Western culture, children have considerably more experience with literature than with any other art form. Unlike music or the visual arts, there is a vast body of literature written especially for the young. Children who rarely see a painting or listen to music are served a daily fare of stories and nursery rhymes. Often children seem insatiable: they listen, spellbound, to a bedtime story and insist on hearing the same story told over again each night.

Given the evident power that literature exerts over children, and given the fact that literature uses the familiar symbol system of language, one might assume that stories and verse are readily accessible to the young. Yet this assumption may not be well founded. To understand the story just begun, children must be able to understand the perceptual metaphors ("Her cheeks were rosy apples") and the nonperceptual ones ("a heart made out of stone"). They must grasp the emotional themes of love between father and daughter, rivalry and jealousy between daughter and stepmother. Upon hearing the beginning of this story, they ought to have an expectation of the events to follow, based on a knowledge of the fairy tale genre: they ought to realize that a conflict will develop which will ultimately be resolved in favor of the princess. And they must be sensitive to the style of the language, recognizing the ominous mood set by the disappearance of the flowers and the appearance of fierce black birds. Finally, they must be sensitive to the characteristics of the medium, such as a book or television, through which the story is encountered.

It is possible that the child's fascination with stories has little to do with their literary aspects, such as figurative language, emotional themes, character development, style, mood, and genre. Parents who assume that their child's interest in stories is due to their literary aspects may, thus, have been fooling themselves all along. Children may be attracted to properties of literature very different from those that attract adults.

Understanding Metaphors

Without the ability to make sense of figurative language, most works of literature would be partially understood at best. No less than adult literature, children's literature is filled with metaphorical language. In fairy tales, kings have wills of iron, stepmothers have hearts of stone, and princesses have apple cheeks. Other kinds of tropes can also be found in children's literature, including hyperbole, understatement, sarcasm, and even irony.

It is not only in literature that children encounter figurative language. Adults often use such language in their speech to children, as in "Your eyes are saucers" (metaphor), "You've made a bit of a mess here" (understatement), and "You are the cutest little boy in the whole world" (hyperbole). Figurative language, especially metaphor, is also used frequently in grade school texts (Arter, 1976). Because of its prevalence, one might assume that figurative language is understood by children. However, any six-year-old, when asked what it means to say that someone has "a hard heart," might well say quite confidently that this person's heart is fashioned out of rock.

Studies of children's understanding of figurative language have focused on the area of metaphor. The results prohibit any simple conclusion about children's ability to understand metaphor. Children's comprehension of metaphor depends on the measures used to assess it as well as the kinds of metaphors whose comprehension is in question.

Some studies of metaphor comprehension have yielded a picture of metaphor as a relatively late acquisition. In one of the first studies, children's understanding of "double-function" adjectives, such a *sweet, hard, cold*, and *crooked*, was examined (Asch and Nerlove, 1960). These adjectives have both a physical and a psychological meaning: a stone is literally hard; an unkind person is metaphorically hard. Children between the ages of three and twelve were tested for their understanding of both senses of these terms, as well as for their ability to explain the link between the two uses.

Children were first able to understand only the physical meaning of double-function terms. Seven- and eight-year-olds understood the psychological sense, but they understood it as entirely separate from the physical meaning and saw no connection between the two. Only the oldest were able to pinpoint the links, explaining, for example, that "hard things and hard people are both unmanageable" (p. 53). These findings were replicated in a later study (Lesser and Drouin, 1975).

While this study examined children's understanding of metaphorical uses of isolated words, another study probed children's understanding of metaphorical sentences in which these words were embedded (Winner, Rosenstiel, and Gardner, 1976). Children between six and fourteen years old were asked to explain sentences such as, "After many years of working at the jail, the prison guard had become a hard rock that could not be moved." The results of this study confirmed that the ability to paraphrase metaphorical language is a late-developing skill. Moreover, very different types of paraphrase were offered for these metaphors by children of different ages.

Six-, seven-, and eight-year-olds favored two types of interpretation. Asked to explain the meaning of the prison guard sentence, they said things like, "The prison guard worked in a hard rock prison" or "The guard had muscles hard as a rock." Thus, they either rephrased the sentence so that the topic and vehicle were associated rather than equated, or they noted a physical way in which a person and a rock could be alike. While six- to eight-year-olds favored such associative and physical interpretations, they also sometimes gave literal responses. Although no age group offered a high rate of literal interpretations, children under eight gave significantly more literal responses than did older children.

By ten, most children were able to articulate the psychological meaning of the sentences, explaining, for instance, that the guard was cruel or unkind. However, as children began to "outgrow" incorrect responses, they sometimes offered interpretations that were almost, but not quite, on the mark. For instance, the guard was sometimes said to be "fussy." However, while an incorrect psychological dimension was sometimes offered, the positive or negative polarity of the double-function term was always respected. Children sensed that *hard*, when applied to a person, had a negative connotation. Though they might conclude that the guard was fussy, they never concluded that he was kind. Thus, a sense of the specific continuum (for instance, kindness versus unkindness) to which a double-function term refers develops after a sense of the polarity (positive versus negative) to which it refers (see also Winner, Wapner, Cicone, and Gardner, 1979).

All of these studies demonstrated that children have considerable difficulty explaining psychological-physical metaphors, which describe psychological properties using physical terms. The problem posed by these metaphors is not due to a lack of knowledge of the psychological domain, for children who were unable to explain metaphors that referred to a person's character by likening it to a physical object, such as a rock, were quite capable of understanding a literal description of a person's character, such as mean, bossy, or stubborn (Cicone, Gardner, and Winner, 1981). One possibility is that children's difficulty with psychological-physical metaphors is due, at least in part, to the abstractness of the link connecting topic and vehicle. Nothing tangible is shared by a hard rock and a hard person: what they share is the abstract property of unyieldingness. Other kinds of metaphors are also grounded in a nonperceptual resemblance, and these, too, prove difficult for children (Mendelsohn, Winner, and Gardner, 1980). However, metaphors based on perceptual links prove much easier. When children encountered a perceptual metaphor, such as a description of snow as shaving cream, they revealed full understanding as young as three or four years old (Winner, McCarthy, and Gardner, 1980).

To conclude that understanding nonperceptual metaphors is a late-developing skill assumes that misunderstanding metaphors stems from a cognitive limitation, such as the inability to perceive abstract resemblances. Another possibility is that misunderstanding arises not from limitations of the child's competence but rather from more superficial problems. Three such problems that might account for misunderstanding metaphor are the linguistic response mode, the lack of context, and the surface form of a metaphor.

In the studies of psychological-physical metaphors, comprehension was assessed through tasks in which the children had to paraphrase the metaphors. But the ability to use language to talk about language, called metalinguistic skill, develops later than the ability simply to understand language. For instance, children can tell the difference between grammatical and deviant sentences long before they can explain why one is correct and the other incorrect (deVilliers and deVilliers, 1978). Thus, the paraphrase studies may tell more about the ability to explain than to understand metaphoric language.

When understanding is assessed nonlinguistically, even preschoolers show some understanding of metaphors based on nonperceptual grounds. In one such study, discussed earlier, a simple matching task was devised (Gardner, 1974a). Subjects from three and a half to nineteen years old heard pairs of opposite adjectives, such as *hard-soft* or *cold-warm,* and were asked to align each member of a pair with a pair of visual stimuli. For instance, *hard-soft* had to be aligned with two colors (brown and blue-gray), two pictured facial expressions (frown and smile), and two sounds (triangle and recorder). A metaphoric response, according to adults, consists of aligning the word *hard* with the color brown, the frowning face, and the sound of the triangle; and the word *soft* with the other member of each pair.

Preschool children were able to match the adjectives to the various stimuli in a metaphoric manner, although they did not do so as consistently as did older children and adults. That they could align *hard* with the frowning face and *soft* with the smiling one indicates that the ability to perceive the abstract connection between a physical and a psychological property is present long before the child can paraphrase metaphors based on such links.

The use of a nonlinguistic response mode not only has demonstrated possible sensitivity to abstract metaphors in preschoolers, but has revealed a form of incipient sensitivity to metaphoric resemblances in prelinguistic infants. For instance, the ability to recognize abstract connections between visual and auditory stimuli was found in infants between nine and twelve months (Wagner, Winner, Cicchetti, and Gardner, 1981). To demonstrate this capacity, infants heard a sound, such as a pulsing tone, that lasted for ten seconds. Three seconds after the onset of the sound, they were shown two slides simultaneously, in this case a picture of a dotted line and a continuous line. Later on, infants saw the same two slides, but this time they viewed them while listening to a continuous tone. On several of the stimulus sets used, infants matched their looking preferences to the sound to which they were simultaneously listening. Thus, while listening to the pulsing tone, they preferred to look at the dotted line; and while listening to the continuous tone, they shifted their preference to the continuous line. Similar findings were reported using a different method of assessment (Lewkowicz and Turkewitz, 1980).

The connections that infants were able to perceive between sounds and patterns are no different, in principle, from those that underlie cross-sensory metaphors linking auditory and visual elements. We refer to colors as "loud" or "quiet" and musical pitches as "high" or "low," presumably because we are able to perceive links between sounds and sights. The finding that even infants can make such connections suggests that many of our common metaphors are determined by nonarbitrary connections which are first perceived nonlinguistically. Further support for this view comes from the finding that in languages which are historically unrelated, double-function terms such as *hot* or *crooked* have closely related psychological meanings (Asch, 1955).

The use of a nonmetalinguistic response mode is not the only way to lower dramatically the age at which metaphoric comprehension is found. When metaphors are presented in a context of some sort, as in a story or a picture, the age at which children can explain abstractly based metaphors is also lowered (Winner, et al., 1979). Thus, the relatively late emergence of comprehension reported elsewhere may be due in part to the response mode used and to the fact that the metaphors were presented out of context.

The late age at which comprehension emerged in other studies may also be due to another potential obstacle: children may not know that it is permissible to use language in a nonliteral way. That is, they may fail on a metaphor task because they do not know what it is that they are supposed to do with a metaphor. Metaphors are an indirect way of pointing out a similarity between two elements. A metaphor asserts that X is Y, but the reader is supposed to understand this as meaning that X is like Y in some respects. If one takes a metaphor literally, it will be misunderstood. No such problems are posed by similes, however, since similes state directly what metaphors state indirectly. If the indirectness of a metaphor is an obstacle, then the child who fails to understand a metaphor ought to be able to understand a corresponding simile.

This proposition was explored by having children ranging from seven to eleven read brief stories and then select what they considered to be the most fitting of four final sentences (Reynolds and

Ortony, 1980). The four choices were either all metaphors, all similes, or all literal statements. Here is a sample story with the range of choices, the starred items indicating the correct choice:

The Old Race Horse

Jack Flash had been a great race horse when he was young, but now he was too old to race. His owner thought Jack Flash wasn't good for anything anymore. None of the other people who worked at the ranch where Jack lived paid any attention to him. No one wanted to ride an old broken-down horse. The owner decided that he did not want Jack around where people could see him.

Literal choices
*Jack was sent to one of the pastures in the back of the farm.

The owner of the ranch played with Jack every day.

Jack was given the best stall on the ranch to stay in.

Jack hated eating oats for breakfast.

Metaphor choices
*The worn-out shoe was thrown into the trash.

The saddle was polished and shiny.

The race was going to begin.

The raincoat was new.

Simile choices
*It was like a worn-out shoe that had been thrown into the trash.

It was like a saddle that was polished and shiny.

It was like a race which was going to begin.

It was like a new raincoat.

Children at all ages chose the correct literal sentences. Choosing the correct metaphor and simile proved more difficult. However, similes were chosen correctly at a level above chance by nine-year-olds, while an equivalent performance on the metaphors was not achieved until one year later. Thus, before children could make sense of the metaphor "The worn-out shoe was thrown into the trash," which refers indirectly to an old, unwanted race horse, they demonstrated the capacity to relate the disparate domains: old race horses and worn-out shoes.

Other manipulations of the surface form of a metaphor also appear to facilitate comprehension. Making the topic of a metaphor specific aids understanding (Reynolds and Ortony, 1980).

Thus, it is easier to understand "The old race horse was a worn-out shoe thrown into the trash" than to understand this same metaphor in a topicless form, "The worn-out old shoe was thrown into the trash." Presumably this is because of the difficulty of finding the appropriate topic given the topicless form. Rephrasing a metaphor in the form of a riddle or an analogy also renders the task of comprehension much easier (Winner, Engel, and Gardner, 1980). Thus, metaphor comprehension may be impeded by the form in which the metaphor is posed. Children may fail on a metaphor task because they do not know the rules of the game. They do not know what it is that they are supposed to do with a metaphor when they see one.

Taken together, the studies suggest that measures of children's ability to understand metaphor may be confounded with factors such as the ability to put one's understanding into words or the knowledge that a metaphor is not to be taken at face value. The purest measure of metaphor comprehension would allow a nonmetalinguistic response mode, present the metaphors in a visual or verbal context, and encode the metaphoric relation in the form of a simile with both topic and vehicle stated. However, by radically simplifying the tasks in this way, researchers may find that they are measuring a relatively primitive form of metaphor understanding. Children who can explain a metaphor presented out of context may not just be demonstrating better metalinguistic skills than the four-year-old who can match but not explain. They may also be demonstrating a fuller understanding of metaphor. Thus, while there may be hints of metaphor comprehension in the crib, these glimmerings should not be confused with the full-grown understanding of the preadolescent.

Understanding metaphor may call upon logical reasoning abilities. Several investigations have tested this hypothesis by exploring the relationship between performance on metaphor tasks and on Piaget's tasks of logical thinking. One such study assumed that to understand the metaphor "Hair is spaghetti," one must recognize that hair and spaghetti are similar because they both belong to the larger class of "long, stringy, tangled things" (Billow, 1975). Thus, to understand metaphors that equate two terms on the basis of a shared property, one must understand the logic of class inclusion, that is, the fact that two different things may belong to the same superordinate category.

This hypothesis was tested by asking children to paraphrase metaphors and to perform Piaget's tasks of class inclusion, which assess the child's awareness that, for instance, a rose is a member of both the subclass of roses and the superordinate class of flowers. With increasing age, children proved able to solve both the metaphors and the class inclusion tasks. However, the hypothesis that the logic of class inclusion is necessary for metaphor understanding was not supported, since a number of children were able to paraphrase the metaphors without demonstrating an understanding of class inclusion.

Another attempt to relate metaphor understanding and logical abilities presumed that the ability to understand metaphors calls upon a different logical ability, that of finding the intersection between two classes which initially do not appear to intersect at all (Eson and Cometa, 1978). For instance, to understand "The guard is a hard rock," one must find the intersection of people and rocks. Their intersection is the class of "inflexible elements."

Piaget's tests of class intersection were administered to children of different ages along with a set of metaphors to be paraphrased. In one of the intersection tests used, children saw a pictured row of green objects—an umbrella, a fish, a book, and a butterfly—at right angles to a row of leaves of various colors. An empty space was left at the point at which the two rows met, and the child was asked to fill in this cell. The correct answer in this case would be a green leaf, as this forms the intersection of the classes of green objects and leaves (Fig. 10.1).

Only those children who could solve such a task proved able both to paraphrase and to explain a series of fairly simple metaphors. The conclusion was reached that the logic required by class intersection tests is the same logic as that required to understand a metaphor.

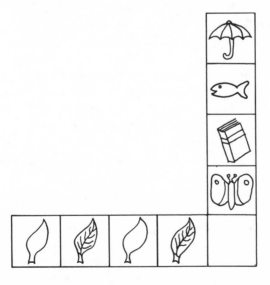

10.1 Class intersection matrix, to be completed by a green leaf intersecting the class of green objects and the class of leaves. This task may call upon the same logic as is required to understand metaphors.

Metaphoric skill may not be entirely a matter of logical abilities. It may also be in part a cognitive style, a certain way of making sense of the world, which is favored by some people more than others. One study demonstrated the existence of individual differences in metaphoric sensitivity (Kogan, Connor, Gross, and Fava, 1980). A picture-grouping task was used in which subjects were shown a triad of pictures and were asked to group the two that went together. One of the triads was composed of pictures of an old man in a wheelchair, a candle going out, and a pipe. Grouping the old man and the candle was considered a metaphoric response, as both are "burning out"; matching the candle and pipe was considered a conventional response, as both belong to the same conventional category—things that can be lit; and matching the old man and the pipe was counted a functional grouping, as a man smokes a pipe. Using this nonverbal measure of sensitivity to metaphoric resemblances, the study revealed individual as well as developmental differences among children. That is, at any given age, some children showed a greater proclivity toward metaphorical groupings than did others.

The Appeal of Metaphors

While metaphor comprehension has been extensively studied, much less is known about the development of the aesthetic appeal of metaphors. Whether children prefer metaphors to literal language, and whether children prefer one kind of metaphor over another has been little investigated. One study explored the comparative appeal of metaphorical and literal descriptions, as well as the basis for a metaphor's appeal at different ages (Silberstein, Gardner, Phelps, and Winner, in press). A multiple choice preference task was used in which children and adults were asked to indicate their preference for literal versus metaphorical statements, and for different types of metaphors. In this study, six- and eight-year-olds preferred literal to metaphorical language. The preference for literal statements then declined steadily with age, with the exception of an unexpected return to literalism among thirteen- and fifteen-year-olds. Unlike the younger children who preferred literal statements, however, the adolescents demonstrated an explicit awareness of what they were rejecting, often articulating a defiance of the nonliteral. For instance, one fifteen-year-old wrote, "I like to be more exact about things and more direct." By seventeen years of age, preference for literal statements had given way to preference for metaphorical ones.

At all ages, when children demonstrated a preference for metaphorical language, metaphors based on two grounds were preferred to those based on only one link. For instance, they preferred "The popped red balloon is an apple peel," based on color and shape, to "The popped red balloon is a limp washcloth," based on shape alone. With respect to single-grounded metaphors, preferences shifted from the static perceptual grounds of shape and color, which are constant features of objects, to the dynamic perceptual grounds of movement and sound, which are transient properties of objects, to nonperceptual grounds such as impermanence, fragility, or explosiveness.

A comparison of these results with findings from comprehension studies suggests that children may understand the basis of a metaphor quite some time before they like the metaphor. While fifth graders typically understand nonperceptual metaphors, and while they demonstrated comprehension of the nonperceptual metaphors that they chose on this preference task, as assessed by the justifications given for their choices, it was not until tenth grade that a preference for these metaphors appeared. Unlike jokes, which children appreciate before being able to explain (Zigler, Levine, and Gould, 1966, 1967) or enjoy most at the time that they initially understand them (McGhee, 1973), metaphor appreciation appears to lag behind comprehension. However, to confirm this preliminary finding, comprehension of all metaphors on the preference task would have to be assessed along with preferences, to determine the understanding of metaphors not chosen as well as those chosen.

The place of metaphor in relation to other tropes is an area ripe for study. Children frequently encounter other forms of nonliteral language in literature, such as hyperbole, sarcasm, and irony. Unlike metaphor, understanding these types of tropes requires not only that they be interpreted nonliterally but also that their motivation be grasped. For instance, suppose that a character in a story is depicted as clumsy. After tripping in a race and falling flat on his face, his friend tells him, "You sure are a great athlete." To make sense of this statement, the reader must realize that the speaker's intent was to tease rather than to falsely compliment the fallen runner, that is, to lie to him. Thus, understanding such tropes requires some awareness of human psychology.

In a study designed to investigate comprehension of hyperbole, understatement, sarcasm, and irony, six-year-olds were found to interpret all such statements literally (Demorest, Silberstein, Gardner, and Winner, 1981). Eight-year-olds recognized these statements as nonliteral but had difficulty grasping their intent. Typically, the child believed that the speaker intended to mislead the listener—that is, to lie through flattery—and failed to see that the speaker and listener might have a shared understanding of the nonliteral truth of the statement. Only the eleven-year-olds were able to recognize a shared perspective between speaker and listener in which both participants are aware of the nonliteral nature of the statement as well as the speaker's intent to tease or to convey a statement with rhetorical impact.

Understanding Story Content

Research on figurative language has shown that children often misunderstand nonliteral uses of language. The kinds of difficulties found at the local level with metaphors might be expected to be paralleled with stories; alternatively, the greater familiarity and interest of stories might render them easier to understand than metaphors. Two approaches to children's understanding of stories have been taken. Those in the psychoanalytic tradition focus entirely on the child's grasp of the content of stories. Cognitive psychologists focus more heavily on the child's understanding of story structure.

The psychoanalytic approach pictures children as creatures beset by powerful emotions and fantasies. Children experience violent jealousy and hatred of any new sibling because they must now share their parents' love with someone else. During the Oedipal period, they experience a sexual longing for the opposite sex parent and consequently harbor murderous wishes toward the same sex parent whom they also greatly fear. Because children cannot understand these powerful and threatening emotions, and because they are extremely fearful of being "caught" with such "evil" wishes, they repress these feelings.

Here, the psychologist Bruno Bettelheim (1976) has argued, fairy tales have an important role to play. Fairy tales touch on all of the child's fantasies. They deal with the gamut of emotions that the young child experiences, such as sibling rivalry, Oedipal desires, and feelings of powerlessness with respect to a seemingly omnipotent parent. Fairy tales deal on a symbolic level with the sexual and aggressive themes that children are confronting and repressing in their own lives. For instance, the theme of the Oedipal conflict between mother and daughter appears in Snow White's conflict with her evil stepmother. The theme of impotence in the face of all-powerful and therefore frightening adults underlies Jack's conflict with the giant in "Jack and the Beanstalk." And "Little Red Riding Hood" concerns the themes of sexuality (the grandmother in bed with the wolf), fear of incorporation (the wolf devouring Little Red Riding Hood and her grandmother), and the conflict between the pleasure principle (yielding to the temptation of the wolf) and the reality principle (delaying gratification in order to resist self-destructive temptations).

Bettelheim argued that even the preschool child can grasp these underlying themes, although only on an unconscious level. Fairy tales are accessible to the very young because these tales speak to children in a language that they can understand. For example, the cast is made up of characters who are either all good or all bad. This is appropriate, for the child cannot make subtle distinctions among motives. Fairy tales end with the meting out of retributive justice: the evil character is punished, and the punishment is often violent death. This too is appropriate, because children believe in retribution and cannot understand the more complicated stance of having mercy for characters who themselves have shown no mercy.

Through these tales of good and evil, violence and revenge, power and powerlessness, children are informed that they are not alone in their feelings of powerlessness and forbidden desires. More important, fairy tales allow the child to feel that good forces exist and that these forces will eventually prevail against destructiveness. Because fairy tales usually end with a reunion or a marriage, they also give the child the healthy message that strength and happiness are to be achieved through the formation of a mature and mutual relationship between two people.

Fairy tales contrast with the typical contemporary stories written for children. Modern children's stories have relatively trivial content, in which no deep threat must be confronted. One such tale discussed by Bettelheim, called "Tootle the Engine," is about a train that wanders off the track and is eventually socialized by the townspeople into staying on the track. Such a story fails to relate to the child's deepest concerns: fairy tales confront the issues that contemporary stories skirt.

By touching symbolically on the powerful, unconscious conflicts that beset young children, fairy tales play an important role in children's psychological well-being, helping them confront and work through their innermost fears. And fairy tales are important not only to the child's mental health, according to Bettelheim, but also to the adult's: "Nothing can be as enriching and satisfying to the child and adult alike as the folk fairy tale . . . more can be learned from them about the inner problems of human beings, and of the right solutions to their predicaments in any society, than from any other type of story within a child's comprehension" (p. 5).

This view of the importance of fairy tales to the child rests on two assumptions that are open to question. First, the child is seen as a creature grappling unconsciously with overwhelming sexual and aggressive emotions. Yet this picture of the child, while based upon rich clinical experience, is not readily susceptible to either proof or disproof. A more serious problem with this theory of fairy tales is its assumption that the child understands the symbolic content of fairy tales and perceives their hidden meaning.

Consider Bettelheim's analysis of "Little Red Riding Hood," which he called "Little Red Cap." Little Red Cap begins as a character dominated by the pleasure principle, who allows herself to be tempted by the wolf. When she emerges from the wolf's belly, she is reborn as a mature person, who presumably can delay gratification because she is governed by the reality principle. The child is said to be able to understand all of this, if only unconsciously: "The child knows intuitively that Little Red Cap's being swallowed by the wolf . . . is by no means the end of the story, but a necessary part of it. The child also understands that Little Red Cap really "died" as the girl who permitted herself to be tempted by the wolf; and that when the story says "the little girl sprang out" of the wolf's belly, she came to life a different person" (p. 179).

Yet all of the evidence gleaned from research in cognitive development suggests that a preschool child cannot understand something as complicated or ambiguous as one character who is really two people (Gardner, 1977). After all, one of the reasons that the child is attracted to fairy tales is that these stories are composed of characters painted in broad strokes of black and white. In general, the evidence from cognitive psychology paints a picture of the young child as unable to apprehend the latent, symbolic meaning of a story. Just as preschoolers find perceptual metaphors much easier to grasp than ones based on intangible, nonphysical connections, so children more readily grasp the perceptible surface details of a story and the overt actions of the characters than the underlying psychological themes. And since preschool children often take psychological metaphors literally, it would be quite surprising if they did not also take fairy tales literally.

In order to determine the extent to which children grasp the emotional content of a story, a test was devised (Damon, 1967). The goal of the test was to determine whether children were "blinded" by the surface aspects of a story, or whether they could see beneath the surface to the inner emotions and motivations of the characters. Children were presented with brief stories adapted from the *Iliad*, from which all terms referring to how a character felt had been deleted. Children then heard other vignettes which were similar to those from the *Iliad* either in their surface content, such as clothing and proper names, or in their emotional content, such as the motivations and feelings suggested by the character's similar behavior. Children were asked to judge which story was most similar to the target story from the *Iliad*.

Children under the age of seven grouped together stories on the basis of surface cues; only children over seven were able to ignore superficial similarities and group stories on the basis of the inferred underlying emotional themes. This finding suggests that the psychoanalytic claims may be unfounded: instead of taking away a deep emotional lesson from a story, children may take away only its overt surface content.

Another study also suggested that the psychoanalytic approach assumes too much ability on the part of the child (Rubin and Gardner, 1977). Children aged six, eight, and eleven were told an unfinished fairy tale about a king who remarried after the death of his wife. He had a very clever daughter whom he loved dearly and of whom the new queen became cruelly jealous. In her jealousy, the queen imposed a series of impossible tasks on the princess. Children heard this unfinished tale in one of two versions. In one version, all mention of motivation and character traits was deleted. Thus, the fact that the queen was jealous was never mentioned. Consequently, there appeared to be neither rhyme nor reason to her actions. In the other version, the story was presented as stories usually are, with motivation explicitly stated. Children were asked to complete the story and then to recall it both immediately and three days later.

Children of different ages responded very differently to the two versions. In retelling the story, six- and eight-year-olds actually did better on the motivation-deleted version. In the motivated version, the queen seemed so overpowering to them that, rather than honor the standard fairy tale ending in which the evil are punished, they proved unable to curtail her power. Only the eleven-year-olds retold the motivation-included version better than the deleted version. They had mastered the fairy tale genre and failed to be overwhelmed by the power of the queen.

Of particular interest was the manner in which the motivation-deleted version was recalled. On the immediate recall task, six-year-olds added some motivation to the story. However, on the delayed recall task, no motivation was included, which suggests the relative unimportance to the child of the psychological themes of the story. Eleven-year-olds did just the opposite: on the immediate recall, they accurately retold the story without motivation; but on the delayed recall, they added motivation to the story. This suggests that they had some grasp of human motivation and could infer the motivation underlying overt behavior.

Taken together, these studies suggest that young children do not grasp the underlying psychological, emotional, or motivational themes of a story. Instead of extracting emotional meaning, children may take in only the literal, external events of a story. To this criticism, the psychoanalytic view would counter that experimental studies do not tap the child's grasp of stories, because the child responds to stories on an unconscious level (Winner and Gardner, 1979). This claim, though perhaps true, is not susceptible to proof and can only be accepted on faith.

Understanding Story Structure

In the field of cognitive development, a number of studies have investigated children's understanding of stories within the framework of story grammars (Mandler, 1978; Mandler and Johnson, 1977; McConaghy, 1980; Stein and Glenn, 1977). The studies in this tradition demonstrated that, like adults, children as young as six years old have a well-formed internal representation of the structure of a typical story. This internalized grammar helps children organize the story as they hear it, store it, and recall it. Like adults, children recall those components of a story defined by the grammar as important more often than those components defined as less important or even optional; well-formed stories are recalled better than deviant ones; and deviant stories are transformed in memory so that they become more grammatical. Moreover, these patterns were confirmed in another culture without formal schooling (Mandler, Scribner, Cole, and DeForest, 1980).

Although the child's internal representation of the structure of a story is very similar to that of the adult, it differs in one respect. While adults recall the internal reactions and psychological states of a character less well than other story units, such as overt actions, children recall almost no internal states at all. This does not seem to be because children are unable to understand psychological states (Berndt and Berndt, 1975; Cicone, Gardner, and Winner, 1981). Moreover, if the characters' intentions are explained to children so that they need not be inferred, children are able to understand these intentions and take them into account in discussing the story (Fitzhenry-Coor, 1977). The problem seems to be one of inference rather than of the ability to understand internal states. The lexical resources needed to describe internal states may also be less readily available to the child than are those needed to describe overt actions.

It seems reasonable to conclude that an important way in which children's understanding of stories differs from adults' understanding is that children do not find the psychology of a story's characters important in their understanding of the story. Rather than focusing on the internal states leading to an outcome, young children emphasize the outcomes themselves. The lack of importance granted to psychological states casts further doubt on the psychoanalytic view of what the young child takes away from a fairy tale.

One objection to the story grammar approach is its insensitivity to the aesthetic aspects of stories (Gardner, 1978). The stories used in the studies have been brief, bare-boned vignettes that lack interest and have little resemblance to "real" stories. "The Old Farmer and His Stubborn Donkey" is a far cry from any tale that usually grips a child. For the most part, the stories used have been calm tales, stripped of struggle, affect, and dialogue. They are just the kind of stories that Bettelheim decried as unable really to speak to children. Moreover, children typically experience stories by hearing them over and over again; yet in the story grammar studies, stories are simply presented once. This hardly mimics the natural experience of a story.

The use of recall as a measure in the studies also ignores a great deal that is important in experiencing a story. This experience involves not only recalling the plot structure but also reacting to mood, style, rhythm, sound properties, and the medium in which the story is told, such as book, radio, or television. In one study, the story included a rhythmic refrain that was repeated several times (Rubin and Gardner, 1977). Although this refrain was marginal to the plot structure of the story, it was well recalled. In brief, while story grammars tell about how the structure of a story is grasped, they tell nothing about the affective appeal of stories. Yet surely it is for its emotional appeal that children insist on hearing the same story over and over.

Nonetheless, the story grammar approach has injected some system into an area virtually bereft of method. There is a rigorous quality to the experiments: delete this, transform that, invert this, add that, and see what happens. Story grammars can tell the same sorts of things about the structure of stories as sentence grammars tell about the structure of sentences. However, given their structural nature, they will probably never be able to capture other aspects, such as mood and style, which are clearly as central to a story as the structure of its plot.

Understanding Mood, Style, and Medium

Works of art typically express moods. Paintings express feelings through both representational content and formal properties, such as color and line; music expresses emotion through such devices as mode, speed, and volume; and literature conveys moods through its content, and through the connotations and sound properties of its language. Just as young children are relatively insensitive to the mood expressed by a picture, so they ignore mood in stories.

Preschoolers' insensitivity to story mood was demonstrated by Dennie Wolf and her colleagues (Rubin and Gardner, 1977). Three- and four-year-olds were presented with two stories similar in subject matter but expressive of opposing moods and were asked to finish the stories. One of the stories consisted of a vignette about a boy who sailed a boat into the middle of an ominous storm and was tossed overboard. Another story told of a girl who sailed a boat on a beautiful sunny day and jumped over the side for a dip in the water. Although preschoolers may have been sensitive at some level to the different tones of these stories, no such awareness was reflected in their endings. Both stories were completed identically: the little boy or girl was said to have climbed back into the boat and gone home to bed. The endings given were thus unaffected by the mood of the story beginning. Since similar studies have not been carried out with older children, the age at which children become aware of, and able to reflect about, mood in stories is not known.

When children first encounter stories and verse, they exhibit little sensitivity to the style in which they are written. In one study, children heard a brief segment of a story or poem and then heard two more literary fragments (Gardner and Lohman, 1975). They were asked to select the one of the fragments that came from the same book as the original story and was written by the same person.

Three different kinds of pairings were used. A third of the time the style ending, which was written in the same style as the first story segment, was paired with a figure ending, which had no stylistic features in common with the original selection but contained similar content. A third of the time the style ending was paired with a neutral ending, which mirrored neither the style nor the content of the original passage. And a third of the time the correct ending was written so that it was similar in content as well as in style to the original story (a style-and-figure ending), and it was paired with a figure ending. A typical opening passage, adapted from a poem by Edward Lear, and the four possible endings are:

Opening passage

How pleasant to know Mr. Peer!
Who has written such volumes of stuff!
Some think him ill-tempered and queer,
But a few think him pleasant enough.

Style ending

> She sits in a beautiful parlour,
> With hundreds of tiles on the wall;
> She drinks a great deal of Marsala,
> But never gets tipsy at all.

Style-and-figure ending

> He reads but he cannot speak Spanish
> He cannot abide ginger beer;
> Ere the days of his pilgrimage vanish
> How pleasant to know Mr. Peer.

Figure ending

> Here's a man who's very nice indeed,
> I'd like to have a book of his to read.
> Sometimes, it's true, he starts to lose his temper.
> Yet Mr. Peer is pleasant each November.

Neutral ending

> Here's a girl who's very nice indeed,
> I'd like to have that dog of hers to feed.
> Sometimes, it's true, she starts to fall asleep,
> Yet she wakes, for her sleep is never deep.

The three combinations of endings were devised to present different levels of difficulty. It was thought that the style ending ought to be relatively easy to select when the other choice was a neutral one. However, when content cues were pitted against stylistic ones, the task was expected to be more demanding. In this case, one must overlook similarities of content and attend only to continuities of style. The case in which two cues (style and content) were pitted against one cue (content) was expected to be intermediate in difficulty.

These predictions were confirmed. The youngest subjects, aged seven years, proved insensitive to style even in the absence of content miscues, randomly selecting either the style or neutral ending. Eleven-year-olds demonstrated some style sensitivity, but only when the correct ending was paired with a neutral ending. When style was pitted against content, they attended only to content and chose on this basis. And when the style-and-figure ending was pitted against a figure ending, they responded at chance level.

Only adolescent and college-age subjects proved able to group on the basis of style in the face of content miscues. College students showed an explicit awareness of style and counted it as more relevant in this task than content. However, adolescents, who chose correctly, seemed to be in conflict: they deliberated longer than college students, and they showed less confidence in their judgments. Thus, there may be little explicit awareness of style before the adolescent years. It is also possible that sensitivity to style would be revealed earlier if simpler literary passages were used.

A comparison of performance across art forms on such tasks reveals that style sensitivity emerges first in music (Gardner, 1973b), then in painting (Gardner, 1970), and last in literature. The reason may lie in the relative importance of content or subject matter in any given art form. For the most part, music has no real plot or subject matter. Thus, there is less to distract attention from style. In tests of musical style sensitivity, preadolescents do as well or better than adolescents do (Gardner, 1973b). In painting, subject matter is very important, although representational content is by no means a necessary feature of the visual arts, as abstract art testifies. In literature, subject matter is far more important than it is in painting. Literature without content is difficult to imagine. And the subject matter of a piece of literature may initially blind a child to its style.

These comparisons reveal that the extent to which various art forms feature representational or denotational content is reflected in the time of emergence of style sensitivity. They also indicate that mere exposure to an art form is not a sufficient condition for the emergence of style sensitivity. Children are more heavily exposed to literature than to any other art form, yet they are quicker to notice the style of a piece of music or a painting than they are to apprehend the style of a story or poem.

Stories can be experienced in a number of different ways. Children may have stories read aloud to them, or they may read the stories themselves. Storybooks may be accompanied by illustrations, or they may contain only words and no pictures. While our grandparents often heard stories on the radio, today's children frequently watch stories enacted on television. The very medium in which the story is encountered may affect how the story is understood.

To determine whether the medium of presentation affects comprehension, the same story was presented in two forms (Meringoff, 1980). One group of children watched the story enacted on television in animated form, while another group heard the story read to them from a storybook as they looked at the pictures in the book. The same style of illustration was used in both cases, and the soundtrack of the video version was identical to the written story.

The "television children" proved more sensitive to the visual detail, even though the "book children" also had pictures to look at. And the television children were more likely to report the characters' actions in their retellings and to make inferences based on actions seen on the screen. In contrast, the book children were more likely to recall auditory patterns, to mention attributes rather than actions of the characters in the retelling, and to make inferences based on knowledge of the world rather than on information presented directly in the book. Thus, the medium in which a story is presented seems to affect how the story is experienced and encoded. A story translated into a different medium becomes, in some respects, a different story. This is yet another aspect of stories that story grammars are powerless to capture.

Recall the fairy tale at the opening of this chapter about a king, his daughter and her stepmother. Young children understand some aspects of this story. Studies suggest that children have a fairly sophisticated knowledge of the story's structure. Even the first time that they hear the opening of this story, they realize that a conflict will develop which must be resolved in some way before the story can end. However, while children may have a fairly good sense that a certain structure must follow because this is a story and not a recounting of actual events, they either ignore or misunderstand other aspects of the story.

To begin with, children may misunderstand the story's metaphorical language. While they may understand the perceptual metaphors, they are likely to misunderstand the psychological ones. Thus, they may realize that the princess' hair was not really made out of silk—it just looked and felt like silk—but misunderstand what it means to say that the queen had a heart of stone. In an attempt to make sense of such an expression, they may imagine that the queen lived in a stony castle, or that she had muscles that were as hard as stone. Children are also likely to see right through the style of this story to its plot, just as they will ignore the ominous mood that is created by the entrance of the big black birds, attending only to the overt events. Finally, they may fail to grasp the underlying psychological themes of Oedipal rivalry (the princess' one-to-one relation with her father is threatened by the arrival of the new queen) and of bitter jealousy.

Children's appreciation of stories presents something of a paradox. They can ignore or misunderstand many fundamental aspects of a story and yet be so fascinated by something in it that they insist on hearing it over and over again. This is a difficult issue to resolve. One possibility is that children are gripped by the one aspect of a story that they seem to understand: its structure. Their attention may be held by the fact that they realize that a conflict is being set up between good and bad characters, and that the story will demonstrate how in the end, after much struggle, good will prevail.

While children may be interested in the story's structure, they may also be captivated by those aspects that they do not quite understand. Perhaps children have an unformed, inchoate sense of the story's style, its mood, its psychological metaphors, and its underlying psychological themes. This understanding may be too vague to be picked up by the tasks devised by experimental psychologists. Nonetheless, such a glimmering of understanding may be what holds children's attention: realizing that there is something that they cannot quite grasp, they may be motivated to make sense of the story.

Perhaps it is for this reason that children insist on hearing the same story over and over again. By hearing it repeatedly, they can begin to assimilate it. If this is the case, then what holds children's attention is not what they can understand, but, paradoxically, what they cannot yet quite understand. In brief, the very effort at understanding what is only vaguely sensed may be what is responsible for the child's unending fascination with stories.

11 First Drafts

It seems to me that, beginning with the age of two, every child becomes for a short period of time a linguistic genius. Later, beginning with the age of five to six, this talent begins to fade . . . If his former talent for word invention and construction had not abandoned him, he would, even by the age of ten, eclipse any of us with his suppleness and brilliance of speech.

—Kornei Chukovsky

The average five-year-old can paint a picture that is strikingly similar to works by contemporary painters. Some of the childhood and adolescent sketches of Klee, Picasso, and Van Gogh seem almost as impressive as drawings made by these same artists much later in their lives. And the autistic child Nadia effortlessly drew pictures that bear an uncanny resemblance to sketches by Renaissance masters.

Examples of early mastery can also be found in music. Mendelssohn wrote one of his greatest pieces, the overture and the incidental music to *A Midsummer Night's Dream,* while still in his teens. Schubert and Mozart died in their thirties, both having left over six hundred compositions, many written while they were adolescents. And the violinist Yehudi Menuhin was internationally famous in the first decade of his life.

The attainment of such high levels of skill at an early age is less often found in literature. Unlike painters, composers, or musicians, poets and novelists often write their best works toward the later years of their lives. While one might conceivably mistake a preschooler's drawing for a Klee sketch, it would be hard to confuse a six-year-old's story with one by Tolstoy.

Perhaps literature stands apart in this way because the content of literary works deals directly with human psychology. Hence, one can not write a great poem or novel until one has lived through—or at least had the opportunity to observe and reflect upon—a number of important experiences. And this most often comes with age. It is difficult to imagine a fifteen-year-old Tolstoy writing *Anna Karenina*, for someone so young could hardly have gained so much insight into life.

While mastery in literature typically emerges later than a comparable level of attainment in the visual arts and music, all pre-schoolers are precocious when it comes to mastering language, the symbol system of literature. By the age of five, most children have acquired the exceedingly complex syntax of their language and learned thousands of words. And all of this occurs without any direct teaching on the part of the adult. Indeed, if adults had to teach children language, they would never learn it. Probably no one would know how to teach it. Moreover, all of the necessary language lessons could not be squeezed into the short space of a few years.

Not only are young children extraordinarily adept at mastering the rules of their native language, but they also often make errors that are extremely inventive. For instance, the Russian children's writer Kornei Chukovsky (1968) reported a child who upon hearing her father's telephone voice for the first time asked, "Daddy, why do you have such a dusky-dusky voice today"(p. 2)? Another child called a stale piece of cake "middle-aged"(p. 3). Still another child called his naked body "barefoot all over" (p. 3). These errors show that children can stretch the meanings of words to fill lexical gaps, and they do so in ways that render their meanings clear.

Thus, although extraordinary precocity is rarely found in literature, it can be said without exaggeration that all children are geniuses when it comes to mastering a first language. Moreover, the seeds of literary skill can be found in the initial stages of language acquisition. As soon as children begin to babble, they play with the sounds of language, stringing them together rhythmically (Chukovsky, 1968; Schwartz, 1980; Weir, 1962). In fact, this early play with sounds is indistinguishable from the infant's first "melodies." Word play—concern with rhythm, rhyme, alliteration, and the like—continues in different forms throughout childhood.

Soon after children utter their first words, they begin to invent novel and intentional metaphors (Carlson and Anisfeld, 1969; Chukovsky, 1968). To be sure, the two-year-old's metaphor is much simpler than a metaphor found in an adult poem. Nonetheless, first metaphors are constructed along the same lines as are the metaphors of any writer: in both cases, the perception of a newly discovered similarity is reflected in a novel use of a word.

Thus, the seeds of poetry are detected in the language of the very young: preschoolers, like poets, play with the sound and the rhythm of words, and they invent novel figures of speech. The seeds of fictional narrative can also be found in childhood. When two- and three-year-olds begin to pretend, the activity that they engage in is called symbolic play: a wooden block becomes a person, a stick becomes a horse, a string becomes a snake. And as children pretend, they begin to weave worlds of fantasy and fiction. Their invented worlds gradually take on the typical plot structure of fictional narrative.

These first glimmerings of literary skill are impressive. In the case of metaphor, the performance of the preschooler is actually more striking that that of the ten-year-old. Early sound play and metaphor have even suggested a special kinship between the young child and the adult poet (Chukovsky, 1968). However, these early instances of word play, metaphor, and fiction are only the first drafts of literary skill, the trappings rather than the substance of literature. They are necessary, but hardly sufficient. What is glaringly lacking is that elaboration of psychological theme, such as love, loss, jealousy, or friendship, worked out on a variety of levels, which is found in mature works of literature. The development of literary skills nevertheless sheds light on the many and variegated component capacities required to produce a work of literature. Of particular importance is the development of three building blocks of literary skill: the capacity to play with the sounds of words, to create metaphors, and to construct fictional worlds.

Poetry in the Crib

Young children are fascinated with the sound properties of language. Rhythm, rhyme, and alliteration are as common to the toddler as to the adult poet (Cazden, 1974; Chukovsky, 1968; Schwartz, 1980). One possible reason that the young child engages in verbal play more than does the typical nonliterary adult is that sound play requires attending primarily to the sound and not to the meaning of words. Perhaps adults, who have more experience with the meanings of words, are unable to ignore their meanings in favor of their sound properties (Cazden, 1974).

In a pioneering study of early sound play, the linguist Ruth Weir (1962) recorded the monologues of her two-and-a-half year old son Anthony as he lay in his crib at night. In his presleep monologues, Anthony played tirelessly with language. Unlike the language Anthony used during the day in order to communicate with another person, his night-time monologues were for himself alone. Because he was not trying to make himself understood, his utterances often seemed to make no sense. Instead of serving communication, his monologues fulfilled two other functions: a metalinguistic function, by drilling himself on phonology, syntax, and word meaning; and a poetic function, by playing with the sounds of words for their own sake (Jakobson, 1960).

Among the common poetic aspects of Anthony's language were alliteration ("*D*addy *d*ance/*b*lue *b*lanket/Like a *p*iggy bank/Like a *p*iggy bank/Had a *p*ink sheet on/The grey *p*ig out") and rhyme ("You take off all the *monkeys*/And kitties/And Phyllis and Humpty *Dumpty*"). His monologues were uttered in a rhythmic pattern, and they often had a rondo-like construction in which a sound pattern introduced in the beginning reappeared later on, creating a symmetrical design. Consider the lines (p. 103):

(1) Look at those pineapple

(2) In a pretty box

(3) And cakes

(4) What a sticks for cakes

(5) For the click

These lines serve little referential function. For example, while Anthony had often eaten pineapple, the pineapple never came "in a pretty box" but rather from a can. Moreover, the final two lines make no sense at all. For this child, more important that the meaning of these lines were their sound properties, in particular their symmetry and rhythm. The symmetrical construction of these lines can be discovered by counting the number of syllables in each line. Line 1 has five syllables (*pineapple* was considered to have only two syllables because of the weak final *l*). All of the other lines also have only five syllables except lines 3 and 5, which have two and three syllables respectively. But the fact that together the syllables of these two lines add up to five can be no accident, for there are too many such examples.

The consonantal pattern of these lines is also symmetrical. Line 1 begins and ends with the sound *l*. This sound is not repeated until the last line, where it reappears in the final word, *click*. Moreover, the first and last words in these lines (*look* and *click*) have an *l* followed by a *k*. Weir believed that Anthony did not know the meaning of *click*; if so, then the only rule guiding its selection must have been its sound properties.

There is also an order to the rhythm of these lines. Each line has one or several stressed syllables. However, whenever a line has only one stress, this stress always falls on the final syllable, as in lines 2, 3 and 5.

In its chaining of sounds, whereby the sounds of one word are contained within another, one of Anthony's frequently uttered group of words is reminiscent of Edgar Allan Poe's "The Raven." Anthony had apparently decided that a certain corner of one of his blankets was like a lipstick. In his monologues he often said the words "blanket like a lipstick." Any referential function of these words appeared to be long since disregarded: Anthony used them primarily in the service of sound play.

The sound chaining is shown by aligning the consonantal sounds of these words:

(1) bl n kt
(2) l   k
(3) l pst k

Each word is composed of the sounds *l* and *k*. The first word, *blanket*, is characterized by the pattern: *b* precedes *l*; *k* precedes *t*. The last word, *lipstick*, has the reverse pattern since *b* and *p* are similar sounds in that both are produced bilabially: *p* follows *l*; *k* follows *t*. This reversal lends internal unity to the utterance: in their consonantal structure, the syllables of *lipstick* are mirror images of the syllable of *blanket*. The use of the same sounds in each word chains together these words as skillfully as Poe's "The Raven." As the linguist Roman Jakobson said of one of Anthony's monologues; "It is a true and beautiful poetic composition tantamount to the masterpieces of infant art—verbal and pictorial" (Weir, 1962, p. 20).

The fascination with sound play in the early years of language acquisition has often been noted (Garvey, 1977). It has even been found in infants who babble in rhythm. For instance, a six-month-old uttered this rhythmic, almost musical sequence: "Uh ooh / Uh ooh / Uh ooh / Uh ooh" (Schwartz, 1980, p. 10).

Sound play, which in young children occurs primarily while they are by themselves, becomes an increasingly social activity with age. Anthony played with words only in his monologues; among older children, sound play begins to appear in their dialogues. This rhyming and rhythmic dialogue took place between two eight-year-olds (Schwartz, 1980, p. 15):

(Child 1) Off my case, potato face.
(Child 2) In your lip, potato chip.
           Up your nose with a rubber hose.
(Child 1) That don't rhyme, Frankenstein.
           I'm the boss, applesauce.

With age, sound play becomes not only more social but also more rule governed. Verbal play now takes such forms as pig

Latin, in which words are systematically distorted, and jump rope rhymes and hand clap games, in which rhyming lines are uttered in a regular beat. These forms of verbal play are taught by one child to another (Opie and Opie, 1960).

First Metaphors

An eighteen-month-old child noticed that his big toe was sticking out of a hole in his sock. He wiggled his toe, pointed at it, and laughingly announced "turtle" (de Villiers and de Villiers, personal communication). The adults who witnessed this were delighted. They could see the resemblance between the toe sticking out of its sock and a turtle's head protruding from its shell. Moreover, no one had ever pointed out to the child such a resemblance. This "renaming" appeared to be a genuinely novel invention.

In the initial stages of language development, children often use words in such unconventional ways. For instance, a two-year-old picked up a red ball, pretended to eat it, and then gleefully announced, "Apple!" A three-year-old pointed to a red and white stop sign and called it a candy cane. And a four-year-old looked up in the sky, saw a streak of skywriting, and said, "Look, the sky has a scar on it!"

Utterances such as these have often been noted in child language (Bowerman, 1976; Carlson and Anisfeld, 1969; Chukovsky, 1968; Clark, 1973; Guillaume, 1927; Nelson, 1974). Such word usage has generally been interpreted as evidence of underdeveloped lexical knowledge: it is assumed that the child who calls the ball "apple" has too broad a meaning for the word "apple." That is, he believes that this word applies literally to all red spheres (Clark, 1973; Gombrich, 1963). Thus, calling the ball "apple" is seen as an instance of "overextension."

The assumption that the child who calls the ball an apple is speaking literally but incorrectly is plausible, but no more so than a rival interpretation. In applying a word to a referent to which the word does not conventionally apply, the child may be creating a metaphor. The child who calls the ball "apple" may know full well that the ball is not really an apple; rather, it reminds him of an apple. Calling the ball "apple" may be his only means, given the fact that he has not yet fully mastered language, of expressing the idea that the ball looks like an apple.

The controversy between those who view early misnomers as metaphors and those who view them as overextensions is difficult to adjudicate. What counts as a convincing example of metaphor in the eyes of one observer may be another investigator's overextension. If these utterances are considered without taking into account the child's lexical development, the context in which the utterance was produced, and the affective components involved, the conflicting interpretations fit the data equally well.

What is needed, then, are not more delightful examples of unconventional word use but the construction of a set of criteria by which early metaphors can reliably be distinguished from unintentional overextensions. In one study, spontaneous speech samples of two boys and one girl between eighteen months and five years of age were analyzed. Instances of unconventional word usage were noted, and a set of guidelines was constructed to distinguish metaphors from mistakes (Winner, 1979; Winner, McCarthy, Kleinman, and Gardner, 1979). For instance, if the child who called the ball "apple" had previously correctly referred to it as a "ball," it could be inferred that he was deliberately overriding the literal name in favor of the novel one. Two other pieces of evidence could indicate that this utterance was not a mistake: if the child laughed as he renamed the ball, and if he did not actually try to eat the ball, but only pretended to.

From this investigation, a profile of early language development emerged in which metaphor played a significant role. Most of the time the children used words according to convention. However, when they did use words unconventionally, by far the major portion of their word use proved genuinely metaphoric, ranging from 72 to 91 percent across all three children.

In the speech samples of the three children studied, two kinds of metaphors were produced. One kind of early metaphor grew out of symbolic play. In such play, children pretend, through gestures, that an object is something else, such as pretending to eat the ball, as if it were an apple. Often, once the children had transformed the object through pretend action, they renamed the object accordingly, in this case "apple." Such metaphors may be called enactive. Examples abound. An eighteen-month-old slithered a toy car up her mother's arm, making it act like a snake, and said, "Snake." A two-year-old put his foot in a wastebasket and said; "Boot." A three-and-a-half-year-old, holding a yo-yo up to his chin, called it a "beard."

A second kind of early metaphor emerged independently of symbolic play. The eighteen-month-old who called his toe a "turtle," the three-year-old who called a red and white stop sign a "candy cane," and the four-year-old who called skywriting a "scar" offer examples of purely perceptual metaphors. Perceptual metaphors stand alone, without the support of action.

In the speech samples of the three children studied, a uniform developmental pattern was found: enactive metaphors declined with age, while perceptual metaphors increased with age. Both kinds of metaphors were found in all three children. But whereas one child's first metaphors were entirely enactive and gave way slowly to perceptual renamings, the other two children's first metaphors included both types, and their later metaphors were almost entirely perceptual. Further evidence for these patterns of individual differences came from a cross-sectional study in which metaphoric renamings of objects were experimentally elicited (Winner, McCarthy, and Gardner, 1980; Winner, McCarthy, Kleinman, and Gardner, 1979). Here, some children were more likely to produce a metaphor when they were allowed to handle the object to be renamed; others did better when permitted only to look at the object to be renamed.

First metaphors are very different from those produced by adults. The preschooler's metaphors consist simply in new names for physical objects. These new names are based on the physical properties of objects—most often on what can be done with them and on their shapes—rather than on affective or psychological aspects of experience. Psychological-physical metaphors, such as calling an angry face "cold," are not found in early language. And early metaphors are uttered only in the immediate tangible presence of the eliciting object. The topic of an adult's metaphor, in contrast, needs only to be imagined; the presence of the eliciting object is not necessary for the production of the metaphor. While early metaphors are thus more restricted in form than those of the adult, this early capacity for playfully renaming objects may be a necessary investment for later, full-blown forms of metaphor. Child metaphors are constructed along the same lines as are those of the adult: both are grounded in a resemblance between disparate elements, and both entail an overriding of the conventional rule governing the extension of a particular word.

Whereas preschoolers delight in giving new names to familiar objects, older children shy away from such unconventional language usage. Ten-year-olds are likely to insist on calling things by their rightful names. When they encounter a metaphor in the speech of another person, they may well protest. For instance, a ten-year-old who heard the expression "a loud tie" announced that words should not be used this way, since clothing does not make any kind of noise at all. And several studies have found that the frequency of spontaneous metaphorical usage declines during the years of middle childhood (Billow, 1981; Marti, 1979; Snyder, 1979).

This decline is not limited to spontaneous metaphors but

occurs as well in tasks designed to elicit metaphorical language. For instance, the production of novel similes was found to decline after the preschool years to a low level in the elementary school and high school years (Gardner, Kircher, Winner, and Perkins, 1975). Asked to complete the sentence, "The room was as quiet as . . . , " one four-year-old responded "as quiet as a magic marker," presumably because of the noiseless way in which a marker can glide over paper. Typical ten-year-old responses, such as "as quiet as a mouse," or "as quiet as a whisper," were less striking, more trite. The production of novel similes rose again among college age subjects. The two populations who produced the highest number of "good" similes were four-year-olds and adults (see also Pollio and Pickens, 1980; Schonberg, 1974). Thus it appears that the course of metaphor, from early renaming to its adult form, is not a directly linear one but follows a U-shaped curve. The preschooler's frequent use of metaphor declines in the years of middle childhood, not to resurface until adolescence.

The years of middle childhood, when metaphoric activity declines so sharply from its preschool level, can be thought of as a period of conventionalism. In language, children seem to want to master the conventional uses of words, just as in drawing they want to master the conventional rules of graphic representation. Increasing reliance on rules can also be found in the moral and social domains (Kohlberg, 1969; Piaget, 1965). Whether this conventionalism is due to formal schooling, which teaches the child to follow rules and give correct answers, or whether it reflects a natural developmental process, is not known. However, evidence from a study of scientific reasoning suggests that this period of rule-governed behavior is not simply due to the influence of schooling (Strauss, 1982). In this study, children were questioned about intensive physical qualities, such as the degree of sweetness of water. Unschooled as well as schooled children progressed from a global, intuitive form of reasoning to a more analytic, rule-governed approach. Thus, the relationship between schooling and conventionalism may well be the reverse of what is expected. Perhaps children are sent to school at six or seven precisely because this is when they begin to want explicitly to identify rules.

Although metaphors are infrequently heard in the speech of elementary school children, the underlying ability to produce metaphors remains intact during middle childhood. The problem seems to be one of motivation. When placed in a situation in which the rules clearly signal that it is desirable to make metaphors, literal age children have no difficulty producing novel figures of speech (Koch, 1970; Winner et al., 1975; Winner, McCarthy, and Gardner, 1980). Moreover, while ten-year-olds are unlikely spontaneously to rename objects as the four-year-old does, they may well create extended analogies. For instance, in trying to understand the concept of side effects caused by medicine, one ten-year-old asked her mother whether side effects were like using a scissors to open a can and bending the scissors in the process (Wolf, personal communication). Such an analogy differs from preschool metaphors in at least two respects. First, it is less risky, because the child has not applied a word in an unconventional way but has simply compared two things. Second, whereas the four-year-old renames physical objects, the ten-year-old analogizes about more abstract concepts, such as side effects.

Yet there are also important similarities between these two behaviors. Renaming objects on the basis of physical similarities may help preschoolers to make sense of the world. By noting resemblances among objects, they make their environment less chaotic and more organized. Similarly, the analogies of older children usually occur as the children are trying to understand a new concept. Relating the new and the abstract to something concrete and familiar helps ten-year-olds, no less than four-year-olds, to make sense of their world.

Early Fictional Worlds

Consider this story told by a preschooler: "Once upon a time there was a giraffe and he saw a bird in a tree and that's the end" (Rubin and Gardner, 1977). This early narrative could be analyzed in a number of different ways. For example, one could describe simply its form and content by counting the kinds of animals named and the number of sentences used. Such a purely descriptive approach was taken in a study of children's stories between the ages of two to five, which detailed typical themes, characters, and settings (Ames, 1966). The chief themes of early stories were found to be violent ones. Preschool children frequently tell stories about harm and disaster in which characters fall down and die, or get devoured by monsters. But children also protect themselves against disaster: bad things happen to other people in the story, but not to the storytellers themselves; or the storyteller "undoes" the disaster at the end of the story.

The giraffe story could also be studied from a psychoanalytic perspective. A study with a theoretical orientation of this kind might explore the phallic imagery of the giraffe and the tree, searching for disguised sexual and aggressive themes as clues to the storyteller's fantasy life. Psychoanalysts have used stories elicited in play therapy to diagnose as well as to treat children with emotional problems. Stories can be used to diagnose because they serve as windows on the storyteller's unconscious. They can also be used to cure because children, in the act of playing out their unconscious fears and wishes, may gain some control over them (e.g. Erikson, 1963; Freud, 1955; Gould, 1972; Singer, 1973).

To the extent that stories have been studied at all, the psycho-analytic perspective represents the major psychological approach to children's literary creations. In one of the most extensive psychoanalytic studies, several hundred stories were collected from children between the ages of two and five (Pitcher and Prelinger, 1963). On the assumption that a story is an interplay between the author's unconscious wishes and the forces striving to disguise these wishes and render them socially acceptable, these stories were used as a means of discovering the children's dominant unconscious fantasies and their characteristic mechanisms of defense. Some stories were found to be almost pure wish fulfillment, with little or no censoring of the wish. For instance, one child, aged two years eleven months, told the story: "Once upon a time there was a dog. He cried. He needs his mommy. The mommy comes. Then she had a bottle" (p. 39).

While this story was interpreted as a tale of direct oral wish fulfillment, other stories were said to present a wish in more disguised, symbolic form, as in the story told by a boy aged three years four months: "Once upon a time there was a cat, and he jumped on a cow. The farmer spanked the cat. The cat went home and was very sad. The cow came over to the cat's house and broke it. That was the next day. The cat spanked the cow for doing that. Then the cat and the cow went to the cow's house, and they were happy, see?" (p. 221). Lurking beneath the disguise of the triangle of farmer, cow, and cat was found the fulfillment of an Oedipal wish. The relationship between the punitive farmer and the naughty cat was said to represent the tension between the little boy and his father. The happy reunion of cat and cow represented the wished-for union of the child with his mother. The storyteller, the investigators reasoned, had used the animals as characters in order to protect himself from the knowledge of what the story was "really" about.

While these two tales were said to represent the fulfillment of wishes, some of which are forbidden, other stories were highly realistic and factual, in which there seemed to be little or no fantasy. These stories were seen as so heavily dominated by censorship and defense that no wish can creep in even momentarily. In a five-year-old's story about a hypothetical trip to outer space, for instance, the storyteller simply described in a factual manner all of the requirements of a space voyage. Such a story was interpreted as revealing that defensive censoring had won out over any manifestation of wish.

Different types of defense were found in the stories. Some revealed the defense of denial. For instance, one child began a story with, "A kitty—he's not a bad boy," and proceeded to describe the kitten's misdeeds. Another child told a story about a tiger which concluded with a pact of friendship between all of the characters. In this way, fears and frightening wishes, represented by the threat of the tiger, were simply denied. The defenses of repression or identification with the aggressor were also found. Examples of the latter type of defense were stories told in the first person, in which the storyteller disciplined naughty animals.

The stories also provided confirmation of the neopsychoanalytic theory of Erik Erikson (1963). According to Erikson's theory, we pass through a number of stages in the course of our lives. At each stage, there is a crisis that can be resolved in either a successful or an unsuccessful way. In infancy, the most important issue is the establishment of a sense of trust. If babies feel loved and if their bodily needs are gratified, a basic sense of trust is established that will serve them throughout life. But if infants feel unloved or abandoned, a sense of mistrust will develop and pervade the rest of their life. During the age of toilet training, in which children experience a significant interference with their bodily pleasures, the major hurdle is to establish a sense of autonomy. If children fail to develop this sense, they will be overcome with shame and doubt. With the increasing independence that comes at about age five, initiative becomes the dominant concern. The world is now something to be explored and conquered. If children are made to feel that their exploration and curiosity are too intrusive, then a sense of guilt rather than self-confidence will develop.

The stories collected provided some support not only for these age-related issues but also for sex differences. Issues of trust were found more often in girls' stories, and themes of initiative and exploration were found more often in boys' stories. While girls told stories about mothering, nurturance, protection, and feeding, boys told of exploration and discovery. Moveover, these themes of exploration became more frequent as boys reached the age of five. Children of both sexes at ages three and five also tended to tell stories related to the problem of autonomy. Although they never related a story that dealt directly with toilet training or other anal concerns, their stories dealt with such issues on a symbolic level, as in stories about characters asserting their independence who came into conflict with parental restrictions. The frequency of such stories at age three is predicted by Erikson's theory, but the resurgence of this issue in the stories of five-year-olds is not.

The psychoanalytic approach to children's stories, though potentially revealing, is beset with weaknesses. Perhaps the main problem is that the evidence on which interpretations of stories are based is usually rather flimsy. Thus, the interpretations often appear far-fetched. For instance, the Oedipal interpretation of the story about the cat, the cow, and the farmer is based on very insubstantial clues. To conclude that this story deals with power relations between parent and child seems much more reasonable.

Another groundless interpretation is the psychoanalytic reading of factual, descriptive stories as indicative of censorship. Simply because a story lacks a fantasy content does not mean that this content has been forcibly kept out of the story. It seems just as likely, if not more so, that the story is about precisely what it purports to be about. That is, the child who told a story about a space voyage may in fact have been genuinely interested in space travel. Not all manifest content needs to be seen as hiding a latent content underneath. Any claim that a story's surface content hides a deeper level must be based on at least some evidence of the latent content lurking beneath the surface. Otherwise, such interpretations remain untestable.

Another way to look at stories is from a cognitive-structural perspective. Rather than using the giraffe story as a way of understanding the child's dominant emotional concerns, a cognitive psychologist might examine the degree to which this vignette possesses the structural components of a story, such as plot, differentiated characters, character development, narrative voice, style, or expressivity (Rubin and Wolf, 1979; Scarlett and Wolf, 1979; Sutton-Smith, 1975). Of these components of a story that the storyteller must eventually master, two must be tackled at the outset. Perhaps most basic is the construction of a boundary between the fictional world of the story and the everyday world of reality. Storytellers must narrate the story, but they must not enter into the story action directly. Thus, the child who tells the giraffe story must realize that he cannot step into the story frame and interact directly with the giraffe or the bird. These story characters must be seen to exist in a separate, bounded, fantasy world, one that is independent of the real world. Failure to respect the boundary between story and reality results in a failure to construct an autonomous fictional world.

Next in importance, the narrator must construct a plot that abides by elementary narrative rules. According to theoretical accounts of narrative, the plot must have a clear beginning, middle, and end, and it must be structured around a problem that the main character confronts and eventually resolves in some way (Aristotle, *Poetics* 1459a; Prince, 1973; Propp, 1968; Todorov, 1969). Thus, in order to make the giraffe story into a legitimate "story," the child must go on to set up some sort of conflict and then resolve this conflict within the story frame. For instance, the bird might come into conflict with the environment by becoming caught in a spider's web. The giraffe might then rescue the bird by using her long neck.

Without a boundary setting off an autonomous fictional world, and without a plot in which a problem is faced and resolved, there is no story. Once these two components have been constructed, the child can be credited with rudimentary story-telling competence. But more sophisticated story-telling skills remain to be mastered. For instance, plot structure can become extraordinarily complex, with a number of problems and resolutions embedded within the main problem to be solved. Thus, in the giraffe story, the main problem to be solved might be for the giraffe to rescue the bird caught in the spider's web in the tree. But first the giraffe must cross a river to get to the bird. And before she can cross the river, she must find a boat. Such a story involves multiple embedded problems. Embedding of this kind is typical of fully formed adult stories.

Other sophisticated skills that must be mastered include a sensitivity to literary genre. Fairy tales must be clearly distinguished from contemporary adventure tales, allegories from fables. Adult writers are aware of the rules of literary genre and do not mix genres unless they are deliberately parodying a genre.

In adult stories, furthermore, characters may be multidimensional. That is, rather than all bad, a villain may be both evil and likable. And multiple voices are constructed: the narrator's voice is distinguished from the voices of the characters in order to create the illusion that the story action is motivated by independent characters rather than by the narrator.

Mastery of Story Boundaries

Even a two-year-old can tell the difference between a story and a nonstory (Leondar, 1977; Pitcher and Prelinger, 1963). Doubters are advised to read a newspaper article to a two-year-old when a bedtime story is requested. Moreover, by the age of two, the child begins spontaneously to invent sequences that sound storylike. While engaged in symbolic play, children begin to narrate pretend events (Rubin and Wolf, 1979). Given toy replicas of a dog and a cat, the child may walk these replicas through a series of events: the dog and cat may go on a walk, the dog bites the cat, the cat protests in a falsetto voice. These episodes narrated in symbolic play are the seeds of stories. Thus, stories no less than metaphors emerge in the arena of symbolic play.

While the two-year-old can be credited with a certain amount of storytelling competence, storytelling skills are still severely limited. Children at this early age do not construct a boundary around the fictional world that they narrate, nor do they yet weave stories with the elementary plot structure that any genuine story must have.

In a study of the development of boundary construction in early narratives, children were told the beginning of a story (Scarlett and Wolf, 1979, 1981). The experimenter stopped the story abruptly in the middle of a crisis and asked the child to furnish an ending. Two kinds of crises were presented: either one character threatened the well-being of the others, or the characters together faced a difficult situation in their environment. In both cases, the story was broken off when the main character was imperiled.

One of the stories opened as a little girl left her house and went for a walk in the woods. As the story was narrated, the experimenter enacted the events, using toy replicas of a little girl, a house, and trees. The little girl spent the afternoon in the forest, picking flowers and talking to the animals. Suddenly she realized that it was growing dark, and she did not know how to find her way home. Here the storyteller stopped and asked the child to take over.

Children of different ages responded to this task in characteristic ways. Eighteen-month-olds simply picked up the toy replicas and explored them. Any sense that there was a story to complete escaped them. Two-and three-year-olds realized there was a story to be finished. They also understood that the story was to be finished by getting the little girl back home. However, this goal was achieved in a rather non-narrative fashion: the toy girl was simply picked up by the children and deposited back home. "Now she's home," they typically announced.

These children had entered into the story world and rescued the main character. Because the children performed the rescue directly, rather than working through the story character, they revealed that they had not yet constructed a boundary that sets off the story world and which cannot be crossed. Examples of such direct intervention abound. In one case, the experimenter called a large round rug "an ocean" and set out one bad fish which was described as wanting to eat all of the other fish. The child was then asked to continue the story. One child solved this task by simply picking up the bad fish, placing him firmly on another rug, and announcing that the bad fish was now in a "different ocean" (Rubin and Gardner, 1977). In another case, the experimenter told a story about some animals in a forest. The forest was described as very hot, because the sun was burning down. A button was used to stand for the sun. The sun was said to become so hot that the animals did not know what to do. At this point, the child was asked to complete the story. One child responded by simply twirling the button around "to make it cold" (Rubin and Gardner, 1977).

Between the ages of three and five, children began to create more autonomous fictional worlds. By five, the story problem was solved within the story itself. Children no longer stepped in and performed the action directly. However, while the problem was solved within the story world, the solution was still very primitive. For example, instead of stepping in and depositing the lost girl back home, children of this age simply made one of the other story characters do this. Thus, a monkey from the forest may pick the little girl up, lift her over the trees, and drop her in her house. Children did not yet deal with the problem of how the animal could do this. A more sophisticated solution, in which the monkey asked a bird to fly over the trees and guide the little girl home, must await later development.

Mastery of Plot Structure

The stories produced by children between two and four do not yet have the basic plot structure that is expected of a story. Consider this example from a three-year-old. "Duckie swam in the water. Then a boat came. The boat has a big whistle. Toot, toot! See, I'm the boat. It went around. Then duckie swam around the boat. Daddy duck came. He gave him a big worm that got dead" (Leondar, 1977, p. 187). Here is another three-year-old's story (Sutton-Smith, 1981, p. 90):

> The little white duck went swimming
> then the crab came
> a lobster came
> then a ice-cream came
> and a popsicle was playing by itself.

These early "stories" do not have a clear beginning (in which a problem is introduced), middle (in which the main character wrestles with the problem), and end (in which the problem is resolved, either successfully or unsuccessfully). Instead, these tales are loosely connected series of events (Applebee, 1978). To be sure, they do not lack all guise of a story. Sometimes they begin and end with the conventional story frames "once upon a time" and "the end"; the events reported are fictional; they are set in some unspecified past; and the events are reported by a narrator who observes everything that is happening. However, the narrators of these first stories are immobile: they do not move around but remain rooted in one spot. As a result, they can only report on events that occur directly in front of them. This immobility is constraining and does not permit the narrators enough space to observe and report the variety of actions necessary to achieve a story with a clear problem-solving structure. Thus, one of the prerequisites for creating stories with a story-like structure may be the release of the narrators from immobility (Leondar, 1977).

Children's first stories not only lack a story-like structure but also possess certain features more typical of poetry than of fiction (Sutton-Smith, 1981). For instance, a two-year-old told this story (p. 48):

> The cat went on the cakies
> the cat went on the car
> the cookie was in my nose
> the cookie went on the fireman's hat
> the fireman's hat went on the bucket
> the cookie went on the carousel
> the cookie was on the puzzle
> the cookie went on the doggie.

This story contains many prosodic elements: it is rhythmic, and full of alliteration (cat, cakies, cookie, carousel). There are many such examples in which the child is clearly more interested in playing with the sounds and the rhythms of sentences than in weaving a plot. These early story-poems recall the presleep monologues of Anthony (Weir, 1962). They also suggest that poetry may be a more natural tongue for the child than the language of stories: poetry is uttered in the crib, whereas narratives that possess the two necessary ingredients of stories—a boundary demarcation and a basic plot structure—are not heard until the later preschool years. This reflects the fact that constructing a story is a more complex task than playing with the sound properties of language. To tell a coherent story demands both an understanding of causality, in order to construct a plot, and the ability to consider two worlds simultaneously—the world of everyday reality and the woven world of the story.

By five, children can construct coherent stories with a beginning, middle, and end. The events of the story are causally connected, and they revolve around a central conflict that the main character must confront. These stories are clearly demarcated from the world of reality, and the boundary between the constructed and the given world is no longer violated.

While the basic skeleton of the story is mastered by five years of age, stories continue to develop throughout the course of childhood. For instance, a clear evolution in both complexity of content and structure can be traced. Folklorists have categorized the types of stories that exist across cultures, and when such taxonomies are imposed on children's stories, they make a developmental pattern discernible.

The hero folktales of various cultures exhibit four types of content (Maranda and Maranda, 1971). In the first type, one power overwhelms another, and the minor power makes no attempt at response. In the second, one power overwhelms another, and the minor power attempts a response but fails. In the third type, one power overwhelms another, who then nullifies the threat. And in the fourth, one power overwhelms another, who nullifies the threat, and the original circumstances are substantially transformed. Although hero tales of all four types exist, in cultures with little belief in control over fate, the fourth kind is seldom found.

Applying this taxonomy to the stories of children between five and ten revealed a progression from level one to level four (Sutton-Smith, 1975). In a typical level one story, the main character is overcome by a powerful, evil figure, and no response is made. In a level two story, the main character responds to the threat but does not succeed in nullifying this threat: while the hero may escape, no provision is made against the return of the danger. The hero may escape from the villain, but the villain is not killed. In level three stories, the threat is nullified when the villain is killed; and at level four, the hero not only slays the villain but also marries the princess and reigns over a now peaceful land.

Some intriguing sex differences were observed in children's stories. Boys tended to tell tales of villainy, in which a high-powered figure overcame one of lower power. Girls, in contrast, told stories in which characters faced a lack, such as hunger or poverty. And girls more often resolved the story conflict with an alliance in which a second figure entered to give help to the main character.

A similar development in complexity was reported in the application of a more structural taxonomy to children's stories. North American Indian stories are constructed upon a primitive dyad: either something is lacking, and this lack is then liquidated; or a villainous deed is carried out, and this villainy is then nullified (Dundes, 1975). More complex narratives are formed by concatenating two or more dyads; the most complex narratives are formed by embedding one dyad within another. In such an embedded structure, as the characters try to solve the main problem, they have to overcome a smaller problem before the major one can be resolved.

Application of this analysis to children's stories revealed that the stories of four- and five-year-olds contained only one nuclear dyad (Botvin and Sutton-Smith, 1977). One story, for example, read: "An astronaut went into space. He was attacked by a monster. The astronaut got in his spaceship and flew away." By seven years old, children began to tell stories which consisted of a concatenation of such dyads. Not until eleven, however, did children embed a subordinate dyad within a superordinate one. Thus, all of the types of stories invented by children can be found in the repertoire of adult folktales; however, children begin by telling only the simplest kinds.

Mastery of Genres

Storytelling skill requires not only that the tellers have a general sense of a story frame but also that they have a sense of genre. They must be able to classify stories, for example, as fairy tales, fables, allegories, or contemporary adventure tales. In the stories they tell, they must establish from the start the particular genre within which they are working, and they must remain within the frame of that genre. The child who begins a story in the fairy tale genre, introducing a king and a queen who lived "once upon a time" in a land far away, and who then goes on to take the king and queen to the movies, has violated the fairy tale frame. Only certain types of characters and activities are appropriate to a given genre. The development of skill within a genre has been almost completely neglected in studies of children's production and comprehension of stories.

One of the few studies of this issue revealed that a developed sense of genre emerges long after the child has acquired a general sense of what it takes to tell a story (Rubin and Gardner, 1977). This study suggested the following picture. When children construct their first stories, they lack any knowledge that stories come in different genres. Almost all of their stories fit a simple "monster" frame. In this kind of a story, characters are divided into broadly defined good and bad characters. Bad characters, which may be anything from lions to alligators to giants, are threatening. Good characters are everyone else. In monster stories, the bad character threatens the good ones, often by chasing them. Typically, the child completes such a story by banishing the evil character. The three-year-old's grasp of this frame is so strong that the child does not admit the possibility of repentance on the part of the bad character.

The monster frame seems to be invented spontaneously by children. The fairy tale genre, on the contrary, is introduced by adults. Although three-year-olds have heard many fairy tales, they rarely invent them on their own. In fact, presented with the stock elements of a fairy tale, such as a king, a queen, and a castle, children initially treat them as ordinary characters, calling them "this guy" and "that guy" and using them to act out a familiar scheme, such as going to the store.

Toward the end of the third year, the first glimmerings of fairy tales can be heard. Given a king, queen, and a castle, one child said that there was a "bridge of water" around the castle, that is, a moat. And a dark forest introduced by the experimenter was said to have "grouchy animals" in it. However, as soon as a dragon was introduced, this child reverted to the monster genre and initiated a chase scene.

While four-year-olds have a notion of some of the stock elements of a fairy tale, such as kings, queens, castles, and forests, as well as some of its stock phrases, such as "once there lived" and "wicked," they do not yet coordinate these elements into a whole. Moreover, they introduce little psychological motivation. Thus, the actions of the characters appear arbitrary.

By middle childhood, children have heard many fairy tales, and they have a fuller understanding of what a story in this genre must be like. Nonetheless, even eleven-year-olds find it difficult to remain entirely within a fairy tale genre. Although they do not violate the genre as blatantly as the three-year-old who takes the king and queen to a fast food restaurant, they sometimes blend fairy tales and modern adventure tales. For instance, one eleven-year-old told the story: "The queen hired a lot of woodsmen to chop down the tree and the daughter started running and hid in the woods . . . and had a wolf with her and she made it attack the queen . . . The wolf bit her and she had an hour or else she'd die . . . Then the only shot for her arm was in another kingdom, miles away. The daughter got on a wild horse and finally got the cure. She got on the back of a cheetah and it ran about sixty miles. She

made it back and saved the queen's life and they were friends."
(Rubin and Gardner, 1977, p. 49). Other eleven-year-olds told fairy
tales with such anachronistic touches as a king who asked for a di-
vorce or a princess who went to the zoo. It is quite possible, however, that children at this age who were thus violating the fairy tale
genre did so intentionally, in order to parody the genre itself.

The ability to parody a genre is one of the best indicators that
the storyteller has fully mastered the genre in question. There is
evidence of children's ability to parody the story frame in general
at a very young age. A four-year-old child of a librarian, who had
heard numerous tales, told this story (Sutton-Smith, 1979, p. 114):

> Once upon a time the once upon a time ate the once
>   upon a time which ate the once upon a time
> and then the once upon a time which ate the once upon
>   a time ate the princess once upon a time with the king
> and then the once upon a times died
> then the end ate the end
> the end
> the end
> then the end died
> then the end died
> then the end died
> then the end died
> and then the end the end the end died
> the end with a the end
> the end
> the end.

Here is a clear parody of the conventional elements of a story
("once upon a time", "the end", kings and princesses, "and then").
Although this four-year-old demonstrated a mastery of the basic
story elements by parodying them, the ability to parody a particular genre, such as a fairy tale, does not emerge until late childhood
(McQuillian, 1975).

Although precocity in literature is much rarer than in music or
the visual arts, the seeds of literary skill can be found in the crib.
The infant plays with the sound and rhythm of words, and the
two-year-old begins to invent striking figures of speech and to
weave rudimentary fictional worlds. The fact that the trappings of
poetry emerge in the form of sound play sometime before the
trappings of fiction suggests that poetry is prior to fiction. The
child's first literary attempts are the kernels of poems rather than

of novels. And even when children first begin to tell stories, the prosodic elements of these stories often render them more like poems than narratives.

It is paradoxical that poetry emerges prior to fiction, since the average adult is much better equipped to tell a story than to create a poem. In cultures with a strong oral storytelling tradition, a wide range of adults can attain impressive storytelling skills (Lord, 1965). But in the case of poetry, the situation is different: while the infant engages in some of the same kinds of sound play as the poet, only a very few adults ever go on to write poetry.

The seeds of literature, though found in the very early years of childhood, blossom in but a few cases, and this only in adulthood. The literary ventures of the preschooler are very different from those of Tolstoy. Children invent the trappings of literature— sound play, metaphor, and the plot structure of a narrative. But many elements are still lacking. While infants play with sound, they do not use sound to enhance meaning. Their metaphors are for the most part perceptually based; never do they work out abstractly grounded metaphors on a number of different levels. And their stories lack complex characters, ambiguity of meaning, and elaborate themes. Although the four-year-old tells stories with themes similar to those in adult novels, these themes are not developed in any complexity. Thus, the four-year-old's tale of love and loss is a far cry from Tolstoy's *Anna Karenina*. More so than musicians or painters, writers must draw upon their life experiences in order to write. It is perhaps for this reason that a literary masterpiece could never be written by a child, or even an adolescent. No matter how sensitive children are to the nuances of language, they lack the richness of experience upon which a work of literature must build.

FIVE Art and Abnormality

12 The Damaged Brain

Since childhood, I have been enchanted by the fact and the symbolism of the right hand and the left—the one the doer, the other the dreamer. The right is order and lawfulness, le droit. Its beauties are those of geometry and taut implication. Reaching for knowledge with the right hand is science. Yet to say only that much of science is to overlook one of its excitements, for the great hypotheses of science are gifts carried in the left hand . . . And should we say that reaching for knowledge with the left hand is art? Again it is not enough, for as surely as the recital of a daydream differs from the well-wrought tale, there is a barrier between undisciplined fantasy and art. To climb the barrier requires a right hand adept at technique and artifice.

—Jerome Bruner

A few years ago, the *New York Times Magazine* ran an article on the brain. Across the cover of the magazine was an eye-catching, attention-grabbing drawing of a human head divided down the middle. The left side of the head was filled with words from a page in a dictionary. This was to suggest the central role of the left hemisphere of the brain in the processing of language. The right half contained whirling dancers from a Degas painting. This was meant to suggest a view of the right hemisphere of the brain as responsible for creative, artistic behaviors.

This magazine picture implied that we have two minds, not one. Freudian theory is based on such a duality—the conscious and unconscious mind. A new, experimentally based theory of the duality of mind has grown out of the laboratory of the neurobiologist Roger Sperry, who studied "split-brain" patients whose two hemispheres had been surgically separated in an effort to control epileptic seizures. Because their two hemispheres could not communicate with each other, it was possible to present tasks to only one hemisphere and observe how the patients solved these various problems. Such study revealed that, while anatomically almost identical, the two sides of the brain contain two distinctly different worlds of consciousness (Gazzaniga, 1970; Sperry, Gazzaniga, and Bogen, 1969).

As a consequence, a new view of the duality of mind began to be espoused by scientists as well as by the popular media. The left brain came to be seen as our rational mind, processing information in a logical, sequential fashion and controlling both linguistic and mathematical reasoning. The right brain came to be seen as our intuitive mind, processing information in a spatial rather than temporal manner and controlling our creative and artistic abilities. According to this increasingly popular account, the left brain is linguistic, analytic, and scientific; the right brain is nonverbal, intuitive, and artistic. Hence, the divided head on the magazine cover.

The possibility that the left brain is the locus of language and scientific reasoning and the right brain is the site of all artistic capacities has radical implications. Among other things, this characterization suggests that art is independent of language and logic. Yet there is questionable truth in such a radically dichotomous picture of mind and brain, and in such a sharp split between art, language, and logic.

Consider one piece of evidence. After suffering a stroke which caused damage only to the left side of his brain, the Russian composer V. G. Shebalin suffered from severe aphasia, an impairment of language caused by brain damage. Despite the severity of the left hemisphere damage, Shebalin's musical abilities were not affected. He continued to compose, to teach, to critically evaluate the performances of his students, and was considered by his critics to be as brilliant a composer as ever (Luria, Tsvetkova, and Futer, 1965).

Consider another piece of evidence. The German expressionist painter Lovis Corinth suffered a right hemisphere stroke. Unlike Shebalin, Corinth's language capacities were unaffected. However, his artistic capacities appeared altered after his stroke. Although he resumed painting after partial recovery, he no longer painted in his old style. The brush strokes had become bolder, rougher, wilder, and the tone of the paintings had become more intensely emotional and expressive (Gardner, 1975; Kuhn, 1925).

The case of Shebalin demonstrates that left hemisphere damage, while causing the disorder of language called aphasia, may leave an artistic capacity unaffected. The case of Corinth reveals that damage to the right side of the brain can fundamentally alter an artistic capacity. These two pieces of evidence are entirely consistent with the magazine cover picture and with a view of the brain in which the right hemisphere is dominant for artistic behavior.

But consider a third piece of evidence, this time based upon healthy rather than brain-damaged individuals. When people both with and without musical training were administered a task in which musical fragments had to be recognized, a surprising difference was found between the two subject populations (Bever and Chiarello, 1974). Those who had no formal music training carried out the task in their right hemispheres. Among those with formal training, however, both hemispheres were involved in processing and recognizing the tunes. These results suggested that those who are trained in music listen in a more left-brain and possibly analytic mode, while those without training listen in a more right-brain, possibly holistic mode. This study alone cautions against an overly simplistic view in which the right hemisphere is equated with art and creativity. Current findings about artistry and the two sides of the brain suggest that, instead of words versus dancers or reason versus artistry, a more complicated picture should have appeared on the magazine cover.

Rather than exploring whether the right brain is the locus of artistry, it is more fruitful to investigate particular artistic skills separately. There is no reason to assume that the right hemisphere is equally involved, or uninvolved, in all artistic skills. Thus, instead of asking whether the right hemisphere is dominant for art, researchers have asked whether it is dominant for particular art forms. The question has been narrowed even further, however, because the right hemisphere might be dominant for one but not for all capacities within a particular art form, such as the ability to perceive and recognize music but not the capacity to compose music. To determine this, the various components of skill within an art form—motivation, creation, performance, perception, criticism, and evaluation—have been separately examined.

Researchers have also asked whether the right hemisphere is dominant not for the arts but rather for a certain way of processing information. Since the right brain is known to process information holistically and the left brain to process information analytically, the two hemispheres may each make different contributions to the arts. To investigate this, artistic skills that call upon analytic processes, such as recognizing the individual pitches of a melody, have been compared to artistic skills that rest upon more global processes, such as recognizing the overall contour of a melody.

Avenues to the Mind

The study of the relationship between brain and behavior constitutes the field of neuropsychology, and the attempt to understand the different functions of the two hemispheres is one of the central concerns of this field. In order to determine how behavioral capacities are represented and organized in the brain, neuropsychologists rely on the study of both normal and brain-damaged individuals. In studying the brain of normal individuals, special techniques must be used which allow investigators to assess the functioning of each hemisphere independently.

One such technique is called dichotic listening. In a typical dichotic listening experiment, two different words are played simultaneously into earphones worn by the listener. One word is played into the left earphone and one into the right. The person is asked to report what is heard. People do not usually report hearing both words. Rather, they usually say that they heard the word played in the right ear (Kimura, 1961). This occurs because the primary neural pathways from the right ear go to the left hemisphere of the brain, and those from the left ear go to the right hemisphere. The fact that the message from the right ear is the one that is reported is evidence that the left hemisphere of the brain is the locus of language. When musical stimuli are presented, however, people report what their left ear, and thus their right hemisphere, heard. This is evidence that music is processed in the right hemisphere.

Another technique which has revealed the different roles of the two hemispheres uses the tachistoscopic test. In a tachistoscopic experiment, the subject is told to fixate on a dot on a screen. Two words, one on either side of the dot, are flashed on a screen for a split second. The word in the subject's right visual field is picked up by the left side of each eye and then goes to the left hemisphere; the word in the left visual field is picked up by the right side of each eye and then goes to the right hemisphere. Thus, the left hemisphere receives information from the right visual field, and vice versa. When asked to report what they saw, subjects typically report the word in the right visual field. This is further evidence for the left hemisphere's dominance in language.

The methodology that has revealed the most information about the roles of the two hemispheres of the brain has been the study of people who have sustained damage to a focal area of the brain. The most common cause of brain damage is the occurrence of a cerebral vascular accident, or stroke, in which the blood supply to part of the brain is temporarily cut off, depriving the brain of vital oxygen and glucose. Without oxygen and glucose for more than a few minutes, brain tissue is irreversibly damaged.

If a stroke reduced all capacities equally, it would tell nothing about the brain. The victim would simply be less proficient than normal at all skills. But because a stroke causes highly selective damage, it provides a unique lens through which to view the organization and functioning of the brain. While some capacities may be wholly destroyed, others remain completely unaffected. By observing the symptoms that cluster together, and by noting those functions that are spared when others are impaired, investigators can learn about which skills are related and which are not. For instance, if damage affects the ability to read musical notation but leaves unharmed the ability to compose, it suggests that the perception and production of music function independently in the brain. The study of selective brain damage makes it possible to disentangle the various component skills that function seamlessly in an intact brain.

Research in neuropsychology, which has focused on language, is only now beginning to examine the arts. Two kinds of brain-damaged populations have been studied in order to determine the organization of artistic capacities in the brain. Artists who have suffered brain damage constitute one group of patients. However, this is a relatively small group, since only a small proportion of any population, artists included, suffers brain damage. Hence, this group must be studied in concert with a second group, composed of people untrained in the arts. Right and left hemisphere damaged patients with no training or previous involvement in the arts are often asked to carry out simple artistic tasks, such as making a drawing, recognizing a melody, or interpreting a metaphor. The role of the two hemispheres in ordinary artistic tasks carried out by people of average levels of competence can thus be determined. A comparison of patients with and without artistic training and talent can reveal whether artistic skills are organized differently in the brains of gifted and average people.

Painting

Striking differences in drawing ability have been found in artistically untrained people with right and left hemisphere damage (Fig. 12.1; Warrington, James, and Kinsbourne, 1966). Asked to draw a picture of a house, a person with left hemisphere damage draws a simple form. Although the overall configuration of the house is captured, few internal details are included. Given the same task, a person with right hemisphere damage draws a confusing picture, in which some details, such as the window panes and chimney bricks, are recorded, but the overall form is distorted. The drawings of the right hemisphere damaged patient exhibit another peculiar symptom: the left side of the house is less detailed than the right side. This left-sided neglect occurs because information from the left visual field is processed by the right hemisphere. Because

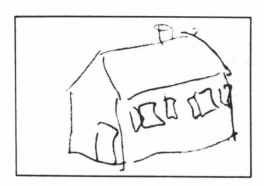

12.1 *Drawings of a house by a right-handed patient with left-hemisphere damage, which omits details but preserves the overall form, and by a right-handed patient with right-hemisphere damage, which includes details (window panes and chimney bricks) but misses the overall form of the object and leaves the left side of the page relatively empty.*

the right hemisphere is dominant for visual-spatial skills, damage to the right hemisphere renders people unaware of the information in their left visual field. The patients could perfectly well see the objects in their visual field by turning their eyes so that these objects move into their right visual field. However, they do not do this because they are completely oblivious to the fact that they neglect their left visual field: to them, it appears as if they are seeing the whole scene. The converse does not occur: left hemisphere damaged people do not suffer right visual field neglect, presumably because their right hemisphere, which is dominant for visual spatial skills, is intact.

Such differences in drawing ability in people with right and left hemisphere damage show that in the ordinary person, both hemispheres play a role in drawing, and each hemisphere makes a different contribution. The left hemisphere analyzes a pattern into its parts. The right hemisphere captures the overall gestalt, or configuration.

Very little neuropsychological research has examined the perception of art. One study, however, demonstrated that the right hemisphere plays an important role in the perception of style (Gardner and Winner, 1981). Patients with unilateral brain damage were given a style-matching task in which, for example, matching a Cézanne landscape with a Cézanne still life constituted a match on the basis of style, while grouping the Cézanne landscape with a Rembrandt landscape constituted a match by content rather than style (Fig. 4.7). Patients with right hemisphere damage and with left hemispheres intact tended to focus on the subject matter and thus to match by content, putting together the two landscapes. Patients with left hemisphere damage but with right hemispheres intact were quite sensitive to style and were able to overlook subject matter and put together the two Cézannes.

Such a result tells something not only about the importance of the right hemisphere in perceiving the style of a painting but also about the nature of style perception itself. Whether this skill involves analysis of details, such as attending to the texture of a painting or to the way in which fingernails and earlobes are depicted, or whether it entails a kind of holistic gestalt pattern recognition, has been heatedly debated. The study supports a view of style perception as one of holistic pattern recognition, since it is this kind of skill, rather than analytic skill, at which the right hemisphere has been shown to excel.

Studies of artistically trained people with brain damage reveal somewhat different findings from studies of untrained people. Studies of painters with left hemisphere damage have suggested that the left hemisphere of a skilled person plays a less crucial role than it does in the unskilled. For instance, a major French painter was rendered severely aphasic by a left hemisphere stroke (Alajouanine, 1948). After the stroke, his artistic activity did not decline, nor did it seem to change in technique or tone, whereas his language was extremely impaired. The painter poignantly described a split between his artistic self and his other selves: "There are in me two men, the one who paints, who is normal while he is painting, and the other one who is lost in the midst, who does not stick to life . . . I am saying very poorly what I mean . . . There are inside me the one who grasps reality, life; there is the other one who is lost as regards abstract thinking . . . These are two men, the one who is grasped by reality to paint, the other one, the fool, who cannot manage words anymore" (Sarno, 1972, pp. 235–236).

The case of a Bulgarian painter confirmed the finding that the ability to paint is not affected by the loss of linguistic skills (Zaimov, Kitov, and Kolev, 1969). The painter suffered a severe aphasia as well as paralysis of the right side of the body as the result of a left hemisphere stroke. Because of the paralysis, the painter began to teach himself to draw with his left hand. He gradually regained his fluency but, unlike the French painter, developed an entirely new style. In his prestroke work, he depicted events occurring over time—in the past, present, and future. His post-stroke work was no longer in such a narrative style but instead was characterized by fantastic, dream-like images, clear colors, and symmetrical patterns. While his post-stroke style was definitely new, it was in no way inferior to his previous work.

These two cases reveal that in skilled painters, graphic skills can function independently of language and other left hemisphere skills. This is not the case with people without exceptional artistic ability, in whom left hemisphere damage results in an impoverishment of detail in their drawings. Perhaps the visual analysis of detail is preserved in the left hemisphere damaged artist because it is overlearned, or possibly it is preserved because it is more widely represented in the brain. But no firm conclusions about the difference between the role of the left hemisphere in normal and gifted painters can be drawn, because the two groups of patients were not matched in terms of lesion site.

As in the case of left hemisphere damage, right hemisphere damage affects painters differently from nonartistic patients. After damage to the right hemisphere, painters do not lose the ability to capture the overall form of objects, as untrained people do. Thus, skilled artists present a clinical picture very different from that of ordinary people.

A study of four twentieth century painters afflicted with right hemisphere damage has been made by the German neurologist Richard Jung (Gardner, 1975). None of these artists stopped painting after brain damage. As with the drawings of normal right-damaged patients, the paintings made soon after the onset of illness were characterized by a neglect of the left side of the picture: the left side of a face, house, or landscape was simply omitted, or it was depicted in a much less detailed way than on the right side (Fig. 12.2). This neglect cleared up within a few months in all of the artists, but a few traces remained: either the paintings were somewhat heavier on the right, or the execution on the left was less careful.

Perhaps the most intriguing finding was that in at least one case, the artist's style underwent a fundamental change after right hemisphere damage. The painter, Lovis Corinth, began to draw in a bolder style, sketching self-portraits that were much more intense, disturbing, and emotionally expressive than those drawn before his stroke (Fig. 12.3). As one critic described Corinth's new style, "characterization is now exaggerated, indeed, often to caricature" (Kuhn, 1925, p. 107). To be sure, a similar kind of stylistic evolution is sometimes noted in the art of healthy artists. Picasso's work, for instance, became more bold, "primitive," and grotesque in his later years. But in Picasso's case the style shift came about gradually; in Corinth's case, the shift was more sudden.

These changes have led art critics to speak of a heightened

12.2 Self-portraits by Räderscheidt before and after a right hemisphere stroke, 1967. (a) Two years prior to stroke. (b) Two months after stroke, brush strokes are sparse and left side of page is totally neglected. (c) Three and a half months after stroke, left side of page is slightly less neglected. (d) Five months after stroke, left side of page still shows some neglect. (e) Six months after stroke, left-side neglect has noticeably improved, but brush strokes are still somewhat formless and the four strokes on the forehead are oriented at an odd angle. (f) Nine months after stroke, left-side neglect is almost completely cleared up, but harsh white brush strokes on the left seem out of place.

12.3 *Self-portraits by Corinth, one year before his right hemisphere stroke (left), and twelve years after the stroke, showing greater emotional expressiveness after the illness.*

emotionality and expressiveness in the style of post-stroke artists. Although these qualities have commonly been attributed to the emotional reaction to the severity of the illness, this cannot be the case because similar increases in expressiveness are not seen in left hemisphere damaged artists. Another explanation is based on evidence that the right hemisphere is dominant for emotional behavior (Geschwind, 1976; Heilman, 1976). If the right hemisphere is central to the emotions, then damage to this hemisphere could lead to a change in personality and in emotional responses. Possibly this could lead to a heightened emotionality in the artist's style (Gardner, 1975).

Once again, the artist appears to react differently to brain damage than does the nonartist. Whereas in the ordinary person, damage to the right side of the brain impairs the ability to depict form, in the artist this ability remains less impaired. In fact, once the left-sided neglect clears up, little problem with form remains. Again, whether this is due to differences in lesion sites between the normal and gifted people studied, to overlearning in the case of artists, or to a wider representation of spatial abilities in the brains of artists is not known.

Literature

At least in the case of painting, some ability to draw remains despite either left- or right-sided damage. This suggests that the visual-spatial abilities involved in the pictorial arts are bilaterally represented in the brain. Less can be expected in the case of an art form that depends on an ability that is extremely lateralized, such as language.

Research into the basic components of language—phonology, semantics, and syntax—has demonstrated that language is one of the most strongly lateralized functions. The central role of the left hemisphere in language is beyond dispute, and it is well known that damage to the left brain causes disorders of language in the case of right-handed people. For a long time, it was commonly believed that only the left hemisphere was involved in language processing. But there is now a great deal of evidence that the right hemisphere also plays some role in language. The right brain is capable of uttering overlearned phrases, such as "How are you?" (Jackson, 1932). It can process vowels, the intonational patterns in which a statement is uttered, and affectively tinged language, such as swear words (Blumstein and Cooper, 1974; Cicone, Wapner, and Gardner, 1980; Heilman, 1976; Kimura, 1973). And it even possesses some vocabulary and syntax (Gazzaniga, 1970; Sperry, 1974; Zaidel, 1977).

Despite all that is known about the organization of basic language skills, it is impossible to predict with confidence what will happen to literary skills after brain damage. Dealing with literature requires far more than syntax, semantics, or phonology. Indeed, the abilities most central to literary competence appear to lie in another area. For instance, to write or to appreciate a piece of literature, one must go beyond the literal and respond to figurative forms of language involving metaphor, irony, or humor. And to perceive or to produce a fictional work requires a sensitivity to the rules of narrative structure and an awareness of the boundary between fact and fiction. Thus, in evaluating the effects of brain damage on literary skill, the important questions do not concern performance on standard linguistic tasks. More important to discover is whether brain damage affects the ability to understand metaphor or the knowledge of what a story is and how it differs from a journalistic account of an actual event.

12.4 Pictures used to test comprehension by brain-damaged patients of the metaphorical sentence, "A heavy heart can really make a difference." Patients with left-hemisphere damage and normal people usually selected the metaphorical picture (person crying); patients with right-hemisphere damage were just as likely to choose the literal picture (person lugging a heart-shaped object) as the metaphorical one.

In the case of left hemisphere damage in a right-handed adult, linguistic abilities are impaired. People with such aphasias exhibit marked difficulties in articulation and in speaking and understanding both grammatically and semantically correct sentences. The particular aspect of language that is impaired depends upon the precise area of the language center that has been destroyed. But such patients, who have intact right hemispheres, may fare better on tasks tapping verbal abilities important to literature. The abilities of the right hemisphere may allow these individuals to grasp figurative language or to apprehend a story.

When aphasics were given sentences containing simple metaphoric expressions like "heavy heart," they had difficulty articulating what this meant (Winner and Gardner, 1977). But this difficulty stemmed simply from an inability to put their understanding into words. Given a nonlinguistic response mode in which they might point to a picture that went with such a metaphorical statement, patients with left-sided damage performed nearly as well as normal people (Fig. 12.4).

Left hemisphere damaged patients thus retain some literary ability, which suggests that the right hemisphere contributes to the understanding of figurative language. Nevertheless, damage to the left hemisphere cripples the writer. The French poet Charles Baudelaire, after suffering a left hemisphere stroke, was never able to write again, and the only words that he could utter were those of an oath (Gardner, 1975). Only if the aphasia recedes do writers go on to write again. The poet William Carlos Williams was able to write some poetry after his partial recovery from aphasia. And a number of doctors who became aphasic and then recovered have gone on to write about their experience. But in no case has an aphasic writer demonstrated the ability to write in the face of a loss of ordinary language ability.

A very different picture is presented by patients with right hemisphere damage. On the surface, patients with right hemisphere damage appear to possess intact language. Yet closer inspection reveals subtle language difficulties. For instance, such people are often unable to relate a statement to its context, and thus they tend to misinterpret the speaker's intended meaning. Upon hearing someone reject an offer of help in hanging a picture by making the statement, "Too many cooks spoil the broth," the patient with right hemisphere damage may fail to recognize that the context of this statement has to do with hanging pictures and not with cooking (Gardner, 1975). Failure to relate this statement to its appropriate context leads to a literal interpretation.

The role of the right hemisphere in attending to context and speaker intention suggests that this hemisphere may make an important contribution in the domain of the literary arts. An inability to relate sentence to context ought to result in a tendency both to interpret figurative language literally, as in taking "heavy-hearted" to mean physically heavy, and to confuse the boundary between a fictive narrative and a straightforward description of actual events, as in believing that a story can describe only events that may occur in reality. Investigation of the role of the right hemisphere in both metaphorical and narrative uses of language reveals just such difficulties.

Unlike left-damaged patients, those with right damage often speak in a manner that sounds metaphorical. For example, a patient might joke about a paralyzed arm, calling it an "old fin." Yet these metaphorical abilities are more apparent than real. When asked to explain proverbs, such patients give literal interpretations. And in a study in which they were asked to paraphrase the metaphorical sentence "He had a very heavy heart," they were initially resistant, often insisting that such language is not English. After a bit of prodding, they revealed no difficulty in paraphrasing the sentence, explaining that it means someone is sad. However, asked to point to the picture that goes with the description, right hemisphere patients were as likely to choose a literal depiction of a person carrying a large heart-shaped object as a picture that captures the metaphorical meaning of the sentence, such as a person crying (Fig. 12.4). Moreover, unlike left hemisphere damaged patients and people with intact brains, they failed to find the literal pictures amusing. Nor did they notice the conflict between their verbal paraphrase and their literal picture choice (Winner and Gardner, 1977).

One way to explain these puzzling findings is to think of the left hemisphere as a "language machine," able to supply verbal paraphrases and definitions of any sentence or word it is given. Thus, the patient with a damaged right hemisphere and an intact left hemisphere has no problem paraphrasing metaphors. Where the right hemisphere appears to be crucial is in alerting the listener to context—recognizing situations in which uttering a particular statement would or would not be appropriate. Thus, those with right hemisphere damage are unable to select the picture depicting the situation in which one would ordinarily say, "He had a very heavy heart."

Sensitivity to context is important not only in understanding figurative language but also in understanding any form of fiction. Understanding a narrative requires, among other things, that one suspend disbelief, willingly enter into the story, and yet retain at all times a clear awareness of the boundary between the fantasy of the story and reality. It appears that these abilities are impaired after right hemisphere damage.

In a study of various aspects of story sensitivity in right hemisphere patients, patients heard a series of brief stories (Wapner, Hamby, and Gardner, 1981). After each tale, the patients were asked to retell it, and they were then posed a set of questions about the main points of the story. Overall, the responses of these patients underscored the importance of the right hemisphere in story understanding. First, in retelling the story, these patients had no difficulty using appropriate phonology and syntax, but they revealed considerable difficulty in both integrating the elements of the story and grasping the narrative structure. For instance, when asked to assemble given story components in their logical order, the patients were markedly impaired. Thus, while unhindered in the basic linguistic processes of phonology and syntax, right hemisphere patients could not organize linguistic information at the higher level of a story.

Further evidence of a lack of sensitivity to narrative form on the part of these patients was their abundance of extraneous additions to the story on the retelling task. A number of these embellishments indicated an unwillingness to accept the story on its own terms and to respect the boundary between fiction and life. For instance, upon hearing a story about a fireman, one patient insisted that the story was "incorrect." The reason given for this odd statement was that the story mentioned an alleyway, and alleyways, he explained, could not be located near a firehouse. Similarly, commenting on a part of the story describing a little girl who sneaked a ride on the fire engine, the patient insisted that this was an impossible occurrence. Other patients changed the story in their retelling so that there was no fire, or they added the experimenter as one of the characters. Such intrusions suggest that the patients failed to respect the story as a separate and integral entity. Constantly violating the boundary between fiction and actuality, they seemed uncertain about the difference between the events related in the story, which are fictional, and those that typically occur in life.

Another dramatic finding concerned the right hemisphere patients' reaction to bizarre elements in several of the stories. For instance, in one story, a boss decided to give a lazy hired hand a raise. While normal people as well as those with left hemisphere damage found such a statement odd and recognized that it was at variance with the description of the employee as lazy, those with right hemisphere damage did not react in this way. Moreover, in retelling the story, they related such elements as faithfully as they did the canonical elements of the story.

The right hemisphere patients thus refused to accept some aspects of stories that normal people have no difficulty accepting, revealing little awareness of a boundary between fantasy and reality. But they also went out of their way to make sense of truly bizarre aspects of stories, revealing an insensitivity to how stories ought to depict characters' motivation. Overall, the right hemisphere patients exhibited striking difficulties in grasping the basic structure of a story and in recognizing the story as a fictional entity.

Neuropsychological studies of literary skill suggest that literary creativity requires both hemispheres of the brain. The left hemisphere is necessary for language, but alone it is sufficient only for context-free language tasks, such as deciding whether a sentence is grammatical ("Grass the is green"; "The boy ate the cake") or judging whether each item in a lexical string is a word ("bat," "plek"). As soon as context affects how a given portion of language is to be interpreted, the right hemisphere also becomes necessary. And it is particularly in the literary arts that context plays a fundamental role.

Music

Music presents a more complex picture than either the visual or the literary arts. First of all, a wider spectrum of roles exists in music, since one can be either a composer or a performer; one can compose directly on an instrument or by writing music notation; and one can perform by playing an instrument from a score, by improvising on an instrument without a score, or by singing, again with or without a score. Each of these roles may require unique types of skill, and some of these roles, such as those involving notation, require formal training. Each of the component skills of music must be separately considered with respect to the role of the two hemispheres. And as in the case of the other arts, both normal and gifted individuals must be examined, for the brains of musicians may well be organized differently from those of average people.

The ability to perceive components of music is carried out by the right hemisphere (Milner, 1962). This was demonstrated by giving subtests of a music test called the Seashore Music Battery to patients who had had either their left or their right temporal lobe surgically removed. After removal of the right but not the left lobe, the ability to detect timbre and intensity was significantly impaired. The finding that music is processed by the right hemisphere has been supported by other studies, including ones with infants (Bogen and Gordon, 1971; Entus, 1975; Gates and Bradshaw, 1977). Rhythm, however, is one facet of music which may be processed by the left hemisphere (Gordon, 1978). This finding is consistent with the frequent claim that the left hemisphere handles temporal sequencing tasks.

The right hemisphere also appears to play a critical role in the storage of musical memories. One study found that the ability to remember tones was impaired in patients with no right temporal lobe (Milner, 1962). Another study demonstrated that right hemisphere damage interferes with the ability to detect errors in familiar tunes (Shapiro, Grossman, and Gardner, 1981). Subjects heard well-known melodies played either correctly or incorrectly and were asked to judge in each case whether an error had been committed. Those with right hemisphere damage performed significantly worse on this task than those with left damage. Right damaged patients were deficient on all items, including those requiring sensitivity to rhythm. This suggests that, regardless of whether rhythm is perceived in the left or right hemisphere, the right hemisphere plays an important role in the storage of the rhythm of a melody.

Further evidence for the claim that the right hemisphere controls the internal representation of a melody comes from the case of an amateur musician with right damage. This patient was unable to determine whether a song's initial note was higher or lower than its second note, suggesting that his internal auditory imagery for known memories was degraded (Gardner, in press).

The ability to situate a familiar melody in the context in which it is ordinarily heard is also a skill carried out by the right hemisphere (Gardner, Silverman, Denes, Semenza, and Rosenstiel, 1977). Patients with right or left damage were asked to match a melody with one of four pictures. The melodies were well-known songs whose lyrics were omitted. For half of the items, the correct answer required a knowledge of the lyrics. For example, to match the melody "Row Row Row Your Boat" to a picture of a boat, one must be able to recall that the lyrics are about a boat. For the other half, getting the correct answer depended on being able to recall the situation in which a particular song is usually sung. For example, to match the melody of "Hail to the Chief" to a picture of the President, one does not need to recall the words or the title, but one does need to recall the situation in which the song is usually played.

Patients with right hemisphere damage performed better than those with left damage on those items in which it was necessary to recall the lyrics. On the situational items, however, right hemisphere damaged patients performed worse. The superior performance of individuals with intact left hemispheres on the verbal items is consistent with the vast amount of evidence that the left hemisphere is dominant for language. The superior performance of individuals with intact right hemispheres on the situational items provides further support for the newly emerging picture of the right hemisphere as particularly attuned to context. This ability has been demonstrated in the domains of metaphor and narrative, and it appears to be true also in the domain of music.

The right hemisphere is crucial not only for the perception of music but also for its production. Patients with nonfunctioning right hemispheres can sing only in a monotone, while those with left damage have much less difficulty producing recognizable melodies (Bogen and Gordon, 1971). This finding is consistent with clinical observations that even severe aphasics remain able to sing (Goodglass and Kaplan, 1972). In fact, a form of therapy called melodic intonation therapy has recently been developed which exploits the aphasic's preserved singing ability as a way of renewing speech (Sparks, Helm, and Albert, 1973). The patient who is totally unable to speak a sentence and who has failed with all other speech therapies can sometimes utter a perfectly grammatical sentence if the sentence is sung rather than spoken.

Several case studies of musicians after brain damage have further underscored the role of the right hemisphere in the production of music and have demonstrated that the ability to produce music can function entirely independently of the ability to perceive it. In one case, an accordion player with an impaired right hemisphere retained intact perceptual but not productive capacities (Botez and Wertheim, 1959). While this musician could recognize pieces, catch slight errors, and criticize his own performance, his productive capacities were severely impaired. He could sing individual pitches but was unable to combine them into a song. And he could not play pieces on his accordion even if asked to repeat a piece that he had just heard.

Not only is the right hemisphere specialized for both productive and perceptive musical skills, but it also may control the artist's emotional involvement in the creative process. In the case of one musician with right hemisphere damage, the ability both to perceive and to produce music was spared. However, after his stroke he no longer felt motivated to compose (Judd, Arslenian, Davidson, and Locke, 1980). He did not like to listen to music as much as he had in the past, and he reported that he no longer experienced the rich set of associations that he used to have while listening to a piece. And he aptly judged his own post-illness compositions as correct but uninspired. It appeared that his right hemisphere damage had robbed him of his interest in the creative process and had stripped music of its emotional resonance (see also Popper and Eccles, 1977). This finding is consistent with suggestions that the right hemisphere is dominant for the emotions.

The musical ramifications of left hemisphere damage range from none at all, to impairment of the ability to read musical notation, to impairment of the ability to compose. The Russian composer Shebalin remained able to compose and teach after a stroke rendered him aphasic (Luria, Tsvetkova, and Futer, 1965). An American composer also remained able to compose and criticize after a left hemisphere stroke (Judd, Gardner, and Geschwind, 1980). This composer, who was unable to read written text, was somewhat able to read musical notation, although his ability was not perfect. In this case, the musician's underlying musical intelligence was spared, and the only skill affected was the ability to read musical notation. His superior performance in reading music as compared to language demonstrates the relative independence of these symbol-decoding capacities.

Other studies have confirmed the independence of reading music and reading language. One patient with left hemisphere damage was able to read music but not language (Souques and Baruk, 1930). Another was found to be able to read language but not music (Dorgueille, 1966). However, while these two skills are not fused, there is some overlap between them, because it is rare to find a patient with a significant aphasia who has not also lost some proficiency at musical reading.

One case has been reported in which left hemisphere damage affected more than the ability to handle notation (Alajouanine, 1948). After a left hemisphere stroke, the French composer Maurice Ravel remained able to recognize music, criticize, and evaluate it. But while his love for music was as strong as ever, he could no longer compose or play the piano. Here is a case, then, which demonstrates the left hemisphere's involvement in the production of music.

All of the studies demonstrating left hemisphere involvement in the ability to read notation and even in the ability to compose have been conducted on skilled musicians. It is thus possible that such left hemisphere involvement is the consequence of formal training in music, training which might result in a more analytic and thus left hemisphere approach to music. In order to investigate this issue, a comparison was made of music perception in two groups of people: musically naive people, who had had less than three years of music lessons at least five years prior to the experiment and who no longer played an instrument or sang, and musically experienced people, who had had at least four years of lessons and were currently playing an instrument or singing (Bever and Chiarello, 1974). The participants in this study heard a series of tonal melodies, twelve to eighteen notes long, presented one at a time to either their left or their right ear. Following each melody, there was a two-second pause. Then a two-note sequence was played, again into only one ear. The first task was to determine whether this two-note sequence was an excerpt from the previously heard melody. Then another melody was played, again monaurally. Sometimes this melody had been heard earlier in the experiment and sometimes it was new. The second task was to judge whether this melody was new or whether it had already been heard.

On the first task, the experienced group had no difficulty, no matter which ear was used; conversely, the naive group failed with both ears. On the second task, an intriguing pattern of results was obtained. Naive listeners performed better when using their left ear and thus their right hemisphere. Experienced listeners performed better when using their right ear and thus their left hemisphere. Most of the differences between the two groups were right ear differences: while both groups performed fairly similarly with their left ear, musically experienced subjects performed considerably better than naive subjects when using their right ear. Thus, naive listeners used their right hemisphere when processing these melodies; trained listeners used both hemispheres.

These results suggest that the two groups were processing music differently. It may be that naive listeners recognize a tune by attending to its overall pattern or gestalt. This kind of global perception is a right hemisphere skill. Listeners with formal training in music may recognize a tune by attending to its component notes. This kind of analytic perception is a left hemisphere skill. Support for the claim that experienced subjects were processing music in a more analytic, left hemisphere fashion comes from the finding that only the experienced group succeeded on the first, analytic task.

This pattern of findings supports a view of the left hemisphere as responsible for any task requiring analytic skills. Presumably, with formal training, one begins to listen to music in an increasingly analytic way. As soon as the task becomes an analytic one, whether or not music is involved, the left hemisphere enters the scene.

Another study demonstrated still greater left hemisphere involvement in tasks requiring complex musical decisions (Shannon, 1980). However, several studies have reported conflicting findings. When listeners were required to recognize dichotically presented chords, musicians were found to have a right hemisphere advantage but nonmusicians had neither a right nor a left advantage (Gordon, 1980). And when people were asked to recognize intervals, right-handed musicians with no left-handers in their families showed a right hemisphere superiority, while nonmusicians showed a left hemisphere superiority (Kellar and Bever, 1980). One possible explanation for these findings is that recognition of chords and intervals is carried out by musicians in a global rather than an analytic manner. Nonmusicians, who do not have an internalized template of an interval such as a fifth, may be forced to use more analytic skills, breaking apart an interval into its component notes.

In short, right hemisphere damage is far more destructive to a musician than is left hemisphere damage. With the exception of Ravel, aphasia leaves the musician with the preserved ability to perceive music, as well as the ability and motivation to create. Its major effect seems to be on the ability to read notation. Right hemisphere damage can impair either productive or perceptual skills, depending on the localization of the damage. It can also alter musicians' emotional relation to music: while their musical technique may remain unimpaired, they may become uninspired. This finding points to an important distinction between the capacity to carry out technical skills, such as naming pitches and reading notation, and the capacity to sustain gratification from this activity.

The evidence suggests that the cover on the *New York Times Magazine* is in need of considerable revision. It is untenable and overly simplistic to see the left brain as linguistic and scientific, and the right brain as responsible for all artistic and creative behaviors. First of all, creativity is as important in the sciences as it is in the arts. Second, one cannot talk about art as a unified whole: one must look separately at the different art forms and at the component skills involved in each. Moreover, one must distinguish between people with and without high levels of skill and formal artistic training.

The major evidence dictates a revised view of the function of the brain hemispheres. In the case of painting, both hemispheres are important for the nonartist. The left captures the parts of the figure to be represented, while the right grasps its overall form. In the case of artists, however, the left hemisphere appears to be less involved, and the right hemisphere is crucial.

In the case of literature, both hemispheres have an important role to play. With left hemisphere damage, the aphasic writer is no longer able to use language to create works of literature. But writers also depend upon the right hemisphere; without this side of the brain, they lose the ability to go beyond the literal, to grasp the sense of figurative language, to apprehend the structure of a narrative, and to distinguish between fact and fiction.

In the case of music, again, both hemispheres make a contribution. While most of the perceptual and productive components of music are lateralized to the right, the left hemisphere remains important in the use of musical notation, which is a symbol system not unlike verbal language. The left hemisphere also contributes to musical perception in the case of the well-trained ear, because through training one comes to listen to music more analytically. Thus, in none of the arts is it possible to rule out left hemisphere involvement. There is no art form which can be attributed entirely to the right hemisphere.

Perhaps the most important contribution of the study of brain damage to an understanding of art is that it helps to disentangle the component skills involved in artistry. To understand the psychology of art, it is important to go beyond a view of artistry as an unanalyzed whole. There are different artistic skills, and they work together in explicable ways to produce artistry of various levels of competence. It is very difficult to determine just what these skills are in the intact person. But studies of brain damage have shown, for instance, that the ability to compose music is independent of the capacity to respond emotionally to music, or that the ability to decode a metaphor is independent of an appreciation of the contexts in which such a figure of speech might be appropriate. Thus, brain damage provides an experiment in nature, teasing apart component skills which may be invisible in great artists, but which actually permit them to go about their business.

13 Mental Illness

Great wits are sure to madness near allied,
And thin partitions do their bounds divide.

—John Dryden

So far from the position holding true, that great wit (or genius, in our modern way of speaking), has a necessary alliance with insanity, the greatest wits, on the contrary, will ever be found to be the sanest writers. It is impossible for the mind to conceive of a mad Shakespeare.

—Charles Lamb

The belief that genius is linked to insanity has persisted at least since the time of the ancient Greeks (Anastasi and Foley, 1941). Plato believed that a common thread linked the poet with the madman and also with the seer, a figure believed to have the power to see into the future: all three were "possessed" by a supernatural force over which they had no control. But despite the similarity, Plato pointed out a difference between artistry and madness: the insanity of the madman was "pathological," that of the artist was "productive" (*Phaedrus* 244a-b, 265b).

Aristotle also had something to say about the matter. "No great genius," he wrote, "was without a mixture of insanity." And the Roman playwright Seneca echoed Aristotle when he stated that "The mind cannot attain anything lofty so long as it is sane" (Rothenberg, 1979, p. 7).

Artists themselves have frequently promoted the belief that insanity and madness are interlocked. In Shakespeare's *A Midsummer Night's Dream*, "the lunatic, the lover and the poet" are said to be alike in imagination (V, 1, 7–8). Writers in the Romantic and Surrealist schools stressed the role of altered states of consciousness, achieved through drugs, alcohol, or physical illness, in fostering creativity. And the playwright August Strindberg believed that he wrote best while hallucinating (Jaspers, 1977).

Those who believe in a bond between artistic genius and mental illness usually use the term *mental illness* to refer to psychosis, a severe disorder quite distinct from the relatively milder condition called neurosis. Most people suffer some degree of neurosis; psychosis is a much rarer disorder. Although there are a variety of forms of psychosis, the most common, and one of the most serious, is schizophrenia. And it is particularly schizophrenia that has been linked to artistry.

Even brief contact with schizophrenics reveals how different they are from people who are merely neurotic. While in extreme cases neurotics may be virtually crippled by anxiety and rigid defenses, they remain in contact with reality. Schizophrenics, on the contrary, have lost touch with the real world. Typically, such patients fail to make contact with others and show inappropriate affect; that is, their emotional responses are inappropriate to the situation. Their thought patterns are often bizarre, illogical, and superstitious: the private, "autistic" world of schizophrenics is enriched with delusions, such as the belief that they are possessed by demons or that they can see into the future, as well as with auditory and visual hallucinations that are experienced as real. Patients typically engage in apparently meaningless, rigid, stereotyped, repetitive behaviors. Language may be impaired (Maher, 1963, 1971; Maher, McKean, and McLaughlin, 1966). And the mechanisms of attention have been reported to be disordered (Callaway, 1970; Kraepelin, 1919; Maher, 1974; McGhie and Chapman, 1961; Mednick, 1958; Mirsky, 1969; Payne, Mattussek, and George, 1959; Shakow, 1962; Venables, 1964). Possibly because of their heightened levels of arousal, schizophrenics seem unable to attend selectively to the environment, to screen out the irrelevant and focus on one event (Tecce and Cole, 1976). Instead, every aspect of the environment competes equally for attention. Schizophrenic patients have made remarks such as: "I can't concentrate. It's diversion of attention that troubles me. I am picking up different conversations. It's like being a transmitter" (McGhie and Chapman, 1961, p. 105). This attentional deficit may account for the delusions of schizophrenia (Maher, 1974). Events that normal people consider insignificant are felt by schizophrenics to be important occurrences in need of explanation. A trace of a frown on a stranger's face, which most people would ignore, might be seen by schizophrenics as a significant event whose cause must be sought. Patients may reason, for example, that this stranger is plotting against them.

The schizophrenic may experience any or all of these symptoms. While a number of hypotheses exist, the etiology of schizophrenia has not been clearly established. According to one view, it develops as a reaction to intolerable family interactions (Laing, 1964; Lidz, 1958; Sullivan, 1953). According to another view, genetic factors also play an important role (Rosenthal, 1970). Among those who posit a genetic component, many believe that the disorder is actually associated with a biochemical imbalance in the brain (Carlsson, 1978; Kety, 1959, 1960, 1969; Maher, 1966; Matthysse, 1977; Meltzer and Stahl, 1976; Snyder, 1976). Although the controversy still rages, it is becoming increasingly evident that there is both a genetic and a biochemical component to this disorder.

A relation between art and schizophrenia is suggested by the fact that some of the behaviors symptomatic of schizophrenia are, in less extreme form, found among artists. For instance, just as schizophrenics have lost contact with reality, artists are often deviant, isolated members of society. Schizophrenics live almost entirely within their own inner world, and artists also allegedly live within their own "dream world." Schizophrenics have hallucinations, and artists have unusual insights or see things in new ways. And schizophrenics fail to screen out "irrelevant" details from their perceptual field, just as artists notice important details that ordinary people ignore as trivial. But these similarities, while seductive, by themselves do not prove that art is cousin to madness.

There are various ways that artistry and schizophrenia could be linked. One hypothesis is that artists are more likely than nonartists to succumb to a mental disorder such as schizophrenia. Perhaps the fact that artists see things in a new and atypical way cuts them off from the rest of humanity, rendering them vulnerable to psychosis. A comparison of the extent of mental illness in artists and nonartists is one way to determine whether artists tend to become schizophrenic.

Rather than artistry leading to schizophrenia, it is also possible that schizophrenia enhances or unlocks artistic abilities. The claim that psychosis enhances artistry can be tested by studying the work of artists before and after the onset of schizophrenia. The claim that psychosis unlocks artistry can be tested by searching for signs of artistic activity among schizophrenics who were not previously artists.

The Link Between Madness and Art

The first attempt to test the general hypothesis that genius and madness are linked was carried out by the nineteenth century psychiatrist and criminologist Cesare Lombroso (1895). Lombroso did not limit his research to artistic geniuses but investigated greatness in a number of fields. Basing his research on the belief at the time that insanity was due to brain degeneration, Lombroso searched for signs of both psychological and physical degeneration among outstanding people who had made their mark in history. Physical degeneration was considered to be a direct reflection of psychological degeneration and thus to be equally indicative of a tendency toward insanity.

A study of facts that had been recorded about great people throughout history showed that geniuses had more than the normal portion of certain physical and psychological "symptoms," such as shortness (Mozart, Beethoven, Plato, Aristotle), rickets (Byron), emaciation (Milton, Newton, Locke), stammering (Darwin), and left-handedness (Michelangelo). Furthermore, various abnormal symptoms, such as contraction of the pulse, fever, and wild eyes, were noted to manifest themselves not only among the insane but also among geniuses while they were deeply immersed in creative activity.

From this survey it was concluded that insanity occurs more frequently among geniuses than among the rest of humanity. This conclusion, however, was unwarranted. The percentage of abnormalities among geniuses was not calculated and compared with the frequency of these symptoms in nongeniuses. Only if the percentage is higher among geniuses can it be concluded that a link exists. Moreover, many of the symptoms regarded as indicative of insanity, such as left-handedness, shortness, and rickets, are in fact unrelated to mental illness.

Whereas Lombroso included physical disorders in his study of genius, others have focused solely on psychological disorders (Rothenberg, 1979). Many artists have thus been shown to be mentally ill. Among such painters are Hieronymus Bosch, Albrecht Dürer, Vincent van Gogh, and Wassily Kandinsky. Among such composers are Hugo Wolf, Camille Saint-Saëns, and Robert Schumann, who is considered either to have been manic depressive or to have had tertiary syphilis. The writers reported to have suffered psychoses are many: Friedrich Hölderlin, August Strindberg, Arthur Rimbaud, Edgar Allan Poe, Charles Lamb, Jonathan Swift, Lewis Carroll, William Blake, Theodore Roethke, Ernest Hemingway, Ezra Pound, Hart Crane, Sylvia Plath, and Virginia Woolf. Dostoevsky is known to have had epilepsy which, though not a form of psychosis, is a neurological disorder that is associated with the presence of psychiatric conditions. For instance, certain forms of epilepsy lead to deepened emotionality, intense concern with religious and philosophical issues, and "hypergraphia," or the tendency to write excessive amounts (Waxman and Geschwind, 1974). It is possible that the disease contributed to Dostoevsky's passionate pages.

Many of these people died centuries ago, long before psychosis was at all understood. Historical records may have mislabeled these people, confusing psychosis with, for example, various neurological diseases (Macalpine and Hunter, 1969). The list is thus suggestive rather than definitive.

Even if one could be certain that all of these artists were in fact mentally ill, such a list is still not evidence for the alliance of genius and insanity, because many geniuses have been perfectly healthy, and many nongeniuses have suffered from mental illness. To verify the link, the actual frequency of mental illness among the great must be compared to the frequency of illness among the nongreat. In the first relatively systematic attempt to document the frequency of mental illness among geniuses, 1030 names were selected from the *Dictionary of National Biography*, and note was made of how many of these people had reportedly been insane (Ellis, 1904). Only 44, or 4.2 percent, of those on the list had suffered from mental illness. Although this percentage was perhaps slightly higher than would be found among average populations, the frequency was low.

In a study that confirmed these findings, the lives and medical histories of 113 artists and 181 scientists, selected by experts in their fields, were investigated (Juda, 1953). Among the artists, 2.8 percent were schizophrenic, 2 percent had unclear forms of psychoses, and 27.3 percent were described as having psychopathic personalities. Among the scientists, a somewhat different trend was found: none were schizophrenic, but 4 percent were manic depressive, and like the artists, a large number, or 19.4 percent, displayed psychopathic personalities. All these percentages are well within normal bounds, except for that found for the category of psychopathic personality. However, the label "psychopathic" may have been used rather loosely, simply to designate eccentric or antisocial behavior. This study challenges the popular notion that insanity and genius are allied.

In short, the hypothesis that geniuses tend to be psychotic has received little support from scrutiny of lists of artists and scientists purported to have been mentally ill. Geniuses do not manifest mental illness at an unusual rate. A weaker version of the hypothesis is that geniuses possess latent, hidden signs of illness. This version has been examined by administering paper and pencil personality tests assessing psychotic tendencies such as the use of bizarre thought processes. In numerous studies, creative people, including artists, scored higher than average people on such tests (Barron, 1953, 1972; Cross, Cattell, and Butcher, 1967; Hartmann et al., 1981; Mackinnon, 1961). This has led researchers to conclude that artists tend to possess latent psychopathology.

However, at least one group of artists, creative writers, also scored extremely high on tests assessing aspects of ego strength such as autonomy and self-confidence (Barron, 1953). In this sense, then, artists are quite distinct from psychotics. Moreover, since the exhibition of many forms of unusual thought process, including idiosyncratic imagery, metaphoric leaps, flights of fancy, or free expression of impulse, would result in high scores on scales assessing psychopathology, these test results do not warrant the conclusion that artists possess latent tendencies toward psychopathology. The results may simply show that artists, like psychotics, tend to display unusual thought processes. The two rival interpretations of artists' performance—as indicative of psychoses or of original thought processes—are equally plausible, and it is not possible to choose between them on the basis of these tests.

The Effect of Schizophrenia on Art

The question of whether artists are more likely to become mentally ill than any other population can be turned on its head: when mental illness strikes, does this disorder bring about an increase in artistic activity? One of the best-known cases of an artist who allegedly became schizophrenic is the Dutch painter Vincent van Gogh. Van Gogh had already established a distinct style when the first signs of psychosis appeared in 1885, at the age of thirty three. The illness became acute for the first time in 1888, and van Gogh committed suicide two years later. During the last two years of his life, he suffered from both hallucinations and delusions.

According to van Gogh, his illness had a valuable effect on his art. "The more I get out of joint, become sicker and more fragile," he wrote, "the more I grow in artistic stature" (Jaspers, 1977, p. 164). His illness undeniably affected the intensity and the speed with which he worked. Although there is no firm evidence about the number of paintings van Gogh produced each year, during the years 1884–1886 he appears to have produced, on the average, four paintings a year (Jaspers, 1977). In 1887 he produced twelve paintings. And in 1888, the year of his first acute attack, which occurred in December, he produced forty-six paintings. This output declined only minimally the next year, when he painted thirty paintings. But in the final half year of his life he produced only seven paintings. Thus, during the beginning of the acute phase, van Gogh became a more prolific painter.

Van Gogh was very aware of his new speed and saw it as an asset. "This is my strength," he wrote about a portrait he had just completed, "namely, to spit out a guy like that in one sitting." He was amazed by his new profusion of ideas: "I am so full of plans . . . The motifs will be countless" (p. 164).

Van Gogh's illness affected his work qualitatively as well as quantitatively. He himself noted a new expressiveness in his style: "Instead of reproducing exactly what I see before me, I use colors rather arbitrarily in order to express myself more forcefully . . . I exaggerate the blond of the hair. I tend toward orange hues, chrome and the light shade of lemon . . . I want to paint in such a manner that everyone who has eyes will have an absolutely clear impression . . . I try with the greatest of effort to bring about something without fine details, to create something else with the brush, nothing but an alternating stroke of the brush" (pp. 167–168).

In general, van Gogh's post-illness style became less realistic. The relatively straightforward portraits painted before his illness had given way, by 1889, to portraits that were more stylized. Trees became swirling flames. Colors grew brighter and less naturalistic. His brushstrokes became so prominent that the forms they described almost disappeared beneath them. The strokes were now geometric—semicircles, coils, spirals—which, along with the increased intensity of color, served to lend his post-illness works a measure of dynamism that they did not possess before (Fig. 13.1).

Whether van Gogh's illness enhanced his artistic abilities is a difficult question to answer. Objective judgments of quality are notoriously difficult to make. It is hard to prove that one style of painting is better than another style. Anyone who knows about van Gogh's illness is likely to be biased in judging the paintings, either wishing to demonstrate that the illness enhanced van Gogh's creativity or the reverse. The closest it would be possible to come to an objective answer to the question would be to ask judges unfamiliar with the fact of van Gogh's illness to evaluate the pre- and post-illness work. In such an event, the post-illness paintings would probably be seen as more interesting and creative than those painted earlier in his life, which would constitute some evidence that schizophrenia can enhance artistry. However, it cannot be proved that the changes were actually caused by the illness. All that is known for sure is that the illness and the stylistic evolution occurred at the same time. Perhaps van Gogh painted such impressive paintings at the end of his life in spite of his illness.

13.1 *Van Gogh*, Two Women Digging, *painted prior to his mental illness, and* Wheatfield with Crows, *painted during his illness.*

Since schizophrenia often involves an impairment of language, it is possible that writers are more adversely affected than painters by this disorder. Studies of writers who have become schizophrenic revealed that the illness did not affect all of them in the same way. In some writers, such as the playwright Strindberg, the illness seemed to affect only the content of his writings but not the style (Jaspers, 1977). In other cases, literary style was also affected.

Consider the case of the nineteenth century Russian novelist Gleb Ivanovic Uspenskij. This writer was reported to have suffered from a "mental illness involving a speech disorder" (Jakobson and Halle, 1956). The symptoms manifested by Uspenskij sound suspiciously like those of a schizophrenic: his language was impaired, and he split his first name, Gleb, and his patronymic, Ivanovic, into names for two different people: Gleb was the good self; Ivanovic the evil one. This fragmentation of personality is reminiscent of certain patterns of splitting found among schizophrenics. Thus, although there is no clear evidence that he was schizophrenic, this diagnosis is highly likely.

Here is a verbal portrait written by Uspenskij after the illness had struck: "From underneath an ancient straw cap with a black spot on its shield, there peeked two braids resembling the tusks of a wild boar; a chin grown fat and pendulous definitively spread over the greasy collars of the calico dicky and in thick layer lay on the coarse collar of the canvas coat, firmly buttoned on the neck. From below this coat to the eyes of the observer there protruded massive hands with a ring, which had eaten into the fat finger, a cane with a copper top, a significant bulge of the stomach and the presence of very broad pants, almost of muslin quality, in the broad ends of which hid the toes of the boots" (Jakobson and Halle, 1956, p. 80). The abundance of detail that is offered here is staggering. According to one Russian student of Uspenskij's writing, "the reader is crushed by the multiplicity of detail unloaded on him in a limited verbal space, and is physically unable to grasp the whole, so that the portrait is often lost" (Jakobson and Halle, 1956, p. 80).

A similar evolution can be seen in another writer reported to have become schizophrenic, the German poet Friedrich Hölderlin. Before he fell ill, Hölderlin wrote poems that were very accessible. But after he became schizophrenic, his style underwent two successive shifts. The first shift was characterized by an accumulation of adjectives used as nouns and the overfrequent use of empty filler words such as "but," "namely," or "as usual." These stylistic characteristics are reminiscent of the multiplicity of details in Uspenskij's style. A few years later, Hölderlin's second style shift occurred. The poems became much more difficult to understand, and some of his writing which was never published is totally incomprehensible. Hölderlin had lost his concentrated discipline and could no longer write intelligible poetry (Jaspers, 1977).

On the basis of the available evidence, therefore, there is only meager support for the hypothesis that schizophrenia is associated with an enhancement of artistic powers in the artist. In the case of van Gogh, his illness appears to have been associated with increased creativity, but the evidence is not overwhelming. And in the case of the writers Uspenskij and Hölderlin, the illness seems to have blocked effective writing.

In the case of the ordinary person who becomes mentally ill, a clearer relation between artistry and schizophrenia can be seen. Schizophrenic patients in mental hospitals commonly display an extraordinary behavior. Patients who, on admission to the hospital, are uninvolved, listless, and passive, sometimes begin spontaneously to demonstrate a strong and active involvement in both visual and literary arts. Those who have never before painted or written suddenly manifest a powerful urge to create (Kris, 1952; Prinzhorn, 1972). Any available scrap of paper is used to make a drawing or to write a composition; when no paper is available, the walls may serve as a canvas. Patients make carvings out of various materials and knead bread into sculptured forms when no wood is available to carve. Without any exposure to art therapy, these patients become virtually addicted to one or another form of artistic activity.

It was not until the last quarter of the nineteenth century that the spontaneous art of mental patients, especially their paintings and drawings, began to be given due attention. As a result of the emergence of the mental asylum and of medicine's interest in mental illness, the works of these patients—previously viewed as uninteresting scribbles or verbal nonsense—came to be prized for their power to reveal the mysteries of the psychotic mind.

It has been estimated that somewhat less than two percent of the inmates of mental hospitals begin to draw, paint, or sculpt (Kris, 1952). This group includes both those whose language is severely impaired and those whose language is intact. A similarly low percentage has been estimated to engage in writing (Arieti, 1974; Kris, 1952). This estimate, however, is not based on hard evidence. For example, it is not clear how many inmates actually had the opportunity to create, nor how many who painted or wrote were observed to have done so. Moreover, the percentage of those who spontaneously turn to art may actually be lower today for two reasons: patients are kept busier, so there is less free time; and most schizophrenics are routinely given drugs that reduce the symptoms of psychosis. Among those symptoms that wane is the spontaneous urge to paint or write (Bader and Navratil, 1976).

The figure of two percent suggests that the vast majority of schizophrenics do not become involved in the arts. The percentage can also be read as high, in view of the fact that those who did begin to create were not previously artistically inclined; they were untrained and unpracticed in art. While a comparable percentage of nonschizophrenics may well also be involved in some form of artistry, in no other population have two percent of the members suddenly and unexpectedly taken up drawing, painting, or writing with such ferocious intensity.

Characteristics of Schizophrenic Art

The spontaneously produced paintings of schizophrenics have characteristic properties that distinguish them from the paintings of all other populations. Perhaps the most immediately noticeable aspect of schizophrenic paintings and drawings is that every inch of available space is densely ornamented (Fig. 13.2). The page is crammed with details which are rarely subordinated to a formal unity. The artists appear to have become so absorbed in the parts that they have forgotten to attend to the integration of the whole. What is left is a string of units, each one competing for attention, and no one unit able to focus attention. This abundance of detail and lack of integration may be related to the attentional deficit that has been reported in schizophrenia. Unable to screen out the irrelevant and focus on one event to the exclusion of another, every aspect of the environment may compete for the schizophrenic artist's attention.

On the surface, this intricacy of detail is reminiscent of two other forms of drawings: the doodles that perfectly healthy people make while on the telephone or otherwise occupied, and the drawings produced by people under the influence of toxins such as LSD or amphetamines (Fig. 13.3; Arieti, 1974; Kris, 1952; Prinzhorn, 1972). But while the schizophrenic's work is the result of intense concentration, normal people appear to create such designs only while distracted or on drugs.

Not only is every inch of schizophrenic paintings filled with details of the same order of importance, but particular details are repeated over and over. Note the repetition of crosses, heads, and dashes in Figure 13.2. Because of this repetitive character, the art

13.2 *Schizophrenic's painting,* Mental Asylum, *showing decorative aspects, profusion of detail, inclusion of writing, numbers, and musical notation, and lack of overall integration.*

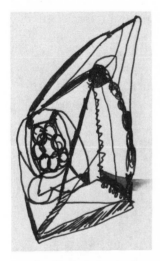

13.3 *Drawings similar to works by schizophrenics: doodle produced by a normal adult while distracted, and drawing made by a person under the influence of a drug, probably LSD. Both types of drawing are characterized by decorative aspects, such as curlicues or swirling lines, and a lack of overall organization.*

works appear stereotyped and rigid. Compulsive, stereotyped, repetitive behavior is typical of schizophrenics in other domains of behavior as well.

In schizophrenic paintings, the composition is sometimes chaotic, and thus there is no order (Fig. 13.4). Or in other cases there is an extremely rigid sense of order, manifesting itself in perfect, chilling symmetry (Arnheim, 1974; see Fig. 13.5). The rigid symmetry may well be related to the compulsive, stereotyped behavior characteristic of schizophrenics.

Concern with realistic representation is rarely found in schizophrenic works. For instance, objects are drawn without boundaries so that they appear to melt into space (Pickford, in press). Bodies are fragmented, and body parts are drawn in isolation from each other, with an arm on one side of the page, a hand on the other side. The rules of perspective are ignored, so that near objects are small and far objects large (Pickford, 1982). Spatial relations are sometimes disintegrated (Billig, 1966; see Fig. 13.6). The use of color bears little relation to the actual colors of objects. One looks in vain for realistic landscapes or still lifes, paintings that convey the forms of the natural world. Instead, schizophrenics seem intent only on capturing their "inner experiences." Objects are of interest only to the extent that they can be used to symbolize. While the works may thus be psychologically real, they are not naturalistically real.

Some schizophrenic works are exceptions to this rule and are quite realistic. Franz Xaver Messerschmidt, an eighteenth century schizophrenic sculptor, sculpted naturalistic portraits (Kris, 1952; see Fig. 13.7). These portraits were intended to portray particular

13.4 *Schizophrenic's drawing,* Holy Sweat Miracle in the Insole, *in which the forms blend into each other, yielding a chaotic composition.*

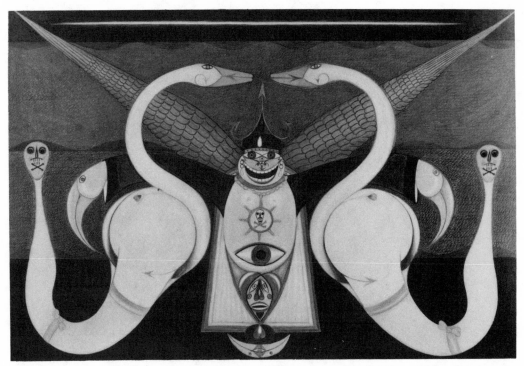

13.5 Schizophrenic's drawing, The Swan Doll's Dance of Death, *showing rigid symmetry.*

emotions, as seen by their titles. However, while the sculptures are clearly meant to be expressive, they do not succeed in conveying the character of anger or scorn. The portraits appear to be studies of muscles rather than emotions. Perhaps this lack of expressiveness occurs because schizophrenics repress their emotions, finding them too threatening to face (Kris, 1952).

Schizophrenic art impresses the observer with its quality of "fascinating strangeness" (Prinzhorn, 1972). Although it is not known whether patients actually depict their hallucinations, the content of their works is eerie and seems to refer to experiences that are foreign to normal people (Arnheim, 1977). One of the reasons for this unintelligibility is the private, idiosyncratic nature of the symbols used. The works are typically filled with objects that seem to have some mysterious, inaccessible symbolic meaning, such as the heads, crosses, and dashes in Fig. 13.2. This quality may be linked to the symbolic significance that these patients attribute to objects in general. Perhaps this tendency to grant trivial

13.6 *Painting by a schizophrenic, showing the disintegration of spatial relations.*

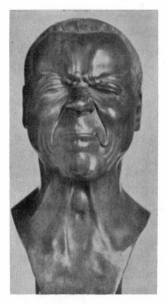 

13.7 *Busts by a schizophrenic artist, Messerschmidt:* The Ill-Humored One *and* The Satirizing One, *which seem more like studies of muscles than of emotions.*

objects a symbolic meaning is due to the disordered attention of the schizophrenic: if everything is given equal attention, then objects or events that seem unimportant to the normal person may take on added import for the schizophrenic.

Two other factors contribute to the unintelligibility of schizophrenic works. One is the curious intermingling of drawing, writing, numbers, and musical notation, as in Fig. 13.2. These notations may well convey a meaning of some sort, but this meaning remains private. The other factor contributing to unintelligibility is that some patients have created entire systems to explain the workings of the universe. It is quite impossible to interpret correctly an individual work without being versed in the entire system.

Finally, there are certain unusual aspects of the process by which schizophrenics paint. First, these patients often begin anywhere on the page and just spin the picture out to the edges. Second, while it is not clear how literally to take such statements, patients often report that they do not create out of choice but are driven to do so. For example, one patient who made carvings out of wood said: "When I have a piece of wood in front of me, a hypnosis is in it—if I follow it something comes of it, otherwise there is going to be a fight" (Prinzhorn, 1972, p. 130).

Evidence for the universality of schizophrenic art comes from cross-cultural studies of schizophrenics who were not artists prior to their illness (Billig and Burton-Bradley, 1975, 1978). Comparison of paintings and drawings produced by schizophrenics in New Guinea and the United States led to the discovery that in the initial stages of psychosis, the paintings bear the imprint of the culture in which they are produced; but as the illness progresses, the paintings begin to lose their cultural characteristics. The paintings by severely ill individuals of New Guinea resemble those of Western schizophrenics more than they resemble works by normal artists of New Guinea. Cultural characteristics are replaced by a universal schizophrenic style. For example, a hospitalized patient in New Guinea began to have delusions of persecution. His dead wife appeared to him in his dreams and warned him not to think about her or he would become mad. To ward off his wife's spirit, he began to paint the ancestral plaques that are typical of New Guinea (Fig. 13.8). In the patient's versions of these plaques, the traditional curlicues were exaggerated. The colors grew wild: instead of the traditional muted red, yellow ochre, black, white, and occasional pink, the artist used bright green, blue, purple, red, and yellow. In some, the borders of the figure disappeared altogether, so that cohesiveness was lost and the eyes appeared to float in space. Such pictures led to the conclusion that, "as the personality disintegrates, an increasing loss of cultural elements and the even-

13.8 Typical Hohao an-
cestral plaque (left) from
the Papuan Gulf, New
Guinea, which is simple
and symmetrical in design,
without bright colors or
complex design elements;
and ancestral plaques
painted by a schizophrenic
(right, from top): basic
structure is preserved but
there is some distortion;
curlicues proliferate and
colors are untraditionally
bright; conventional boundaries have disappeared,
colors are bright, and the
painting bears little resemblance to the traditional
plaque.

tual appearance of universal elements occur" (1975, p. 38). As patients begin to recover, these bizarre characteristics begin to dissolve, and the paintings become increasingly coherent and realistic (Billig and Burton-Bradley, 1978).

The characteristics of schizophrenic paintings seem to be attributable to something about the disorder of schizophrenia itself, rather than to factors such as mental illness per se, institutionalization, or lack of formal training. People with mental disorders other than schizophrenia create very different kinds of pictures. The schizophrenic's odd distortions in content and spatial relations are not found in works by depressives, hysterics, or neurotics (Hardi, 1972; Pickford, 1970, 1982). Such distortions are also absent from the works of other institutionalized people, such as alcoholics, tuberculosis patients, and prisoners (Hardi, 1962, 1969; Laing, 1964; Schaefer-Simmern, 1948). Moreover, other types of untrained adults have taken up painting, yet their works display a simplicity of style absent from the paintings of schizophrenics (Jones, 1980; Schaefer-Simmern, 1948).

Many questions about the artistic products of schizophrenics clamor for experimental investigation. For instance, it is not known whether patients who engage in artistic activity constitute a special, atypical group of schizophrenics. If schizophrenics who do not paint or write were asked to do so, perhaps their works would differ from those of schizophrenics who take up painting or writing spontaneously. Nor is it known what would happen if those who create spontaneously were requested to produce a drawing or a poem. Perhaps they are not able to create on command but must wait until the urge overtakes them. Because the area of schizophrenic art is bereft of experimental intervention, these questions cannot yet be answered. It is also not known why the works of established painters who become schizophrenic do not resemble the works of people who begin to paint for the first time after falling ill. In van Gogh's work, for instance, the abundance of details so typical of the paintings of untrained schizophrenics is absent. In fact, the details appear to be lost in the thickness of the brush stroke. Van Gogh's post-illness paintings remained integrated, and his style continued to evolve until his death. His post-illness works resemble those of his healthier days far more than they resemble those of untrained schizophrenics.

As with established artists, in the case of schizophrenics who begin to create for the first time after becoming ill, the disorder appears to have a more adverse effect on the verbal than the visual arts. Schizophrenic language appears highly metaphorical (Arieti, 1974). However, whether patients realize that they are using language figuratively is not clear. One piece of evidence that they are not using metaphorical language intentionally is that they frequently interpret metaphors and proverbs literally (Arieti, 1974).

This poem was written by a schizophrenic patient (Arieti, 1974):

> I think a little
> even a chittle
> if don't mittle
> on the tittle
> in the middle
> of a diddle
> of a kiddle
> in my middle
> don't you taddle
> or I'll saddle
> then goodbye goodbye.

A predominant concern here is with the phonetic effect of the words, which is reminiscent of the sound play of very young children. The writer focuses on the sounds of the words—properties such as assonance and rhyme—to the exclusion of their meaning. Neologisms or invented words are rampant. To be sure, poets also play with sounds. But even when word play is rampant, in nonschizophrenic poems such play is usually in the service of some kind of intelligible meaning.

Because of the focus on sound over meaning and the resultant neologisms in this schizophrenic poem, it fails totally to communicate. In its lack of an overall unity to which the rhymes are subordinated, its rigidity, and its unintelligibility, this poem is reminiscent of schizophrenic paintings. Schizophrenic poems have an incoherent, disintegrated character, and it is difficult to see any links between schizophrenic poetry and that of nonschizophrenic writers. Schizophrenic writing seems to possess only one of the raw materials of poetry—the sound effects. Without an overall integration, and without a subordination of the sound effects to some kind of meaning, the poetry flounders.

Psychoanalytic Approaches to Schizophrenic Art

Schizophrenic art has been interpreted in various ways. From a psychoanalytic viewpoint, schizophrenic art is seen as the result of a deep regression to primary process or irrational thinking. This interpretation of schizophrenic art is articulated in the writings of Ernst Kris (1952), a psychoanalytic theorist who was initially a student of art history. According to Kris, the healthy individual temporarily regresses to the level of primary process thinking while dreaming. Primary process thinking accounts for the strange characteristics of dreams, such as condensation, in which two opposite images are fused (a male body with a female head); displacement, in which a dream image symbolizes something very different (one's father symbolizing one's husband); or multiplicity of meaning, in which one image symbolizes several things (a house symbolizing one's body as well as the womb). These same aspects of primary process thinking make possible such activities as joking, punning, and creating novel works of art. But in all of these cases, the regression to the primary process level is temporary. And it is always carried out in the service of the ego. The ego remains in ultimate control, and it does not allow the individual to lose sight of the boundary between inner and outer reality.

According to this view, schizophrenics too have regressed to primary process thinking. But this regression is neither temporary nor in the service of the ego. Because the ego of schizophrenics is not intact, they lose the distinction between fantasy and reality, and they interpret their primary process images as literal reflections of reality. It is for this reason that the images of schizophrenic art are so bizarre.

According to psychoanalytic theory, the schizophrenic begins to create art only as an attempt at restoring mental health. An example is a patient who began to carve sculptures after the onset of schizophrenia and then ceased sculpting after his condition improved (Kris, 1952). Schizophrenics are said to gravitate to art because of art's healing powers.

Aesthetic Approaches to Schizophrenic Art

Countering the psychoanalytic view of schizophrenic art is the aesthetic approach which views schizophrenic art not as the product of deep regression to primary process thinking but as the product of universal aesthetic urges running out of control. According to this view, study of schizophrenic art can elucidate the basic mechanisms of imaginative and creative behavior as it manifests itself in all individuals, whether healthy or ill, child or adult. This belief is based on the assumption that the same psychological mechanisms underlie normal and abnormal art.

Such an aesthetic approach has been articulated by Hans Prinzhorn (1972). A student of art history and philosophy before becoming a psychiatrist, Prinzhorn was appointed to the Heidelberg Psychiatric Clinic in Germany in 1918. After his appointment,

Prinzhorn began to collect the spontaneous paintings, drawings, and sculptures produced by inmates of psychiatric institutions throughout Europe. Most of the patients whose work he collected suffered from what was believed to be schizophrenia. And almost none had any prior training or practice in the arts. Prinzhorn also studied children's art, primitive and folk art, and twentieth century Expressionist and Surrealist art.

Striking affinities were found among these different art forms. Prinzhorn concluded that all art works, both psychotic and normal, are manifestations of healthy urges, including the desire to play, to decorate, to create order, and to symbolize. These aesthetic urges are basic and universal. They manifest themselves first in the spontaneous play and art of children, and then decline during the school years. But they do not die; they remain latent, capable at all times of being reactivated. And one way in which they can become reactivated is by the onset of schizophrenia.

On this account, schizophrenia activates aesthetic urges by cutting people off from the external world. Schizophrenics are forced to create their own world through art, a world that is sensorily richer than the real world. Once these universal aesthetic urges are awakened in schizophrenics, however, they do not run their normal course; instead, they erupt in an uncontrolled manner. This accounts for the insistence on filling every inch of space and for the idiosyncratic and abundant use of symbols. Psychotic art is thus a manifestation of healthy urges gone awry.

The view that schizophrenic paintings are the product of universal aesthetic urges accords them status as works of art. Indeed, the works of schizophrenics have come increasingly, and somewhat romantically, to be valued as genuine works of art. Artists such as Paul Klee proclaimed the paintings of psychotics to be sources of inspiration (F. Klee, 1968); and museums and galleries in both the United States and Europe have exhibited works by mental patients (Anastasi and Foley, 1941).

Certainly many schizophrenic works of art are "beautiful." But evaluative properties such as beauty do not determine whether something qualifies as a work of art. A more useful gauge of these works is whether they possess properties typically found in a work of art, such as repleteness or expression. But applying such criteria to schizophrenic art is difficult. As with the drawings of chimpanzees or children, schizophrenic works may seem replete and expressive to the observer, but these properties may have been produced quite unintentionally. Only if schizophrenics are sensitive to such properties as repleteness or expression and if they introduce these symptoms into their works deliberately can their works be said to function aesthetically for them. Such investigations, unfortunately, have not been carried out.

Whether works by schizophrenics qualify as "art" is one question. Another question asks whether schizophrenic works are as powerful or appealing as "great" works of nonschizophrenic art. This calls for a value judgment. The paintings of schizophrenics do bear a resemblance to Expressionist and Surrealist art. All three depict the artist's inner world rather than the external, public world. And both Surrealist and schizophrenic art make abundant use of private, strange symbols. Yet schizophrenic art is set apart from these schools in several ways.

First, the schizophrenic painter seems unable to paint in any other than a private, autistic way. Expressionist and Surrealist painters, however, deliberately choose to paint in this style. Second, because schizophrenic art often displays a lack of integration, it is difficult to look at schizophrenic paintings for extended periods of time. While details in a Surrealist painting are subordinated to an overall framework, those in a schizophrenic work are not. The observer's attention is thus constantly shifting, unable to decide where to come to rest.

Finally, because of its extreme unintelligibility, schizophrenic art fails to communicate. This is much less so in Expressionist and Surrealist art. Expressionist and Surrealist works are attempts to communicate about the psychological aspects of existence in an age of anxiety. Schizophrenic art does not seem to be directed at others, and it is intelligible only to the artist, or perhaps not even to the artist. Art deals with experiences universal to humanity. But schizophrenia cuts people off from humanity and in this sense impairs them in the artistic realm.

The Healing Power of Art

In the pictorial arts, schizophrenia both awakens artistic activity in the untrained and sometimes enhances the creative powers of established artists, allowing them to produce paintings that are more interesting than those produced in earlier, healthier times. One possible reason that schizophrenics throw themselves into artistic activity with unusual intensity is because such activity may be therapeutic. Art may help to heal mental illness: sensing this on some level, patients who have never before made a work of art may naturally gravitate to the arts; and established artists may increase their output. Of course, this self-imposed therapy is not necessarily successful. Van Gogh did not get better even though his output after the onset of his illness sharply increased. Nevertheless, engaging in artistic activity of some sort may provide relief and thereby dull the anguish of mental illness.

The belief that art has the power to heal has as long a history as the belief that genius and insanity are linked. Support for this possibility comes from the testimony of mentally ill artists, who state that their work helps them through their most difficult periods. In one of van Gogh's letters written near the end of his life from his hospital room, he wrote: "Work strengthens the will and consequently leaves less hold for my mental weaknesses; it distracts me infinitely better than anything else. If I could once really throw myself into it with all my heart it might be the best remedy" (Stone and Stone, 1960, p. 524). Van Gogh's comments are similar to those of the writer Graham Greene: "Writing is a form of therapy. Sometimes I wonder how all those who do not write, compose or paint can manage to escape the madness, the melancholia, the panic fear which is inherent in the human situation" (1980, p. 285).

Art has been used both to diagnose and to cure mental illness. The first studies of the spontaneous works of mental patients were attempts to use the patients' art as a diagnostic tool (Lombroso, 1895; Simon, 1888). In twentieth century psychiatry, art works have been increasingly used in this way. Drawing tests have been invented for use in diagnosis (Anastasi and Foley, 1941; Naumburg, 1950, Pickford, 1963, 1970), and art therapy has been instituted as part of the treatment for the mentally ill (Wadeson, 1980). Patients are encouraged to draw, paint, sculpt, write, make music, and dance. The works that are produced are used to help to diagnose the particular form of disorder from which the patient is suffering. For instance, drawings by schizophrenics possess certain hallmarks, while drawings by depressives possess quite different qualities. Paintings typical of depressed patients show little investment of effort, are often colorless, empty, and lacking in detail, and appear incomplete, although many exceptions can be found (Fig. 13.9; Dax, 1953; Plokker, 1965; Wadeson, 1980). These characteristics are similar to other aspects of the depressed personality: inhibition of affect and low energy and productivity. Manic depressive patients make similar kinds of pictures when in a depressed phase. But when they enter into a manic phase, the paintings they produce are vividly colored, filled to the edges of the page, and emotionally exuberant (Wadeson, 1980).

Because the pictures that patients make reflect their illness, patients' art work can be used to help make an accurate diagnosis. Furthermore, once a broad diagnosis is made, such as schizophrenia, depression, or manic depression, the therapist can gain insight into the particular conflicts of individual patients by examining the

13.9 Drawing by a depressed patient, which is empty and colorless.

properties of their paintings. Patients who are unwilling or unable to talk about their feelings may allow these feelings to reveal themselves in their art work. Anger long suppressed may manifest itself unwittingly in a patient's drawing, thus allowing the therapist to realize that the patient is angry. Art works are used in art therapy in the same way as dreams are used in traditional psychotherapy: both are seen as windows on the unconscious. In this sense, art serves as a form of communication from patient to therapist.

The fact that patients may unwittingly reveal unconscious feelings in their drawings allows art to be used as a means of cure as well as diagnosis. First of all, art works grant therapists insight into patients. Therapists can thus help the patients to come to terms with their unconscious conflicts. Second, by externalizing their unconscious feelings in a work of art, patients by themselves can come to recognize these feelings. In one case, a patient who had painted an angry face looked at it and said that he had no idea why he had made such an angry looking face, since he himself was not at all angry (Wadeson, 1980). Eventually, however, he came to realize that in fact he had been angry after all. By consciously recognizing his anger, he was able to accept his feelings and integrate them, rather than deny them and split them off from himself.

Art therapy is also believed to have healing powers because it provides a way of releasing pent-up feelings. Just as Freud believed that dreams allow a certain degree of tension reduction, art therapists argue that, by expressing their feelings through art, patients can ventilate suppressed emotions and thus achieve a calmer state.

For all of these reasons, the artistic activity of the "sane" artist may also be therapeutic. Artistry may serve as a defense against latent psychosis by providing a way of gaining insight into one's problems, as well as by providing a means of release. Perhaps artists do in fact have latent psychotic tendencies, as the paper and pencil personality tests suggest, and making art helps to prevent the latent disorder from becoming manifest.

Art therapy is used with a wide variety of individuals (Wadeson, 1980). It is used with hospitalized patients suffering from such disorders as schizophrenia, depression, or manic depression. It is used in the treatment of neurotics and even in family therapy, where family members make joint pictures in an effort to explore family dynamics. It is used with many kinds of institutionalized people who are not mentally ill: people in nursing homes, those suffering from drug and alcohol addiction, and with retarded and physically handicapped people. Such therapy is even beginning to be used with normal children as a means of growth through self-expression.

Many case studies have demonstrated that involvement in the arts correlates with improvement in the mental health of the people involved (Anastasi and Foley, 1941; Gaston, 1968; Naumburg, 1950; Plokker, 1965; Schaefer-Simmern, 1948; Wadeson, 1980). These studies show that as patients begin to get better, their art works dramatically reflect this improvement. Schizophrenics whose paintings are a mass of unintegrated details begin, as they get better, to make paintings which are less bizarre and more normal. Depressives whose paintings are empty and colorless begin to make pictures that are more colorful and detailed and show greater investment of effort (Fig. 13.10).

Such correlations do not constitute evidence that art therapy works. They do not prove that the artistic activities of these patients are causally related to their cure. It may simply be that the patients' art works reflect rather than induce the changing course of the illness. The problem with studies showing that a regular program of art therapy correlates with improvement in the patients' condition is that these studies usually lack a control group of similar patients who were engaged in some other form of activity besides art. Thus, it is not known whether improvement would have occurred in any case (Anastasi, 1941). And when a control group has been employed, the patients in the control group were

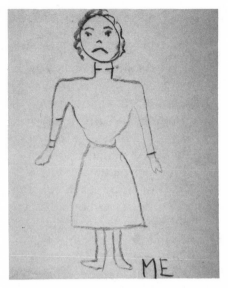

13.10 *Drawings by a depressed patient: self-portrait drawn during a severe depression, showing neck and wrist wounds from a suicide attempt the previous day, and colorful picture made after the depression had lifted.*

left entirely alone, without any form of therapy (Gardner, 1973a). Thus, it is possible that improvement in the group that received therapy could simply be the result of engaging in any acvitity with a therapist.

Yet the potential value of art therapy should not be lightly dismissed. Studies of other forms of psychotherapy have also failed to prove definitively that the treatments in question have an effect (Eysenck, 1960). Moreover, any cure is most likely produced by a variety of factors, and artistic activity may well contribute to restoration of health. If the arts are a natural means of self-expression, the mentally ill may find it easier to communicate through art than through other forms of communication, such as ordinary language. Since some patients gravitate spontaneously to the arts, this is probably a sign that the arts have meaning for them and play a positive role in their lives.

Biochemical Links Between Schizophrenia and Artistry

In addition to the healing powers of art, there is another possible explanation why artistry is associated with schizophrenia. Perhaps schizophrenia unlocks latent artistic creativity. The very symptoms of schizophrenia themselves may facilitate artistry. For instance,

hallucinations, heightened levels of arousal, and the inability to ignore what most people consider to be irrelevant may lead to the
novel insights and visions characteristic of the artist.

A preliminary study has suggested a biochemical mechanism
by which schizophrenia may unlock artistic creativity (Hartmann et
al., 1981). In an investigation of disorders of sleep, an intriguing
connection between nightmares, schizophrenia, and artistry was
suggested. Ads were placed in several newspapers asking for people over eighteen years of age who frequently experienced nightmares. A group of thirty-eight adults who reported having nightmares more than once a week was selected for study. Each subject
was given one or two extensive psychiatric interviews and a battery
of personality tests assessing neurotic and psychotic symptoms.

Considerable psychopathology was found in these subjects as
assessed by the tests. Moreover, the life histories of these people
revealed a great deal of mental disturbance. Four had been hospitalized for a psychiatric illness, probably schizophrenia. Twenty-
nine were or had been in psychotherapy. Many were often depressed: fifteen had seriously thought about suicide, and seven had
actually tried to kill themselves. Four of the subjects met the criteria for schizophrenia, nine were assessed as borderline, and six
were schizotypal personalities. Many of the subjects had relatives
who had been diagnosed as schizophrenic. Strikingly, no typically
neurotic people were found among the group.

This finding is hardly surprising. One might expect severe
nightmare sufferers to be disturbed. The surprising finding was
that almost all of the subjects had occupations or career plans related to the arts. They were painters, poets, musicians, and art
therapists. And those who had more conventional jobs thought of
themselves as artists even if they could not support themselves
through art. This group was thus unusually involved in the arts.

Hartmann (1980) boldly speculated about a possible link between the schizophrenic tendencies of these subjects, their nightmares, and their artistic inclinations. He suggested that a biochemical imbalance in the brains of this group caused their
predisposition toward schizophrenia, their excessive nightmares,
and their artistic interests. There is some indirect evidence to suggest that in the schizophrenic brain, the cells that transmit dopamine, a naturally produced chemical which conducts impulses between neurons of the brain, are hyperactive (Carlsson, 1978;
Matthysse, 1977; Meltzer and Stahl, 1976; Snyder, 1976). And high
dopamine levels have been found to cause vivid dreams and nightmares. For instance, when given a drug called L-Dopa, which raises
the dopamine level in the brain, people experienced more night-

mares than those in a control group given a placebo (Hartmann, Russ, and Skoff, 1978).

Thus, high dopamine levels are associated both with schizophrenia and with vivid nightmares. Perhaps high levels of dopamine also predispose people to the arts, though this speculation remains untested. One way to test it would be to examine the effects of amphetamines on nonschizophrenics. Through the administration of amphetamines, scientists have been able to create conditions in the nonschizophrenic brain similar to heightened levels of dopamine (Alpert and Friedhoff, 1980). The effect is to produce a psychosis in nonpsychotic individuals. It would be important to determine whether people become artistically inclined while under the influence of amphetamines. Another, more indirect way to test the hypothesis about dopamine levels would involve determining whether artists throughout history have had an excessive number of nightmares.

Even if it could be shown that high dopamine levels contribute both to artistry and to schizophrenia, this would prove only that artistry and schizophrenia have a common cause. Such evidence would not prove that schizophrenia itself unlocks artistry, for it may be that schizophrenia both works against the artist and is correlated with artistry. That is, it may turn out that the best artists are those with high dopamine levels who, for some other reason, are not as schizophrenic as the typical person afflicted with this disorder. Compounding the difficulty is the fact that the role of dopamine in schizophrenia has itself been contested and remains a controversial and unresolved issue (Alpert and Friedhoff, 1980). Nonetheless, the hypothesis about dopamine levels is one of the few attempts to suggest a biochemical link between madness and artistry.

From the available evidence, tentative conclusions can be drawn. First, there is no good evidence that artists become manifestly psychotic at an above average rate. However, there is some suggestive, though by no means conclusive, evidence that, on the average, artists as compared to nonartists possess latent psychotic tendencies.

Second, the psychosis of schizophrenia has an effect on artistry. In the case of the visual but not the verbal arts, there is some evidence that it may enhance the artistic powers of the patient. Schizophrenia affects artistry differently in the case of an established painter and in the case of someone who begins to paint for the first time after becoming schizophrenic. The style of the established painter may change, but his post-illness works will resemble his pre-illness works more than they will resemble works of untrained mental patients.

Third, art may have an effect on psychosis. Its use as a diagnostic tool is beyond dispute, and it is even possible that involvement in artistic activity may contribute to the cure or alleviation of various forms of mental illness.

Finally, there is at least the hint of a biochemical link between schizophrenia and artistry. Schizophrenia may be associated with high dopamine levels, and this may possibly enhance artistic creativity. However, even if a biochemical link is demonstrated between artistic creativity and schizophrenia, the key psychological questions are still left unanswered. Where is the connection between biochemistry and artistry? That is, what are the actual mechanisms by which a chemical in the brain yields artistic impulses? And what is the aesthetic significance of this activity?

Because of the difficulty of working with schizophrenics, research on these questions will not be easy. The studies carried out to date remain far from conclusive. But now that the questions have been defined and appropriate instruments to answer them have been suggested, it is in principle possible to examine large populations of schizophrenics and appropriate control groups in order to understand the creative impulses of laymen and established artists who have the misfortune to become schizophrenic.

Solving the Puzzle of Art

The psychology of art confronts a number of broad questions. With respect to the creation of art, the questions concern how and why the artist creates—what skills the artist must possess, and what drives someone to become an artist. A parallel set of questions having to do with the perception of art asks how and why people respond to works of art—what skills are required to make sense of them, and what effect they have on people. A final overarching question asks whether there are processes common to the production and perception of all forms of art, or whether each form requires different answers to the questions of how and why.

Although these are the major issues in the psychology of art, researchers have rarely addressed them directly. Instead, as is the case with other scientific fields, narrower questions are usually posed, since these are more readily susceptible to empirical investigation. For instance, rather than carrying out a research program designed to reveal how people make sense of works of art, psychologists have sought to understand how certain kinds of people—such as children, average adults, connoisseurs, and brain-damaged adults—respond to certain forms of art—such as simple stories, metaphors, representational paintings, nudes, or atonal melodies. And rather than trying to answer the question of why the artist creates, psychologists have sought to understand the personality differences between particular kinds of artists—such as highly creative writers versus average writers, and problem solvers in the visual arts versus problem finders. Putting together the answers to these smaller questions holds the promise of eventually illuminating the broader questions. But there is an ever-present danger: if, in the interest of conducting empirical tests, psychologists formulate questions that are too narrow in scope, the answers they discover may never be able to illuminate the larger questions.

Constructing a psychology of art is like building a house. A house cannot be put up all of a piece but must be built up out of smaller units: cement, bricks, glass, plaster, doors. Yet if one begins with units that are too small—atoms instead of bricks, doors, and cement—the task will never be accomplished. The builder must select components of just the right size. Similarly, the answers to major psychological questions about art cannot be discovered by asking the questions directly. One must begin with issues that are more manageable. Yet they must also be significant, more like bricks than atoms. There must be a fit between the ultimate questions to be answered and the data collected: if the data are too microscopic, they will never contribute to the understanding sought.

Progress toward answering basic questions in the psychology of art has certainly been made, but the history of such work reveals a continual tension between those who have tried to build their houses all at once and those who have tried to build them out of atoms. As a general rule, the big builders have tended to use nonexperimental methods, while the atomists have insisted on rigorous laboratory methods. Among the first to pose psychological questions about art were the ancient Greeks. Plato developed a theory of how the artist creates, and Aristotle considered the power that art exerts over the perceiver. Such questions went to the heart of the psychology of art. But these philosophers tried to build the house all at once, posing questions of only the broadest kind. Moreover, they proposed no objective means to test the validity of their theories, relying instead on logic and intuition.

Over the centuries, philosophers and artists followed in the footsteps of the Greeks, posing fundamental questions about art without providing empirical evidence. Freud was the first thinker to attempt to answer these questions empirically. He formulated a theory of human nature which purported to account for all of human behavior, including that of the artist. This bold attempt to place art within an entire theory of personality perhaps comes closer to a commonsense expectation of what it means to understand art than does any other psychological theory. However, once the problem is framed so broadly, it is difficult to make progress. Although Freud based his theory on clinical observations of neurotic people, he did not systematically test his conclusions. Thus, his answers were scarcely more reliable than the Greeks'.

At the same time that Freud was delving into the ultimate questions about art, other psychologists were setting themselves a very different task. Toward the end of the nineteenth century, psychology became a laboratory science, and for the first time hypotheses about artistic behavior were proposed that were readily susceptible to empirical test. Experimental psychologists such as Gustav Fechner restricted themselves to questions that could be subjected to quantitative measure, specifically to the properties of art that people find appealing. Not only was the focus of their study a narrow one, but the units that they studied, such as color patches, geometric forms, and isolated tones, were often so small that the discoveries could never contribute to an understanding of the broader psychological questions. Thus, these early experimental psychologists missed the essence of art: instead of trying, like Freud, to build the house all at once, they tried to build it from atoms.

It is easy, of course, to look back and accuse psychoanalysts of choosing units that were too large and experimental psychologists of choosing ones that were too small. But after all, one cannot know at the outset just what the right units are. The appropriate components can be discovered only after considerable exploration. That stage of discovery was reached in the psychology of art with the work of such investigators as Daniel Berlyne and Rudolf Arnheim, and the work of cognitive psychologists. Berlyne developed a theory, grounded in empirical evidence, of why art exerts power over us. Arnheim demonstrated the kinds of perceptual organization we impose on works of art. And cognitive psychologists have tried to discover the mental skills required by participation in the arts. These investigators have posed hypotheses more readily susceptible to empirical test than those of Freud, yet not nearly so narrow as those of Fechner. Thus, they offer some hope of illuminating the fundamental questions.

Because it is extremely difficult to understand the mental proccesses involved in producing or understanding a work of art as a whole, cognitive psychologists typically analyze works into their components and study how one comes to produce or understand these components. For instance, instead of asking how one understands poetry, they ask how one responds to the sound properties of poetry and how one comes to understand a metaphor. Once these component skills involved in understanding a literary text have been pinpointed, they can be combined to form a picture of the entire operation of reading literature. What is hopeful about this approach is that the components selected for study are likely to be the actual rather than the apparent building blocks of works of art, because the units studied are defined by students of the art forms themselves. Thus, it is possible to generalize with confidence from the findings of cognitive psychology to real works of art.

Cognitive psychologists have for the most part addressed only one of the fundamental questions of art. They have focused more on perception than on production, and more on the question of how than why. Because most cognitive research addresses the question of how art works are perceived, quite a bit is now known on this subject. Much less effort has been expended to discover how art works are produced, why artists create, and why audiences are drawn to the arts. The reasons for all this selective focus are, first, that psychological questions about the perceiver are more susceptible to empirical study than are psychological questions about the artist. Everyone, after all, perceives the arts, whereas the artist is an exceptional person. It is easier to study the ordinary skill of the typical perceiver than the extraordinary skill of the artist. And second, questions about the how of art are answerable in cognitive terms. Questions about the why have more to do with issues of motivation and personality, and the field of psychology has progressed less in these domains than in more prototypically cognitive areas.

Studies of the perception of art have revealed the extremely active, problem-solving stance that perceivers adopt when attempting to make sense of a work of art. To cite examples from different art forms, viewers of representational painting supplement the information coming to their senses in order to perceive the objects represented and the depth depicted; music listeners construct an internal grammar of tonality by which melodies are assimilated and understood; and readers extract and internalize the grammar of stories for use in assimilating and remembering new stories. These are things that the perceiver cannot help but do. They do not require conscious effort. Nonetheless, if the perceiver were not actively organizing the incoming stimuli and imposing a structure on them, works of art would appear to be meaningless.

Although the reasons art exerts power over us and the ways it is created remain relatively mysterious, some insights have been gained. The active stance required by viewers may be related to the pleasure experienced in contemplating works of art. The challenge of trying to make sense of a work of art is itself enjoyable. Perhaps this is the reason that people with independent, active, inquiring minds and a high tolerance for complexity prefer works of art considered to be of high quality by art experts, while more passive people prefer those considered by experts to be somewhat hackneyed.

As for the creation of art, there is evidence that the process occurs largely on a conscious level. Studies of artists at work have helped to demystify creativity by revealing that artists use logical, rational thought processes in order to solve the problems that they set for themselves. But a great deal more than logic and problem solving goes into the creation of a work of art. Not only are artists skilled at problem solving, but they are constantly seeking problems to solve. Indeed, problem finding may be the trait that sets the truly creative artist apart from the mediocre one. Moreover, creative artists are deeply engaged in multiple pursuits at the same time, which enables them to see connections that were never seen before. Forging such links is at the heart of creating an original and lasting work of art.

A playful, daring attitude also characterizes the artist, a desire to experiment and to violate conventions. And this willingness to experiment must be coupled with an unusual amount of motivation. Without a high degree of ego strength, autonomy, and sheer drive, as well as the ability to persevere in the face of apparent failure and popular derision, the artist could never make it through the years of toil and training that are necessary for creation.

Future studies of artists at work will probably reveal that there are not one but many creative processes. Because works of art are unique, aspects of the process by which they are made may be specific to the artist in question. Although there certainly are common features to how artists create, individual differences may characterize artistic creativity to a far greater extent than ordinary domains such as perception, language, and memory.

Why an artist makes art is probably the most mysterious question of all. Yet there is evidence that the drive to create has something to do with the quest for knowledge. When asked why they create, artists repeatedly answer in terms of knowledge and discovery. These introspective reports are supported by the fact that the most creative artists tend to set difficult problems for themselves to solve, whereas the less original artists seem to accept problems as given and solve them within ordinary confines.

The question of why artists create is undoubtedly related to the as yet unanswered question of the neuropsychology of talent. If the brain of an artistic genius is atypical in certain ways, then creating works of art may simply be what artists do naturally, just as constructing a first language is what all humans do effortlessly. Perhaps it is not necessary to posit a special source of energy that explains the artist's drive to create, any more than it is necessary to posit a special source of motivation to learn a first language or to learn to walk. In the words of the composer Camille Saint-Saens, "I produce music as easily as an apple tree produces apples."

Cross-cultural studies are sorely needed to test the universality of all these claims. They are especially needed to test the universality of explanations for why people like art and why artists make art, because these motivational issues are most likely to be subject to cultural influences. For instance, studies in nonindustrialized societies will probably reveal that the artist as a solitary, driven creature is a Western invention, a creation of a culture that values Faustian exploration. Such artists are found almost exclusively in industrialized societies, although accomplished craftsmen exist everywhere.

The broadest question to be posed is whether there are psychological processes common to the perception and production of all forms of art. Are there any "pan-artistic" skills that are called upon in all forms of art? Is there such a thing as one "artistic intelligence," or are there instead different kinds of artistic intelligence—musical, literary, and visual? These questions must be answered before it can be determined whether there is a single "psychology of art," as opposed to a psychology of painting, of music, or of literature.

Some pan-artistic skills may well exist in the areas of repleteness, expression, and composition, which are arguably the three most important properties to attend to in a work of art. It is likely that sensitivity to these three qualities is called upon in the perception and production of all forms of art, but is relatively unimportant in the perception and production of nonartistic objects. Fortunately, sensitivity to these properties can be studied using the methods of cognitive psychology. For instance, studies could determine whether perceiving the composition of a melody calls upon the same skills as grasping the composition of a story, or whether sensitivity to repleteness in a drawing is the same skill as sensitivity to repleteness in music. Thus, it should prove eminently possible to determine whether there are any psychological processes that cut across the arts.

Progress in the psychology of art depends greatly upon progress in other areas of psychology. In the past few decades, cognitive psychology has made major advances, from which the psychology of art has reaped the benefits. Much less progress has been made in answering questions about personality, motivation, and the emotions. When advances are made in these relatively noncognitive areas, we will have better tools and models with which to explore such issues in connection with the arts. Yet psychologists of art are not waiting idly to reap the benefits of advances in other areas of psychology; they are forging ahead on their own. Eventually, the more traditional areas of psychology may in turn benefit from advances made in the psychology of art.

Illustration Sources

References

Index

Illustration Sources

1.1   Musée du Louvre.

1.2   Copyright © Museo del Prado, Madrid, and SPADEM, Paris/VAGA, New York, 1982.

2.1   D. E. Berlyne, "The Influence of Complexity and Novelty in Visual Figures on Orienting Responses," *Journal of Experimental Psychology* 55 (1958): 289–296, copyright 1958 by the American Psychological Association, reprinted by permission of publisher.

2.2   K. O. Götz, A. R. Borisy, R. Lynn, and H. J. Eysenck, "A New Visual Aesthetic Sensitivity Test: I. Construction and Psychometric Properties," *Perceptual and Motor Skills* 49 (1979): 795–802, Fig. 1. Reprinted by permission of authors and publisher.

2.3   The Toledo Museum of Art, Gift of Edward Drummond Libbey; Photograph Collection, Art and Architecture Library, Yale University.

2.4   Fogg Art Museum, Harvard University, bequest of Grenville L. Winthrop; Skulpturengalerie, Staatliche Museen Preussischer Kulturbesitz, Berlin (West), photograph from Reinhard Friedrich, Berlin.

2.5   Copyright © Museo del Prado, Madrid.

3.1   Widener Collection, National Gallery of Art, Washington.

3.2   Oil on canvas, with sequins, 63⅝ x 61½". Collection, The Museum of Modern Art, New York, acquired through the Lillie P. Bliss Bequest.

3.3   Staatliche Museen Preussischer Kulturbesitz Kupferstichkabinett, Berlin.

3.4   Beverlee Seronick.

3.7   E. H. Gombrich, *Art and Illusion: A Study in the Psychology of Pictorial Representation* (Princeton, N.J.: Princeton University Press, and Oxford: Phaidon Press Limited, 1960), reprinted by permission of Princeton University Press.

3.8   Beverlee Seronick.

3.14   E. H. Gombrich, *Art and Illusion: A Study in the Psychology of Pictorial Representation* (Princeton, N.J.: Princeton University Press, and Oxford: Phaidon Press Limited, 1960), adapted by permission.

3.15   D. N. Perkins, "The Perceiver as Organizer and Geometer," in J. Beck, ed., *Representation and Organization in Perception* (Hillsdale, N.J.: Lawrence Erlbaum Associates, 1982).

3.17   Oil on canvas, 50 x 50". Collection, The Museum of Modern Art, New York; Collection, Mr. and Mrs. Armand Bartos.

4.1   T. G. R. Bower, "The Visual World of Infants," copyright © 1966 by Scientific American, Inc., all rights reserved.

4.2   Research conducted by Dr. W. Hudson in conjunction with The National Institute for Personnel Research, cited in J. B. Deregowski, "Pictorial Perception and Culture," copyright © 1972 by Scientific American, Inc., all rights reserved.

4.3   T. Carothers and H. Gardner, "When Children's Drawings Become Art: The Emergence of Aesthetic Production and Preferences," *Developmental Psychology* 15 (1975): 570–580, copyright 1975 by the American Psychological Association, reprinted by permission of publisher and authors.

4.4   Oil on canvas, 29 x 36¼". Collection, The Museum of Modern Art, New York, acquired through the Lillie P. Bliss Bequest.

4.5   S. Chipman and M. J. Mendelson, "Sensitivity to Visual Structure," *Journal of Experimental Child Psychology* 20 (1975): 411–429.

4.6   Hill-Stead Museum, Farmington, Connecticut; Worcester Art Museum, Worcester, Massachusetts; The National Museum, Naples, and Alinari/Editorial Photocolor Archives; Museu de Arte de São Paulo.

4.7   The Phillips Collection, Washington; Collection of the Art Institute of Chicago; Isabella Stewart Gardner Museum, Boston; Musée du Louvre; Isabella Stewart Gardner Museum, Boston; Sterling and Francine Clark Institute, Williamstown, Massachusetts.

5.1   (Fold-out drawing) J. Goodnow, *Children Drawing* (Cambridge: Harvard University Press, and London: William Collins Sons, Ltd., 1977), reprinted by permission; (X-ray drawing) R. Arnheim, *Art and Visual Perception: A Psychology of the Creative Eye* (Berkeley: University of California Press, 1974).

5.3   L. Selfe, *Nadia: A Case of Extraordinary Drawing Ability in an Autistic Child* (1977), copyright by Academic Press Inc. (London) Ltd., reprinted by permission; The Royal Library, Windsor Castle, reproduced by gracious permission of Her Majesty Queen Elizabeth II.

5.4–5.6 R. Kellogg, *Analyzing Children's Art*, reproduced by permission of Mayfield Publishing Company, copyright © 1969, 1970, by Rhoda Kellogg.

5.8   (Mandala with multiple crosses) B. Lark-Horovitz, H. Lewis, and M. Luca, *Understanding Children's Art for Better Teaching*, 2nd ed. (Columbus: Charles E. Merrill, 1973).

5.11   Photographie Giraudon, Paris.

5.12   N. H. Freeman, *Strategies of Representation in Young Children: Analysis of Spatial Skills and Drawing Processes* (1980), copyright Academic Press Inc. (London) Ltd., reprinted by permission.

5.13   Collection, Stedelijk Museum, Amsterdam.

5.14   J. Willats, "How Children Learn to Draw Realistic Pictures," *Quarterly Journal of Experimental Psychology* 29 (1977): 367–382.

5.15   R. Arnheim, *Art and Visual Perception* (Berkeley: University of California Press, 1974).

5.16   H. Schaeffer-Simmern, *The Unfolding of Artistic Activity* (Berkeley: University of California Press, 1970).

5.17   David Brown.

5.18   Copyright © 1982 by COSMOPRESS, Geneva, and ADAGP, Paris; H. Gardner, *The Arts and Human Development* (New York: John Wiley and Sons, 1973); copyright © Museo del Prado, Madrid, and SPADEM, Paris/VAGA, New York, 1982; Sylvia Fein, *Heidi's Horse* (Pleasant Hill, Cal.: Exelrod Press, 1976).

5.19   T. Carothers and H. Gardner, "When Children's Drawings Become Art: The Emergence of Aesthetic Production and Preferences," *Developmental Psychology* 15 (1975): 570–580; copyright 1975 by the American Psychological Association, reprinted by permission of publisher and authors.

5.20–
5.21   Thomas Carothers and Howard Gardner.

5.22   D. Morris, *The Biology of Art* (New York: Knopf, 1962).

5.23   Beatrice Gardner.

5.24   D. Morris, *The Biology of Art* (New York: Knopf, 1962).

5.25   L. Selfe, *Nadia: A Case of Extraordinary Drawing Ability in an Autistic Child*, 1977; copyright by Academic Press Inc. (London) Ltd., reprinted by permission.

5.26   Copyright © SPADEM, Paris/VAGA, New York, 1981.

5.27   Paul Klee Foundation Museum of Fine Arts, Bern, copyright © 1982 by COSMOPRESS, Geneva, and ADAGP, Paris.

5.28   Charles Clemons.

7.1   J. Bamberger, "Revisiting Children's Drawings of Simple Rhythms," in S. Strauss, ed., *U-shaped Behavioral Growth* (in press), copyright Academic Press Inc. (London) Ltd., reprinted by permission.

8.1–8.2 L. Bernstein, *The Unanswered Question* (Cambridge: Harvard University Press, 1976), reprinted by permission.

8.3–8.5 P. McKernon, "The Development of First Songs in Young Children," *Early Symbolization, New Directions for Child Development*, no. 3 (1979): 43–58.

Ch. 9   "It Bids Pretty Fair," *The Poetry of Robert Frost*, ed. Edward Connery Lathem, copyright 1947, © 1969 by Holt, Rinehart and Winston, copyright © 1975 by Lesley Frost Ballantine, reprinted by permission of Holt, Rinehart and Winston, Publishers.

9.1   D. E. Rumelhart, "Understanding and Summarizing Brief Stories," in D. LaBerge and J. Samuels, eds., *Basic Processes in Reading: Perception and Comprehension* (Hillsdale, N.J.: Lawrence Erlbaum and Associates, 1982), reprinted and adapted by permission of author and publisher.

Ch. 9   "I Heard a Fly Buzz," *The Poems of Emily Dickinson*, ed. Thomas H. Johnson (Cambridge: Harvard University Press), copyright 1951 © 1955, 1979 by the President and Fellows of Harvard College, reprinted by permission of the publishers and the trustees of Amherst College.

10.1   Michael Cometa.

12.1   H. Gardner, *The Shattered Mind* (New York: Knopf, 1975).

12.2   R. Jung, *Psychiatrie der Gegenwart*, 2nd ed. (Berlin-Heidelberg-New York: Springer, 1980).

12.3   Thomas Corinth.

13.1   Collection, National Museum Vincent van Gogh, Amsterdam.

13.2   Copyright Adolf-Wölfli-Stiftung Kunstmuseum, Bern, photograph from Adolf-Wölfli-Foundation, Museum of Fine Arts, Bern.

13.3   Michael Moore. (Drawing produced under influence of a drug) Stanislav Grof, M.D., and Joan Halifax-Grof, *Realms of the Human Unconscious*, copyright by Stanislav Grof and Joan Halifax-Grof, reprinted by permission of Viking Penguin, Inc., New York, and Souvenir Press Limited, London.

13.4   H. Prinzhorn, *Artistry of the Mentally Ill*, trans. Eric von Brockdorff (New York: Springer-Verlag, 1972).

13.5   Private collection.

13.6   O. Billig, "Spatial Structure in Schizophrenic Art," *Psychiatry and Art*, 1966, pp. 1–66.

13.7   E. Kris, *Psychoanalytic Explorations in Art* (New York: International Universities Press, 1952).

13.8   Field Museum of Natural History, Chicago, Illinois. O. Billig, and B. G. Burton-Bradley, "Cross-cultural Studies of Psychotic Graphics from New Guinea," *Psychiatry and Art* 4 (1975): 18–47.

13.9–
13.10   H. Wadeson, *Art Psychotherapy* (New York: John Wiley and Sons, 1980).

References

Ackerman, J. 1962. A theory of style. *The Journal of Aesthetics and Art Criticism* 20 (3):227–237.

Alajouanine, T. 1948. Aphasia and artistic realization. *Brain* 71:229–241. Reprinted in M. T. Sarno, ed. *Aphasia: selected readings.* New York: Appleton-Century Croft, 1972, pp. 231–239.

Albers, J. 1963. *Interaction of color.* New Haven: Yale University Press.

Alpert, M., and Friedhoff, A. 1980. An un-dopamine hypothesis of schizophrenia. *Schizophrenia Bulletin* 6 (3):387–390.

Altshuler, R., and Hattwick, L. 1969. *Painting and personality: a study of young children.* Chicago: University of Chicago Press.

Ames, A. 1955. *An interpretive manual for the demonstrations in the Psychology Research Center, Princeton University.* Princeton: Princeton University Press.

Ames, L. 1966. *Children's stories. Genetic Psychology Monographs* 73:337–396.

Anastasi, A., and Foley, J., Jr. 1941. A survey of the literature on artistic behavior in the abnormal: I. Historical and theoretical background. *The Journal of General Psychology* 25:111–142.

Anwar, M., and Child, I. 1972. Personality and esthetic sensitivity in an Islamic culture. *Journal of Social Psychology* 87:21–28.

Apel, W. 1969. *Harvard Dictionary of Music.* 2nd ed. Cambridge: Harvard University Press.

Applebee, A. 1978. *The child's concept of story: ages two to seventeen.* Chicago: University of Chicago Press.

Arieti, S. 1974. *Interpretation of schizophrenia.* New York: Basic Books.

Arnheim, R. 1949. The Gestalt theory of expression. *Psychological Review* 56:156–171.

———. 1962. *The genesis of a painting: Picasso's Guernica.* Berkeley: University of California Press.

———. 1969. *Visual thinking.* Berkeley: University of California Press.

———. 1972. *Toward a psychology of art.* Berkeley: University of California Press.

———. 1974. *Art and visual perception.* Berkeley: University of California Press.

———. 1977. The art of psychotics. *Art Psychotherapy* 4:113–120.

———. 1980. Problems of space in early forms of art. Paper presented at National Symposium for Research in Art, University of Illinois, Urbana-Champaign, October.

Arter, J. 1976. The effects of metaphor on reading comprehension. Ph.D dissertation, University of Illinois, Urbana-Champaign.

Asch, S. 1955. On the use of metaphor in the description of persons. In H.

Werner, ed. *On expressive language.* Worcester: Clark University Press.

——. 1956. Studies of independence and conformity: a minority of one against a unanimous majority. *Psychological Monographs* 70 (9), no. 416.

Asch, S., and Nerlove, H. 1960. The development of double-function terms in children: an exploratory investigation. In B. Kaplan and S. Wapner, eds. *Perspectives in psychological theory: essays in honor of Heinz Werner.* New York: International Universities Press.

Attneave, F. 1954. Some informational aspects of visual perception. *Psychological Review* 61:183–193.

——. 1972. Representation of physical space. In A. W. Melton and E. Martin, eds. *Coding processes in human memory.* New York: Wiley.

Attneave, F., and Olson, R. K. 1971. Pitch as medium: a new approach to psychophysical scaling. *American Journal of Psychology* 84:147–166.

Bader, A. 1958. Psychotics and their paintings: the human soul laid bare. *CIBA Symposium* 6:152–155.

Bader, A., and Navratil, L. 1976. *Zwischen Wahn und Wirklichkeit.* Lucerne: Bucher.

Bamberger, J. 1982. Revisiting children's drawings of simple rhythms: a function for reflection-in-action. In S. Strauss, ed. *U-shaped behavioral growth.* New York: Academic Press.

Bamberger, Jr., and Brofsky, H. 1979. *The art of listening: developing musical perception.* 4th ed. New York: Harper and Row.

Bamberger, J., Duckworth, E., and Lampert, M. 1981. Final report: an experiment in teacher development. NIE Grant G-78-0219, M.I.T., March.

Bamberger, M., and Hildebrandt, C. 1979. Claps and gaps. Unpublished paper, M.I.T., Cambridge.

Barron, F. 1952. Personality style and perceptual choice. *Journal of Personality* 20 (4):385–401.

——. 1953. Complexity-simplicity as a personality dimension. *Journal of Abnormal and Social Psychology* 48:162–172.

——. 1958. The psychology of imagination. *Scientific American* 199 (3):151–166.

——. 1963a. *Creativity and psychological health: origins of personality and creative freedom.* Princeton: Van Nostrand.

——. 1963b. The needs for order and for disorder as motivation in creative activity. In C. W. Taylor and F. Barron, eds. *Scientific Creativity: its recognition and development.* New York: Wiley.

——. 1969. *Creative person and creative process.* New York: Holt, Rinehart, and Winston.

——. 1972. The creative personality: akin to madness? *Psychology Today,* July, pp. 42–44, 84–85.

Barron, F., and Welsh, G. 1952. Artistic perception as a possible factor in personality style: its measurement by a figure preference test. *Journal of Psychology* 33:199–203.

Bartlett, J., and Dowling, W. 1980. Recognition of transposed melodies: a key-distance effect in developmental perspective. *Journal of Experimental Psychology: Human Perception and Performance* 6 (3):501–515.

Beebe-Center, J. 1932. *The psychology of pleasantness and unpleasantness.* Princeton: Van Nostrand.

Beebe-Center, J., and Pratt, C. C. 1937. A test of Birkhoff's aesthetic measure. *Journal of General Psychology* 17:335–350.

Bell, C. 1913. *Art.* New York: F. A. Stokes.

Berlyne, D. 1960. *Conflict, arousal, and curiosity.* New York: McGraw Hill.

————. 1970. Novelty, complexity, and hedonic value. *Perception and Psychophysics* 8:279–286.

————. 1971. *Aesthetics and psychobiology.* New York: Appleton-Century-Crofts.

————, ed. 1974. *Studies in the new experimental aesthetics: steps toward an objective psychology of aesthetic appreciation.* New York: Wiley.

Berlyne, D. and Lawrence, G. 1964. Effects of complexity and uncongruity variables on GSR, investigatory behavior and verbally expressed preference. *Journal of General Psychology* 71:21–45.

Berlyne, D., and Ogilvie, J. 1974. Dimensions of perception of paintings. In D. E. Berlyne, ed. *Studies in the new experimental aesthetics: steps toward an objective psychology of aesthetic appreciation.* New York: Wiley.

Berndt, T., and Berndt, E. 1975. Children's use of motives and intentionality in person perception and moral judgment. *Child Development* 46:904–912.

Bernstein, L. 1976. *The unanswered question: six talks at Harvard.* Cambridge: Harvard University Press.

Bettelheim, B. 1967. *The empty fortress: infantile autism and the birth of self.* New York: The Free Press.

————. 1976. *The uses of enchantment: the meaning and importance of fairy tales.* New York: Knopf.

Bever, T., and Chiarello, R. 1974. Cerebral dominance in musicians and nonmusicians. *Science* 185:137–139.

Billig, O. 1966. Spatial structure in schizophrenic art. In I. Jakab, ed. *Psychiatry and art: proceedings of the IVth International Congress of Psychopathology of Expression.* Basel: S. Karger.

Billig, O., and Burton-Bradley, B. 1975. Cross-cultural studies of psychotic graphics from New Guinea. In I. Jakab, ed. *Transcultural aspects of psychiatric art,* vol. 4: *Psychiatry and Art.* New York: S. Karger.

————. 1978. *The painted message.* Cambridge: Schenkman.

Billow, R. 1975. A cognitive-developmental study of metaphor comprehension. *Developmental Psychology* 11:415–423.

Billow, R. 1981. Observing spontaneous metaphor in children. *Journal of Experimental Child Psychology* 31 (3):430–445.

Birkhoff, G. 1933. *Aesthetic measure.* Cambridge: Harvard University Press.

Black, J., and Wilensky, R. 1979. An evaluation of story grammars. *Cognitive Science* 3:213–230.

Black, M. 1962. *Models and Metaphors.* Ithaca: Cornell University Press.

Blackwell, H., and Schlosberg, H. 1943. Octave generalization, pitch discrimination, and loudness thresholds in the white rat. *Journal of Experimental Psychology* 33:407–419.

Blumstein, S., and Cooper, W. 1974. Hemispheric processing of intonation contours. *Cortex* 10:146–158.

Bogen, J., and Gordon, H. 1971. Musical tests for functional lateralization with intra-carotid amabarbital. *Nature* 230:524–525.

Bonaparte, M., Freud, A., and Kris, E., eds. 1954. *The origins of psychoanalysis.* Trans. Eric Mosbacher and James Strachey. New York: Basic Books.

Bond, E. 1972. Perception of form by the human infant. *Psychological Bulletin* 77:225–245.

Bornstein, M. 1975. Qualities of color vision in infancy. *Journal of Experimental Child Psychology* 19:401–419.

Boswell, S. 1974. The development of verbal and spatial organization for material presented tachistoscopically. Ph.D. dissertation, University of Colorado, Boulder.

Botez, M., and Wertheim, N. 1959. Expressive aphasia and amusia following right frontal lesion in a right-handed man. *Brain* 82:186–201.

Botvin, G. 1974. Acquiring conservation of melody and cross-modal transfer through successive approximation. *Journal of Research in Music Education* 22 (3):226–233.

Botvin, G., and Sutton-Smith, B. 1977. The development of structural complexity in children's fantasy narratives. *Developmental Psychology* 13:377–388.

Bower, G. 1976. Comprehending and recalling stories. Division 3 Presidential Address, American Psychological Association, September.

Bower, T. 1964. Discrimination of depth in premotor infants. *Psychonomic Science* 1:368.

———. 1966. The visual world of infants. *Scientific American* 215:80–92.

———. 1972. Object perception in infants. *Perception* 1 (1):15–30.

Bowerman, M. 1976. The acquisition of word meaning: an investigation of some current conflicts. In N. Waterson and C. Snow, eds. *Proceedings of the Third International Language Symposium.* New York: Wiley.

Boyd, R. 1979. Metaphor and theory change: what is "metaphor" a metaphor for? In A. Ortony, ed. *Metaphor and Thought.* Cambridge, Eng.: Cambridge University Press.

Braine, L. 1972. A developmental analysis of the effect of stimulus orientation on recognition. *American Journal of Psychology* 85:157–188.

Bransford, J., and Johnson, M. 1973. Considerations of some problems of comprehension. In W. Chase, ed. *Visual information processing.* New York: Academic Press.

Brehmer, F. 1925. *Melodie Auffassung un melodische Begabung des Kinders.* Leipzig: J. A. Barth. Cited in R. Francès. *La Perception de la musique.* Paris: Vrin, 1958.

Brighouse, G. 1939. Variability in preferences for simple forms. *Psychological Monographs* 51 (5):68–74.

Brittain, W. 1968. An exploratory investigation of early adolescent expression in art. *Studies in Art Education* 9 (2):5–12.

Brody, G. 1970. The development of visual aesthetic preferences in young children. *Sciences de l'Art: Scientific Aesthetics* 7 (1–2):27–31.

Brown, R. 1958. *Words and things.* New York: The Free Press.

———. 1981. Music and language. In *Documentary report of the Ann Arbor Symposium: applications of psychology to the teaching and learning of music.* Reston, Va.: Music Educators National Conference.

Brown, R., Black, A., and Horowitz, A. 1955 Phonetic symbolism in natural languages. *Journal of Abnormal and Social Psychology* 50:388–393.

Brown, R., and Herrnstein, R. 1975. *Psychology.* Boston: Little, Brown.

Bruner, J. 1962. *On knowing: essays for the left hand.* Cambridge: Harvard University Press.

———. 1966. The conservation of liquids. In J. Bruner, R. Olver, and P. Greenfield, eds. *Studies in cognitive growth.* New York: Wiley.

Burns, E., and Ward, W. 1974. Categorical perception of musical intervals. *Journal of the Acoustical Society of America* 55 (2):456 (A).

Burt, C. 1939. The factorial analysis of emotional traits. *Character and Personality* 7:285–300.

Bush, M. 1967. The problem of form in the psychoanalytic theory of art. *The Psychoanalytic Review* 54 (1):5–35.

Cabe, P. 1976. Transfer of discrimination from solid objects to pictures by pigeons: a test of theoretical models of picture perception. *Perception and Psychophysics* 19:545–550.

Callaway, E., III. 1970. Schizophrenia and interference. *Archives of General Psychiatry* 22:193–208.

Carlson, P., and Anisfeld, M. 1969. Some observations on the linguistic competence of a two-year-old child. *Child Development* 40:565–575.

Carlsson, A. 1978. Does dopamine have a role in schizophrenia? *Biological Psychiatry* 13 (1):3–21.

Carothers, T., and Gardner, H. 1979. When children's drawings become art: the emergence of aesthetic production and perception. *Developmental Psychology* 15 (5):570–580.

Cassirer, E. 1957. *Philosophy of symbolic forms.* New Haven: Yale University Press.

Cazden, C. 1973. Problems for education: language as curriculum content and learning environment. *Daedalus* 102 (3):135–148.

————. 1974. Play with language and metalinguistic awareness: one dimension of language experience. *International Journal of Early Childhood* 6:12–24.

Chang, H., and Trehub, S. 1977a. Auditory processing of relational information by young infants. *Journal of Experimental Child Psychology* 24:324–331.

————. 1977b. Infants' perception of temporal grouping in auditory patterns. *Child Development* 48:1666–1670.

Child, I. 1962. Personal preferences as an expression of aesthetic sensitivity. *Journal of Personality* 30:496–512.

————. 1964. Development of sensitivity to aesthetic values. Cooperative Research Project No. 1748, Yale University.

————. 1965. Personality correlates of esthetic judgment in college students. *Journal of Personality* 33:476–511.

————. 1968–1969. Esthetics. In G. Lindzey and E. Aronson, eds. *Handbook of social psychology,* vol. 3. 2nd ed. Reading, Mass.: Addison-Wesley.

————. 1978. Aesthetic Theories. In E. Carterette, ed. *Handbook of Perception,* vol. 10. New York: Academic Press.

Child, I., Hansen, J., and Hornbeck, F. 1968. Age and sex differences in children's color preferences. *Child Development* 39 (1):237–247.

Child, I., and Iwao, S. 1968. Personality and esthetic sensitivity: extension of findings to younger age and to different culture. *Journal of Personality and Social Psychology* 8:308–312.

————. 1977. Young children's preferential responses to visual art. *Scientific Aesthetics/Sciences de l'Art* 1 (4):291–307.

Child, I., and Schwartz, R. 1966. Exploring the teaching of art values. *Journal of Aesthetic Education* 1 (2):41–54.

Child, I., and Siroto, L. 1965. Bakwele and American esthetic evaluations compared. *Ethnology* 4:349–360.

Chipman, S., and Mendelson, M. 1975. The development of sensitivity to visual structure. *Journal of Experimental Child Psychology* 20:411–429.

Chomsky, N. 1957. *Syntactic structures.* The Hague: Mouton.

————. 1965. *Aspects of the theory of syntax.* Cambridge: MIT Press.

Chukovsky, K. 1968. *From two to five.* Berkeley: University of California Press.

Cicone, M., Gardner, H., and Winner E. 1981. Understanding the psychology in psychological metaphors. *Journal of Child Language* 8:213–216.

Cicone, M., Wapner, W., and Gardner, H. 1980. Sensitivity to emotional expressions and situations in organic patients. *Cortex* 16:145–158.

Clark, A. 1896–1897. The child's attitude toward perspective problems. *Studies in education.* Stanford: Stanford University Press.

Clark, E. 1973. What's in a word? In T. E. Moore, ed. *Cognitive development and the acquisition of language.* New York: Academic Press.

Clark, H. 1979. Responding to indirect speech acts. *Cognitive Psychology* 11:430–477.

Cockrell, J., and Sadacca, R. 1971. *Training individual image interpreters using team consensus feedback.* Technical Research Report 1171, U.S. Army Behavior and Systems Research Laboratory.

Cole, M., and Scribner, S. 1974. *Culture and thought: a psychological introduction.* New York: Wiley.

Collingwood, R. 1938. *The principles of art.* Oxford: Clarendon Press.

Connor, K., and Kogan, N. 1980. Topic-vehicle relations in metaphor: the issue of asymmetry. In R. P. Honeck and R. R. Hoffman, eds. *Cognition and figurative langauge.* Hillsdale, N.J.: Lawrence Erlbaum Associates.

Cooper, B. 1977. Development of sensitivity to geometric information for viewing shapes and sizes in pictures. In R. N. Haber, ed. *Proceedings of the tenth symposium of the Center for Visual Sciences.* Rochester: University of Rochester.

Copland, A. 1939. *What to listen for in music.* New York: McGraw Hill.

———. 1977. *Music and imagination.* Cambridge: Harvard University Press.

Corcoran, A. 1954. Color usage in nursery school painting. *Child Development* 25 (2):107–113.

Cross, P., Cattell, R., and Butcher, H. 1967. The personality patterns of creative artists. *British Journal of Educational Psychology* 37:292–299.

Crozier, J. 1980. Absolute pitch. Paper presented at International Society for Empirical Aesthetics, Montreal, Canada, August.

Daehler, M., Perlmutter, M., and Myers, N. 1976. Equivalence of pictures and objects for very young children. *Child Development* 47:96–102.

Damon, W. 1967. The child's conception of literary emotion. Honors thesis, Harvard College.

Daniels, P. 1933–34. Discrimination of compositional balance at the preschool level. *Studies in the Psychology of Art, Psychological Monographs* 18:45.

Davenport, R., and Rogers, C. 1971. Perception of photographs by apes. *Behavior* 39:318–320.

Davidson, L., McKernon, P., and Gardner, H. 1981. The acquisition of song: a developmental approach. In *Documentary report of the Ann Arbor symposium: applications of psychology to the teaching and learning of music.* Reston, Va.: Music Educators National Conference.

Davis, R. 1936. An evaluation and test of Birkhoff's aesthetic measure formula. *Journal of General Psychology* 15:231–240.

Dax, E. 1953. *Experimental studies in psychiatric art.* London: Faber and Faber.

Day, H. 1965. Exploratory behavior as a function of individual differences and level of arousal. Ph.D. thesis, University of Toronto.

———. 1966. Looking time as a function of stimulus variables and individual differences. *Perceptual and Motor Skills* 22:423–428.

DeLoache, J., Strauss, M., and Maynard, J. 1979. Picture perception in infancy. *Infant Behavior and Development* 2:77–89.

Demorest, A., Silberstein, L., Gardner, H., and Winner, E. 1981. From understatement to hyperbole: recognizing nonliteral language and its intent. Paper presented at Biennial Meetings of the Society for Research in Child Development, Boston.

De Myer, K. 1976. The nature of neuropsychological disability in autistic children. In E. Schopler and R. Reichler, eds. *Psychopathology and child development: research and treatment.* New York: Plenum Press.

Dennis, N. 1978. Portrait of the artist. *New York Review of Books* 25 (May 4):8–15.

Deregowski, J., Muldrow, E., and Muldrow, W. 1972. Pictorial recognition in a remote Ethiopian population. *Perception* 1:417–425.

Deutch, D. 1972. Octave generalization and tune recognition. *Perception and Psychophysics* 11:411–412.

De Villiers, J., and de Villiers, P. 1978. *Language acquisition*. Cambridge: Harvard University Press.

Dewar, K., Cuddy, L., and Mewhort, D. 1977. Recognition memory for single tones with and without context. *Journal of Experimental Psychology: Human Learning and Memory* 3:60–67.

Dewey, J. 1934. *Art as experience*. New York: Minton, Balch.

Dirks, J., and Gibson, E. 1977. Infants' perception of similarity between live people and their photographs. *Child Development* 48:124–130.

Dissanayake, E. 1974. A hypothesis of the evolution of art from play. *Leonardo* 7:211–217.

Dorgueille, C. 1966. Introduction a l'étude des amusies. Ph.D. dissertation, Paris. Cited in M. Critchley and R. Henson, eds. *Music and the brain*. London: William Heinemann Medical Books, 1977.

Dowling, W. 1972. Recognition of melodic transformations: inversion, retrograde, and retrograde inversion. *Perception and Psychophysics* 12:417–421.

———. 1978a. Musical scales and psychophysical scales. *Ethnomusicology* 22:229–244.

———. 1978b. Scale and contour: two components of a theory of memory for melodies. *Psychological Review* 85 (4):341–354.

———. 1979. The cognitive psychology of music. *Humanities Association Review* 30 (1–2):58–67.

———. 1981. Mental structures through which music is perceived. In *Documentary report of the Ann Arbor symposium: Applications of psychology to the teaching and learning of music*. Reston, Va.: Music Educators National Conference, pp. 144–151.

———. In press. Melodic information processing and its development. In D. Deutsch, ed. *The psychology of music*. New York: Academic Press.

Dowling, W., and Fujitani, D. 1971. Contour, interval, and pitch recognition in memory for melodies. *Journal of the Acoustical Society of America* 49 (2):524–531.

Dowling, W., and Hollombe, A. 1977. The perception of melodies distorted by splitting into several octaves: effects of increasing proximity and melodic contour. *Perception and Psychophysics* 21:60–64.

Dreistadt, R. 1969. The use of analogies and incubation in obtaining insights in creative problem solving. *Journal of Psychology* 71:159–175.

Drevdahl, J., and Cattell, R. 1958. Personality and creativity in artists and writers. *Journal of Clinical Psychology* 14:107–111.

Drexler, E. 1938. A study of the development of the ability to carry a melody at the preschool level. *Child Development* 9:319–332.

Dundes, A. 1975. *Analytic essays in folklore*. The Hague: Mouton.

Ecker, D. 1963. The artistic process as qualitative problem solving. *The Journal of Aesthetics and Art Criticism* 21:283–290.

Edwards, B. 1979. *Drawing on the right side of the brain*. Los Angeles: J. P. Tarcher.

Ehrenzweig, A. 1953. *The psychoanalysis of artistic vision and hearing*. London: Routledge and Kegan Paul.

Eimas, P., Siqueland, E., Jusczyk, P., and Vigorito, J. 1971. Speech perception in infants. *Science* 171:303–306.

Elkind, D. 1970. Developmental studies of figurative perception. In L. Lipsitt and

H. Reese, eds. *Advances in child development and behavior,* vol. 4. New York: Academic Press.

Elkind, D., Anagnostopoulou, K., and Malone, S. 1970. Determinants of part-whole perception in children. *Child Development* 41:391–397.

Elllis, H. 1904. *A study in British genius.* London: Hurst and Blackett.

Entus, A. 1975. Hemispheric asymmetry in processing of dichotically presented speech and nonspeech stimuli by infants. Paper presented at Society for Research in Child Development, Denver.

Erikson, E. 1963. *Childhood and society.* New York: Norton.

Eson, M., and Cometa, M. 1978. Logical operations and metaphor interpretation: a Piagetian model. *Child Development* 49 (3):649–659.

Eson, M., and Shapiro, A. 1980. When 'don't' means 'do': pragmatic and cognitive development in understanding an indirect imperative. Unpublished paper, State University of New York, Albany.

Eysenck, H. 1940. The general factor in aesthetic judgments. *British Journal of Psychology* 31:94–102.

———. 1940–1941. Some factors in the appreciation of poetry and their relation to temperamental qualities. *Character and Personality* 9:160–167.

———. 1941a. "Type" factors in aesthetic judgments. *British Journal of Psychology* 31:262–270.

———. 1941b. The empirical determination of an aesthetic formula. *Psychological Review* 48:83–92.

———. 1942. The experimental study of the "good gestalt"—a new approach. *Psychological Review* 49:344–364.

———. 1960. *Uses and abuses of psychology.* Harmondsworth, Eng.: Penguin books.

Eysenck, H., and Castle, M. 1970. Training in art as a factor in the determination of preference judgments for polygons. *British Journal of Psychology* 61:65–81.

Eysenck, H., and Eysenck, S. 1976. *Psychoticism as a dimension of personality.* London: Hodder and Stoughton.

Eysenck, H., and Iwawaki, S. 1971. Cultural relativity in aesthetic judgments: an empirical study. *Perceptual and Motor Skills* 32:817–818.

Fagan, J. 1970. Memory in the infant. *Journal of Experimental Child Psychology* 9:218–226.

Fairley, I. 1977. Experimental approaches to language in literature: reader responses to poems. Paper presented at XII International Congress of Linguists, Vienna, Austria.

Fantz, R., Fagan, J., and Miranda, S. 1975. Early visual selectivity. In L. Cohen and P. Salapatek, eds. *Infant Perception,* vol. 1. New York: Academic Press.

Fantz, R., and Miranda, S. 1975. Newborn infant attention to form of contour. *Child Development* 46:224–228.

Fechner, G. 1876. *Vorschule der Ästhetik.* Leipzig: Breitkopf & Hartel.

Feshbach, S., and Singer, R. 1971. *Television and Aggression.* San Francisco: Jossey-Bass.

Festinger, L., Burnham, C., Ono, H., and Bamber, D. 1967. Inference and the conscious experience of perception. *Journal of Experimental Psychology Monograph* 74:1–36.

Field, J. 1976. Relation of young infants' reaching behavior to stimulus distance and solidity. *Developmental Psychology* 12:444–448.

Fish, S. 1980. *Is there a text in this class?* Cambridge: Harvard University Press.

Fitzhenry-Coor, I. 1977. Children's comprehension and inference in stories of intentionality. Paper presented at Society for Research in Child Development, New Orleans, April.

Ford, C., Prothro, E., and Child, I. 1966. Some transcultural comparisons of aesthetic judgment. *Journal of Social Psychology* 68:19–26.

Foucault, M. 1973. *Madness and civilization: a history of insanity in the age of reason.* New York: Random.

Francès, R. 1954. Recherches expérimentales sur la perception de la mélodie. *Journal de Psychologie* 3:439–457.

———. 1958. *La perception de la musique.* Paris: Vrin.

———. 1968. *Psychologie de l'esthétique.* Paris: Presses Universitaires de France.

Francès, R., and Voillaume, H. 1964. Une composante du jugement pictural: la fidelité de la representation. *Psychologie Française* 9:241–256.

Fraser, B. 1979. The interpretation of novel metaphors. In A. Ortony, ed. *Metaphor and thought.* Cambridge, Eng.: Cambridge University Press.

Freeman, N. 1980. *Strategies of Representation in young children.* London: Academic Press.

Freeman, N., and Janikoun, R. 1972. Intellectual realism in children's drawings of a familiar object with distinct features. *Child Development* 43:1116–1121.

Freimuth, M., and Wapner, S. 1979. The influence of lateral organization on the evaluation of paintings. *British Journal of Psychology* 70:211–218.

Freud, A. 1955. *The psychoanalytical treatment of children.* New York: International Universities Press.

Freud, S. 1905. Three essays on the theory of sexuality. In J. Strachey, ed. *The standard edition of the complete psychological works of Sigmund Freud,* vol. 7. London: Hogarth Press, 1953.

———. 1908. Creative writers and day-dreaming. In J. Strachey, ed. *The standard edition,* vol. 9. 1959.

———. 1910. Leonardo da Vinci and a memory of his childhood. In J. Strachey, ed. *The standard edition,* vol. 11. 1957.

———. 1911. Formulations of the two principles of mental functioning. In J. Strachey, ed. *The standard edition,* vol. 12. 1958.

———. 1913a. The claims of psychoanalysis to scientific interest. In J. Strachey, ed. *The standard edition,* vol. 13. 1955.

———. 1913b. The theme of the three caskets. In J. Strachey, ed. *The standard edition,* vol. 12. 1958

———. 1913c. Totem and taboo. In J. Strachey, ed. *The standard edition,* vol. 13. 1955.

———. 1914. The Moses of Michelangelo. In J. Strachey, ed. *The standard edition,* vol. 13. 1953.

———. 1925. An autobiographical study. In J. Strachey, ed. *The standard edition,* vol. 20. 1959.

———. 1928. Dostoevsky and parricide. In J. Strachey, ed. *The standard edition,* vol. 21. 1961.

Friedman, S., and Stevenson, M. 1980. Perception of movement in pictures. In M. Hagen, ed. *The perception of pictures,* vol. 1: *Alberti's window: the projective model of pictorial information.* New York: Academic Press.

Fucigna, C., and Wolf, D. 1981. The earliest two-dimensional symbols: the onset of graphic representation. Paper presented at Eleventh Annual Conference of the Jean Piaget Society, Philadelphia, May.

Gablick, S. 1976. *Progress in art.* New York: Rizzoli.

Gardner, H. 1970. Children's sensitivity to painting styles. *Child Development* 41:813–821.

———. 1971. The development of sensitivity to artistic styles. *The Journal of Aesthetics and Art Criticism* 29 (4):515–527.

------. 1972. The development of sensitivity to figural and stylistic aspects of paintings. *British Journal of Psychology* 63:605–615.

------. 1973a. *The arts and human development.* New York: Wiley.

------. 1973b. Children's sensitivity to musical styles. *Merrill-Palmer Quarterly* 19:67–77.

------. 1974a. Metaphors and modalities: how children project polar adjectives onto diverse domains. *Child Development* 45:84–91.

------. 1974b. The contributions of color and texture to the detection of painting styles. *Studies in Art Education* 15:57–62.

------. 1975. *The shattered mind.* New York: Knopf.

------. 1977. Review of B. Bettelheim, *The uses of enchantment: the meaning and importance of fairy tales. Semiotica,* 21:363–380.

------. 1978. From Melvin to Melville: on the relevance to aesthetics of recent research on story comprehension. In S. Madeja, ed. *The arts, cognition, and basic skills.* St. Louis: Cemrel.

------. 1979. Children's art: Nadia's challenge. *Psychology Today* 13 (4):18–23.

------. 1980. *Artful scribbles: the significance of children's drawings.* New York: Basic Books.

------. 1981. Breakaway minds: an interview with Howard Gruber. *Psychology Today* 15 (7):64–71.

------. In press. Artistry following damage to the human brain. In A. Ellis, ed. *Normality and pathology in cognitive functions.* London: Academic.

Gardner, H., and Gardner, J. 1973. Developmental trends in sensitivity to form and subject matter in paintings. *Studies in Art Education* 14:52–56.

Gardner, H., Kircher, M., Winner, E., and Perkins, D. 1975. Children's metaphoric productions and preferences. *Journal of Child Language* 2:125–141.

Gardner, H., and Lohman, W. 1975. Children's sensitivity to literary styles. *Merrill-Palmer Quarterly* 21 (2):113–126.

Gardner, H., Silverman, J., Denes, G., Semenza, C., and Rosenstiel, A. 1977. Sensitivity to musical denotation and connotation in organic patients. *Cortex* 13:243–256.

Gardner, H., and Winner, E. 1981. Artistry and aphasia. In M. Sarno, ed. *Acquired aphasia.* New York: Academic Press.

Gardner, H., and Winner, E. 1982. First intimations of artistry. In. S. Strauss, ed. *U-shaped behavioral growth.* New York: Academic Press.

Gardner, H., Winner, E., and Kircher, M. 1975. Children's conceptions of the arts. *Journal of Aesthetic Education* 9 (3):60–77.

Gardner, H., and Wolf, D. 1979. First drawings: notes on the relationships between perception and production. In C. F. Nodine and D. F. Fisher, eds. *Perception and pictorial representation.* New York: Praeger.

Gardner, R., and Gardner, B. 1969. Teaching sign language to a chimpanzee. *Science* 165:664–672.

Gardner, R., and Gardner, B. 1978. Comparative psychology and language acquisition. *Annals of the New York Academy of Sciences,* 309:37–76.

Garfunkel, G. 1980. The development of compositional balance in children's drawings. Paper presented at Annual Meeting of American Educational Research Association, Boston, April.

Garvey, C. 1977. Play with language and speech. In S. Ervin-Tripp and C. Mitchell-Kernan, eds. *Child discourse.* New York: Academic Press.

Gaston, T., ed. 1968. *Music therapy.* New York: Macmillan.

Gates, A., and Bradshaw, J. 1977. The role of the cerebral hemispheres in music. *Brain and Language* 4:403–431.

Gazzaniga, M. 1970. *The bisected brain.* New York: Appleton-Century-Crofts.

Geick, K. 1980. Unpublished research. Boston College, Chestnut Hill, Mass.

Geschwind, N. 1976. Approach to a theory of localization of emotion in the human brain. Paper presented at International Neuropsychological Symposium, Roc-Amadour, France.

Gesell, A., and Ilg, F. 1946. *The child from five to ten.* New York: Harper.

Getzels, J., and Csikszentmihalyi, M. 1976. *The creative vision: a longitudinal study of problem finding in art.* New York: Wiley.

Getzels, J., and Jackson, P. 1962. *Creativity and intelligence: explorations with gifted students.* New York: Wiley.

Ghent, L. 1956. Perception of overlapping and embedded figures by children of different ages. *American Journal of Psychology* 69:575–587.

Ghiselin, B., ed. 1952. *The creative process.* New York: Mentor.

Gibson, E. 1969. *Principles of perceptual learning and development.* New York: Appleton-Century-Crofts.

Gibson, J. 1950. *The perception of the visual world.* Boston: Houghton Mifflin.

———. 1954. A theory of pictorial perception. *Audio-Visual Communication Review* 1:3–23.

———. 1960. Pictures, perspective, and perception. *Daedalus* 89:216–227.

———. 1966. *The senses considered as perceptual systems.* Boston: Houghton Mifflin.

———. 1971. The information available in pictures. *Leonardo* 4:27–35.

———. 1979. *The ecological approach to visual perception.* Boston: Houghton Mifflin.

Gibson, J., and Yonas, P. 1968. A new theory of scribbling and drawing in children. In H. Levin, E. J. Gibson, and J. J. Gibson, eds. The analysis of reading skill. Washington, D.C.: U.S. Dept. of Health, Education, and Welfare, Office of Education (Final Report).

Glucksberg, S., Gildea, P., and Bookin, H. In press. On understanding nonliteral speech: can people ignore metaphors? *Journal of Verbal Learning and Verbal Behavior.*

Gollin, E. 1960. Developmental studies of visual recognition of incomplete objects. *Perceptual and Motor Skills* 11:289–298.

———. 1961. Further studies of visual recognition of incomplete objects. *Perceptual and Motor Skills* 13:307–314.

Golomb, C. 1973. Children's representation of the human figure: the effects of models, media, and instruction. *Genetic Psychology Monographs* 87:197–251.

———. 1974. *Young children's sculpture and drawing.* Cambridge: Harvard University Press.

———. 1981. Representation and reality: the origins and determinants of young children's drawings. In *Review of Research in Visual Arts Education* 14:36–48.

Gombrich, E. 1960. *Art and illusion: a study in the psychology of pictorial representation.* Princeton: Princeton University Press.

———. 1963. *Meditations on a hobby horse and other essays on the theory of art.* London: Phaidon Press.

Goodglass, H., and Kaplan, E. 1972. *The assessment of aphasia and related disorders.* Philadelphia: Lea and Febiger.

Goodman, N. 1968. *Languages of art.* Indianapolis: Bobbs-Merrill. 2nd ed. Indianapolis: Hackett, 1976.

———. 1972. *Problems and projects.* Indianapolis: Bobbs-Merrill. Repub. Indianapolis: Hackett, 1976.

———. 1975. The status of style. *Critical Inquiry* 1 (3–4):799–811.

———. 1977. When is art? In D. Perkins and B. Leondar, eds. *The arts and cognition.* Baltimore: Johns Hopkins University Press. Rpt. in *Ways of worldmaking.* Indianapolis: Hackett, 1978.

Goodnow, J. 1971. Auditory-visual matching: modality problem or translation problem? *Child Development* 42:1187–1201.

————. 1977. *Children drawing.* Cambridge: Harvard University Press.

Gordon, H. 1978. Left-hemisphere dominance for rhythmic elements in dichotically presented melodies. *Cortex* 14:58–70.

————. 1980. Degree of ear asymmetries for perception of dichotic chords and for illusory chord localization in musicians of different levels of competence. *Journal of Experimental Psychology: Human Perception and Performance* 6:516–527.

Gordon, I. 1982. *Left and right in art.* In D. O'Hare, ed. *Psychology and the arts.* Atlantic Highlands, N.J.: Humanities Press.

Götz, K., Borisy, A., Lynn, R., and Eysenck, H. 1979. A new visual aesthetic sensitivity test: I. Construction and psychometric properties. *Perceptual and Motor Skills* 49:795–802.

Gough, H. 1961. Techniques for identifying the creative research scientist. In *Proceedings of the Conference on "the creative person."* Berkeley: University of California Extension.

Gould, R. 1972. *Child studies through fantasy.* New York: Quadrangle Books.

Granger, G. 1955a. An experimental study of colour harmony. *Journal of General Psychology* 52:21–35.

————. 1955b. The prediction of preference for color combinations. *Journal of General Psychology* 52:213–222.

————. 1955c. An experimental study of colour preferences. *Journal of General Psychology* 52:3–20.

Graves, M. 1946. *Design judgment test.* New York: Psychological Corporation.

Greene, G. 1980. *Ways of escape.* New York: Simon and Schuster.

Gregory, R. 1977. Review of *Nadia. New Statesman,* Dec. 1, p. 57.

Gruber, H. 1974. *Darwin on man: a psychological study of scientific creativity.* New York: E. P. Dutton. 2nd ed. Chicago: University of Chicago Press, 1981.

————. 1978. Darwin's "tree of nature" and other images of wide scope. In J. Wechsler, ed. *On aesthetics in science.* Cambridge: MIT Press.

Guilford, J. 1934. The affective value of color as a function of hue, tint, and chroma. *Journal of Experimental Psychology* 17:342–370.

————. 1940. There is a system in color preferences. *Journal of the Optical Society of America* 30:455–459.

————. 1967. *The nature of human intelligence.* New York: McGraw Hill.

Guillaume, P. 1927. The development of formal elements in the child's speech. In C. Ferguson and D. Slobin, eds. *Studies of child language development.* New York: Holt, Rinehart, and Winston, 1973.

Haber, R., and Haber, R. 1964. Eidetik imagery: I. frequency. *Perceptual Motor Skills* 19:131–138.

Hagen, M. 1978. An outline of an investigation into the special character of pictures. In H. Pick and E. Saltsman, eds. *Modes of perceiving and processing information.* Hillsdale, N.J.: Lawrence Erlbaum Associates.

Hagen, M., and Jones, R. 1978. Cultural effects on pictorial perception: how many words is one picture really worth? In R. Walk and H. Pick, Jr., eds. *Perception and experience.* New York: Plenum.

Haith, M. 1966. Response of the human newborn to visual movement. *Journal of Experimental Child Psychology* 3:235–243.

Hardi, I. 1962. The effect of psychotropic drugs on drawing. In G. Macagnani, ed. *Psicopatologia dell 'expressione.* Imola: Galeati.

————. 1966. Dynamic drawing tests applied in psychotropic medication. *Third conferentia Hungarica pro therapia et investigatione in pharmacologia.* Budapest: Kultura.

————. 1972. Reflection of manic-depressive psychoses in dynamic drawing tests. *Confinia Psychiatrica* 15:64–70.

Haritos-Fatouros, M., and Child, I. 1977. Transcultural similarity in personal significance of aesthetic interests. *Journal of Cross-Cultural Psychology* 8:285–298.

Harlow, H. 1953. Mice, monkeys, men, and motives. *Psychological Review* 60:23–32.

Harris, D. 1963. *Children's drawings as measures of intellectual maturity.* New York: Harcourt Brace & World.

Hartmann, E. 1980. Quoted in *Harvard Gazette*, Jan. 18, p. 3.

Hartmann, E., Russ, D., van der Kolk, B., Falke, R., and Oldfield, M. 1981. A preliminary study of the personality of the nightmare sufferer: relationship to schizophrenia and creativity? *American Journal of Psychiatry* 138 (6):794–797.

Hartmann, E., Russ, D., and Skoff, B. 1978. The biochemistry of the nightmare: possible involvement of dopamine. *Sleep Research* 7:1078.

Hayes, C. 1951. *The ape in our house.* New York: Harper.

Hayes, K., and Hayes, C. 1953. Picture perception in a home-raised chimpanzee. *Journal of Comparative and Physiological Psychology* 46:470–474.

Heider, F., and Heider, G. 1941. Studies in the psychology of the deaf, No. 2. *Psychological Monographs* 53:1–158.

Heilman, K. 1976. Affective disorders associated with right hemisphere disease. Address to Aphasia Academy, Florida, October.

Helmholtz, H. von. 1863. *On the sensations of tone as a physiological basis for the theory of music.* Ed. and trans. A. Ellis. New York: Dover, 1954.

————. 1867. *Handbook of physiological optics.* Ed. and trans. J. Southall. New York: Optical Society of America.

Helson, H. 1948. Adaptation level as a basis for a quantitative theory of frames of reference. *Psychological Review* 55:297–313.

Helson, R., and Crutchfield, R. 1970. Creative types in mathematics. *Journal of Personality* 38:177–197.

Hevner, K. 1936. Experimental studies of the elements of expression in music. *American Journal of Psychology* 48:246–268.

————. 1937. The affective value of pitch and tempo in music. *American Journal of Psychology* 49:621–630.

Hochberg, J. 1978. Art and perception. In E. Carterette and M. Friedman, eds. *Perceptual ecology.* New York: Academic Press.

Hochberg, J., and Brooks, V. 1960. The psychophysics of form: reversible-perspective drawings of spatial objects. *American Journal of Psychology* 73:337–354.

————. 1962. Pictorial recognition as an unlearned ability: a study of one child's performance. *American Journal of Psychology* 75:624–628.

Hochberg, J. and McAlister, E. 1953. A quantitative approach to figural goodness. *Journal of Experimental Psychology* 46:361–364.

Holland, N. 1968. *The dynamics of literary response.* New York: Oxford University Press.

————. 1975. *Five readers reading.* New Haven: Yale University Press.

Hudson, W. 1960. Pictorial depth perception in subcultural groups in Africa. *Journal of Social Psychology* 52:183–208.

Hulsker, J., ed. 1970. *Van Gogh's "Diary."* Amsterdam: Meulenhoff International.

Humphreys, L. 1939. Generalization as a function of method of reinforcement. *Journal of Experimental Psychology* 25:361–372.

Hussain, F. 1965. Quelques problemes d'esthétique experimentale. *Sciences de l'art* 2:103–114.

Imberty, M. 1969. *L'acquisition des structures tonales chez l'enfant.* Paris: Klincksieck.

Inhelder, B., and Piaget, J. 1964. *The early growth of logic in the child.* New York: Norton.

Iser, W. 1978. *The act of reading.* Baltimore: Johns Hopkins University Press.

Ittelson, W. 1952. *The Ames demonstrations in perception: a guide to their construction and use.* Princeton: Princeton University Press.

Iwao, S. and Child, I. 1966. Comparison of esthetic judgments by American experts and by Japanese potters. *Journal of Social Psychology* 68:27–33.

Iwao, S., Child, I., and Garcia, M. 1969. Further evidence of agreement between Japanese and American esthetic evaluation. *Journal of Social Psychology* 78:11–15.

Iwawaki, S., Eysenck, H., and Götz, K. 1979. A new visual aesthetic sensitivity test (VAST): II. Cross-cultural comparison between England and Japan. *Perceptual and Motor Skills* 49:859–862.

Jackson, J. 1932. *Selected writings.* London: Hodder and Stoughton.

Jahoda, G., Deregowski, J., Ampene, E., and Williams, N. 1977. Pictorial recognition as an unlearned ability: a replication with children from pictorially deprived environments. In G. Butterworth, ed. *The child's representation of the world.* New York: Plenum.

Jahoda, G., and McGurk, H. 1974. Pictorial depth perception in Scottish and Ghanaian children: a critique of some findings with the Hudson test. *International Journal of Psychology* 9 (4):225–267.

Jakobits, L. 1969. The affect of symbols: towards the development of a cross-cultural graphic differential. *International Journal of Symbology* 1:28–52.

Jakobson, R. 1945. Commentary. *Afanas'ev,* pp. 629–651.

———. 1960. Closing statement: linguistics and poetics. In. T. A. Sebeok, ed. *Style in language.* Cambridge: M.I.T. Press.

Jakobson, R., and Halle, M. 1956. *Fundamentals of language.* The Hague: Mouton.

Jaspers, K. 1977. *Strindberg and Van Gogh.* Trans. O. Grunow and D. Woloshin. Tucson: University of Arizona Press.

Jeannerod, M., Gerin, J., and Pennier, J. 1968. Déplacements et fixations du regard dans l'exploration libre d'une scène visuelle. *Vision Research* 8:81–97.

Jersild, A., and Bienstock, S. 1934. A study of the development of children's ability to sing. *Journal of Educational Psychology* 25:481–503.

Johnson, M. 1967. Syntactic position and rated meaning. *Journal of Verbal Learning and Verbal Behavior* 6:240–246.

Johnson, N., and Mandler, J. 1980. A tale of two structures: underlying and surface forms in stories. Technical Report 80. Center for Human Information Processing, University of California, San Diego.

Jones, E. 1976. *Hamlet and Oedipus.* New York: Norton.

Jones, J. 1980. *Teaching art to older adults: guidelines and lessons.* Atlantic: Georgia Department of Administrative Services.

Juda, A. 1953. *Höchstbegabung: Ihre Erbverhältnisse sowie ihre Beziehungen zu psychischen Anomalien.* Munich: Urban and Schwarzenberg.

Judd, T., Arslenian, A., Davidson, L., and Locke, S. 1980. Unpublished research, Boston Veterans Administration Hospital.

Judd, T., Gardner, H., and Geschwind, N. 1980. Alexia without agraphia in a composer. Project Zero Technical Report No. 15., Harvard Graduate School of Education, Cambridge.

Julesz, B., and Spivack, C. J. 1967. Stereopsis based on vernier acuity cues alone. *Science* 157:563–565.

Jung, C. G. 1960. *Psychology and religion.* New Haven: Yale University Press.

Kagan, J. 1970. The determinants of attention in the infant. *American Scientist* 58 (3):298–306.

Kallman, H. J., and Massaro, D. W. 1979. Tone chroma is functional in melody recognition. *Perception and Psychophysics* 26 (1):32–36.

Kamman, R. 1966. Verbal complexity and preferences in poetry. *Journal of Verbal Learning and Verbal Behavior* 5:536–540.

Kanner, L. 1943. Autistic disturbances of affective contact. *Nerv. Child* 2:217–250.

Kant, I. 1892. *Critique of judgment.* New York: London, Macmillan & Co.

Kellar, L. A., and Bever, T. G. 1980. Hemisphere asymmetries in the perception of musical intervals as a function of musical experience and family handedness background. *Brain and Language* 10:24–38.

Kellogg, R. 1969. *Analyzing children's art.* Palo Alto: National Press Books.

Kennedy, J. E. 1961. The paired-comparison method and central tendency effect in esthetic judgments. *Journal of Applied Psychology* 45 (2):128–129.

Kennedy, J. M. 1974. *A psychology of picture perception.* San Francisco: Jossey-Bass.

Kennedy, J. M., and Ross, A. 1975. Outline picture perception by the Songe of Papua. *Perception* 4:391–406.

Kessen, W., Levine, J., and Wendrich, K. 1979. The imitation of pitch in infants. *Infant Behavior and Development* 2:93–99.

Kety, S. 1959. Biochemical theories of schizophrenia. *Science* 129:1528–1532, 1590–1596.

———. 1960. Recent biochemical theories of schizophrenia. In D. D. Jackson, ed. *The etiology of schizophrenia.* New York: Basic Books.

———. 1969. Biochemical hypotheses and studies. In L. Bellak and L. Loeb, eds. *The schizophrenic syndrome.* New York: Grune.

Keyser, S. In press. There is method in their adness: the form of advertisement. *New Literary History.*

Kilpatrick, R. 1954. Two processes in perceptual learning. *Journal of Experimental Psychology* 47:362–370.

Kimura, D. 1961. Cerebral dominance and the perception of verbal stimuli. *Canadian Journal of Psychology* 15:166–171.

———. 1973. The asymmetry of the human brain. *Scientific American* 228:70–78.

Kinney, D., and Kagan, J. 1976. Infant attention to auditory discrepancy. *Child Development* 47:155–164.

Kintgen, E. 1980. The perception of poetry. *Style* 14 (1):22–40.

Klee, F., ed. 1968. *The diaries of Paul Klee, 1898–1918.* Berkeley and Los Angeles: University of California Press.

Knapp, R. 1957. Achievement and aesthetic preference. In J. Atkinson, ed. *The assessment of human motives.* Princeton: Van Nostrand.

Knapp, R., McElroy, L., and Vaughn, J. 1962. On blithe and melancholic aestheticism. *Journal of General Psychology* 67:3–10.

Koch, K. 1970. *Wishes, lies and dreams.* New York: Chelsea House.

Koffka, K. 1935. *Principles of Gestalt psychology.* New York: Harcourt Brace.

Kogan, N., Connor, K., Gross, A., and Fava, D. 1980. Understanding visual metaphor: developmental and individual differences. *Monographs of the Society for Research in Child Development* 45:1

Kohlberg, L. 1969. Stage and sequence: the cognitive-developmental approach to socialization. In D. A. Goslin, ed. *Handbook of socialization theory and research.* New York: Rand McNally.

Köhler, W. 1929. *Gestalt psychology.* New York: Liveright.

———. 1937. Psychological remarks on some questions of anthropology. *American Journal of Psychology* 50:271–288.

Kosslyn, S. 1980. *Image and mind.* Cambridge: Harvard University Press.

Kraepelin, E. 1919. *Dementia praecox and paraphrenia.* Trans. R. M. Barclay. Edinburgh: E. and S. Livingstone.

Kreitler, H., and Kreitler, S. 1972. *Psychology of the arts.* Durham: Duke University Press.

Kris, E. 1952. *Psychoanalytic explorations in art.* New York: International Universities Press.

Krumhansl, C. 1979. The psychological representation of musical pitch in a tonal context. *Cognitive Psychology* 11:346–374.

Krumhansl, C., and Shepard, R. 1979. Quantification of the hierarchy of tonal functions within a diatonic context. *Journal of Experimental Psychology: Human Perception and Performance* 5:579–594.

Kubie, L. 1958. *Neurotic distortion of the creative process.* Lawrence: University of Kansas Press.

Kuhn, A. 1925. *Lovis Corinth.* Berlin: Im Propyläen-Verlag.

Kuhn, R. 1979. Metaphor in science. In A. Ortony, ed. *Metaphor and thought.* Cambridge, Eng.: Cambridge University Press.

Laing, J. 1964. Tuberculous paintings. *CIBA Symposium* 12:135–143.

Laing, R. 1964. *Sanity, madness, and the family.* New York: Basic Books.

Lakoff, G., and Johnson, M. 1980. *Metaphors we live by.* Chicago: University of Chicago Press.

Lamb, C. 1951. Sanity of genius. In *The last essays of Elia.* London: Oxford Clarendon Press.

Langer, S. 1942. *Philosophy in a new key.* Cambridge: Harvard University Press.

———. 1953. *Feeling and form.* New York: Scribner.

Lark-Horowitz, B. 1937. On art appreciation of children: I. Preference of picture subjects in general. *Journal of Educational Research* 31 (2):118–137.

———. 1938. On art appreciation of children: II. Portrait preference study. *Journal of Educational Research* 31 (8):572–598.

———. 1939. On art appreciation of children: III. Textile pattern preference study. *Journal of Educational Research* 38 (1):7–35.

Lark-Horowitz, B., Lewis, H., and Luca, M. 1973. *Understanding children's art for better teaching.* 2nd ed. Columbus: Merrill.

Lawler, C., and Lawler, E. 1965. Color-mood associations in young children. *Journal of Genetic Psychology* 107:29–32.

Leondar, B. 1977. Hatching plots: the genesis of storymaking. In D. Perkins and B. Leondar, eds. *The arts and cognition.* Baltimore: Johns Hopkins University Press.

Lesser, H., and Drouin, C. 1975. Training in the use of double-function terms. *Journal of Psycholinguistic Research* 4:285–302.

Lévi-Strauss, C. 1970. *The raw and the cooked: introduction to a science of mythology,* vol. 1. Trans. J. and D. Weightman. New York: Harper and Row.

Lewis, H. 1963. The relationship of picture preference to developmental status in drawing. *Journal of Educational Research* 57:43–46.

Lewkowicz, D. J., and Turkewitz, G. 1980. Cross-modal equivalence in early infancy: auditory-visual intensity matching. *Developmental Psychology* 16 (6):597–607.

Liberman, A. 1960. *The artist in his studio.* New York: Viking Press.

Liberman, A. M., Cooper, F., Shankweiler, D., and Studdert-Kennedy, M. 1967. Perception of the speech code. *Psychological Review* 74:431–461.

Lidz, T. 1958. Schizophrenia and the family. *Psychiatry* 21:21–27.

Lombroso, C. 1895. *The man of genius.* London: Scott.

Lord, A. 1965. *Singer of tales.* New York: Atheneum.

Lowenfeld, V., and Beittel, K. 1959. Interdisciplinary criteria of creativity in the arts and sciences: a progress report. *Research Yearbook, National Art Education Association,* pp. 35–44.

Lowenfeld, V., and Brittain, W. 1970. *Creative and mental growth*. 5th ed. New York: Macmillan.

Lowery, H. 1966. *A guide to musical acoustics*. New York: Dover.

Lundholm, H. 1921. The affective tone of lines. *Psychological Review* 28:43–60.

Luria, A., Tsvetkova, L., and Futer, D. 1965. Aphasia in a composer. *Journal of Neurological Science* 2:288–292.

Macalpine, I., and Hunter, R. 1969. Porphyria and King George III. *Scientific American* 221 (1):38–46.

Machotka, P. 1966. Aesthetic criteria in childhood: justifications of preference. *Child Development* 37:877–885.

———. 1979. *The nude: perception and personality*. New York: Irvington.

MacKinnon, D. 1961. The study of creativity and creativity in architects. In *Proceedings of the Conference on "the creative person."* Berkeley: University of California Extension.

———. 1962. The nature and nurture of creative talent. *American Psychologist* 17:484–495.

———. 1965. Personality and the realization of creative potential. *American Psychologists* 20:273–281.

Maher, B. 1963. The shattered language of schizophrenia. *Psychology Today* 2 (6):30–33, 60.

———. 1966. *Principles of psychopathology: an experimental approach*. New York: McGraw.

———. 1971. The language of schizophrenia: a review and interpretation. *British Journal of Psychiatry* 120:3–17.

———. 1974. Delusional thinking and perceptual disorder. *Journal of Individual Psychology* 30:98–113.

Maher, B., McKean, K., and McLaughlin, B. 1966. Studies in psychotic language. In P. Stone, D. Dunphy, M. Smith, and D. Ogilvie, eds. *The general inquirer: a complete approach to content analysis*. Cambridge: M.I.T. Press.

Mandler, J. 1978. A code in the node: the use of a story schema in retrieval. *Discourse Processes* 1:14–35.

Mandler, J., and Johnson, N. 1977. Remembrance of things parsed: story structure and recall. *Cognitive Psychology* 9:111–151.

Mandler, J., Scribner, S., Cole, M., and DeForest, M. 1980. Cross-cultural invariance in story recall. *Child Development* 51 (1):19–26.

Maranda, E., and Maranda, P. 1971. *Structural models in folklore and transformational essays*. The Hague: Mouton.

Marshal, M. 1981. Musical wunderkinds. *Boston Globe Magazine*, July 26, pp. 8–9, 28–33, 41.

Marti, E. 1979. La pensée analogique chez l'enfant de 2 à 7 ans. Ph.D. dissertation, University of Geneva.

Matthysse, S. 1977. The role of dopamine in schizophrenia. In E. Usdin, D. Hamburg, and J. Barchas, eds. *Neuroregulators and psychiatric disorders*. New York: Oxford University Press.

McConaghy, S. 1980. Developmental differences in story comprehension. Paper presented to New England Child Language Association, Tufts University, November.

McGhee, P. 1973. Children's appreciation of humor: a test of the cognitive congruency principle. Paper presented at Society for Research in Child Development, Philadelphia.

McGhie, A., and Chapman, J. 1961. Disorders of attention and perception in early schizophrenia. *British Journal of Medical Psychology* 34:103–116.

McKernon, P. 1979. The development of first songs in young children. *New Directions for Child Development* 3:43–58.

McQuillian, M. 1975. A study of parody. Unpublished manuscript, Project Zero, Harvard Graduate School of Education, Cambridge.

Mednick, S. 1958. A learning theory approach to research in schizophrenia. *Psychological Bulletin* 55:316–327.

———. 1962. The associative basis of the creative process. *Psychological Review* 69:220–232.

Meier, N. 1940. *The Meier art tests: I. Art judgment.* Iowa City: Bureau of Educational Research and Service, University of Iowa.

Melson, W., and McCall, R. 1970. Attentional responses of five-month girls to discrepant auditory stimuli. *Child Development* 41:1159–1171.

Meltzer, H., and Stahl, S. 1976. The dopamine hypothesis of schizophrenia: a review. *Schizophrenia Bulletin* 2:19–76.

Mendelsohn, E., Winner, E., and Gardner, H. 1981. Sorting out similarity. Unpublished manuscript, Project Zero, Harvard Graduate School of Education, Cambridge.

Meringoff, L. 1980. Influence of the medium on children's story apprehension. *Journal of Educational Psychology* 72 (2):240–249.

Meyer, L. 1956. *Emotion and meaning in music.* Chicago: University of Chicago Press.

———. 1979. Toward a theory of style. In B. Lang, ed. *The concept of style.* Philadelphia: University of Pennsylvania Press.

Millar, S. 1975. Visual experience or translation rules? Drawing the human figure by blind and sighted children. *Perception* 4:363–371.

Milner, B. 1962. Laterality effects in audition. In V. B. Mountcastle, ed. *Interhemispheric relations and cerebral dominance.* Baltimore: Johns Hopkins Press.

Mirsky, A. 1969. Neuropsychological bases of schizophrenia. In D. L. Farnsworth, ed. *Annual review of psychology,* vol. 20. Palo Alto: Stanford University Press.

Moorhead, G., and Pond, D. 1941. *The music of young children: I. Chant.* Pillsbury Foundation Studies.

Morris, D. 1967. *The biology of art.* Chicago: Aldine-Atherton.

Munsinger, H., and Kessen, W. 1964. Uncertainty, structure, and preference. *Psychological Monographs* 78 (9), no. 586.

Murray, D., and Deabler, H. 1957. Colors and mood-tones. *Journal of Applied Psychology* 41:279–283.

Murray, H. *Endeavors in psychology: selections from the personology of Henry A. Murray.* Ed. E. S. Schneidman. 1981. New York: Harper and Row.

Murray, J. 1973. Television and violence: implications of the surgeon general research program. *American Psychologist* 28:472–478.

Mursell, J. 1937. *The psychology of music.* New York: W. W. Norton.

Naumburg, M. 1950. *Schizophrenic art: its meaning in psychotherapy.* New York: Grune & Stratton.

Nelson, K. 1974. Concept, word and sentence: interrelations in acquisition and development. *Psychological Review* 81:267–285.

Nettl, B. 1956a. Infant musical development and primitive music. *Southwestern Journal of Anthropology* 12:87–91.

———. 1956b. *Music in primitive culture.* Cambridge: Harvard University Press.

Newhall, S. 1940. Measurement of simultaneous contrast. *Psychological Bulletin* 37:500.

Newman, S. 1933. Further experiments in phonetic symbolism. *American Journal of Psychology* 45:53–75.

Nisbett, R., and Wilson, T., 1977. Telling more than we can know: verbal reports on mental processes. *Psychological Review* 84 (3):231–259.

Nodine, C. 1982. Compositional design as a perceptual determinant of aesthetic judgment. *Review of Research in Visual Arts Education* 15:43–54.

Normore, L. 1974. Verbal responses to visual sequences varying in uncertainty level. In D. Berlyne, ed. *Studies in the new experimental aesthetics.* New York: Wiley.

O'Connor, N., and Hermelin, B. 1961. Like and cross-modality recognition in subnormal children. *Quarterly Journal of Experimental Psychology* 11:48–52.

O'Hare, D., and Gordon, I. 1976. An application of repertory grid technique to aesthetic measurement. *Perceptual and Motor Skills* 42:1183–1192.

Olson, R. 1975. Children's sensitivity to pictorial depth information. *Perception and Psychophysics* 17 (1):59–64.

Olson, R., Pearl, M., Mayfield, N., and Millar, D. 1976. Sensitivity to pictorial shape perspective in 5-year-old children and adults. *Perception and Psychophysics* 20 (3):173–178.

Olton, R. 1979. Experimental studies of incubation: searching for the elusive. *Journal of Creative Behavior* 13 (1):9–22.

Olton, R., and Johnson, D. 1976. Mechanisms of incubation in creative problem solving. *American Journal of Psychology* 89 (4):617–630.

Opie, I., and Opie, P. 1960. *The lore and language of school children.* Oxford: Clarendon Press.

Orff, C. 1978. *The Schulwerk,* vol. 3. Trans. M. Murray. New York: Schott.

Ortony, A. 1975. Why metaphors are necessary and not just nice. *Educational Theory* 25:45–53.

———. 1979a. Beyond literal similarity. *Psychological Review* 86:161–180.

———. 1979b. The role of similarity in similes and metaphors. In A. Ortony, ed. *Metaphor and thought.* Cambridge, Eng.: Cambridge University Press.

———. 1980. Some psycholinguistic aspects of metaphor. In R. P. Honeck and R. R. Hoffman, eds. *Cognition and figurative language.* Hillsdale, N.J.: Lawrence Erlbaum Associates.

Ortony, A., Schallert, D., Reynolds, R., and Antos, S. 1978. Interpreting metaphors and idioms: some effects of context on comprehension. *Journal of Verbal Learning and Verbal Behavior* 17:465–477.

Osgood, C. 1960. The cross-cultural generality of visual-verbal synesthetic tendencies. *Behavioral Science* 5:6–69.

Otswald, P. 1973. Musical behavior in early childhood. *Developmental Medicine and Child Neurology* 15:367–375.

Paraskevopoulas, I. 1968. Symmetry, recall and preference in relation to chronological age. *Journal of Experimental Child Psychology* 6:254–264.

Pariser, D. 1979. A discussion of Nadia: a case study of extraordinary drawing ability in an autistic child. Project Zero Technical Report No. 9. Harvard Graduate School of Education, Cambridge.

Park, C. 1978. Review of L. Selfe, *Nadia: a case of extraordinary drawing ability in an autistic child. Journal of Autism and Childhood Schizophrenia* 8 (4):457–472.

Parsons, M., Johnston, M., and Durham, R. 1978. Developmental stages in children's aesthetic responses. *Journal of Aesthetic Education* 12 (1):83–104.

Patrick, C. 1935. Creative thought in poets. *Archives of Psychology,* no. 178.

———. 1937. Creative thought in artists. *Journal of Psychology* 4:35–73.

Patterson, F. G. 1977. Linguistic capabilities of a young lowland goulla. Paper presented at Symposium of the American Association for the Advancement of Science, Denver.

Payne, R. W., Mattussek, P., and George, E. 1959. An experimental study of schizophrenic thought disorder. *Journal of Mental Science* 105:627–652.

Peckham, M. 1965. *Man's rage for chaos.* Philadelphia: Chitton.

Peel, E. 1944. On identifying aesthetic types. *British Journal of Psychology* 35:61–69.

———. 1946. A new method for analyzing aesthetic preferences: some theoretical considerations. *Psychometrika* 11:129–137.

Perkins, D. 1979. Pictures and the real thing. Paper presented at Conference on Processing of Visible Language 2, Niagara-on-the-Lake, Canada, Sept. 3–7.

———. 1981. *The mind's best work.* Cambridge: Harvard University Press.

———. In press. The perceiver as organizer and geometer. In J. Beck, ed. *Representation and organization in perception.* Hillsdale, N.J.: Erlbaum.

Perkins, D., and Cooper, R. 1980. How the eye makes up what the light leaves out. In M. Hagen, ed. *The perception of pictures,* vol. 2. New York: Academic Press.

Peters, G., and Merrifield, P. 1958. Graphic representation of emotional feelings. *Journal of Clinical Psychology* 14:375–378.

Pflederer, M. 1964. The responses of children to musical tasks embodying Piaget's principle of conservation. *Journal of Research in Music Education* 12 (4):251–268.

Phillips, W., Hobbs, S., and Pratt, F. 1978. Intellectual realism in children's drawings of cubes. *Cognition* 6:15–34.

Piaget, J. 1952. *The child's conception of number.* New York: Humanities.

———. 1963. *The origins of intelligence in children.* New York: Norton.

———. 1965. *The moral judgment of the child.* New York: The Free Press.

Piaget, J., and Inhelder, B. 1967. *The child's conception of space.* New York: Norton.

Pickering, G. 1974. *Creative malady.* London: George Allen & Unwin.

Pickford, R. 1963. *Pickford projective pictures.* London: Tavistock.

———. 1970. Psychiatric art. In H. Osborne, ed. *Oxford companion to art.* Oxford: Clarendon Press.

———. 1972. *Psychology and visual aesthetics.* London: Hutchinson.

———. 1982. Art and psychopathology. In D. O'Hare, ed. *Psychology and the arts.* London: Harvester.

Pine, F., and Holt, R. 1960. Creativity and primary process: a study of adaptive regression. *Journal of Abnormal and Social Psychology* 61:370–379.

Piston, W. 1933. *Principles of harmonic analysis.* Boston: E. C. Schirmer.

Pitcher, E., and Prelinger, E. 1963. *Children tell stories: an analysis of fantasy.* New York: International Universities Press.

Platt, W. 1933. Temperament and disposition revealed in young children's music. *Character and Personality* 2:246–251.

Plokker, J. 1965. *Art from the mentally disturbed.* Boston: Little, Brown.

Poffenberger, A., and Barrows, B. 1924. The feeling value of lines. *Journal of Applied Psychology* 8:187–205.

Pollio, H., and Burns, B. 1977. The anomaly of anomaly. *Journal of Psycholinguistic Research* 6:247–260.

Pollio, M., and Pickens, J. 1980. The developmental structure of figurative competence. In R. Honeck and R. Hoffman, eds. *Cognition and figurative language.* Hillsdale, N.J.: Erlbaum.

Poore, H. R. 1967. *Composition in art.* New York: Dover.

Popper, K. 1968. *The logic of scientific discovery.* London: Hutchinson.

Popper, K., and Eccles. 1977. The self and its brain. New York: Springer-Verlagg.

Potter, M. 1966. On perceptual recognition. In J. Bruner, R. Olver, and P. Greenfield, eds. *Studies in cognitive growth.* New York: Wiley.

Powers, J., III, Brainard, R., Abrams, R., and Sadacca, R. 1973. *Training techniques for rapid target detection.* Technical Paper 242, U.S. Army Research Institute for the Behavioral and Social Sciences.

Pratt, C. 1931. *The meaning of music: a study in psychological aesthetics.* New York: McGraw-Hill.

Prince, G. 1973. *A grammar of stories.* The Hague: Mouton.

Prinzhorn, H. 1972. *Artistry of the mentally ill.* New York: Springer.

Propp, V. 1968. *Morphology of the folk tale.* Austin: University of Texas Press.

Rank, O. 1945. *Will therapy: truth and reality.* Trans. J. Taft. New York: Knopf.

Rao, H. 1923. *The psychology of music.* Bangalore, India: Guruvilas Printing Works.

Reimers, D. 1927. Untersuchungen uber die Entwickelung des Tonalitätsgefühls. In Laufe des Schulzeits, *Zeitschr. f. angew. Psychol.* 28. Cited in R. Francès, *La perception de la musique.* Paris: Vrin, 1958.

Révész, G. 1925. *The psychology of a musical prodigy.* New York: Harcourt Brace.

——. 1954. *Introduction to the psychology of music.* Norman: University of Oklahoma Press.

Reynolds, R., and Ortony, A. 1980. Some issues in the measurement of children's comprehension of metaphorical language. *Child Development* 51 (4):1110–1119.

Richards, I. A. 1929. *Practical criticism.* New York: Harcourt Brace.

——. 1936. Metaphor. In I. A. Richards. *The philosophy of rhetoric.* London: Oxford University Press.

——. 1960. Variant readings and misreadings. In T. A. Sebeok, ed. *Style in language.* Cambridge: M.I.T. Press.

Richter, J., ed. 1970. *The literary works of Leonardo da Vinci,* vol. 1. 3rd ed. London: Phaidon Press.

Rigg, M. 1940. Speed as a determiner of musical mood. *Journal of Experimental Psychology* 27:566–571.

——. 1942. *The Rigg poetry judgment test.* Iowa City: Bureau of Educational Research and Service, University of Iowa.

Rimland, B. 1964. *Infantile autism.* New York: Appleton-Century-Crofts.

Rosch, E. 1975. Cognitive reference points. *Cognitive Psychology* 7:532–547.

Rose, G. 1980. The power of form. *Psychological Issues,* Monograph 49. New York: International Universities Press.

Rose, S. 1977. Infants' transfer of response between two-dimensional and three-dimensional stimuli. *Child Development* 48:1086–1091.

Rosenberg, J. 1964. *On quality in art: criteria of excellence, past and present.* Princeton: Princeton University Press.

Rosenblatt, L. *The reader, the text, the poem: the transactional theory of the literary work.* Carbondale: Southern Illinois University Press, 1978.

Rosenstiel, A., Morison, P., Silverman, J., and Gardner, H. 1978. Critical judgment: a developmental study. *Journal of Aesthetic Education* 12 (4):95–107.

Rosenthal, D. 1970. *Genetic theory and abnormal behavior.* New York: McGraw.

Rosinski, R., Mulholland, T., Degelman, D., and Farber, J. 1980. Picture perception: an analysis of visual compensation. *Perception and Psychophysics* 28 (6):521–526.

Rothenberg, A. 1971. The process of Janusian thinking in creativity. *Archives of General Psychiatry* 24:195–205.

——. 1979. *The emerging goddess.* Chicago: University of Chicago Press.

Rothenberg, A., and Hausman, C. 1976. *The creativity question.* Durham: Duke University Press.

Rubin, S., and Gardner, H. 1977. Once upon a time: the development of sensitivity to story structure. Unpublished manuscript, Project Zero, Harvard Graduate School of Education, Cambridge.

Rubin, S., and Wolf, D. 1979. The development of maybe: the evolution of social roles into narrative roles. In E. Winner and H. Gardner, eds. Fact, fiction, and fantasy in childhood. *New Directions for Child Development* 6:15–28.

Ruff, H., Kohler, C., and Haupt, D. 1976. Infant recognition of two- and three-dimensional stimuli. *Developmental Psychology* 12:455–459.

Rumelhart, D. 1977. Understanding and summarizing brief stories. In D. La Berge and S. Samuels, eds. *Basic processes in reading: perception and comprehension*. Hillsdale, N.J.: Lawrence Erlbaum.

———. 1979. Some problems with the notion of literal meanings. In A. Ortony, ed. *Metaphor and thought*. Cambridge, Eng.: Cambridge University Press.

Ryan, T., and Schwartz, C. 1956. Speed of perception as a function of mode of representation. *American Journal of Psychology* 69:60–69.

Saddock, J. M. 1979. Figurative speech and linguistics. In A. Ortony, ed. *Metaphor and thought*. Cambridge, Eng.: Cambridge University Press.

Sapir, E. 1929. A study in phonetic symbolism. *Journal of Experimental Psychology* 12:225–239.

Sarno, M., ed. 1972. *Aphasia: selected readings*. New York: Appleton-Century-Crofts.

Scarlett, G. 1981. Problems in make-believe: real or pretend? Paper presented at Orthopsychiatry Conference, New York City.

Scarlett, G., and Wolf, D. 1979. When it's only make-believe: the construction of a boundary between fantasy and reality in storytelling. In E. Winner and H. Gardner, eds. Fact, fiction, and fantasy in childhood. *New Directions for Child Development* 6:29–40.

Schaefer-Simmern, H. 1948. *The unfolding of artistic activity*. Berkeley: University of California Press.

Schapiro, M. 1962a. Leonardo and Freud: an art historical study. In P. Wiener and A. Noland, eds. *Ideas in cultural perspective*. New Brunswick: Rutgers University Press.

———. 1962b. Style. In S. Tax, ed. *Anthropology today*. Abridged ed. Chicago: University of Chicago Press.

Scheerer, M., and Lyons, J. 1957. Line drawings and matching responses to words. *Journal of Personality* 25:251–273.

Schiller, P. 1951. Figural preferences in the drawings of a chimpanzee. *Journal of Comparative and Physiological Psychology* 44:101–111.

Schoenberg, A. 1978. *Theory of harmony*. Berkeley: University of California Press.

Schonberg, R. 1974. Adolescent thought and figurative language. Ph.D. dissertation, University of Tennessee.

Schopenhauer, A. 1891. *The art of literature*. London: S. Sonnenschein.

Schwartz, J. 1980. Metalinguistic awareness: a study of verbal play in young children. Unpublished manuscript, Queens College, City University of New York.

Searle J. 1979. Metaphor. In A. Ortony, ed. *Metaphor and thought*. Cambridge, Eng.: Cambridge University Press.

Seashore, C. 1967. *Psychology of music*. New York: Dover.

Seashore, C., Lewis, D., and Saetveit, J. 1960. *Manual of instructions and interpretations for the Seashore measures of musical talents*. 2nd rev. New York: The Psychological Corporation.

Segall, M., Campbell, D., and Herskovits, M. 1966. *The influence of culture on visual perception*. Indianapolis: Bobbs-Merrill.

Selfe, L. 1977. Nadia: a case of extraordinary drawing ability in an autistic child. London: Academic Press.

Serafine, M. 1979. A measure of meter conservation in music based on Piaget's theory. *Genetic Psychology Monographs* 99:185–229.

Sergeant, D., and Roche, S. 1973. Perceptual shifts in the auditory information processing of young children. *Psychology of Music* 1 (2):39–48.

Sessions, R. 1951. *Harmonic practice.* New York: Harcourt, Brace.

Shakow, D. 1962. Segmental set: a theory of formal psychological deficit in schizophrenia. *Archives of General Psychiatry* 6:1–17.

Shanon, B. 1980. Lateralization effects in musical decision tasks. *Neuropsychologia* 18:21–31.

Shapiro, B., Grossman, M., and Gardner, H. 1981. Selective musical processing deficits in brain-damaged patients. *Neuropsychologia* 19:161–170.

Shuter, R. 1968. *The psychology of musical ability.* London: Methuen.

Siegel, J. 1981. Culturally defined learning experience and musical perception. In *National Symposium on the Applications of Psychology to the Teaching and Learning of Music.* Reston, Va.: Music Educators National Conference.

Siegel, J., and Siegel, W. 1977a. Categorical perception of tonal intervals: musicians can't tell *sharp* from *flat. Perception and Psychophysics* 21 (5):399–407.

———. 1977b. Absolute identification of notes and intervals by musicians. *Perception and Psychophysics* 21:143–2.

Silberstein, L., Gardner, H., Phelps, E., and Winner, E. In press. Autumn leaves and old photographs: the development of metaphor preferences. *Journal of Experimental Child Psychology.*

Silverman, J., Winner, E., Rosenstiel, A., and Gardner, H. 1975. On training sensitivity to painting styles. *Perception* 4:373–384.

Simon, H., Newell, A., and Shaw, J. 1962. The processes of creative thinking. In H. Simon. *Models of thought.* New Haven: Yale University Press, 1979.

Simon, M. 1888. Les écrits et les dessins des alienés. *Archives de l'Anthropologie Criminelle* 3:318–355.

Singer, J. 1973. *The child's world of make-believe.* New York: Academic Press.

Singer, J., and Singer, D. 1979. Television viewing, family style and aggressive behavior in preschool children. Paper presented at Meeting of American Association for the Advancement of Science, Houston, January.

Skinner, B. F. 1972. A lecture on having a poem. In B. F. Skinner. *Cumulative record.* 3rd ed. New York: Appleton-Century-Crofts.

Slater, E., and Meyer, A. 1959. Contributions to a pathography of the musicians. I. Robert Schumann. *Confinia Psychiatria,* 2:65–94.

Smith, N. 1972. The origins of graphic symbolization in children 3–5. Ph.D. dissertation, Harvard University, Cambridge.

———. 1980. Development and creativity in American art education: a critique. *High School Journal,* May, pp. 348–352.

Smith, P., and Smith, D. 1961. Ball-throwing responses to photographically portrayed targets. *Journal of Experimental Psychology* 62:223–233.

Snyder, J. 1979. The spontaneous production of figurative language and word play in the grade school years. Ph.D. dissertation, Boston University.

Snyder, S. 1976. The dopamine hypothesis of schizophrenia: focus on the dopamine receptor. *American Journal of Psychiatry* 133 (2):197–202.

Soueif, M., and Eysenck, H. 1972. Factors in the determination of preference judgments for polygonal figures: a comparative study. *International Journal of Psychology* 7:145–153.

Souques, A., and Baruk, H. 1930. Autopsie d'un cas d'amusie (avec aphasie) chez un professeur de piano. *Revue Neurologique* 1:545–556.

Sparks, R., Helm, N., and Albert, M. 1973. Melodic intonation therapy. Paper presented at Academy of Aphasia, Albuquerque, October.

Sperry, R. 1974. Lateral specialization in the surgically separated hemisphere. In F. Schmitt and F. Worden, eds. *The neurosciences third study program.* Cambridge: M.I.T. Press.

Sperry, R., Gazzaniga, M., and Bogen, J. 1969. Interhemispheric relationships: the neocortical commisures: syndromes of hemispheric disconnection. In P. J. Vinken and G. W. Bruyn, eds. *Handbook of Clinical Neurology,* vol. 4. Amsterdam: North Holland Publishing.

Spiro, R. 1977. Inferential reconstruction in memory for connected discourse. In R. C. Anderson, R. J. Spiro, and W. E. Montague, eds. *Schooling and the acquisition of knowledge.* Hillsdale, N.J.: Lawrence Erlbaum Associates.

Springbett, B. 1960. The semantic differential and meaning in nonobjective art. *Perceptual and Motor Skills* 10:231–240.

Steck, L., and Machotka, P. 1975. Preference for musical complexity: effects of context. *Journal of Experimental Psychology: Human Perception and Performance* 1:170–174.

Stein, N., and Glenn, C. 1977. An analysis of story comprehension in elementary school children. In R. Freedle, ed. *Multidisciplinary approaches to discourse comprehension.* Hillsdale, N.J.: Ablex.

Stokes, A. 1955. Form in art. In M. Klein, ed. *New directions in psychoanalysis.* London: Tavistock.

Stone, I., and Stone, J., eds. 1960. *Dear Theo: the autobiography of Vincent van Gogh.* New York: Grove Press.

Strauss, S., ed. 1982. *U-shaped behavioral growth.* New York: Academic Press.

Sullivan, H. 1953. *The interpersonal theory of psychiatry.* Ed. H. Perry and M. Gawel. New York: Norton.

Sutton-Smith, B. 1975. The importance of the storytaker: an investigation of the imaginative life. *Urban Review* 8:82–95.

———. 1979. Presentation and representation in fictional narrative. In E. Winner and H. Gardner, eds. Fact, fiction, and fantasy in childhood. *New Directions for Child Development* 6:53–65.

———. 1981. *The folkstories of children.* Philadelphia: University of Pennsylvania Press.

Suzuki, S. 1969. *Nurtured by love: a new approach to education.* New York: Exposition Press.

Swinney, D., and Cutler, A. 1979. The access and processing of idiomatic expressions. *Journal of Verbal Learning and Verbal Behavior* 18:523–534.

Szonyi, E. 1973. *Kodaly's principles in practice.* London: Boosey and Hawkes.

Tecce, J., and Cole, J. 1976. The distraction-arousal hypothesis, CNV, and schizophrenia. In D. I. Mostofsky, ed. *Behavior control and modification of physiological activity.* Englewood Cliffs, N.J.: Prentice Hall.

Teplov, B. M. 1966. *Psychologie des aptitudes musicales.* Paris: Presses Universitaires de France.

Thiel, C. 1927. An investigation of the drawings of deaf and dumb children. *Z. Kinderforsch* 33:138–176.

Thorndyke, P. 1977. Cognitive structures in comprehension and memory of narrative discourse. *Cognitive Psychology* 9:77–110.

Tighe, T. 1968. Concept formation and art: further evidence on the applicability of Walk's technique. *Psychometric Science* 12:363–364.

Todd, J. 1943. Preferences of children for modern and older paintings. *Elementary School Journal* 44:223–231.

Todorov, T. 1969. *Grammaire du Décaméron.* The Hague: Mouton.

———. 1971. The two principles of narrative. *Diacritics,* Fall, p. 39.

Tolstoy, L. 1930. *What is art?* Oxford: Oxford University Press.

Torrance, E. 1962. *Guiding creative talent.* Englewood Cliffs, N.J.: Prentice-Hall.

Tourangeau, R., and Sternberg, R. 1981. Aptness in metaphor. *Cognitive Psychology* 13:27–55.

Turbayne, C. 1962. *The myth of metaphor.* New Haven: Yale University Press.

Tversky, A. 1977. Features of similarity. *Psychological Review* 84:327–352.

Valentine, C. 1962. *The experimental psychology of beauty.* London: The Camelot Press, Methuen.

Vayo, J. 1977. A microgenetic study of metaphor comprehension in college students. Unpublished research, Project Zero, Harvard Graduate School of Education, Cambridge.

Venables, P. 1964. Input dysfunction in schizophrenia. In B. Maher, ed. *Progress in Experimental Personality Research,* vol. 1. New York: Academic Press.

Verbrugge, R. 1974. The comprehension of analogy. Ph.D. dissertation, University of Minnesota, Minneapolis.

———. 1980. Transformations in knowing: a realist view of metaphor. In R. P. Honeck and R. R. Hoffman, eds. *Cognition and figurative language.* Hillsdale, N.J.: Erlbaum.

Verbrugge, R., and McCarrell, N. 1977. Metaphoric comprehension: studies in reminding and resembling. *Cognitive Psychology* 9:494–533.

Vinegrad, M. 1972. A direct magnitude scaling method to investigate categorical vs. continuous modes of speech perception. *Language and Speech* 15:114–121.

Vitz, P., and Todd, T. 1971. Preference for tones as a function of frequency (H_2) and intensity (db). *Psychological Review* 78 (3):207–228.

Voss, M. 1936. A study of conditions affecting the functioning of the art appreciation process at the child-level. In N. C. Meier, ed. *Studies in the Psychology of Art,* vol. 2. *Psychology Monographs* 48 (1):1–39.

Wadeson, H. 1980. *Art psychotherapy.* New York: Wiley.

Wagner, R. 1924. *My life.* New York: Dodd, Mead.

Wagner, S., Winner, E., Cicchetti, D., and Gardner, H. 1981. "Metaphorical" mapping in human infants. *Child Development* 52:728–731.

Walk, R. 1967. Concept formation and art: basic experiment and controls. *Psychometric Science* 9:237–238.

Wall, J. 1959. The base line in children's drawings of self and its relationship to aspects of overt behavior. Ph.D. dissertation. The Florida State University, Tallahassee.

Wallach, M. 1960. Two correlates of symbolic sexual arousal: level of anxiety and liking for esthetic material. *Journal of Abnormal and Social Psychology* 61:396–401.

Wallach, M., and Kogan, N. 1965. *Modes of thinking in young children.* New York: Holt, Rinehart, and Winston.

Wallas, G. 1926. *The art of thought.* New York: Harcourt, Brace.

Walton, W. 1936. Empathic responses in children. In N. C. Meier, ed. *Studies in the Psychology of Art,* vol. 2. *Psychological Monographs* 48 (1):40–67.

Wapner, W., Hamby, S., and Gardner, H. 1981. The role of the right hemisphere in the apprehension of complex linguistic materials. *Brain and Language* 14:15–33.

Warrington, E. K., James, M., and Kinsbourne, M. 1966. Drawing disability in relation to laterality of cerebral lesion. *Brain* 89:53–82.

Waxman, S. G., and Geschwind, N. 1974. Hypergraphia in temporal lobe epilepsy. *Neurology* 24:629–636.

Weiner, M. 1956. Perceptual development in a distorted room: a phenomenological study. *Psychological Monographs* 70:16.

Weir, R. 1962. *Language in the crib.* The Hague: Mouton.

Weitz, M. 1956. The role of theory in aesthetics. *Journal of Aesthetics and Art Criticism* 15:27–35.

Werner, H. 1961. *Comparative psychology of mental development.* New York: Wiley.

Werner, H., and Kaplan, B. 1963. *Symbol Formation.* New York: Wiley.

Wertheimer, M. 1945. *Productive thinking.* New York: Harper.

Wexner, L. 1954. The degree to which colors (hues) are associated with mood-tones. *Journal of Applied Psychology* 38:432–435.

Wheelwright, P. 1954. *The burning fountain: a study in the language of symbolism.* Bloomington: Indiana University Press.

White, R. 1959. Motivation reconsidered: the concept of competence. *Psychological Review* 66:297–331.

Wild, C. 1965. Creativity and adaptive regression. *Journal of Personality and Social Psychology* 2:161–169.

Willats, J. 1977. How children learn to represent three-dimensional space in drawings. In G. Butterworth, ed. *The child's representation of the world.* New York: Plenum Press.

Wilson, B. 1966. An experimental study designed to alter fifth and sixth grade students' perception of paintings. *Studies in Art Education* 8 (1):33–42.

Wilson, B., and Wilson, M. 1977. An iconoclastic view of the imagery sources in the drawings of young people. *Art Education* 30:5–11.

Wimsatt, W. 1967. *The verbal icon: studies in the meaning of poetry.* Lexington: University of Kentucky Press.

Wing, H. 1948. Tests of musical ability and appreciation. *British Journal of Psychology,* Monograph Supplement, 27.

Winn, M. 1979. The pleasures and perils of being a child prodigy. *New York Times Magazine.* Dec. 23, pp. 12–17, 38–45.

Winner, E. 1979. New names for old things: the emergence of metaphoric language. *Journal of Child Language* 6 (3):469–491.

———. 1980. Unpublished research, Boston College.

Winner, E., Engel, M., and Gardner, H. 1980. Misunderstanding metaphor: what's the problem? *Journal of Experimental Child Psychology* 30:22–32.

Winner, E., and Ettlinger, E. 1979. Do chimpanzees recognize photographs as representations of objects? *Neuropsychologia* 17:413–420.

Winner, E., and Gardner, H. 1977. The comprehension of metaphor in brain-damaged patients. *Brain* 100:719–727.

Winner, E., and Gardner, H. 1979. Investigations of the imaginative realm. *New Directions for Child Development* 6:vii–xii.

Winner, E., McCarthy, M., and Gardner, H. 1980. The ontogenesis of metaphor. In R. Honeck and R. Hoffman, eds. *Cognition and figurative language.* Hillsdale, N.J.: Lawrence Erlbaum Associates.

Winner, E., McCarthy, M., Kleinman, S., and Gardner, H. 1979. First metaphors. In D. Wolf, ed. Early symbolization. *New Directions for Child Development* 3:29–41.

Winner, E., Mendelsohn, E., Garfunkel, G., Arangio, S., and Stevens, S. 1981. Are children's drawings balanced? Paper presented at Society for Research in Child Development, Boston.

Winner, E., Rosenstiel, A., and Gardner, H. 1976. The development of metaphor understanding. *Developmental Psychology* 12:289–297.

Winner, E., Wapner, W., Cicone, M., and Gardner, H. 1979. Measures of metaphor. In *New Directions for Child Development* 6:67–75.

Wittgenstein, L. 1953. *Philosophical investigations.* New York: Macmillan.

Wohlwill, J. 1965. Texture of the stimulus field and age as variables in the perception of relative distance in photographic slides. *Journal of Experimental Child Psychology* 2:166.

Wölfflin, H. 1932. *Principles of art history.* London: G. Bell and Sons.

Wollheim, R. 1979. Pictorial style: two views. In B. Lang, ed. *The concept of style.* Philadelphia: University of Pennsylvania Press.

Woodworth, R. S. 1938. *Experimental psychology.* New York: Holt.

Yonas, A. 1979. Attached and cast shadows. In C. F. Nodine and D. F. Fisher, eds. *Perception and pictorial representation.* New York: Praeger.

Yonas, A., Goldsmith, L., and Hallstrom, J. 1978. Development of sensitivity to information provided by cast shadows in pictures. In *Perception* 7 (3):333–341.

Yonas, A., and Hagen, M. 1973. Effects of static and motion parallax depth information on perception of size in children and adults. *Journal of Experimental Child Psychology* 15:254–265.

Zaidel, E. 1977. Unilateral auditory language comprehension on the Token Test following cerebral commissurotomy and hemispherectomy. *Neuropsychologia* 15:1–8.

Zaimov, K., Kitov, D., and Kolev, N. 1969. Aphasie chez un peintre. *Encephale* 68:377–417.

Zenatti, A. 1969. Le développement génétique de la perception musicale. *Monographies Françaises de Psychologie*, no. 17.

Ziff, P. 1953. The task of defining a work of art. *Philosophical Review* 62:58–78.

Zigler, E., Levine, J., and Gould, L. 1966. Cognitive processes in the development of children's appreciation of humor. *Child Development* 37:507–518.

Zigler, E., Levine, J., and Gould, L. 1967. Cognitive challenge as a factor in children's humor appreciation. *Journal of Personality and Social Psychology* 6:332–336.

Zimmerman, R., and Hochberg, J. 1963. Pictorial recognition in the infant monkey. *Proceedings of the Psychonomic Society* 46.

Zimmerman, R., and Hochberg, J. 1971. The facilitation of picture discrimination after object discrimination learning in the neonatal monkey and probably vice versa. *Psychonomic Science* 24 (5):239–241.

Index

Billig, O., 366, 369, 371
Billow, R., 291, 313
Binocular cues, 83, 84, 88, 92, 120, 121
Biochemistry, 379–381, 382
Birkhoff, George, 58
Black, A., 251
Black, M., 256
Blackwell, H., 205
Blake, William, 356
Blumstein, S., 341
Body-proportion effect, 154
Bogen, T., 331, 346, 347
Bonaparte, M., 276
Bond, E., 127
Bookin, H., 259
Book stories, vs. television, 303
Borisy, A., 66
Bornstein, M., 137
Bosch, Hieronymus, 356
Boswell, S., 127
Botez, M., 348
Botvin, G., 219, 324
Boundary, fiction/reality, 318, 319–321, 344–345
Bower, G., 269, 271
Bower, T., 115, 118
Bowerman, M., 311
Boyd, R., 253
Bradshaw, J., 346
Brainard, R., 118
Braine, L., 117
Brain field, 96
Brain studies, 11, 332–352, 387
Bransford, J., 271
Brehmer, F., 222
Brighouse, G., 138
Brittain, W., 154, 161, 163, 168
Broadway Boogie Woogie, 106
Brody, G., 138
Brooks, V., 98, 113
Brothers Karamazov, 19, 54–55
Brown, David, 167
Brown, R., 186, 212, 213, 250, 251
Bruner, Jerome, 131, 331
Burnham, C., 90
Burns, B., 256
Burns, E., 203, 204
Burt, C., 72
Burton-Bradley, B., 369, 371
Butcher, H., 26, 358
Byron, G., 356

Cabe, P., 116
Callaway, E., 3, 354
Calm perceivers, 74
Calvino, Italo, 247

Campbell, D., 117
Canfield, Dorothy, 38
Carlson, P., 307, 311
Carlsson, A., 355, 380
Carothers, T., 109, 124, 170, 175
Carroll, Lewis, 356
Cartoons, 161
Cassirer, Ernst, 65, 105
Castle, M., 58
Categorical perception, 202–205
Catharsis, 53, 55–56, 58, 275
Cattell, R., 26, 358
Cazden, C., 308
Cézanne, Paul, 130–131, 336–337
Chang, H., 217, 218
Chapman, J., 354
Characters, in stories, 272, 319
Chiarello, R., 333, 349
Child, Irvin, 57, 68–69, 70, 71, 134–141 *passim*
Children, 66–67; drawings by, 92, 144–191; picture perception by, 112–143; music perception by, 217–228; singing by, 229–243; literary sensitivity of, 284–305; literature production by, 306–327
Chimpanzees, 176–180, 191
Chinese, 251
Chipman, S., 127
Chopin, F., 209
Chromas, 206, 207
Chromatic scales, 196, 234
Chukovsky, Kornei, 306, 307, 308, 311
Cicchetti, D., 124, 288
Cicone, M., 287, 299, 341
Circles, 153, 155, 164
Clark, A., 158
Clark, E., 311
Clark, H., 260
Class inclusion tasks, 291–292
Class intersection tests, 292
Closed concepts, 5
Closure law, 209
Cockrell, J., 118
Cocteau, Jean, 38, 51
Cognitive processes: of artists, 9, 12, 15–16, 28–50, 163, 180, 318–319, 357–358, 373, 385–388; of perceivers, 9, 12, 59–71 *passim,* 132, 142, 211, 266, 283–299 *passim,* 385–386, 388
Cole, J., 354
Cole, M., 122, 299
Collative variables, 59
Collingwood, R. G., 4

Color preferences, 137, 138, 139, 140
Color use, in drawing, 151–152
Combines, 149–150
Cometa, M., 292
Communication, 52
Complexity, 59–64, 70, 71, 136, 138–139, 164–167
Composition, 388; pictorial, 125–129, 142; music, 236–237, 238, 239–242, 243, 348–349; stories, 299–300
Comprehension, *see* Understanding
Computer, mind as, 253
Concepts, open/closed, 5–6
Congo, 177, 179
Connor, K., 258, 293
Conscious craft, 37, 42–49, 386–387
Conservation: of visual quantity, 131; musical, 218–219
Constable, John, 49, 81–92 *passim,* 100, 104, 112–113, 129
Constructivist theory, 89–109 *passim,* 123
Content, vs. form, 4, 55
Context, color, 139
Continuation principle, 103, 209
Contour, melodic, 206–208, 217–218, 219, 220, 234, 235
Contradictions, pictorial, 83
Control, 170
Conventionalism: in pictorial perception, 93–95, 107–109, 123; and drawing, 160–161, 176, 190–191; in children's language, 314–315
Convergent thinking, 29
Cooper, B., 121
Cooper, F., 202
Cooper, R., 97
Cooper, W., 341
Copland, Aaron, 15, 216, 217
Corcoran, A., 152
Corinth, Lovis, 332, 338
Crane, Hart, 356
Cro-Magnon humans, 1
Cross, P., 26, 358
Crozier, J., 222
Crutchfield, R., 23
Csikszentmihalyi, Mihaly, 30, 32
Cubes, 102–103, 187
Cubism, 129
Cuddy, L., 197
Culture, 387–388; and pictorial perception, 68, 122, 143; and

music, 196, 198, 204–205, 215, 221, 229–232, 235, 236, 239, 242; and stories, 299, 323, 327; and schizophrenia, 369–371. *See also* Conventionalism
Cutler, A., 260
Czech, 251

Daehler, M., 114
Damon, W., 297
Daniels, P., 129
Darwin, Charles, 48, 229, 356
Darwinian tradition, 52
Davenport, R., 116
Davidson, L., 233, 234, 235, 348
Davis, R., 58
Dax, E., 376
Day, H., 61
Daydreaming, 18
Deabler, H., 109
Deaf people, 185, 213
Defenses: of readers, 279, 281; of storytellers, 316–317
Definitions: of art, 2–8; of psychology of art, 8–10
DeForest, M., 299
Degelman, D., 121
Delay, Dorothy, 241
Deliberation, 2, 3
DeLoache, J., 114, 115, 141
Demorest, A., 294
De Myer, K., 181
Denes, G., 347
Denial, in storytelling, 317
Dennis, N., 183
Denotation, 10
Depressives, 376
Depth cues, 83–84, 86, 88, 92, 118–123
Deregowski, J., 114, 118
Designs, prerepresentational, 147, 148–150. *See also* Representation, pictorial
Detail, in schizophrenic art, 361–362, 363, 371
Deutsch, D., 206, 207
de Villiers, J., 181, 288, 311
de Villiers, P., 181, 288, 311
Dewar, K., 197
Dewey, J., 42
Diagrams, in children's drawing, 149–150, 153, 177
Diatonic scales, 196, 202, 234
Dichotic listening, 334
Dickinson, Emily, 277–278
Dictionary of National Biography, 357

Differences: individual, 66–73, 275–282, 293; sex, 317–318, 323
Differentiation, 139, 164–167. *See also* Discrimination
Direct registration theory, 84–88, 92–93, 95, 97, 98–99, 108
Dirks, J., 115
Discipline, with music, 239–240
Discrimination, 65, 76–77, 204, 208
Discursive symbols, 65, 211
Dissanayake, E., 52
Dissonance, musical, 214
Divergent thinking, 29–30
Divine inspiration, 9, 10
Dominant note, 199, 222
Dopamine, 380–381, 382
Dorgueille, C., 349
Dostoevsky, F., 19, 54–55, 356
Double-function terms, 286–288
Dowling, W., 197, 198, 205, 206, 207, 219, 220
Dramatic perceivers, 74–75
Drawing, 144–191, 225–227, 229, 363, 369, 376
Dreams, 40, 378, 380–381
Dreistadt, R., 41
Drevdahl, J., 26
Drexler, E., 233
Drouin, C., 286
Drugs, 363, 380–381
Dryden, John, 353
Duality, of mind, 331–352
Duchamp, Marcel, 3
Duckworth, E., 198
Dundes, A., 324
Dürer, Albrecht, 356
Durham, R., 140
Dynamic Hieroglyphic of Bal Tabarin, 82–83, 104

Ecker, D., 42
Ecological properties, of art, 58
Education, art, 11. *See also* Training, musical
Edwards, B., 187
Ego, 23–26, 373
Egyptian painting, 158
Eidetic imagery, 185–186, 223
Eimas, P., 202
Elkind, D., 116
Ellis, H., 357
Embodied meaning, 208–210
Emotions, 3, 4–5, 28, 52–54, 74–75; paintings expressing, 2; visual arts evoking, 51–52, 65–66, 77; music evoking,

195–196, 201, 212–215, 348; music expressing, 210–212, 214–215; for music production, 240, 241, 242, 348, 350; literature evoking, 248, 283, 300; literature expressing, 297–299; and brain hemispheres, 340, 348
Enactive metaphors, 312, 313
Engel, M., 291
Entus, M., 346
Epilepsy, 356–357
Erikson, Erik, 316, 317, 318
Ernst, Max, 36
Eson, M., 261, 292
Essay on Criticism, 248
Etc. principle, 91
Ettlinger, E., 116
Expectation, musical, 209–210, 213–214, 215
Experience, reading, 273–282, 283
Experimental aesthetics, 35–36, 53, 56–58, 385; new, 58–64, 65, 75, 138–139
Exploration, 317
Expression, 7–8, 388; pictorial, 10–11, 104–111, 123–125, 142, 170–173; musical, 10–11, 106, 208–209, 210–212, 214, 215, 300–301; in literature, 10–11, 272, 300–301; in schizophrenic art, 374–375
Expressionists, 375
Extramusical meaning, 208–209, 210–212
Eysenck, Hans, 58, 66, 68–69, 72, 379
Eysenck, S., 69

Fagan, J., 114, 115
Fairley, I., 279
Fairy tales, 284–285, 295–299, 304, 324, 325–326
Familiarity: and preference, 66, 68–70, 135–136; with pictorial arts, 66, 68–70, 101–102, 110, 113, 122, 130, 135–136; with music, 209–210, 213–214. *See also* Training, musical
Fan motif, 179
Fantasies, 71, 279, 281
Fantz, R., 115, 137
Farber, J., 121
Faulkner, William, 280–282
Fava, D., 293
Fechner, Gustav, 56, 57, 385
Feshbach, S., 55